D0893560

Evaluating Welfare and Training Programs

Evaluating Welfare and Training Programs

Edited by

**Charles F. Manski and
Irwin Garfinkel**

Harvard University Press
Cambridge, Massachusetts
London, England   1992

Library of Congress Cataloging-in-Publication Data

Evaluating welfare and training programs / edited by Charles F. Manski
  and Irwin Garfinkel.
    p. cm.
  Includes bibliographical references and index.
  ISBN 0-674-27017-7
  1. Public welfare—United States—Evaluation—Congresses.
  2. Welfare recipients—Employment—United States—Evaluation—
  Congresses. 3. Occupational training—United States—Evaluation—
  Congresses. I. Manski, Charles F. II. Garfinkel, Irwin.
HV95.E94 1992   91-19132
362.5'84'068—dc20   CIP

Preface

This nation has long struggled to develop welfare and training programs that bring its disadvantaged citizens into the economic mainstream. The programs enacted to date have reflected a variety of assumptions about what works best in reducing dependency and increasing attachment to the labor force. Some programs have stressed basic education, while others have provided job training and counseling. Participation in some programs has been voluntary, in others mandatory.

How can we learn from our experience, so that we may improve the effectiveness of future programs? This basic question of evaluation is addressed here. In the Introduction we explain the scientific and practical issues that make program evaluation a challenging task. The nine chapters that follow were all specifically commissioned for this volume; the authors were asked to investigate aspects of evaluation in which they had substantial expertise and interest.

Preliminary versions of these chapters were presented in April 1990 at a national conference cosponsored by the Institute for Research on Poverty (IRP) of the University of Wisconsin–Madison and the Office of the Assistant Secretary for Planning and Evaluation (ASPE), U.S. Department of Health and Human Services. Held at the Airlie Conference Center, Airlie, Virginia, the conference gathered leading experts in evaluation methodology to address the complex problem of assessing welfare and training programs. In addition to those presenting and commenting on the commissioned papers, representatives of federal agencies, congressional staff, and foundation personnel participated in the conference.

We expect that this book will be valuable to several audiences: policy researchers, evaluation professionals, social scientists, federal and state government officials, and citizens concerned with social policy. Because the methodological issues examined here arise in the evaluation of all social programs, the book should be useful beyond the community directly interested in the evaluation of welfare and training programs.

Elizabeth Evanson, Assistant Director for Public Information at IRP, provided superb assistance in all phases of the project. Her contribution warrants special recognition. Michael Fishman, William Prosser, and Steven Sandell of the ASPE staff provided valued advice in setting the theme and organization of the Airlie House conference. A highlight of the conference was the ASPE staff presentation of the government's plans for evaluating the nation's most recent major effort at welfare reform, the Family Support Act of 1988. Elizabeth Uhr, Senior Editor at IRP, offered many good suggestions that improved the writing of our introductory essay. Finally, we thank Michael Aronson of Harvard University Press for his strong interest in and commitment to the publication of this volume.

C.F.M.

I.G.

Contents

Evaluating Welfare and Training Programs

Introduction

Charles F. Manski and Irwin Garfinkel

It may seem self-evident that social programs should regularly be assessed and revised in the light of lessons drawn from experience. Nevertheless, systematic program evaluation is a recent development. Modern evaluation practice is generally agreed to have begun in the middle 1960s, when attempts were made to evaluate the impacts of programs proposed as part of the War on Poverty. Earlier efforts were largely limited to descriptions of how enacted programs were administered.[1]

Concern with program evaluation has spread rapidly since the 1960s. Today almost every substantial social program is subjected to some form of evaluation. Findings from evaluations not only fill many professional journals but are reported routinely in the media, where they presumably influence public thinking on social policy.

Evaluation requirements now appear in major federal statutes. Evaluation is prominently featured in the recently enacted Family Support Act of 1988, which revised the Aid to Families with Dependent Children (AFDC) program. In Title II of this statute, Congress mandated separate implementation and effectiveness studies of training programs initiated by the states under the new Job Opportunities and Basic Skills Training Program (JOBS). Taking unusually specific action, Congress even stipulated the mode of data collection for the effectiveness study: "A demonstration project conducted under this subparagraph shall use experimental and control groups that are composed of a random sample of participants in the program."[2]

---

1. The development of modern evaluation practice is discussed in Aaron (1978), Haveman (1987), and Lampman (1976). Modern practice does have some historical precursors. For example, the Children's Bureau of the U.S. Department of Labor studied the impact on infant mortality of the Sheppard-Towner Act (Public Law 97, 67th Congress; 42 Stat. 224), a 1921 statute establishing programs to improve infant and maternal health and hygiene (see U.S. Department of Labor, Children's Bureau, 1931). We are grateful to Linda Gordon for bringing this early evaluation to our attention.

2. Public Law 100-485, October 13, 1988, Section 203, 102 Stat. 2380. A contract to perform the mandated effectiveness study has been awarded to the Manpower Demonstration Research Corporation. The Secretary of the U.S. Department of Health and

1

Growth in the demand for program evaluation has been accompanied by the development of an industry specializing in the performance of evaluations. The major evaluations of the 1960s and early 1970s were designed and conducted by academic social scientists, in collaboration with early evaluation professionals. While some analysis continues to take place in universities, program evaluation has increasingly become the domain of private firms.[3]

Although there now exists a consensus that program evaluation is important and should be an integral part of the policy process, no similar consensus exists regarding the proper conduct and interpretation of evaluations. Evaluation methodology is the subject of continuing controversy.

In part, the problem is organizational. Successful evaluation of social programs requires the integrated efforts of three broad communities with differing perspectives and modes of analysis: social scientists, including economists, sociologists, political scientists, and statisticians; public officials at the federal, state, and local levels; and professionals in the consulting firms that execute evaluations. Evaluation suffers when, as is often the case, these communities (and the subcommunities within) do not appreciate one another's perspectives and do not collaborate effectively.

In part, the problem is a persistent, sometimes heated dispute about scientific method. The dispute is often framed as a question about data: Should evaluators attempt to interpret observations of actual program outcomes, or should they analyze findings from controlled social experiments? The underlying question, however, concerns the role of social science in program evaluation: Should evaluators attempt to understand the complex social processes that make programs work as they do, or should they focus on inputs and outputs, treating programs as "black boxes"?

Human Services has also appointed an Advisory Panel for the Evaluation of the JOBS Program, composed of public officials and academic experts. Although Congress specified the mode of data collection for the effectiveness study, it did not stipulate the method of data analysis. Later in the chapter we explain the central issues in evaluation methodology and describe past and current practices.

3. The evaluation industry now includes such large firms as Abt Associates, Lewin/ICF, the Manpower Demonstration Research Corporation, and Mathematica Policy Research, among others.

This volume is the result of the contributors' collective effort to improve communication and collaboration among the communities that design, perform, and utilize program evaluations. The reader will find that the contributors, each of whom is a leading expert on some aspect of evaluation, do not speak with one voice. Taken together, however, their chapters convey well the range of perspectives found among active evaluators.

The volume also reflects the contributors' desire to increase general awareness of the deep scientific questions and difficult practical problems that confront all attempts to evaluate social programs. Policymakers and the public can intelligently appraise the findings reported by evaluators only if they appreciate the nature of the evaluation enterprise.

The substantive focus of the book is, of course, the evaluation of welfare and training programs. The importance of these programs is indisputable; their cost to the government is large, and even larger is their hold on the nation's attention. The book should be useful as well to those concerned with the evaluation of programs in education and public health. Indeed, the methodological questions examined here arise in the evaluation of all social programs.

The book is divided into three parts. The four chapters in Part I describe evaluation practice during the past decade and report findings from some notable recent evaluations. The three chapters in Part II are concerned with evaluation methodology, in particular, the role of social science in evaluation. The two chapters in Part III examine the institutions that administer social programs.

The remaining sections of this Introduction present the editors' personal perspective on the issues that surround evaluation today. Our discussion draws heavily on the revealing descriptions of evaluation practice and the insightful analyses of methodological questions found in the chapters that follow.[4] But the views expressed here are our own; we are not attempting to formulate a consensus position among the contributors to the volume.

To focus attention, we first outline the structure of a typical program. The next section considers the practical problem of specifying the domain of an evaluation. We question sharply the conventional separation of process and impact evaluations. The following section examines the

4. The discussion also draws on material in Manski (1990b).

methodological controversy concerning the role of social science in program evaluation. We conclude that evaluations cannot, in general, avoid asking how programs work. In the final section we call attention to political and funding considerations that influence the conduct of evaluations today.

Schematic of a Federally Mandated Welfare or Training Program

Figure I.1 depicts a typical federal welfare or training program. Such programs as AFDC and the Job Training Partnership Act (JTPA) share the structure shown in the figure. Arrows 1, 2, and 3b trace the process by which a program is fleshed out. Federal statutes and regulations sketch the program, leaving a state with substantial discretion in the way it will comply with the federal mandate. Negotiations between the state and the federal government yield an accepted state program. The state-federal agreement specifies major program provisions but inevitably leaves many details to be settled by the state as it administers the program.[5]

Program administration may itself be a multi-tiered process, involving state, county, and local agencies as well as private service providers. This subprocess is omitted from the figure for the sake of simplicity. In the end, decisions about program eligibility and specification of treatments may be made by individual caseworkers in local welfare offices and by service providers operating under government contract.

Arrows 3a, 3b, and 3c describe the determination of program participation. A participant emerges from the population when a potentially eligible person applies for entry into the program. Eligibility is not determined solely by the program's formal rules; in practice, the rules are interpreted by local officials. Moreover, initially ineligible persons may become eligible by modifying their behavior appropriately. For example, a woman can choose to become eligible for AFDC through her marriage, childbearing, and labor supply decisions.

---

5. The degree of state latitude in program design increased with the federalism drive of the 1980s. For example, Hotz in Chapter 2 describes how the centralized manpower training programs of the 1960s and 1970s were replaced by the decentralized JTPA program in 1982. Similarly, the Family Support Act of 1988 gives states new discretion in their AFDC programs.

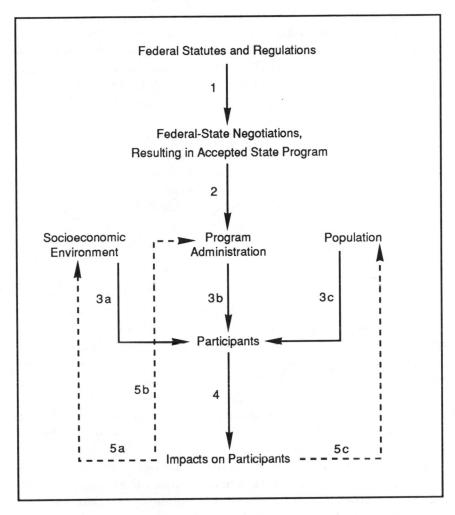

Figure I.1. A federal welfare or training program. Dotted lines indicate feedback effects.

   The participation process takes place in an environment shaped by
the local economy and social norms. In particular, a person's economic
options and the social stigma associated with program participation will
be influential as a person decides whether to become eligible and to
apply to the program. Robert Moffitt discusses the participation process
in Chapter 6.

Arrows 4, 5a, 5b, and 5c show the program's impacts. The term "impact" is sometimes applied only to the program's direct effect on participants. But attention must also be given to feedback effects, shown by the dotted arrows. For example, a training program may have effects on the operation of the labor market; a program for the homeless may affect the housing market. The social stigma associated with a program may change with the number of persons who participate. A state may revise the way it administers a program as it observes how the program affects participants. A program may even alter the composition of the population of an area; for example, it is often asserted that a relatively liberal AFDC program makes a state a "welfare magnet." We discuss feedback effects in Chapter 7 (written with Charles Michalopoulos).

The Domain of Evaluation

To be useful in policy formation, evaluations should seek to answer *counterfactual* questions: What would happen if some aspect of a program were changed? In principle, an evaluation should seek to characterize the effect of specified program changes on the entire process depicted in Figure I.1. In practice, evaluators simplify their task by restricting attention to part of the process shown in the figure. The implicit assumption is that other parts of the process either are unaffected by the program change under study or are perfectly controllable by the policymaker. Evaluators also simplify their task by limiting the set of program options to be compared.

Efforts to limit the domain of evaluation are clearly essential. At the same time, one must be careful not to oversimplify the evaluation problem. Of the process shown in Figure I.1, the only parts regularly subjected to counterfactual analysis are program participation (arrows 3a, 3b, and 3c) and the direct impact of a program on participants (arrow 4). The federal-state negotiation of an agreed program (arrow 1) is generally ignored entirely. Program administration (arrows 2 and 5b) is often described but is rarely compared with alternatives. Feedbacks to the socioeconomic environment and to the population (arrows 5a and 5c) may be noted as possibilities but are almost always ignored in actual evaluations.

In Chapter 7 we call attention to the adverse consequences of ignoring feedbacks. Here we question the logic of the traditional distinction between "process" and "impact" evaluation and then ask how the set of program options under consideration comes to be specified.

Process as Part of Treatment

It has long been the practice in the evaluation of social programs to distinguish between a program and its administration. *Impact* (or *effectiveness*) evaluations seek to learn the consequences of alternative programs. *Process* (or *implementation*) evaluations describe the administration of programs; they generally do not ask counterfactual questions. Impact evaluations have been conducted primarily by economists with a quantitative orientation, while process evaluation has been the province of qualitatively trained political scientists.

The separation of a program from its administration makes sense if a program's administration can be controlled perfectly or if administrative practices remain the same as programs change. It does not make sense if, as is typically the case, administrators have scope to interpret programs in accordance with their own perceptions. Although it is common to speak of the federal government as imposing "mandates" on the states, in reality mandates only establish rules and incentives intended to influence the behavior of the states, whose objectives may differ from those of the federal government. Similarly, a state cannot perfectly control the behavior of the local agencies and service providers that ultimately carry out a program. The lesson is that, from the perspective of policymaking, a program is not defined solely by its treatment of participants; it is also defined by the rules and incentives it establishes for the governmental units and service providers that administer the program. Thus, process is part of treatment.

Whereas process evaluations have generally been limited to descriptions of program administration, policy formation requires answers to counterfactual questions. Evaluators need to ask how outcomes would change if the rules and incentives operating on program administrators were altered. Two examples follow.

The Effects of Alternative Case Management Systems. Fred Doolittle and James Riccio in Chapter 9 describe a range of systems used in the management of AFDC cases. At one extreme is the "generalist" system, in which each AFDC recipient is assigned to a single case manager who oversees all aspects of the recipient's interaction with the welfare system. At the other extreme is the "sequential specialist" system, in which the

AFDC recipient interacts with a series of specialists, each of whom is responsible for one aspect of the case. Observing that we know little about the outcomes associated with these and intermediate case management systems, Doolittle and Riccio cogently argue the need for research into their relative effectiveness. In addition to not knowing the consequences of alternative case management systems, we also do not know the effect on program outcomes of the varied strategies taken by individual case managers in dealing with their caseloads.[6]

The Effects of Performance Standards. The federal government, aware that its ability to monitor and control the administration of social programs is limited, sometimes uses monetary or other incentives to influence the behavior of states, localities, and service providers. In such "performance standard" systems, rewards or sanctions are related to observable performance in achieving specified goals. Burt Barnow describes in Chapter 8 how performance standards are used in the JTPA program in an effort to improve job training outcomes. Section 203 of the Family Support Act requires that the Secretary of the U.S. Department of Health and Human Services submit to Congress by October 1, 1993, recommendations for performance standards for the JOBS program of AFDC.

Successful application of performance standards and other incentive systems presupposes an understanding of the manner in which these systems affect the behavior of program administrators. Unfortunately, we possess little or no such understanding. Because process evaluations have failed to ask counterfactual questions, Barnow can only speculate

---

6. Wisconsin's "Learnfare" program offers an apt example of the ability of administrators to affect outcomes. Since 1988, Learnfare has required that teenagers included in an AFDC grant (that is, teen dependents of parents receiving AFDC or teen mothers on AFDC) be enrolled in school and meet strict attendance standards. Failure to meet the requirements results in a reduction in benefits. Corbett et al. (1989) describe the program. Enforcement of the Learnfare provisions relies on the attendance records transmitted from teachers to their school administrations, from school administrations to their districts, and from school districts to county welfare offices. Since the program began, it has become clear that attendance recording practices vary widely. More important, initiation of the Learnfare program may have changed prevailing practices. It has been reported that, in some schools, types of absences that previously were recorded as "unexcused" are now being recorded as "excused" or are not being recorded at all. In other schools, attendance recording may have been tightened. The explanation offered is that Learnfare has altered the incentives to record attendance accurately. Some teachers and administrators, believing the program to be unfairly punitive, do what they can to lessen its effects. Others, supporting the program, act to enhance its impact.

in Chapter 8 about the effects the JTPA performance standards have had on the administration of the program.

The Range of Program Options

Evaluations invariably consider only a small set of program options. Innovations cannot depart too far from the status quo if they are to be politically feasible. Having somehow specified a set of alternatives, policymakers want to know which is likely to work best. The immediate objective of evaluation is to help society choose among the options under consideration at the time.

For example, Daniel Friedlander and Judith Gueron in Chapter 4 address the question: Are high-cost services more effective than low-cost services? The Family Support Act of 1988 reinforces a growing emphasis on programs that seek to help AFDC recipients move into the labor force. Two very different strategies have been proposed, basic education and job search assistance. The former strategy is much more intensive and expensive than the latter. In an effort to inform policymaking, Friedlander and Gueron assess what recent evaluations tell us about the relative merits of the two strategies.

Static and Dynamic Evaluation. Policymaking, however, is only partially a matter of choosing the best among a given set of options. It is also a matter of developing new programs that may work better. There is a tension between the *static* sense of evaluation, which compares a set of specified program options, and the *dynamic* sense, which seeks to improve future social decisions by developing new programs. From the static perspective, a program should be abandoned if, given the available information, the program is judged to yield inferior outcomes. From the dynamic perspective, it may be worthwhile to continue an "inferior" program if it yields information that may aid in the design of new programs.

Perhaps the most vibrant expression of the dynamic sense of evaluation is the idea that the fifty American states serve as "laboratories" where experiments with new ideas are initiated, the lessons eventually benefiting all of society.[7] In our federal system, a wide variety of pro-

---

7. The idea that the states are laboratories for policy experimentation is deeply ingrained in American thinking. For example, Louis Brandeis (1932) wrote: "It is one of the happy incidents of the federal system that a single courageous State may, if its citizens choose, serve as a laboratory; and try novel social and economic experiments without risk

grams may be operated simultaneously. Given the information available at any one time, a newly proposed program may be judged inferior to the status quo or insufficiently promising to warrant widespread adoption. But one or more states may wish to put the new program into operation, and observing the outcome may yield information valuable to the nation as a whole. The program may work better than expected. Or even if the program does not work well, analysis of its outcomes may reveal facts that are useful in the design of future programs.

Unfortunately, this book has little to say about the dynamic sense of evaluation. We understand only vaguely how new program options come to be proposed and taken seriously. This should not be surprising; we also know relatively little about how new commercial products appear and how new scientific ideas evolve. The development of new social policy is certainly no less complex a process.

Evaluation Methods

Reduced-Form and Structural Evaluation

Program evaluations have the pragmatic objective of learning what works best. The reasons welfare and training programs work as they do are rooted in basic social processes: individual labor supply and fertility behavior; the operation of the labor market; the formation of social norms; the way states, localities, and service providers organize and administer the programs. The central methodological question facing the evaluator is this: What must one understand about how programs work in order to reach conclusions about their merits?

The answer to this question depends on the available data. Suppose that one wishes to compare a given set of programs, all of which have actually been operated in the environment of interest. In this case, one need not understand how programs work in order to learn what they accomplish. The pragmatic evaluator can simply observe what they accomplish, treating the program as a black box. This *reduced-form* ap-

---

to the rest of the country." Theodore Roosevelt (1912) wrote: "Thanks to the movement for genuinely democratic popular government which Senator La Follette led to overwhelming victory in Wisconsin, that state has become literally a laboratory for wise experimental legislation aiming to secure the social and political betterment of the people as a whole" (p. vii).

proach to evaluation is infeasible, however, if one wants to compare programs that have not actually been operated in the environment of interest. In these cases, one does not possess the data necessary to compare programs directly. Evaluation requires that one somehow extrapolate from the available data.

Extrapolation is possible if one is able to characterize the environment of interest and if one understands the social processes that generate program outcomes in this environment. Then one can forecast the consequences of programs that have been proposed but not yet operated. Applying an understanding of social processes to forecast program outcomes in specified environments is referred to as *structural* evaluation.

The Methodology Controversy

The foregoing discussion suggests that the reduced-form and the structural approaches to evaluation both have their uses. Reduced-form evaluation is feasible if programs have actually been operated in the environment of interest; structural evaluation is feasible if one is able to characterize the environment of interest and if one understands the social processes at work well enough to permit forecasting with confidence. But what should one do if, as is often the case, neither reduced-form nor structural evaluation is feasible?

One answer is to initiate research that seeks to improve our understanding of the environment and of relevant social processes, in order to enable better structural evaluation. Advances may come from new data collection, from new analyses of available data, or from new theoretical insights. A second answer is to obtain data that enable better reduced-form evaluation. Although a proposed program may not have been operated in the environment of interest, one may observe that a similar program has somewhere, at some time, been operated in a similar environment. If no suitable *observational data* can be found, one might try to create a similar environment and initiate a similar program as a *social experiment.*

Disagreement about the relative merits of these two answers has made evaluation methodology a subject of debate. Researchers disagree on whether we can learn enough about the environment of social programs and about the social processes at work to make structural evaluation credible. And they disagree on whether we can find observational data or perform social experiments in which the environment and program are similar enough to the ones of interest to make reduced-form evaluation credible.

Questions about the credibility of structural and reduced-form evaluation often spill over into arguments about the usefulness of observational and experimental data. Structural evaluations have generally been based on observational data, whereas reduced-form evaluations increasingly use evidence from social experiments. It is important to understand that the mode of data collection per se is not the issue. Observational data may be used in reduced-form evaluations, and experimental data may be used to obtain a better understanding of social processes.[8] The issue is the manner in which the data are interpreted.

The New Orthodoxy. Until the early 1980s, the norm in the evaluation of welfare and training programs was to use observational data to perform structural evaluations.[9] Some studies analyzed cross-sectional variation in outcomes across states with different programs. Others analyzed "before-and-after" data; that is, time-series variation within a state that alters its program.

In the past decade, reduced-form analysis of social experiments has become the new orthodoxy, dominating the evaluations commissioned by the federal government and by the major foundations. In Chapter 2 Joseph Hotz describes how dissatisfaction with the evaluations of job training programs performed in the 1970s led the U.S. Department of Labor to commission an experimental evaluation of JTPA in the mid-1980s. David Greenberg and Michael Wiseman in Chapter 1 describe how a set of experiments, sponsored by the Ford Foundation and executed by the Manpower Demonstration Research Corporation, influenced the federal government to choose reduced-form experimental analysis as the preferred approach to evaluations of AFDC reforms.[10]

8. Reduced-form interpretations of observational data are sometimes referred to as analyses of "natural experiments." The use of data from social experiments to support structural evaluations is advocated by Orcutt and Orcutt (1968) and by James Heckman in Chapter 5.

9. From the mid-1960s through the late 1970s, social experiments were used to evaluate such programs as the negative income tax and time-of-day electricity pricing. Various experiments of this period are described in Hausman and Wise (1985). Welfare and training programs, however, were generally evaluated using observational data. One significant experimental evaluation was the National Supported Work Demonstration. See Manpower Demonstration Research Corporation (1980).

10. A series of articles in the academic literature may also have influenced government and foundation thinking. In the mid-1980s, a group of researchers expressed very pessimistic views regarding the feasibility of reliable structural evaluation and, contrariwise,

In Chapter 3 Michael Fishman and Daniel Weinberg provide a rare insiders' view of the government's deliberations as they describe the efforts of the federal Interagency Low-Income Opportunity Advisory Board to encourage experimental evaluation of AFDC reforms proposed by the states.

What led the government and foundations to abandon structural evaluation and to embrace reduced-form experimental evaluation? Is the recent transformation of evaluation practice warranted? In addressing these questions, we begin by explaining the selection problem that plagues structural evaluations based on observational data.

The Selection Problem

Structural evaluation based on observational data is widely recognized to pose a difficult scientific task. One observes the outcomes associated with some programs operated in some locations, with participants selected by some process. One would like to learn the impacts other programs would have if operated in other locations, with other participation processes.

Evaluation is obviously difficult if the program of interest has never been operated anywhere. We shall not consider this problem here. Instead, we restrict attention to the more limited task of forecasting outcomes when an observed program is moved to another location or operated with another participation process.[11]

Extrapolation from observational data is problematic for at least two reasons. First, the states or locales that operate a given program presumably do so because they expect the program to produce favorable outcomes. Second, in each location where a program is operated, the people

---

expressed optimism regarding the power of reduced-form experimental evaluation. Some went so far as to assert that only experimental evidence should be used to evaluate welfare and training programs. See, for example, Betsey et al. (1985), Bassi and Ashenfelter (1986), LaLonde (1986), Barnow (1987), and Fraker and Maynard (1987). Recently, the same assertion has been made with respect to the evaluation of public health programs. A National Research Council study of AIDS prevention programs, citing the difficulty of interpreting observational data, has concluded that only evidence from social experiments should be used to evaluate such programs. See Coyle, Boruch, and Turner (1991).

11. Evaluators sometimes use a single broad label, such as "job search," to characterize a range of heterogenous programs. The discussion here and in the following section assumes more than that the observed program and the new one share the same label; they must, in all substantive respects, provide the same treatment.

who choose to become eligible and apply presumably are those who
expect the program to have favorable impacts on them. It follows that,
if expected impacts are related to actual ones, then the outcomes that
would occur if the program were operated elsewhere, with a different
participation process, could well differ from those actually observed.

The extent to which extrapolation is possible depends on how well
one understands the process that determines the selection of participants into observed programs. Consider, for example, the task of forecasting the impact an observed program with voluntary participation
would have if participation in this program were made mandatory. It
can be shown that this task is only partly feasible in the absence of prior
information on how the program participants were selected. Observational data alone imply bounds on the impact of a mandatory version
of the program. These bounds can be tightened if prior information is
brought to bear. Given sufficiently strong information, the impact of a
mandatory version of the program can be measured.[12]

The practice in structural evaluation has been to invoke assumptions
strong enough to permit extensive extrapolation of program impacts.
Usually this is done through the medium of models that seek jointly to
explain program participation and impacts.[13] The problem is that the
stronger are the assumptions necessary to support an analysis, the less
credible is that analysis. Credibility is further diminished when, as is
often the case, social scientists have divergent opinions about the validity
of the prior information invoked in structural program evaluations.
Credibility is especially at risk when, as sometimes happens, the results
of a structural evaluation are found to be sensitive to the assumptions
made. For these reasons, criticisms of structural evaluations based on
observational data have been frequent and difficult to deflect.

Extrapolation from Social Experiments

Reduced-form evaluation of social experiments seeks to avoid the difficulties inherent in structural analysis of observational data. In the idealized experiment, a program is initiated at a set of randomly selected

12. See Manski (1989, 1990a, 1991) for a theoretical treatment of the identification
problem. Manski, Sandefur, McLanahan, and Powers (1990) provide an empirical case
study showing what can be learned in the absence of prior information.
13. See, for example, Heckman and Robb (1985) or Maddala (1983).

sites. Persons drawn from a specified population are randomly assigned
to a "treatment group" who participate in the program and to a "control
group" who do not. Random selection of sites and random assignment
to treatment break the tie between program operation, participation,
and outcome that is inherent in observational data. The outcomes in
the treatment group are then ostensibly the same as would occur if the
program were available to all members of the specified population; the
outcomes in the control group are those that would occur if the program
were not available to this population.[14]

The basic premise of reduced-form experimental evaluation is that
the experimental version of a program is operated under conditions
that approximate well the conditions under which the program would
be operated in practice. It is this premise which allows one to extrapolate
from the experiment to the real world.[15] There are, however, numerous
reasons to question this premise, as discussed in the following para-
graphs.

Program Administration. Reduced-form experimental analysis assumes
that program administration under the experiment does not systematically differ from administration of the program in practice. But experiments typically do not produce the same field conditions as do actual
program implementations; nor do they provide program administrators
and participants with the same information about program features.
Particularly problematic is the fact that social experiments cannot be
performed using the double-blind protocols of medical trials, in which
neither experimenters nor subjects know who is in the treatment and
control groups. Program administrators necessarily know who is in each
group and cannot be prevented from using this information to influence
outcomes.

Macro Feedback Effects. Full-scale programs change the environment
in which they operate in ways that may alter the effects of the programs.
In Chapter 7 we describe several such "macro" feedback effects, includ-

14. The impact of the program is typically measured by the difference between the
mean outcomes in the treatment and control groups. Given that the presence of the
program is the only systematic factor distinguishing the two groups, the difference in
mean outcomes can be attributed only to the program or to random fluctuations. For this
reason, randomized experiments are said to be "internally valid." See Cook and Campbell
(1979).

15. When the premise holds, an experiment is said to be "externally valid." See Cook
and Campbell (1979).

ing labor market—equilibrium effects, information-diffusion effects, and norm-formation effects. The scale of the typical social experiment is too small to discern these effects, which may become prominent when a program is actually implemented. The existence of macro feedback effects undermines the basic experimental premise that one can extrapolate from the experiment to the real world.

Site Selection. The experimental paradigm calls for random selection of sites. But because evaluators generally do not have the power to compel localities to cooperate, experiments are typically conducted at sites selected jointly by evaluators and local officials. A site, which may be a city, county, or other unit, is selected if it is judged suitable by the evaluators and if the relevant local officials agree to participate in the experiment.

Hotz describes in Chapter 2 how the JTPA evaluators originally sought to select sites randomly but, being unable to secure the agreement of the randomly drawn sites, were ultimately required to provide large financial incentives to nonrandomly selected localities in order to obtain their cooperation. Perhaps as a result of this chastising experience, the JOBS evaluation planned by the federal government makes no attempt to select sites randomly. Rather, sites will be chosen among those localities that apply to participate in the experiment.[16]

Program Participation. The usual social experiment randomly assigns program applicants to treatment and control groups. Extrapolation of outcomes from the experiment to the real world requires the evaluator to assume that the population of applicants would not change if the program were actually implemented. It must also be assumed that the attrition process by which people leave the program would not change if the program were implemented.

Heckman in Chapter 5 observes that the assumption of an unchanged applicant pool and attrition process is not plausible, because the value of participating in a program with randomized treatment is not the same as that of participating in a program with known treatment. He makes the point well when he observes that social experimentation is intrinsically different from experimentation in the biological sciences and agriculture: "Plots of ground do not respond to anticipated treatments of fertilizer, nor can they excuse themselves from being treated."

Thus, although an idealized experiment escapes the selection problem

---

16. See Manpower Demonstration Research Corporation (1990).

that afflicts analysis of observational data, actual social experiments must confront this problem.[17]

Implications of Extrapolation Problems

The difficulty of extrapolating from a social experiment to the real world has long been known. Extrapolation problems arising in the social experiments of the 1970s led evaluation researchers of that period to become quite cautious in interpreting experimental evidence. For example, attrition was a major concern in the analysis of outcomes in the negative income tax experiments.[18]

Extrapolation problems have been downplayed or ignored in recent experimental evaluations. The impression has taken hold that reduced-form analysis of experimental data does not require assumptions. It is said that randomization makes it possible to perform evaluations without understanding the social processes at work.[19]

In fact, reduced-form experimental evaluation actually requires that a highly specific and suspect structural assumption hold: Individuals and organizations must respond in the same way to the experimental version of a program as they would to the actual version. Unfortunately, the evaluation community has not made a systematic effort to ascertain the circumstances in which this assumption is justified and to determine the implications of invoking the assumption when it is not justified. Hence there is, at present, no basis for the popular belief that extrapolation from social experiments is less problematic than extrapolation from observational data.

As we see it, the recent embrace of reduced-form social experimentation, to the exclusion of structural evaluation based on observational data, is not warranted. The diversity of our federal system makes observational data a powerful source of evidence on program outcomes and on the social processes that generate those outcomes. The collection

17. Moffitt, in Chapter 6, addresses the problem of designing an experiment that properly recognizes the voluntary nature of program participation. He concludes that the usual sampling protocol would need to be changed. Whereas the practice is to assign program applicants randomly to treatment and control groups, one should instead randomly assign members of the general population to program-eligible and incligible groups. This protocol is never implemented, possibly because of its high cost.

18. Many of the extrapolation problems mentioned in the previous section are discussed in Hausman and Wise (1985).

19. See, for example, Coyle, Boruch, and Turner (1991).

of observational data is sometimes inexpensive relative to the cost of conducting a social experiment; some such data are collected routinely for purposes of administering programs. It is unwise for the government and foundations to commit all of their evaluation resources to social experiments, while leaving diverse, inexpensive observational data unanalyzed.

Experimentation should certainly continue. Social experiments constitute an important source of data for evaluation. But analyses of experimental data must confront openly the problem of extrapolating from the experimental setting to the real world.

Special Problems Confronted in Evaluating Social Programs

Program evaluations are efforts to learn from experience in order to improve social decisions. Individuals, firms, and other private-sector organizations routinely learn from experience. To conclude this chapter, we ask whether social program evaluation has unique characteristics that influence current evaluation practices.

Entitlements and the Ethics of Social Experimentation

Private experimentation and social experimentation are alike in many respects; for example, both must confront the problem of extrapolation discussed earlier. In some respects, however, social experimentation raises issues not occurring in the private sector.

Some social programs achieve the status of "entitlements," whether through law or through popular consensus. Suppose that one wants to compare the outcomes observed under an entitlement program with those that would occur if the program were not in place. An experiment making this comparison may be valuable to society for the information it yields about the merits of the program. But such an experiment must select some individuals to be members of a control group who are denied the benefits of the program. Denying some individuals their entitlement raises an ethical problem not occurring in private experiments.

The implication of this ethical problem for evaluation practice is that some potentially informative social experiments are not conducted. The courts may halt a planned experiment. More commonly, evaluators restrict their attention to experiments thought not to raise serious ethical issues.

Experimentation does not always create an ethical problem; in some cases it solves one. Often a locality does not possess sufficient funds to make a program an entitlement. A means must then be found to allocate the available funds among the eligible applicants. In the absence of consensus on a systematic allocation rule, random selection of program participants is appealing.

The Credibility of Evaluations

Social programs are important to a population composed of people with widely divergent personal concerns and political ideologies. Program evaluations can influence policymaking only if they are conducted and reported in a manner that makes their findings credible to the majority of this population. In this respect, the evaluation of social programs differs fundamentally from private-sector evaluation, where findings need be credible only to the individual or organization initiating the evaluation.

The desire to increase the general credibility of program evaluations has been largely responsible for the recent decline of interest in structural evaluations based on observational data and the associated rise of interest in reduced-form experimental evaluation. The evaluation literature using observational data has, for the most part, been explicit about its structural assumptions. In this literature, it is common to find soul-searching and debate on the validity of assumptions and on the sensitivity of results to variation in assumptions. The literature using experimental data, on the other hand, has tended to leave its assumptions implicit and unquestioned.

Open scrutiny of the assumptions that underlie evaluations is healthy. Ironically, however, such scrutiny tends to diminish the credibility of evaluations, especially to policymakers who may not appreciate the inherent difficulty of the evaluation enterprise.[20] As a consequence, the influence of reduced-form experimentation has risen in recent years while that of structural evaluations has declined. The proper balance between structural and reduced-form analysis will be found only when the evaluation community holds both to the same standard.

20. Henry Aaron, who participated in evaluation both as a researcher and as a federal government official, provides a perceptive discussion in Aaron (1978).

Funding

Finally, we call attention to what we see as the most disturbing aspect of evaluation today: the funding-induced imbalance between applications and basic research. From the mid-1960s through the 1970s, evaluations of social programs nicely blended applications and basic research. Specific programs were analyzed and policy implications drawn. At the same time, innovation in evaluation methods took place and a base of empirical knowledge guiding future evaluations was established. Social scientists, evaluation professionals, and public officials not only worked together but sometimes traded hats.

Since 1980, government and foundation funding for basic evaluation research has almost disappeared. At the same time, the public has increasingly demanded proof of the effectiveness of existing social programs. The consequence is that evaluation today is dominated by tightly focused applications with short horizons. Government and foundation funding is allocated largely through contracts calling on the evaluator to provide specified deliverables on a fixed schedule. The contractor's task is to compare the short-run direct impact of a given program with that of a particular alternative, often the absence of that program.

The existing funding environment has negative implications for the long-term health of evaluation practice. Present contractual funding encourages assembly-line evaluations, executed with conventional procedures, reported in a standardized format. It discourages innovation in methods, efforts to understand the complex set of processes that define a program, evaluation of long-term program impacts, and creative thinking about program design.

The present funding imbalance between applications and basic evaluation research must be corrected. Effective collaboration of social scientists, evaluation professionals, and public officials is necessary to make the evaluation of social programs a creative enterprise with both immediate and long-term benefits to society.

References

Aaron, Henry. 1978. *Politics and the Professors: The Great Society in Perspective.* Washington, D.C.: Brookings Institution.

Barnow, Burt. 1987. "The Impact of CETA Programs on Earnings: A Review of the Literature." *Journal of Human Resources,* 22: 157–193.

Bassi, Laurie, and Orley Ashenfelter. 1986. "The Effect of Direct Job Creation and Training Programs on Low-Skilled Workers." In *Fighting Poverty: What Works and What Doesn't*, ed. Sheldon H. Danziger and Daniel H. Weinberg. Cambridge, Mass.: Harvard University Press.

Betsey, Charles L., Robinson G. Hollister, and Mary R. Papageorgiou, eds. 1985. *Youth Employment and Training Programs*. Washington, D.C.: National Academy Press.

Brandeis, Louis. 1932. Dissenting Opinion in *New State Ice Co. v. Liebmann*, 285 U.S. 311.

Cook, Thomas, and Donald Campbell. 1979. *Quasi-Experimentation*. Chicago: Rand McNally.

Corbett, Thomas, Jeannette Deloya, Wendy Manning, and Liz Uhr. 1989. "Learnfare: The Wisconsin Experience." *Focus* (newsletter of the Institute for Research on Poverty), 12 (no. 2): 1–10.

Coyle, Susan L., Robert F. Boruch, and Charles F. Turner, eds. 1991. *Evaluating AIDS Prevention Programs*. Washington, D.C.: National Academy Press.

Fraker, Thomas, and Rebecca Maynard. 1987. "The Adequacy of Comparison Group Designs for Evaluations of Employment-Related Programs." *Journal of Human Resources*, 22: 194–227.

Hausman, Jerry, and David Wise, eds. 1985. *Social Experimentation*. Chicago: University of Chicago Press.

Haveman, Robert. 1987. *Poverty Policy and Poverty Research: The Great Society and the Social Sciences*. Madison: University of Wisconsin Press.

Heckman, James J., and Richard R. Robb. 1985. "Alternative Methods for Evaluating the Impact of Interventions." In *Longitudinal Analysis of Labor Market Data*, ed. Heckman and Burton Singer. New York: Cambridge University Press.

LaLonde, Robert. 1986. "Evaluating the Econometric Evaluations of Training Programs with Experimental Data." *American Economic Review*, 76: 604–620.

Lampman, Robert. 1976. "The Decision to Undertake the New Jersey Experiment." Foreword to *The New Jersey Income Maintenance Experiment*, ed. David Kershaw and Jerilyn Fair. Vol. 1. New York: Academic Press.

Maddala, G. S. 1983. *Limited-Dependent and Qualitative Variables in Econometrics*. Cambridge: Cambridge University Press.

Manpower Demonstration Research Corporation, 1980. *Summary and Findings of the National Supported Work Demonstration*. Cambridge, Mass.: Ballinger.

——— 1990. *The JOBS Evaluation: Questions and Answers*. New York: MDRC.

Manski, Charles F. 1989. "Anatomy of the Selection Problem." *Journal of Human Resources*, 24: 343–360.

———— 1990a. "Nonparametric Bounds on Treatment Effects." *American Economic Review,* 80 (no. 2): 319–323.

———— 1990b. "Where We Are in the Evaluation of Federal Social Welfare Programs." *Focus* (newsletter of the Institute for Research on Poverty), 12 (no. 4): 1–5.

———— 1991. "The Selection Problem." In *Advances in Econometrics,* ed. Christopher Sims. New York: Cambridge University Press.

Manski, Charles F., Gary D. Sandefur, Sara McLanahan, and Daniel Powers. 1990. "Alternative Estimates of the Effect of Family Structure during Adolescence on High School Graduation." Institute for Research on Poverty, Discussion Paper No. 929-90, University of Wisconsin-Madison.

Orcutt, Guy, and Alice Orcutt. 1968. "Experiments for Income Maintenance Policies." *American Economic Review,* 58: 754–772.

Roosevelt, Theodore. 1912. Introduction to Charles McCarthy, *The Wisconsin Idea.* New York: Macmillan.

U.S. Department of Labor, Children's Bureau. 1931. "Seven Years' Work of the Cooperating States under the Maternity and Infancy Act." In *The Promotion of the Welfare and Hygiene of Maternity and Infancy.* Bureau Publication No. 203. Washington, D.C.: U.S. Government Printing Office.

PART I

Evaluation Today

1 What Did the OBRA Demonstrations Do?

David Greenberg and Michael Wiseman

A Tale of Two Decades

Here is a paradox: Welfare reform failed in the Nixon-Carter era despite ardent pursuit and commitment to pay by both administrations. In contrast, welfare reform was accomplished in the Reagan years in the face of considerable executive skepticism and a burgeoning federal deficit. Here is another: At least in retrospect, it appears that social science research confounded policymaking in the 1970s, but facilitated consensus-building in the 1980s. The contrast between welfare policy developments during the two decades illustrates the episodic character of welfare reform and suggests, perhaps, that the relation between social science and public policy may have changed.

Consider the contrast further. From the perspective of welfare policy, the 1970s effectively began in 1969 with President Nixon's Family Assistance Plan (FAP) proposal and the first reports from what was to be a series of experiments aimed at assessing the consequences of adoption of a national system of income maintenance for low-income families. The decade effectively ended with congressional rejection of modest incremental reforms of the AFDC system proposed in 1979 by the Carter administration in an attempt to save some aspects of the comprehensive Program for Better Jobs and Income (PBJI) that the President had proposed in 1977. During the decade, policy-related research seemed to add to, rather than reduce, confusion about appropriate welfare policy (Munnell, 1986).

The 1980s began with a determined attempt by the Reagan administration to reduce federal involvement in welfare and to increase the latitude granted states in welfare system operation. Like the negative income tax initiatives of the 1970s, this movement also produced a remarkable quantity of policy-related research. But at the end of the decade the result was much different: instead of a collection of dead proposals suitable only for postmortem, we had the Family Support Act (FSA) of 1988, a major (if modest) national initiative passed by commanding majorities in both houses of Congress. And observers and participants alike credit the research produced during the decade with significant effects on both the design and political support for this new legislation (Baum, 1989; Haskins, 1989; Szanton, 1989).

We are interested in the connection between research and policy and the lessons learned from the Reagan years for future welfare program evaluation and policymaking. To study this, we focus on research covering the consequences of programs of employment or employability enhancement for welfare applicants or recipients that resulted from the Omnibus Budget Reconciliation Act of 1981 (OBRA) and subsequent OBRA-related legislation. OBRA was the foundation of the Reagan reform program. In the remainder of this section, we set the stage by reviewing the OBRA innovations.

The act made a major contribution toward development of methods of integration of income maintenance with employability enhancement. Like most welfare innovations, OBRA was the product of compromise. President Reagan and his associates came to the White House with a program for welfare reform based on what they believed had been accomplished by then-Governor Reagan in California in 1971 (Levy, 1978). The California reform package featured reduction of the financial incentives for employment incorporated in the calculation of benefits. But it also included a work requirement, the California Work Experience Program (CWEP), which was designed to link AFDC payments to mandatory community service without pay. The Reagan administration proposed similar innovations for the country as a whole. Congress agreed to changes in the benefits-calculation procedures, but instead of mandating state implementation of work-for-welfare, OBRA provided a collection of possible building blocks or tools for an enhanced employment-oriented welfare system. CWEP (now Community, not California, Work Experience) was but one of these tools.

The OBRA toolkit was expanded and modified by subsequent legislation, but the basic components have remained the same: the consolidation of authority for AFDC-related employment operations within state welfare agencies; community work experience; a work supplementation program that permitted use of welfare grants to subsidize client employment in public, private nonprofit, and (after 1984) private for-profit organizations and businesses; and expanded authority for requiring participation in job search programs by both AFDC applicants and recipients.

Many states responded to the OBRA opportunities by constructing welfare employment programs from the OBRA toolkit. Although interesting as an example of creative federalism, the outpouring of innovation from the "thousand flowers" welfare policy encouraged by OBRA was potentially a disappointment for those interested in systematic improvement of policy. To identify innovations worthy of evaluation, we need to know what the consequences of such policies are for the behavior of families and individuals at risk of poverty and welfare dependence. While a multiplicity of approaches potentially provides many degrees of freedom for assessment of the consequences of the various OBRA-related tools and the processes created to manage them, a priori there was no reason to believe that a sufficient quantity of reliable data would be produced to allow the potential information gains from so many experiments to be realized. In fact, we have learned a great deal.

Operation of most OBRA-based programs required that the states be granted waivers of certain Social Security Act requirements for AFDC. In particular, since operations typically could not be implemented statewide, SSA restrictions on variation in treatment of recipients within states had to be waived. Granting of waivers requires an evaluation plan. Thus, one result of OBRA-based innovations has been a substantial number of evaluations of the consequences of such activities.

The quality of many of these OBRA evaluations is very high. There are at least two reasons for this, one historical, the other entrepreneurial. While OBRA reformers were in part motivated by dissatisfaction with top-down approaches to welfare reform inherited from a decade of Washington-spawned welfare reform proposals, they were heirs as well to the results of fifteen years of welfare experimentation. Much of this work—most notably the four income maintenance experiments (Munnell, 1986) and the Supported Work Demonstrations—was based on sophisticated research studies that featured comparisons of outcomes for participants ("experimentals") assigned at random to receive some reform-related "treatment" to outcomes for individuals who did not receive such treatment (controls). The legacy of this tradition was a growing academic consensus that random assignment was a methodologically superior approach to program evaluation and evidence that such studies could in fact be carried out.

No matter how strong academic support for impact evaluation on the basis of random assignment of participants to experimental and control groups might have been, it is unlikely that states would have, on their own, adopted this approach. The translation of consensus into action is attributable to the aggressive entrepreneurship of the Manpower Demonstration Research Corporation (MDRC). As architect of the National Supported Work Demonstration, MDRC was committed to random assignment as the foundation of evaluation of employment policy innovations. The firm organized private grants for the OBRA evaluation effort and offered states subsidized research in return for a state commitment to an evaluation based on random assignment of clients to control and treatment groups. Once these techniques caught on, the MDRC delivered the research reports that became required reading for welfare administrators nationwide, the number of MDRC-evaluated experiments grew rapidly.

The upshot is that we are beginning the last decade of the twentieth century with a remarkable collection of new information on the consequences of employment-related welfare innovations, much of which has been produced in a common and comparable format. This chapter and a larger and more detailed companion report (Greenberg and Wiseman, 1991) surveys 24 evaluations of individual OBRA-related state demonstration programs, 13 of which were conducted by MDRC. In addition, we have reviewed a large collection of related research, both cross-cutting and targeted at complementary, but not specifically OBRA-based, policies. Our objective is to assess what has been learned from this work about the efficacy of both the interventions themselves and the institutional and methodological procedures that have been used for their evaluation.

We begin with an overview of issues in demonstration design and evaluation, then study the welfare processes created by the OBRA demonstrations, review what is known about their impact, and conclude with some reflections on the lessons learned and the work still needed.

An Approach to Demonstration Evaluation

This section sets out an organization scheme for the OBRA studies and presents an overview of the evaluation reports we reviewed. We refer to all the programs developed in response to OBRA opportunities as Welfare Employment Programs, or WEPs. Figure 1.1 is a flow diagram

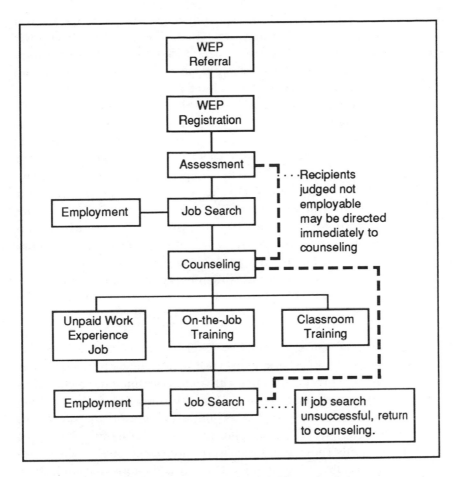

Figure 1.1. Flow chart, hypothetical welfare employment program. Circumstances prompting *referral* vary; it may be subsumed in the welfare application process. *Assessment* typically covers "barriers" to employment, including service needs and basic as well as specific skills deficiencies. *Job search* uses individual and/or group search methods. In the *counseling* stage, more thorough counseling and barriers-to-employment assessment are performed; activities may include a "contract." The *work experience and training* stage covers a wide variety of activities; assignment to a work experience job is rarely the initial activity.

for a stylized WEP. Diagrams similar to this one are a common feature of the evaluation reports we have reviewed. The diagram depicts the sequence of activities a client experiences, with flow from top to bottom of the chart. WEPs vary considerably from one to another; no actual program flow diagram matches this figure exactly.

The figure illustrates three properties shared by many of the programs we reviewed. First, this WEP is a *process* rather than a condition. Traditionally, saying that a client was "on welfare" sufficed as a description of his or her condition because welfare was a stationary state. But welfare employment processes are time-dependent, and as a result, saying "in WEP" leaves something more to be described. Second, most of these programs may be divided, like traditional casework, into a series of steps, or components, from which the process is constructed. It is often the case that components are provided by other agencies or non-profit organizations. Finally, the process may be tailored to individual characteristics, and this tailoring will show up in variation in the sequence of steps recipients take. To the extent that the differences in these sequences are systematic, they may be termed "tracks."

A WEP evaluation may be focused on any or all of several levels. In the organizational sense, the highest level is the political/institutional process that creates such a system. OBRA and concurrent budgeting decisions basically presented states with an opportunity and a change in resources. States responded to this offer with programs that mixed the opportunities in varying ways. But it is important to note that we do not have information on *all* state responses; we have in hand evidence on outcomes for only those states that were induced to submit their programs to the scrutiny of evaluators. If the jurisdictions that undertook evaluations of OBRA-based demonstrations are exceptional—and they are—then making inferences for the consequences of similar programs for the nation as a whole from the results of these demonstrations is hazardous at best. The odds that three draws in a random sample of 24 OBRA-related demonstrations nationwide would come from San Diego County—as is true for our survey—are extremely low!

The hazard of selection bias is reduced if we can uncover the "recipes" that are at the heart of the various WEPs created as a result of the OBRA opportunity. This is the second possible evaluation focus, and it can be looked at in two ways. One approach is to emphasize structure, including contributing organizations, bargains struck between the managing agency and contributors, effects of the innovation on the sponsoring organizations, and public presentations of the program. The alternative is to emphasize the experience of individual WEP participants, that is, to describe the WEP "treatment." It is identification of the treatment that is essential if replication of effects is to be assured. The investigations of both organization and treatment have been termed "process analysis."

A third possible emphasis of evaluation is the effect of the recipe upon client behaviors and outcomes. This is often termed "impact analysis." Traditionally, the outcomes of interest for impact studies have included employment, earnings, and welfare utilization. While such evaluations may concentrate on broad-based comparisons of the effects of one general system to another (or perhaps to no system at all), once a WEP is in place, the decisions that count from the local agency perspective are those that marginally change program operation—for example, substituting one method of job search for another.

Once a substantial number of evaluations of various types are in hand, a fourth object of evaluation can be the evaluations themselves: What policies were tested? Why? What designs were utilized?

Finally, for policy purposes, the object is often some sort of cost-benefit analysis in which program outcomes are summarized to whatever extent possible in dollar terms. This common unit allows assessment of the efficiency of the project—whether the value of resources gained exceeds resources lost. Cost-benefit analysis of programs still in a development phase may not be conclusive, however, because of significant potential for both costs and impacts to change as agencies, clients, and the local economy adjust to the innovation, and as learning-by-doing occurs.

Our interest concerns lessons for policy evaluation and insights into the consequences of WEPs for clients. Accordingly, we omit political and organizational analysis and focus instead upon review of WEP client processes, demonstration research designs, and client impacts. While useful political and organizational analysis of individual OBRA-related programs exist (see Behn, 1989), a comparative political/organizational analysis of state programs is, to our knowledge, not yet available. An assessment of cost-benefit studies of OBRA innovations is included in our larger study (Greenberg and Wiseman, 1991) but is omitted here because of space considerations as well as our perception that such studies may be premature given the continuing evolution of welfare employment program design and operation.

Our sample was defined solely on the basis of availability of data. We began by asking the Office of the Assistant Secretary for Planning and Evaluation in the U.S. Department of Health and Human Services (HHS) for all OBRA-related demonstration evaluation reports submitted to HHS through December 31, 1989, and we added all of the reports produced by the MDRC Work/Welfare Initiatives project. In two cases (Maryland and West Virginia), one report covered two quite different demonstrations, and we have treated them separately.

All told, we accumulated 24 evaluations, which are summarized in the appendix at the end of the chapter. We consider the following nine observations and conclusions drawn from our survey to be particularly important for understanding OBRA's lessons.

Most Evaluations Are by MDRC. Thirteen of the 24 evaluations we studied were conducted by MDRC. The remaining evaluations were either conducted in-house by the state or by research firms other than MDRC. Because findings from the OBRA demonstrations are dominated by the analyses of MDRC and the techniques it adopted, an important objective of this chapter must be to assess the degree to which the MDRC approach serves public ends.

Geographic Coverage Varies. The 24 evaluations cover demonstrations in 19 states, and this variety is reflected in substantial program diversity and considerable variation in the economic environments in which innovation was carried out. However, while some of the OBRA demonstrations were conducted over the entire state, others were limited to sub-areas such as counties or welfare office jurisdictions.

Participation Was Generally Mandatory. The evaluated OBRA demonstrations were generally directed toward adults whose participation in the Work Incentive Program (WIN) was a requirement for AFDC eligibility. At a minimum, WIN required certain adult recipients to register for job search and other employment-related activities with the local office of their state's job service. The most significant group typically exempted from WIN participation was single parents with children under age 6.[1] However, in five of the programs mandatory participation was extended to parents with no children under age 3. Except for the Employment and Training-Choices (ET) program in Massachusetts and the Greater Avenues for Independence (GAIN) program in California, failure of those for whom participation was mandatory to comply with

1. Other situations conferring exemption include enrollment in school (for teenagers), illness, incapacity, lack of access to transportation or remote location, and responsibility for care of a sick person.

program requirements was supposed to be met with a "sanction": elimination of the noncompliant adult from the household's grant computation in the case of AFDC-R (single or disabled parent) and loss of welfare eligibility altogether for AFDC-U (two-parent, unemployed) cases. In contrast, Massachusetts allowed AFDC recipients to decide for themselves whether or not to participate at all in its program and, if they did so decide, to select among a menu of available program components. And California has experimented with reduction of client expenditure discretion—third-party management of household expenditures—as an alternative to deregistration and grant reduction.

Demonstration Targets Vary. OBRA demonstration programs varied substantially with respect to the subset of potential eligibles actually targeted. For some WEPs, welfare application initiated WEP treatment (this target client pool is identified as "APPs" in discussions that follow). Alternatively, the WEP might be introduced at the point when welfare eligibility was formally obtained ("New Recipients," or NRs). A third port of entry occurs when circumstances change—for example, when the youngest child in the household of a woman who otherwise satisfies the criteria for WIN participation reaches the age of 6 (or, in some WEPs, 3)—and recipients who formerly were not mandatory participants become so ("NDMRs," for "Newly Determined Mandatory Recipients"). Finally, some WEPs served all AFDC recipients who were eligible for WIN at the time the program was initially established ("CMRs," for "Continuing Mandatory Recipients").

These distinctions have at least three important consequences. First, applicants are not recipients, and some WEP proponents believe that early interception of persons applying for public assistance will dissuade some from taking up welfare at all. This possibility, however, was not explicitly analyzed in any of the studies we considered. Second, in a newly initiated or expanded WEP, it may initially be necessary to restrict the rate of intake of eligibles in some way in order to avoid swamping the system. Taking only *new* mandatories—either APPs, NRs, or NDMRs—has the advantage of allowing the agency to deal with a flow of clients that is smaller than the stock of CMRs. The OBRA demonstrations thus provide information pertinent to evaluation of such a strategy. Finally, adults in the existing AFDC caseload are typically more disadvantaged and more isolated from the labor market than adults in the applicant families. Differences in outcomes among the various groups may reflect this.

Structure Varies. Distinctions may be drawn among WEPs on the basis of the nature of and importance attached to the sequence of program activities. Programs generally fall between two extremes. In one, all participants go through the same steps; in the other, virtually nothing is prespecified. For example, the San Diego Employment Preparation Program/Experimental Work Experience Program (EPP/EWEP) had a fixed participation sequence—job search followed by CWEP. In contrast, the Baltimore Options program utilized a variety of components and allowed caseworkers to tailor services to individual needs. Some programs, such as California's GAIN effort, begin with a relatively rigid sequence and then increase caseworker and client discretion at later stages in the process.

Focus Varies. A broad distinction can be made between demonstrations that concentrate on implementation of an alternative to the minimal services provided by WIN and demonstrations designed to provide evidence on the impact of alternative tracks within a richer WEP process. Some do both. We count as tests of components the EPP/EWEP project in San Diego (the effectiveness of adding CWEP), Florida's TRADE (Trade Welfare for Work) program, the Illinois WDP (WIN Demonstration) program, Maine's TOPS (Training Opportunities in the Private Sector), the New Jersey OJT (On-the-Job Training) demonstration, the Virginia ESP (Employment Services) program, and one of the two Washington state experiments, although, as discussed later, not all of these experiments yielded useful information.

Circumstances Vary. The earliest intake of client data for evaluation of one of the OBRA demonstrations began in June of 1982 (one of the Washington demonstrations); the most recent data were collected for the third quarter of 1988 (12-quarter observations from the San Diego SWIM program). Many changes occurred in the economy during this interval. Overall, conditions improved markedly, with the national unemployment rate falling from 9.2 percent in 1982 to 5.5 percent in 1988. At the same time, prices and wages went up. We have not, however, attempted adjustment in this chapter for price effects or place-to-place and time-to-time variation in labor market conditions.

Results Have Many Dimensions. The evaluations of the OBRA demonstrations have as a useful by-product important information heretofore unavailable on the experience of households receiving public assistance. In particular, they provide the richest data available on the experience of welfare-dependent families over time—data that are reported at quarterly, in some cases monthly, intervals. Moreover, these data are probably more reliable than survey-provided information, at least with respect to transfers and participation in the above-ground economy, because much of the information is taken directly from institutional sources. Of particular importance is the fact that the OBRA demonstrations provide an exceptional body of information on AFDC-U families, since virtually every AFDC-U family included a WIN mandatory adult. Intact families have long been on the frontier for income maintenance expansion, and, as a result, particular interest is attached to the consequences of OBRA-type intervention for this group.

There Are Many Degrees of Freedom. Variation in the design, implementation, and evaluation of WEPs is substantial. As a result we can anticipate that, even given 24 WEPs with which to work, the likelihood of identifying relations between outcomes and inputs sufficiently clear-cut to serve as a basis for forecasting the consequences of national replication of such innovations is small.

The Demonstrations: Process

While the requests published by agencies seeking to fund program evaluations often include calls for process analysis, the meaning and objective of this requirement are generally ambiguous. In our review we developed a client-oriented process analysis that had two objectives: (1) assessment of the effects of the various WEPs studied on the type of service provided clients; and (2) identification of the consequences of such programs for what those applying for or receiving public assistance can expect to experience over a given interval of time. Our analysis indicates that WEP effects on client outcomes occur through the consequences of such systems for labor market information, participant skills, and the costs of dependency. These objectives of our process analysis reflect our understanding of the avenues whereby WEP effects occur.

Many of the demonstration reports did not include data for even rudimentary statistical analysis of process, although others, especially the MDRC reports, did. In cases where the necessary statistics were not provided, we were forced to rely on general descriptions of procedures to make inferences about the incidence and timing of WEP activities.

Nonetheless, our reading suggests that five important conclusions regarding services actually received emerge from process analyses of the OBRA demonstrations.

Job Search Is the Major Treatment. Within the OBRA demonstrations and client subsamples for which statistical information on service receipt was available, only about half of the treatment-group members participated in any component activity over an interval of nine to twelve months following assignment. Of these activities, job search was by far the most common. With the exception of West Virginia's CWEP saturation experiment, the odds were generally less than 1 in 5 that a member of a "treatment" group became involved in CWEP or training during the nine to twelve months following WEP registration.

Turnover Is Substantial. In the demonstrations for which data were available, more than *half* of AFDC applicants eventually deregistered from the WEP. Interpretation of this number is complicated, however, by the fact that so many applicants never apparently achieved welfare eligibility. Deregistration rates are also appreciable for AFDC-R recipients. Deregistration, however, can come about for reasons other than employment; our understanding of OBRA outcomes would be aided by better information on the reasons for these transitions.

Sanctioning Occurs. There are in the demonstration reports frequent references to difficulties encountered in securing client cooperation and attendance in WEP-related activities (as well as to the eagerness of some clients to receive WEP services). In practice, a small but significant proportion of those for whom participation has been mandated have been sanctioned.

Service Receipt Is Often Selection-Dependent. A very low incidence of receipt of particular services in complex programs—for example, training in the Baltimore Options and Virginia ESP demonstrations—means that someone's discretion is exercised in determining who gets what. As a result, whatever impacts are observed are potentially the product of both the services delivered and an unobserved assignment procedure.

Circumstances of Controls Vary. In some of the OBRA demonstrations, services received by controls were minimal; in others, controls received more. This is particularly true in component-oriented demonstrations such as Maine's TOPS, the New Jersey Grant Diversion program, and the Virginia ESP demonstration. Indeed, in the Virginia experiment, controls received sufficient training to contaminate one part of the outcome, leading to its exclusion from analysis.

By and large, the focus of most WEP process data is upon service receipt. Far less attention has been paid to measurement of the time cost of WEPs or to identifying the expected sequence of services a client might be expected to receive and the likely timing of this sequence. In analyzing the consequences for behavior, it may also be important to study what clients *believe* will happen. In many of the OBRA demonstrations, it is not clear what participants were led to believe about the program process. In the first of the San Diego demonstrations, for example, clients in the job search/CWEP track were not told that CWEP was in their future until they were well into job search. Other demonstration reports provide little information at all about what recipients were told. In the absence of better information, the best approach would be to study the actual experience of clients who remain program-eligible. What is the expected sequence of activity and time commitment generated for a recipient, given continued participation? We rarely know. Of course, because of the now familiar problem of selection bias, answering this question is not simple. Those recipients who stay WEP-eligible are themselves exceptional.

A cruder, but nonetheless useful, approach to investigation of WEP participation is to focus on the likelihood of activity at a point in time. Obviously, for example, if all eligibles in a WEP do something every month, then the prospect for new participants who stay on welfare is most likely the same. These point-in-time incidence measures are available for a small subset of the OBRA demonstrations. They are usually calibrated on a monthly basis, so any activity within a month makes that month count as active. Data in the MDRC report on Arizona's WID (Work Incentive Demonstration) program, for example, indicate that over the interval covered, about 25 percent of WID eligibles were active in each month on average, a number comparable to the 23 percent achieved in the Minnesota CWEP program. Rates about twice as high were achieved in both the San Diego SWIM program and the West Virginia CWEP demonstrations, but in these cases "saturation" was an objective of the demonstration.

The welfare employment program established by the Family Support Act of 1988—the Job Opportunities and Basic Skills Training programs, JOBS—includes a participation goal. By 1995, states are to achieve a monthly activity rate of 20 percent. Compared to the participation rates reported for the OBRA demonstrations, the requirement defined in program regulations appears at once generous and restrictive. It is generous in that the percentage is low, phase-in is gradual, and the statutes allow the numerator of the ratio to include both mandatory participants and volunteers, while the denominator covers only those required to participate. It is restrictive in that only recipients who are scheduled for an average of 20 hours or more per week in approved activities over the month and who actually attend at least 75 percent of their scheduled hours can be counted in the numerator. In contrast, the OBRA reports count any activity, regardless of how brief, as participation. Thus, the OBRA demonstrations give only weak evidence on the feasibility of mandating rates of participation for agencies.

The Demonstrations: Impact

Given process, did the OBRA demonstrations achieve the anticipated effects? Impact analyses designed to address this question were conducted as part of all but a few of the OBRA demonstration evaluations. In this section we examine these impact analyses. We begin by briefly enumerating the demonstration outcomes or impacts that the impact analyses attempted to measure; we then describe the numerous ways in which the evaluation designs associated with the various demonstrations influenced the estimates of these impacts. This is followed by a discussion of findings from those impact analyses in which we place some confidence.

Impacts of Interest

The goal of most of the OBRA demonstrations was to improve the labor market performance of AFDC recipients and, thereby, reduce their dependence on welfare. The measures of impacts used in the evaluations reflect this goal. These measures include changes in the employment status, earnings, welfare status, and transfer payments of AFDC recipients, and, at a more aggregate level, changes in caseload size and welfare expenditures.

In measuring and reporting on these impacts, evaluators of the OBRA demonstrations have placed the greatest emphasis on effects on the welfare population as a whole, or at least that part of the population eligible for treatment under the demonstration programs. However, because resources to fund programs aimed at reducing welfare dependency are scarce, some effort has been made, especially in those demonstrations evaluated by MDRC, to determine whether treatment impacts differ among various subgroups. If they do, then program resources can be targeted on members of those subgroups for which the treatment has the greatest payoff.

Researchers have been particularly interested in the relationship between program impacts and case characteristics associated with long-term dependence in studies of welfare. Since some welfare cases ("movers") leave more rapidly than others ("stayers"), there tends to be a systematic difference between the average characteristics of all cases that are ever open during, say, a year, and the characteristics of those cases that are ever open on any given day. Specifically, the point-in-time caseload tends to have a higher proportion of "stayers" than is true for any cohort of new openings. Compared to movers, stayer cases account for a disproportionate share of welfare costs. These considerations focus attention on differences between employment program effects upon the job-ready and those who are not job-ready, and also upon differences in program effects upon new entrants—presumably more likely to include movers—and upon long-term recipients, a group dominated by stayers. An additional important subgroup comparison is between AFDC recipients with preschool or younger children and those with only children in school. To some extent this, too, is a distinction between movers and stayers, since women with younger children might be expected to face greater barriers to employment and to view the opportunity costs of working outside the home as more substantial.

In interpreting impact estimates from the evaluations, it is important to keep in mind the population to which they are applicable. This point has received little emphasis in the OBRA evaluation literature, but it has an important bearing on judgments concerning how "large" or "small" the measured impacts are. The reason for this is that impacts are inevitably reported as a change in a ratio—for example, a dollar increase in earnings per person or a percentage-point reduction in numbers of persons receiving welfare. The demonstration programs, however, were usually targeted at only a subset of the full AFDC population—often those who were WIN-mandatory. And of the targeted population for a particular program, typically only a subset actually participated. Hence, there were three obvious alternative candidates for use in the denominators of the impact ratios: all recipients, all members of the target population, and only those persons who actually participated in the demonstration program. Since each of these groups is successively smaller than the preceding one, measured impacts will become increasingly large as one moves from the first candidate to the second and then to the third.

These three alternative impact denominators can be used to address three quite distinct policy questions: (1) Can the demonstration treatments substantially reduce the size of the welfare caseload or total expenditures on welfare, and can they appreciably increase earnings among the welfare population? (2) Did the demonstrations have substantial impacts on those at whom the treatments were directed? (3) Did the demonstrations have substantial impacts on those who actually received the program treatments?

Each of the OBRA evaluations tended to focus exclusively on only one of the three questions. Several—particularly those that emphasized program effects on overall caseload size—measured impacts relative to the entire recipient population. In general, the demonstrations on which MDRC focused were designed to answer question 2. As will be seen, this choice was made, in part, for solid statistical reasons. But often the demonstrations are interpreted as if they were designed to answer the third question. It is this one that is of particular interest if participation in the demonstration services is itself a policy variable. However, only a few evaluations attempted to measure impacts for only those who actually received treatment services under the programs, and, as discussed later, these studies were highly flawed.

We address these issues in more detail below. Our point here is that in examining findings from the OBRA evaluations, it is important to recognize that the effect of the choice of denominator on the magnitudes of the impact estimates is potentially quite substantial. In the case of the Virginia Employment Service Program, for example, 46 percent of the AFDC caseload in the 11 participating counties was excluded from the demonstration's target group (MDRC: Riccio et al., 1986, p. 29), and of the target group, 42 percent never participated in any of the treatment components (p. 56).

Evaluation Design Issues

Experimental versus Nonexperimental Designs. Several alternative evaluation designs were used to assess the various OBRA demonstrations in our sample. The most prevalent of these was an experimental design in which the targeted adults were randomly assigned to a treatment or a comparison group. In principle, only persons in the treatment group were to participate in the activities and receive the services being tested in the demonstration. (In practice there were some exceptions to this rule, but these exceptions were usually minor.) Because of random assignment, the characteristics of the cases in the two types of groups should have been similar, and differences that occurred by chance could be at least partially adjusted through standard statistical techniques. Consequently, the impacts of the treatment(s) could be measured by simply comparing average outcomes for the two groups.

This experimental design, which was used in all but one of the MDRC impact analyses and in several of the other evaluations as well, can be usefully contrasted to some of its alternatives. The most important of these, which we shall call the "treatment-comparison site" design, has been utilized in evaluations where the demonstration sites covered only part of a state. Under these circumstances, a treatment group can be constructed of cases located in the demonstration sites and a comparison group of cases located in other sites. The obvious shortcoming of this evaluation design is that the treatment and comparison sites may differ from one another in aspects other than treatment status, including local labor market conditions, characteristics of the AFDC caseload, and approaches to and philosophy in administering welfare. Differences in outcomes that are observed in comparing cases at the two types of sites may be attributable to these other factors, rather than to the demonstration treatment.

This shortcoming can be at least partially overcome by using statistical techniques to adjust for those site differences that can be observed and measured. This was not done in all the studies we reviewed that used the treatment-comparison site design, however, and even when it was, there was no assurance that all systematic differences between sites could, in fact, be observed and measured. This latter problem can be mitigated somewhat by placing the sites themselves into matched pairs and then randomly assigning one member of each pair to treatment status and the other to comparison status. This approach was used for the evaluation of West Virginia's AFDC-U CWEP Demonstration and Washington State's Intensive Applicant Employment Services Demonstration. Its limitation is that relatively few sites may be available for random assignment. In West Virginia, for example, there were only four pairs of matched sites. Thus, complete randomization may not occur.

Although the advantages of the randomized experimental design over the treatment-comparison site design are apparent, it is important to recognize that the latter does offer certain potential advantages of its own. Specifically, a demonstration may have site-wide effects that will be missed by an impact analysis that relies on an experimental design, but might be captured by an analysis based on a treatment-comparison site design. For example, the very existence of a demonstration at a site may cause workers administering the AFDC program to change their attitudes toward *all* applicants and recipients, both those in and those outside the target population. Given the presence of a large-scale WEP, for instance, eligibility workers might begin to administer AFDC regulations more stringently. Moreover, it is also possible that the very existence of a demonstration program at a site, especially one with a CWEP component, may deter some persons who would otherwise be eligible to receive AFDC benefits from applying. Alternatively, a program that stresses training and education may attract persons into AFDC. Since these effects are site-wide, they can only be captured by an evaluation design that compares demonstration sites with sites where the demonstration program has not been implemented.

Another alternative to a randomized experimental design is to compare persons who have elected to participate in a treatment program with persons at the same sites who have elected not to participate. Although this design has been widely used in the past to evaluate human resources programs, it has been used in only one of the OBRA evaluations—an evaluation of the Massachusetts ET-Choices program recently completed by the Urban Institute (Nightingale et al., 1991).

Yet another evaluation design that has been used in the OBRA demonstrations is to compare actual outcomes to what would have been expected on the basis of past experience. In its simplest and probably least reliable form, this amounts to attributing all of the change in (say) earnings or welfare payments between the date of the experimental observation and the date used for reference to the demonstration. This is the approach used in evaluations of Oregon's WIN Waiver Jobs Program and Utah's Emergency Work and Employment Program. The problem is, of course, that in the world of public assistance things change even in the absence of a demonstration. A more sophisticated approach is to develop statistical models capable of controlling for the influence of such developments and then evaluating the consequences of experimental developments on the basis of the difference between actual outcomes of interest (dependency, for example) and those which the models would have predicted given all other developments *except* for the intervention. This is the approach used in a second evaluation of the Massachusetts program, one recently completed by June O'Neill (1990) that extends earlier work by Garasky (1990). Forecast-based approaches to program evaluation are viewed skeptically by many, however, in part because of questions about whether or not past experience provides adequate control in the context of rapidly changing economic and social circumstances and because of less-than-successful attempts to use such models to forecast one key outcome measure, welfare caseloads, in the past.[2]

Self-Selection of Sites. Two types of site self-selection occurred in the OBRA demonstrations: interstate and intrastate. Interstate selection occurs because under the OBRA regulations, individual states could decide whether or not to conduct a demonstration and, if they did so decide, they had considerable leeway in determining what sort of treatment to offer and what kind of evaluation to conduct. Presumably, each of the demonstration states tended to select treatment combinations for which sufficient political and administrative enthusiasm could be mustered and which appeared administratively feasible.[3] If the same treatment combination were transferred to another state and different circumstances, the results could be very different.

Intrastate site self-selection results because, in most of the demonstration states, the treatment was not implemented on a statewide basis. Instead, only a subset of local offices became demonstration sites. While site selection is generally poorly documented, it appears to have been common to pick locations thought to have compatible and motivated administrations. Consequently, findings from demonstrations in these sites may not be generalizable to the rest of the state, since the demonstration sites may not be very representative of the state as a whole. In North Carolina's CWEP Demonstration Program, for example, the demonstration sites were six small, rural counties that together accounted for only 7 percent of the state's total caseload. Even in the case of Virginia's Employment Services Program, where there is good information on how the sites were selected and where considerable ef-

---

2. See Plotnick and Lidman (1987) for a discussion of caseload forecasting.

3. Blum (1990) discusses factors motivating state welfare administrators who agreed to the use of random assignment to evaluate welfare employment programs.

fort was made to select sites that as a group were representative of the entire state, the demonstration sites had "all expressed a strong interest in taking part in the study" (MDRC: Riccio et al., 1986, p. 9).

Length of the Study Period. The period of time covered by the OBRA evaluations was typically relatively short, and for good reason. Agencies running demonstration programs are understandably anxious to learn about the impacts of these programs. Moreover, the longer an evaluation is continued, the more expensive it becomes. Thus, to cite just one fairly typical example, MDRC began to draw its research sample for its evaluation of the San Diego Job Search and Work Experience Demonstration two months after the demonstration began and completed this process eleven months later (MDRC: Goldman et al., 1986, p. 249). Follow-up information was collected for two years on the members of the sample selected earliest and for one and one-half years for members of the sample selected last.

The fact that the evaluation of the OBRA demonstrations usually covered a period of time close to when the treatment was first implemented may cause the impact measured by the evaluation to understate the ultimate impact of the treatment. It takes times to implement a new program fully and to learn how to do the job well. Whenever data collection is initiated, if the data collected span only a short follow-up period, an additional problem will result: it will be difficult to determine how the demonstration treatment affects program participants over the longer run.

Drawing a Representative Research Sample. Most of the OBRA demonstrations were pilot studies that limited treatment to only a subset of a state's total AFDC caseload. It is obviously important that this subset of cases be reasonably representative of the demonstration program's ultimate target population. For example, as suggested earlier, when a demonstration is limited to only a few of a state's welfare offices, the demonstration sites should be as similar as possible to sites in the rest of the state.

A somewhat similar issue is suggested by the fact that evaluation of several of the demonstration programs—for example, the San Diego Job Search and Work Experience Demonstration and the Washington State Intensive Applicant Employment Services Demonstration—was limited to only new AFDC applicants. There is nothing wrong with doing this, but if policymakers later become interested in extending the demonstration treatment to the ongoing caseload—a group that differs in many important respects from new applicants—it is important to recognize that any attempt to use evaluation results based on applicants to predict impacts on current AFDC recipients is highly suspect.

Program Participation. In every WEP demonstration at least some AFDC recipients were excluded from the target populations. Although the excluded groups varied considerably, they typically included single parents with young children, persons with language barriers or health problems, and persons who lived in inaccessible rural areas. However, this systematic exclusion poses less of a problem for interpretation of the results than does the frequent absence of treatment for persons who were in principle eligible. In every evaluation, substantial proportions of persons in the treatment groups typically did not actively participate in the demonstration program for which they were eligible. For example, although participation in the OBRA demonstrations conducted in San Diego, Baltimore, Virginia, Arkansas, and Cook County was supposedly mandatory, the percentage of persons in the five treatment samples who actually ever participated in any program activity ranged from a high of 58 percent in Virginia to a low of 38 percent in Arkansas (MDRC: Friedlander, 1988, p. 19).

There are many reasons why participation rates fall well below 100 percent. Probably the most important is that members of the treatment group drop out of AFDC prior to being required to participate, undoubtedly, in some instances, to avoid participating. In addition, sanctioning may be ineffective or weakly enforced; budgets to pay for WEP activities may be constrained; there may be administrative impediments to more full participation; and some persons may be excused from participating—for example, because of ill health or family responsibilities.

Given treatment and comparison groups, estimates of impacts are made by comparing the two. Because the treatment group contains both program participants and nonparticipants, however, the impact estimates obtained from this procedure are a weighted average of program effects on persons who received the services incorporated in the treatment and persons who did not. Given this, one would anticipate that the magnitude of impact estimates from the OBRA demonstrations is partially driven by the magnitude of demonstration participation rates; in general, the larger the latter, the larger will be the former. Consequently, it should be of interest to measure demonstration program impacts in terms of their effects on only those who were actually treated under the program, especially if participation rates can be manipulated by changes in policy. There has been little attempt in the OBRA evaluations to do this, however, because of the substantial statistical problems involved in measuring treatment effects on only participants when participation is itself an experimental outcome.

This issue becomes especially important if an impact analysis is used to predict what would happen if a demonstration program were to become permanent. Such a prediction will become increasingly less accurate, the greater the extent to which the demonstration and the permanent program differ from each other in terms of any of the three following variables: (1) program participation rates; (2) quantity of program services received per individual, given participation; (3) the mix of service types received by each participant. It is possible that two demonstrations, or a demonstration and a full-scale implementation, could be identical in terms of the ostensible characteristics reported in the appendix at the end of the chapter, but differ profoundly in, for example, participation rates and the number of hours of job training or supervised job search received by those who participate. Again, the potential for such variation suggests that generalizing from a demonstration program to a permanent program should be done only with great caution.

We now turn to a somewhat different implication of the fact that in the OBRA demonstrations the quantity and type of services received varied across members of the treatment groups. As mentioned earlier, considerable effort has been made in some of the OBRA evaluations to determine whether treatment impacts vary across subgroups—for example, applicants and recipients, persons with and without lengthy welfare histories, persons with and without previous work experience, and cases that are located in different types of geographic areas. When impact differences are found among subgroups, however, it is difficult to know exactly what to make of this. The subgroups obviously differed in terms of personal characteristics; but, even within the same demonstration, they typically also differed in terms of the three participation variables listed above. The latter differences may, in turn, have been necessitated by the differences in personal characteristics or, alternatively, they may have reflected policy and administrative choices. Hence, one cannot be certain whether an estimated difference in demonstration impacts between two subgroups is attributable to differences between the two in personal capability or motivation or to policy and administrative factors that resulted in differences in the way they were treated under the program.

Comparisons of Alternative Treatments. The states that conducted the OBRA demonstrations experimented with a wide variety of treatments and treatment combinations. Determining which of these treatments or combinations of treatments tended to produce the greatest impacts is obviously of great policy importance. There are two potential means of doing this: comparisons across demonstrations and comparisons within demonstrations.

The first of these approaches exploits the fact that the OBRA demonstrations did vary considerably in the treatments they offered. However, although comparisons of impact estimates for different demonstrations can be instructive, they should be interpreted with considerable caution, for in addition to treatment variation there were other important differences among the demonstrations. The states conducting the demonstrations differed in terms of labor market conditions, population density, AFDC payment levels, characteristics of the welfare population, and approaches toward administering welfare. It is clearly difficult to untangle all these factors in order to isolate the influence of treatment variation on observed differences in program impact. Indeed, sometimes the environment in which a demonstration is conducted may dominate program outcomes. For example, different variants of CWEP were tested in San Diego and West Virginia. Since San Diego's unemployment rate first peaked at about 10 percent and then fell to 6 percent during the demonstration study period, while West Virginia's unemployment rate peaked at 18 percent and then declined only to 13 percent, it is not too surprising that earnings impacts were found to be substantial in San Diego, but nonexistent in West Virginia.

The second means of comparing the impacts of alternative treatments, comparisons within demonstrations, is potentially superior to the first. This approach requires that there be two or more treatment groups rather than just one, with each group receiving a different treatment. The treatment groups can be compared to one another as well as to a comparison group. Thus it is possible to determine which treatment had the larger impact. Unfortunately, the research design just described was utilized relatively rarely in the OBRA demonstrations, and in only one or two instances were impact estimates produced that are useful in comparing alternative treatments.

It may be useful to comment on one potential treatment variation that was essentially ignored in developing the research designs of the OBRA demonstrations: the use of monetary sanctions. Almost all the programs tested in the demonstrations were mandatory, and the use of sanctions to enforce participation in such programs has been widely discussed. The impact of sanctions might have been tested in one of the demonstrations by using a two-treatment-group research design similar to that described above and vigorously enforcing strong sanctions on one of the treatment groups, but not the other. This was not done, however. Although there was some variation among demonstrations in the use of sanctions, the demonstrations also varied in so many other respects that it is not possible to draw any conclusions concerning the impact of sanctions.

Data Sources. In general, the data required to conduct the OBRA impact evaluations were readily obtained. The data necessary to measure the independent variables needed for the regression model typically used in the OBRA evaluations pertain to the characteristics of individuals at the time of their assignment to the research sample. Since these persons were either receiving or applying for AFDC benefits at this time, the required data could be easily obtained directly from them. In fact, much of the necessary information was routinely collected in administering the welfare system.

Measuring outcomes of the demonstrations required information on individuals after their initial assignment to the research sample. The data needed to measure two of these outcome variables—welfare status and amount of welfare received—could of course be readily obtained from the administrative records of the agencies conducting the demonstrations. Two alternative sources of data were available to measure the outcome variables pertaining to employment status and earnings.

The first of these data sources is follow-up interviews with members of the treatment and comparison groups. This approach is expensive and time-consuming, and it leads, if those who cannot be found or will not participate in interviews differ in earnings or employment from those who do participate, to "attrition bias." This problem can occur, for example, if the treatment provided by a demonstration program helps members of the treatment group secure employment and, thereby, leave the welfare rolls, and it is easier to obtain interviews with those still on the rolls than with those who are off. Under such circumstances, the impact of the demonstration treatment on employment would be understated.

The second source for employment and earnings data is state Unemployment Insurance (UI) earnings records. These records are constructed from quarterly earnings reports that are required from employers for the purpose of administering state unemployment insurance programs. In general, the UI earnings data are preferable to interview based earnings data, since UI data are less expensive to obtain and are less subject to attrition bias. They may also be more accurate, since they are not subject to recall errors. However, although all states are now required to maintain UI earnings files, some states did not have these data bases during the time period covered by the OBRA evaluations.

Findings from the Impact Analyses

Of the 24 OBRA demonstration evaluations reviewed, impact analyses had been completed for 19 by the end of 1989. We now turn to their findings. We limit our discussion to only 13 of the available 19 sets of findings—those in which we place some confidence. Of the 13 sets of findings we discuss, 10 were obtained from evaluations conducted by MDRC; the remaining three are from evaluations of Massachusetts' Employment and Training-Choices Program, North Carolina's CWEP Demonstration Program, and Washington State's Intensive Applicant Employment Services Project. The first of these three evaluations was conducted by June O'Neill, an academic. The other two were conducted in-house by state agency personnel.

Before proceeding, a few comments are in order about the six excluded evaluations: Ohio's Work Experience Program, Minnesota's Work Experience Program, Oregon's WIN Waiver Jobs Program, Utah's Emergency Work and Employment Program, Florida's Trade Welfare for Work Program, and Washington State's Community Work Experience Program. Our lack of confidence in impact findings from these evaluations stems from a variety of causes. Findings from the Ohio Work Experience impact analysis were subject to important econometric problems. Impact findings from the Minnesota, Oregon, and Utah demonstrations are based on relatively crude comparisons between two sets of sites, those with and without the treatment, or between two points in time, prior to and after introduction of the treatment. These comparisons are subject to confounding differences between the two sets of sites or the two points in time that are inadequately controlled for by the analyses. Consequently, reliable inferences as to impacts cannot be drawn. In contrast to the Minnesota, Oregon, and Utah demonstrations, the Florida and Washington demonstrations utilized an experimental design. Unfortunately, after random assignment, numerous cases were dropped from the samples selected in both demonstrations, in large part because of missing data. Since the cases that were dropped differed systematically between the treatment and comparison groups, the integrity of the random assignment was violated and, as a consequence, the impact findings, which are based on comparisons between the restricted treatment and comparison groups, are unreliable.

We now consider the findings from the 13 impact analyses in which we do place some confidence. We have summarized many of the salient results from the 10 analyses conducted by MDRC in Tables 1.1 through 1.3. (Results from the three non-MDRC evaluations do not lend themselves to the format used in these tables, but will be briefly described later.) Within subcategories, these results are reported in the chronological order of the beginning of experimental treatment. Thus, for AFDC recipients, San Diego I, for which experimental assignment began in October 1982, is first, and San Diego II, initiated in July 1985, is last. The intent in these three tables is to restrict the volume of reported numbers to a manageable level, yet convey important information from the MDRC impact analyses. Thus, while MDRC uses four measures of impacts, we focus only upon earnings (in Table 1.1) and welfare status (in Table 1.2). These two measures would appear to capture adequately how well the OBRA demonstrations met the major objective of increasing the earnings of AFDC recipients, thereby allowing them to leave the welfare rolls. Parentheses are used to indicate estimates of treatment impacts that came out the opposite from this goal—that is, when earnings were found to decrease or persons remaining on AFDC were found to increase.

Tables 1.1 and 1.2 contain five similar columns. The first column in each table reports the control-group mean value for the impact measure over an extended period. The intent here is to provide a benchmark, an estimate of the value of the impact measure in the absence of the treatment. The second column presents MDRC's estimates of the impacts themselves. Since data in MDRC reports are reported on the basis of calendar quarters, the numbers found in the first two columns in each table are averages that are computed over several quarters. In making these computations, we began with the third calendar quarter after an individual was assigned to the evaluation sample and included every additional quarter thereafter for which impact estimates existed. The first two quarters were not used in the computations because calendar quarter 1 can include experience before experimental assignment, and services and activities for most of the demonstrations extended at least through quarter 2. The next two columns report impact estimates for two individual calendar quarters: the third and the last available. These estimates can be compared with each other or, better, with the average impact estimates in the second column to obtain a rough idea of how the impact of each demonstration treatment varied over time. The last column indicates the total number of calendar quarters over which the averages were computed and the number of these quarters for which the impact estimates were statistically significant at least at the 10 percent level. Thus, for example, the average estimate of impact on earnings that appears in the first row of the second column of Table 1.1 is based on individual impact estimates for the last four of the six calendar quarters for which MDRC provided estimates. And of these four individual impact estimates, only one was statistically significant at least at the 10 percent level.

The two columns of Table 1.3 respectively indicate the sample sizes upon which the impact estimates are based and program costs per experimental. The reported sample sizes are based on members of both treatment and control groups. As can be seen, all but a few of the sample sizes are relatively large. However, in analyses of treatment impacts on subgroups, a topic we will discuss shortly, the samples in some of the demonstrations were sometimes stretched rather thin.

The estimates of program costs per experimental were obtained from the cost-benefit sections of various MDRC reports. These figures include estimates of program operating costs, allowances paid to program participants (mainly for day care and transportation expenditures), and, in the case of the New Jersey and Maine demonstrations, wage subsidies paid to private sector employers. The estimates are net of similar expenditures on comparison group members. The purpose of providing these estimates is to try to take account of the fact that participation levels varied widely among various treatment groups, an issue discussed earlier in this section. By measuring the government's *average* investment in each member of the different treatment groups, the cost estimates provide a rough gauge of the number and type of services received by these persons.

The results in the three tables are reported separately for the AFDC-R and the AFDC-U programs. In addition, whenever possible, impact estimates are reported separately for new program applicants (that is, those designated earlier as APPs or NRs) and prior program recipients (those

Table 1.1 Summary of earnings effects found in MDRC evaluations of various OBRA demonstrations (earnings received in a calendar quarter-year, current dollars)

Treatment group	Control group: Average earnings in absence of program	Program impact (treatment group minus control group)			
		Average impact[a]	Impact in third quarter	Impact in last quarter	Significant quarters among available quarters[b]
AFDC-R Applicants					
San Diego I:					
Job Search Only	$683	$33	$118**	$26	1/4
Job Search/CWEP	683	140	163***	161***	4/4
Baltimore	823	181	94	194	9/10
Arkansas	186	(−6)	(−6)	(−6)	0/1
West Virginia	228	(−40)	(−21)	(−55)	0/4
Virginia	526	78	69	87	0/2
Cook County:					
Job Search Only	690	(−61)	(−84)*	(−19)	1/4
Job Search/CWEP	690	(−48)	(−62)	(−24)	0/4
San Diego II	685	90	76	29	2/7
AFDC-R Recipients					
Baltimore	427	40	48	18	0/3
Arkansas	42	42	42**	42**	1/1
West Virginia	124	14	38**	10	1/4

Virginia	273	19	19	20	0/2
Maine	590	207	39	209*	8/9
New Jersey	988	109	40	123	2/5
Cook County:					
Job Search Only	266	39	18	46*	3/4
Job Search/CWEP	266	45	37*	44*	4/4
San Diego II	402	172	87**	221***	7/7
AFDC-U Applicants					
San Diego I:					
Job Search Only	1,580	59	136	15	0/4
Job Search/CWEP	1,580	23	69	7	0/4
San Diego II	1,096	139	183	145	0/7
AFDC-U Recipients					
San Diego II	542	91	105	110	0/7
AFDC-U Combined					
Baltimore	1,499	(−416)	(−400)	(−551)	2/3
West Virginia	608	(−38)	(−16)	(−102)***	1/4

Source: Various final and supplemental reports on individual state work/welfare demonstrations published by the Manpower Demonstration Research Corporation. A complete annotation is available from the authors.

Note: Estimated effects in parentheses have unanticipated sign.

a. Averaged from quarter 3 through last quarter available.

b. Number of quarters with a statistically significant increase or decrease, from quarter 3 through last quarter available.

* Statistically significant at the 10% level using a 2-tailed *t*-test.

** Statistically significant at the 5% level using a 2-tailed *t*-test.

*** Statistically significant at the 1% level using a 2-tailed *t*-test.

Table 1.2 Summary of effects on AFDC receipt found in MDRC evaluations of various OBRA demonstrations (percentage receiving AFDC in a calendar quarter-year)

Treatment group	Control group: Average receipt in absence of program	Program impact (treatment group minus control group)			
		Average impact[a]	Impact in third quarter	Impact in last quarter	Significant quarters among available quarters[b]
AFDC-R Applicants					
San Diego I:					
Job Search Only	45.9%	−1.8%	−6.0%*	(0.0)%	1/4
Job Search/CWEP	45.9	−2.8	−6.4**	−1.2	1/4
Baltimore	50.1	−2.4	−1.4	−1.1	0/10
Arkansas	48.5	−3.3	−3.3	−3.3	0/1
West Virginia	51.6	−0.2	(0.8)	−3.5	0/5
Virginia	43.0	−1.7	−1.0	−2.4	0/2
Cook County:					
Job Search Only	67.9	−4.3	−3.5**	−5.3***	4/4
Job Search/CWEP	67.9	(2.4)	(2.6)	−2.1	0/4
San Diego II	52.4	−6.3	−4.5*	−6.9***	8/8
AFDC-R Recipients					
Baltimore	74.0	(0.3)	(0.1)	(1.3)	0/10
Arkansas	85.7	−11.4	−11.4***	−11.4***	1/1
West Virginia	75.7	−2.5	−1.8	−2.5	2/5

Virginia	77.8	−0.5	−2.3	(1.2)	0/2
Maine	68.6	(1.9)	(1.0)	(6.0)	0/9
New Jersey	60.7	−3.5	−0.9	−1.8	1/6
Cook County:					
Job Search Only	84.7	−2.3	−0.9	−3.1***	3/4
Job Search/CWEP	84.7	−1.3	−1.0	−1.5	0/4
San Diego II	76.8	−6.4	−1.5	−7.0***	7/8
AFDC-U Applicants					
San Diego I:					
Job Search Only	40.4	−4.7	−7.0***	−5.1**	3/4
Job Search/CWEP	40.4	−5.0	−7.4***	−2.9	3/4
San Diego II	49.7	−3.2	−1.7	−1.7	1/8
AFDC-U Recipients					
San Diego II	73.4	(4.0)	−7.6	−4.6	1/8
AFDC-U Combined					
Baltimore	43.0	(4.8)	(4.9)	(2.8)	0/3
West Virginia	59.0	−5.3	−4.8***	−6.9***	5/5

Source: See Table 1.1.

Note: Estimated effects in parentheses have unanticipated sign.

a. Averaged from quarter 3 through last quarter available.

b. Number of quarters with a statistically significant increase or decrease, from quarter 3 through last quarter available.

* Statistically significant at the 10% level using a 2-tailed t-test.

** Statistically significant at the 5% level using a 2-tailed t-test.

*** Statistically significant at the 1% level using a 2-tailed t-test.

Table 1.3 Summary of program costs in MDRC evaluations of various OBRA demonstrations

Treatment group	Sample size	Program cost per treatment group member[a]
AFDC-R Applicants		
San Diego I:		
Job Search Only	1,729	$558
Job Search/CWEP	2,375	636
Baltimore	1,380	708
Arkansas	667	158[b]
West Virginia	1,078	228
Virginia	1,285	253
Cook County:		
Job Search Only	2,631	127[b]
Job Search/CWEP	2,668	158[b]
San Diego II	1,258	700
AFDC-R Recipients		
Baltimore	1,377	913
Arkansas	452	158[b]
West Virginia	2,601	293
Virginia	1,897	548
Maine	444	3,060
New Jersey	994	921
Cook County:		
Job Search Only	5,231	127[b]
Job Search/CWEP	5,187	158[b]
San Diego II	1,953	1,068
AFDC-U Applicants		
San Diego I:		
Job Search Only	1,644	587
Job Search/CWEP	2,189	727
San Diego II	798	660
AFDC-U Recipients		
San Diego II	543	1,025
AFDC-U Combined		
Baltimore	337	634
West Virginia	5,630	136

Source: See Table 1.1.

a. Additional government expenditures on treatment group members, relative to expenditures on comparison group members.

b. Separate program cost estimates for applicants and recipients were not available for Cook County and Arkansas.

designated as CMRs or NDMRs). Not only did treatment impacts tend to differ substantially between these two groups, but, as the last column of Table 1.3 suggests, the average cost of treatment did also. For two of the demonstrations—the one in Cook County and the first one in San Diego—there were two separate treatment groups, and impact findings are reported separately for each.

The impact estimates reported for earnings and welfare receipt vary considerably from one demonstration to another. This is not surprising, given the variety of treatments offered by the demonstrations, differences in participation rates among the demonstrations, variations in the target groups covered by the demonstrations, and variations in the economic and institutional environments in which the demonstrations were conducted. Moreover, many of the impacts are estimated with little precision and are therefore statistically insignificant. Nevertheless, with only a few exceptions, they are in the hoped-for direction. That is, they imply that the demonstration treatments really did increase earnings and reduce the size of the welfare rolls.

On the other hand, most of the impact estimates indicate that the demonstration treatment effects were relatively small. For example, only 6 of the 24 earnings impact estimates appearing in the second column of Table 1.1 imply that average earnings were raised by over $100 per calendar quarter by the treatment, and only one of these impact estimates exceeded $200 per quarter. On an annual basis, it would appear that in no case were earnings increased by as much as $1,000 a year. As pointed out earlier, however, these earning impacts are averaged over those who participated in treatment under the demonstrations and those who did not; they would almost certainly be higher if estimated only for those who actually received the program treatment. Nevertheless, one is left with the impression from Table 1.1 that, although some of the treatments tested in the OBRA demonstrations did raise the earnings of some program participants, overall these effects are quite limited. Since most treatment impacts on rates of employment are well under ten percentage points in any given calendar quarter, it would appear that whatever earnings increments occurred were concentrated among relatively few persons.

Table 1.2 shows that the demonstration treatments were also successful in reducing the incidence of welfare receipt, but again only to a limited degree. For example, only 4 of the 23 impact estimates exceeded five percentage points and only one, that for AFDC recipients enrolled in the Arkansas WORK Program, exceeded ten percentage points. More-over, program success in reducing the size of the welfare rolls was sub-stantially smaller than these estimates might at first glance appear to imply. The reason for this is that not all welfare recipients were included in the target populations of any of the demonstration programs. For example, 38 percent of those in Arkansas' AFDC caseload had children under the age of 3 and, consequently, were not required to participate in that state's WORK Program. Had these persons been included in the evaluation sample, the estimated impact of the treatment on welfare status would have been considerably smaller.

The results for non-MDRC OBRA evaluations are broadly similar to those reported by MDRC. Both Washington State's Intensive Applicant Employment Services Project and North Carolina's CWEP Demonstra-tion Program also apparently reduced the size of the welfare rolls. For example, the Washington State project, which was limited to new AFDC applicants, appeared either to reduce the amount of time during which new applicants, once accepted, remained on the rolls or to reduce the likelihood that these persons ever got on the rolls to begin with. During the 10 months after originally applying for AFDC, members of the com-parison group received assistance for 3.5 months, on average, while members of the treatment group received assistance for only 3.1 months, on average (Washington State Department of Health and Social Services, 1983, table B-1). The impact analysis of North Carolina's CWEP Demonstration Program, which covered both applicants and re-cipients, implied that the AFDC caseload was around 4 percent lower than it would have been in the absence of the program (North Carolina Department of Human Resources, 1985, table 13). There is also some evidence that this program had a small positive effect on earnings. On the other hand, from O'Neill's study (1990, chap. 5) it appears that the Massachusetts ET program had little, if any, effect on the size of that state's AFDC caseload or on the earnings of its AFDC recipients.

The impact data support several additional inferences. First, both new AFDC applicants and persons already receiving AFDC were treated under most of the OBRA demonstrations evaluated by MDRC. Tables 1.1 and 1.2 suggest that, although some of these demonstrations were more successful in affecting outcomes for one group rather than the other, a clear pattern does not emerge. As Table 1.3 indicates, however, program expenditures per member of the recipient treatment group considerably exceeded those per member of the applicant groups. Prob-ably the major reason for this is that applicants were more likely than recipients to leave the AFDC rolls early in the treatment process. Indeed, some never became eligible for welfare at all.

Second, several of the OBRA demonstrations evaluated by MDRC covered both the AFDC-R and the AFDC-U populations. With one exception, it does not appear that these demonstrations were more successful in treating one of these population groups than the other. The major exception occurred under the demonstration in Baltimore, where the lack of success in treating AFDC-U participants is striking. The reader should note, however, that results for AFDC-U participants in Baltimore are based on a relatively small sample.

Third, four pairwise comparisons can be made in Table 1.3 that allow one to examine the incremental effect of adding CWEP to job search. Only in the case of AFDC-R applicants in San Diego did this addition appear to have a positive incremental impact. Positive incremental effects are not apparent for either AFDC-U applicants in San Diego or AFDC-R applicants or recipients in Cook County.

Fourth, it is of considerable importance to determine whether the impacts of demonstration programs tend to persist or decay over time. Tables 1.1 and 1.2 provide mixed evidence concerning this issue. Some of the measured impacts reported in the tables do appear to decay, but others seem to persist or even grow over time. It should be emphasized, however, that most of these impacts are measured over relatively few calendar quarters. If program impacts could be observed for a longer period of time, it might be possible to provide more definitive evidence concerning time trends.

Impacts on Subgroups

Some attempts have been made, notably by Daniel Friedlander (1988), to estimate WEP impacts for selected subsets of treatment group members. Typically these studies disaggregate overall effects by subdividing the samples on the basis of certain recipient characteristics, usually pre-experiment earnings or welfare history. Subgroups defined in this way are of interest because such criteria could be applied in the field. If individuals in a particular subgroup were found to be more responsive to the demonstration treatments than others, scarce program resources could be targeted at them.

It is difficult to draw conclusions with any confidence from existing studies of subgroup effects. Perhaps the most important observation is that no truly clear patterns concerning subgroup impacts emerge. There is a hint that employment impacts are somewhat greater for applicants who have previously been on AFDC and somewhat smaller for applicants who have not. They are also, perhaps, smaller for applicants who earned over $3,000 during the year prior to application. There is also some suggestion that treatment impacts on AFDC payments were greater for treatment group members with modest amounts of prior earnings than for treatment group members with either relatively large amounts of prior earnings or no prior earnings at all. None of these relationships, however, is found consistently across all the demonstration programs. Moreover, even those patterns that might be discerned must be interpreted cautiously. As pointed out earlier, both the number and types of services received by various subgroups may have differed, and this may have caused differences in subgroup impacts. Thus, it would appear that evidence from the OBRA demonstrations concerning targeting strategies is highly tentative at best.

An additional subgroup of interest is made up of the heads of AFDC-R recipient units with children between 3 and 5 years of age. There has been concern that parents of young children could not be adequately served by WEPs because of difficulties in arranging for day care. Prior to OBRA, such parents could not be required to participate in WIN. These parents were part of the client target pool in five of the OBRA demonstrations. The impact analyses for these demonstrations consistently implied that program effects on single parents with children between ages 3 and 5 were similar to those on single parents with only older children.

Reflections on the Outcomes

We return now to the question introduced at the beginning of this chapter: Why was welfare reform successfully accomplished in the 1980s, under fiscal circumstances far less hospitable than those which attended the failure of the Family Assistance Plan and the Program for Better Jobs and Income? More to the point, what, if any, was the role of the OBRA demonstrations in bringing reform about?

OBRA and the Family Support Act

At first glance, the Family Support Act seems to bear only a tenuous relation to the state initiatives we have reviewed. The legislation begins not with welfare employment policy, but with new initiatives for child support. Like OBRA, the Job Opportunities and Basic Skills program mandated by Title III of the act extends consolidation of authority for AFDC-related employment operations nationwide, but the requirements placed upon state welfare agencies and the program opportunities presented are significantly different. For example, JOBS requires participation of single parents with no children younger than 3 (or 1, at state option); only five of the OBRA demonstrations had this feature. JOBS provides funds for extensive education services; among the demonstration evaluations available to Congress in 1987, only Baltimore had this feature, and the consequences of the inclusion of education cannot be determined from the outcomes measured there. JOBS provides funds for extended Medicaid and day care for welfare recipients who become employed; none of the OBRA demonstrations evaluated with random assignment had this feature (although services of this type are provided in the ET-Choices and GAIN initiatives). The Family Support Act also establishes a point-in-time participation target for JOBS eligibles; most of the OBRA demonstrations did not involve participation targets, and indeed, for many it is difficult to assess just what participation was. And finally, FSA mandates that states without AFDC-U adopt that program (with the option of limiting benefits to no more than six months during any calendar year) and, eventually, that all states require 16 hours per week of CWEP participation for AFDC-U parents. While some experiments included AFDC-U families and required their participation in CWEP, none included an obligation of this type.

Nonetheless, there exists a substantial consensus among persons active in welfare policy that the OBRA demonstrations, particularly MDRC's evaluations of them, had a major effect on the course of the debate and, possibly, the success of the effort. In a review of MDRC's work that was commissioned by the Ford Foundation, Peter Szanton (1989) summarized a common theme in this way: "MDRC's work and welfare studies . . . were relevant, they were convincing, and they showed that something worked. They offered a solid basis for policy change and they helped to produce it" (p. 15). In a similar vein, Ronald Haskins (1989), a minority staff member on the House Ways and Means Committee with responsibility for welfare-related legislation, writes: "Because their research methods were so compelling, MDRC studies gave rise to very little criticism. As a result, the conclusions that states could conduct cost-beneficial job search and work experience programs did not give rise to the seemingly endless bickering among social scientists that accompanies most studies of welfare" (pp. 35–36). And finally, Erica Baum (1989), Senator Daniel Patrick Moynihan's principal assistant for welfare policy at the time the Family Support Act was prepared, writes that MDRC's work was a significant factor in the design and passage of the legislation: "MDRC's findings were unambiguous [and] not subject to challenge on methodological grounds" (p. 19).

As is surely evident from our discussions of the MDRC reports, we concur in much of the praise directed toward them (see Wiseman, 1991). But in studying the outcomes, we have come to an interpretation that is somewhat at variance with the positions of Szanton, Haskins, and Baum. As we see it, the critical aspects of the research's impact on policy involve the image of process and what Baum has called the "sheer dumb luck" of timing.

Regarding process, as mentioned earlier, the foundation of much of the welfare reform effort of the 1970s had been the presumption that significant change required a "complete overhaul" of the welfare system. The alternative to radical change was incremental reform within the system, but in the words of the title of one paper on the subject, incremental reform was "a strategy whose time has passed" (Lynn and Worthington, 1977, p. 49). A posture that called for radical reform had a number of corollaries. One was that there was not much to be learned about strategies for dealing with poverty from study of existing welfare institutions. A second was that since AFDC was a product of federal legislation, reform itself was a matter of national political initiative. The action was in Washington, and the focus of research in the various negative tax experiments was on what were believed to be questions central to national income support policy. Barbara Blum, the president of MDRC during the period in which the OBRA demonstrations were initiated, has pointed out that few state welfare administrators paid attention to, or apparently were much aware of, the various negative tax experiments (Blum, 1990).

In contrast, the OBRA initiatives were specifically oriented toward state welfare operations. The theme repeatedly emphasized by MDRC was not that significant reform at the state level was infeasible—indeed, it was the very feasibility of such initiatives that MDRC wished to stress—but that if new initiatives were to have any impact, their effects would have to be evaluated in the style of the negative tax experiments. What was achieved was both a sense of the feasibility of state-initiated policy modifications at existing welfare agencies and a sense that those changes which were feasible were worthy of laurels as reform. Moreover, the specifics were not as important as the concept of process: linking welfare receipt with obligation. States might construct their systems in a variety of ways, but for the most part such variation did not seem to violate common sense or to compromise human dignity. MDRC thus played the role of both messenger and medium, serving to communicate the message of the significance of the research design to the states and acting as a medium for conveying a broad sense of outcomes from state initiatives to Congress.

Rationalization had long been a theme of welfare reform efforts at the federal level. What MDRC seemed to be saying was that when given flexibility, states could achieve considerable rationalization of welfare systems by themselves. But it was not necessary to go as far as the Reagan administration had proposed early in the decade, that is, lumping virtually all poverty-related programs into a single block grant. Furthermore, given the platform of process, it was not necessary that all services be universal. After OBRA, incremental reform meant enhancing the toolkit by providing states with a menu of services, some of which they could potentially adopt. And enhancing the welfare employment program toolkit is very much what the Family Support Act is about.

Timing was also essential to MDRC's impact. What Baum, Haskins, and Szanton all fail to note is that the perceived lack of ambiguity in MDRC's findings comes in significant part precisely because of timing. In the years 1987–1988, virtually the only researchers familiar with the details of MDRC's work were at MDRC. Results were communicated to Congress practically as they were developed. Had more time passed, it is likely that more criticism would have arisen, and, indeed, MDRC's findings would have been challenged on methodological grounds, just as we have done in this overview. More important, critics might have been able to focus better on the important distinctions between what was done in the OBRA demonstrations and what has been incorporated in JOBS. In 1987–1988, however, fortuitous timing made the MDRC results seem more compelling than they actually were. What Haskins fails to understand is that it requires time for social scientists to organize a good bicker.

Lessons from the OBRA Evaluations

What judgments, then, are justified from the OBRA results? We feel that a number of both negative and positive ones are appropriate. The first is that, even with 24 observations, what went on in the OBRA demonstrations remains something of a "black box." Although in a number of instances we have what appear to be reliable estimates of the impacts of particular demonstrations, we are not very confident about what produced them, and we cannot predict with much certainty how the measured impacts would change if the demonstration were replicated in another location or if the demonstration program were expanded or made permanent in the same location. For example, moving from one location to another may change the level of participation, the intensity of treatment, the treatment mix, and the characteristics of the people receiving a particular treatment mix. This, in turn, may result in very different outcomes. Our suspicion that results from any specific OBRA demonstration may not be replicable is heightened by consideration of the special economic and political conditions that produced the demonstration data we now have.

Nevertheless, as stressed by participants in the FSA debates, it is reassuring that impacts from the demonstrations were usually in the desired direction—employment and earnings increased and (with somewhat less certainty) welfare dependency seemed to decline. However, these impacts were typically rather small in magnitude, although in interpreting their magnitudes it is important to recognize that, as measured, such effects are diluted by the presence in the treatment groups of many welfare applicants and recipients who in fact received no services. It is not apparent from the comments by various participants that members of Congress or congressional staff ever grasped this distinction.

We are skeptical of attempts to glean information on subgroup effects from the OBRA research—for example, investigation of differential program effects on persons with long versus short welfare histories or persons with and without previous work histories. Even where differences in impacts do seem to exist across such groups, it is not clear whether they are attributable to different responses to the same treatment or to differences in the treatment actually received.

Although the basis for our judgment is not developed here, the conclusion of our larger work (Greenberg and Wiseman, 1991) is that the findings from the benefit-cost analyses are less reliable than those from the impact analyses. One reason for this is the inherent difficulty of measuring benefits and costs associated with complicated programs such as the ones tested. Some benefits and costs (for example, the value of output produced in CWEP and net changes in the utility levels of program participants) are subject to potentially important biases. Moreover, benefit-cost analyses of many of the demonstration programs produced net gains for taxpayers and net losses for recipients, leaving us with a distributional quandary.

Truth can endure repetition, so we gladly repeat ourselves and echo what many others have said: policymakers owe a great debt to the Manpower Demonstration Research Corporation for imposing order on what almost certainly would have been chaotic in their (and the Ford Foundation's) absence. But a price has been paid. The MDRC approach to analysis is basically atheoretical, and the firm's approach to data has been proprietary. According to some observers, the monopoly established by MDRC's innovation served the public interest by clarifying issues and by focusing available information upon congressional concerns. But in the end, it is not clear that social science has been served. To our knowledge, not a single piece of research has yet been conducted by persons outside of MDRC using primary data from the OBRA demonstrations collected by MDRC.

The problem arises in part from a factor that has contributed immensely to MDRC's success: the firm acts as an agent of the states with which it is working. This seems, among other things, to increase local willingness to assist and to motivate much greater interest in the evaluation findings than might otherwise be the case. But while it may be in California's interest to contract with MDRC for evaluation of GAIN, for most Californians, development of a public use sample is not a major object of concern. Indeed, many contracts appear specifically to forbid the dissemination of data, and certainly funding is never provided for it. But we are not convinced that, at least until recently, MDRC sought funding for preparation of data for public use or that a major effort has been exerted with contractors to authorize such distribution. The challenge for national policy is to find ways to support firms like MDRC in their efforts (and to assure the motivation of their employees), while also assuring that as soon as possible the data upon which their results are based are made accessible and subject to the evaluation of the social science community at large. Of course, it is not MDRC's fault that the federal government did not choose to mount a systematic evaluation of the OBRA demonstrations, and the approach adopted by the firm may reflect the objectives of the foundations that have provided support. The failure to produce public use data was universal among the OBRA demonstrations. It was not unique to the evaluations conducted by MDRC. But the federal government is involved in upcoming WEP evaluations, most notably of the JOBS program, and such matters must be considered.

Future Research

We conclude this chapter by providing a brief list of ways in which we believe future designs for evaluating employment-oriented programs for the welfare population could be improved.

1. *Site Randomization.* We have emphasized at several points in this chapter that sites in the OBRA demonstrations were typically self-selected, thereby reducing the extent to which results from the demonstrations could be generalized. This problem might be ameliorated somewhat by random selection of sites in which to test various treatments. Although such an approach is probably infeasible at the state level, it would appear possible to select randomly welfare offices within a state as test sites.

2. *Analysis of Individual Treatment Components.* In all but a few of the OBRA demonstrations, those who were eligible were offered services in a package containing several individual components. We believe that in future evaluations, the interests of program operators as well as the larger policy community would be best served by emphasis on evaluation of specific components, perhaps in multi-site demonstrations. Consequently, we strongly endorse evaluation designs in which program packages for which members of different treatment groups are eligible differ in terms of only a single program component.

3. *Evaluation of Sanctioning.* An important characteristic of the OBRA demonstrations is that most of the tested programs were mandatory. However, little was learned about the impact of sanctioning itself. We recommend that attention be given to the design of alternative, more graduated sanctioning procedures and that such graduations be tested in the context of a WEP operation. As long as the country is committed to obligation as a component of welfare policy, sanctions will be an instrument. Present procedures appear excessively cumbersome, and the sanctions available may be unnecessarily harsh.

4. *Modeling the Selection Process.* We have emphasized throughout this chapter that there seems to have been considerable variability in the treatment actually received among persons who were eligible to participate in any specific OBRA demonstration program, even when adjustment is made for the fact that some recipients stay eligible for only short

periods of time. In future demonstrations, it would be very useful to investigate specifically how these treatment variations come about (for example, the role of the AFDC recipient versus the role of program administrators), and the association between such variation and client characteristics. Among other things, such study would allow detection of changes in service management procedures and, in consequence, treatments over time.

5. *Comparison of Subgroup Impacts.* To allocate resources more efficiently, it is obviously important that we learn more about how treatment impacts vary among different subgroups. This, however, requires that members of different subgroups be treated as similarly as possible under the program being tested. We think it imperative that attention be devoted to the design of experiments, and the creation of incentives for governments to conduct experiments, in which discretion in service allocation is minimized and, in consequence, genuine service effects can be observed separately from the consequences of "creaming" or other administrative behaviors.

6. *Labor Market Intermediation.* One of the most striking features of the OBRA demonstration results is the regular discovery of positive payoffs from what might at first glance seem relatively trivial interventions related to job search and employment preparation. To us, these research results confirm what traditional labor market economists have long argued: namely, that various features of labor markets pose significant barriers to low-productivity workers, and that information both about jobs and about potential employee productivity is often hard to come by. More complex forms of assistance for workers moving into unsubsidized employment than those used in the OBRA demonstrations are available, including the efforts by some private firms to act as intermediaries between welfare offices and private employers. Investigation of the impacts of these innovations would seem to be as justifiable as focusing attention on the consequences of adding more basic skills training.

7. *The Research Match.* Part of MDRC's success is attributable to the financial support provided by the Ford Foundation. Currently, state funds spent on research on welfare innovations are typically matched with federal dollars on exactly the same basis as all other management expenditures. There seems to be no theoretical or practical justification for this. Attention needs to be given to the design of research support systems that will exchange a more generous federal match for requirements that certain design and reporting criteria be met and for evalua-

tion efforts directed at important, unresolved policy issues—for instance, the consequences of individual WEP components for system outcomes. In its sponsorship of MDRC's OBRA evaluations, the Ford Foundation created something of great value. But ultimately program evaluation is the business of government, and the problem of finding ways of getting this job done well by government deserves more attention.

Appendix: The Projects

This appendix presents capsule summaries of the 24 OBRA-related work-welfare demonstrations reviewed in this chapter. A more detailed summary appears in Greenberg and Wiseman (1991). Only the principal reference is cited; Greenberg and Wiseman (1991) includes a more detailed bibliography. Aside from name, date of initiation, and reference, no attempt is made at systematic inclusion of information, so the fact that a feature is not cited does not mean that it was absent. Where used, abbreviations follow conventions cited in the text. Programs are summarized in alphabetical order by state.

The Arizona Work Incentive Demonstration Program. Initiated in June of 1982, this program provided job search, training, and placement assistance for WIN-eligible AFDC-R recipients without children younger than age 3. No impact evaluation was attempted, but an organizational study by MDRC (Sherwood, 1984) includes useful process and background data.

The Arkansas WORK Program. This program focused on APPs or NDMRs in, or applying for, AFDC-R. As in the Arizona WID program, adults were exempted from participation if their youngest child was under age 3. Job search assistance and some "work experience" jobs were provided. The program began in October of 1982, and impacts were assessed by random assignment of some eligibles to a control group receiving no services. The WORK evaluation was done by MDRC (Friedlander et al., 1985a); the impacts are surprisingly large, given the nature of the services.

San Diego I: The Employment Preparation/Experimental Work Experience Program (EPP/EWEP). This program began in August of 1982. The evaluation of the impact on applicants for public assistance was conducted by MDRC (Goldman et al., 1986) on the basis of a random assignment experimental design. The treatment features two "tracks," one with job search assistance only and the other featuring job search followed by community work experience. This was one of the first experiments providing data on impacts for AFDC-U, as well as AFDC-R, clients.

San Diego II: Saturation Work Initiative Model (SWIM). SWIM succeeded EPP/EWEP (see above) in July 1985. The services provided were more comprehensive, and participants included all adults in the caseload or applying for public assistance who met basic WIN eligibility restrictions. The evaluation was conducted on the basis of random assignment by MDRC (Hamilton and Friedlander, 1989). This is the most comprehensive of the OBRA reports; the data on participation and process are unique. The measured impacts are exceptionally large.

California Greater Avenues for Independence. Impact estimates for GAIN were not available at the time of this survey. However, since the GAIN program is constructed from OBRA tools, the program and process descriptions already available are important. The GAIN program includes an exceptionally rich service package oriented toward basic skills. A random assignment evaluation, by MDRC, is under way (Riccio et al., 1989).

Florida TRADE Welfare for Work Program. Initiated in 1984, TRADE was planned to evaluate the impact of alternative wage subsidy schemes on the employment of AFDC-R recipients who had unsuccessfully completed job search programs. The original plan called for evaluation by random assignment; the program (described in Florida DHRS, 1987) was an administrative failure.

Illinois WIN Demonstration Program (WDP). WDP operations began in Cook County in January 1984. Participants included both applicant and NDMR adults from AFDC-R households. The service provided was minimal—principally individual job search in one track, job search plus work experience assignment in a second. Impact—or, more precisely, lack of impact—was evaluated by MDRC on the basis of random assignment (Friedlander et al., 1987). This experiment is important because it is treated in subsequent MDRC literature as a case in point supporting arguments that minimal expenditures get minimal effects.

Maine Training Opportunities in the Private Sector (TOPS). TOPS provided work experience and on-the-job training to volunteers drawn from AFDC-R recipients who had been receiving welfare for at least six months. The program, which began in September 1983, is interesting as an example of evaluation of a service option (OJT) that is a component of many general welfare-to-work schemes. The evaluation, based on random assignment, was done by MDRC (Auspos, 1988).

Maryland Baltimore Options. The Options program, which began in October 1982, is important because of the contrast between the service-rich program it presented to a fixed number of clients and the more minimalist strategies occurring at the same time elsewhere (cf. San Diego EPP/EWEP, above). The program included both AFDC-R, AFDC-U applicants, and NDMRs and was operated by a well-known nonprofit community agency in Baltimore. The evaluation was conducted by MDRC (Friedlander et al., 1985b) on the basis of random assignment.

Maryland Basic Employment and Training (BET). The BET demonstration was introduced at the same time as the Baltimore Options program, but in a different county. The program differed from Options in requiring job search as a first step for all participants. Random assignment was not attempted, but the report on the program (included in Friedlander et al., 1985b) is valuable because of attention to process.

Massachusetts Employment and Training (ET) Choices. ET-Choices was initiated in October 1983; clients include all adult welfare recipients who, following orientation, volunteer. The program offered a variety of training, placement, and general education services. Random assignment evaluation was deliberately avoided; first available evaluations other than state reports are based on time-series analysis of caseload trends (O'Neill, 1990). This program is important because of associated controversy over evaluation methodology.

Minnesota Community Work Experience Program. Begun in early 1983, this program combined job search and CWEP for all eligible adults in AFDC-UP. The state unsuccessfully attempted an impact assessment based on simple caseload trend comparisons between counties with the program and matched counties without the program (Minnesota DHS, 1987).

New Jersey Grant Diversion. Like Maine's TOPS, this program provided on-the-job training to a select set of volunteer AFDC-R recipients. The program was initiated in April 1984. Fewer resources were used than in TOPS, and earnings impacts (measured on the basis of random assignment) were lower (Freedman, Bryant, and Cave, 1988).

North Carolina Community Work Experience Program. This demonstration is a somewhat routine test of a job search/CWEP program similar to the first San Diego experiment. The program started in July 1982. The evaluation was based on a comparison of actual annual caseloads in the six counties involved with forecasts based on pre-CWEP trends. The report (North Carolina DHR, 1985) is a particularly interesting and useful example of an in-house evaluation.

Ohio Community Work Experience Program. This CWEP program was initiated in April 1984. "Treatment" for participants included job search, community work experience, and on-the-job training. The evaluation (Potomac Institute for Economic Research, 1988) is based on a pooled time-series regression analysis of caseload trends in counties with and without the program. The analysis is seriously flawed.

Oregon JOBS. In January 1982, Oregon began requiring applicants for AFDC to undertake a job search as a condition for obtaining assistance. The in-house (Oregon DHR, 1988) evaluation is based on comparison of caseload trends in Oregon with trends in Washington state. The report is of little value; unfortunately, it is more typical of state welfare agency evaluation than the North Carolina CWEP evaluation cited earlier.

Pennsylvania Community Work Experience Program. This is another example of the wave of state CWEP demonstrations that began in 1982 in the wake of OBRA. The state's report (Pennsylvania DPW, 1986) is mainly descriptive, with some data on participation incidence.

South Carolina Community Work Experience Program. This is yet another example of the wave of state CWEP demonstrations begun in 1982 in the wake of OBRA. The state's report (Clarkson Co., n.d.) is remarkable for its vacuity.

Utah Emergency Work Experience Program (EWEP). This program is exceptional because its work requirement is unmitigated: beginning in 1983, EWEP replaced AFDC-U and offered only a wage for work plus some services. The evaluation (Janzen et al., 1987) concerns impact, comparing EWEP caseloads to those experienced under AFDC-U.

Virginia Employment Services Program (ESP). ESP offered job search, community work experience, and miscellaneous training to AFDC-R recipients. The program began in 1983; the evaluation, by MDRC, is based on random assignment (Riccio et al., 1986). The results are useful despite a partial failure to implement the original evaluation design.

Washington Applicant Employment Services. This is a mandatory job search program for AFDC-R applicants without children under age 3 that began in April of 1982. The in-house evaluation (Washington DHS, 1983) is based on comparison of client outcomes in "treatment" counties with control counties. The evaluation is exceptional in that it is the sites (counties) themselves that are randomly assigned. The final report is disappointingly brief given the apparent quality of the research design.

Washington Community Work Experience Program. Beginning in October 1982, this program randomly assigned registrants for the WIN program selected by WIN offices to control groups or one of two different experimental groups. Two separate treatments, CWEP and job search, were used. The implementation violated the integrity of the random assignment and failed to produce adequate sample sizes for impact evaluation (Washington DHS, 1984).

West Virginia AFDC-R CWEP. This program, initiated in July of 1983, is treated in this study as a separate experiment from a related innovation for AFDC-U, which is described below. In this experiment, AFDC-R recipients were required to take CWEP jobs. The impact evaluation was conducted by MDRC on the basis of random assignment of eligibles to a control group not required to participate and an experimental group which was (Friedlander et al., 1986). This is a classic test of the effect of a welfare work requirement imposed in the context of a weak economy.

West Virginia AFDC-U CWEP. This program, a companion to the AFDC-R CWEP demonstration cited above, was begun in 1982. In this case eligibility was confined to AFDC-U parents (fathers). The two experiments are analyzed separately because the AFDC-U innovation was evaluated on the basis of comparison of caseload trends in counties randomly assigned to demonstration or to control status. Like San Diego's SWIM, this is a saturation effort (Friedlander et al., 1986).

References

Auspos, Patricia, George Cave, and David Long. 1988. *Maine: Final Report on the Training Opportunities in the Private Sector Program.* New York: Manpower Demonstration Research Corporation.

Baum, Erica. 1989. "Social Science and the Family Support Act of 1988." Manuscript. Forthcoming in Wiseman, 1991.

Behn, Robert D. 1989. *The Management of ET CHOICES in Massachusetts.* Durham, N.C.: Duke University Institute of Policy Sciences and Public Affairs.

Blum, Barbara. 1990. "Bringing Administrators into the Process. *Public Welfare,* 48 (no. 4): 4–12.

Clarkson Co., M. H., Inc. n.d. *Final Report on the Evaluation of the South*

Carolina Work Experience Program. Columbia, S.C.: M. H. Clarkson Co., Inc.

Florida Department of Health and Rehabilitative Services. 1987. *Evaluation of the TRADE Welfare for Work Program.* Report E-87-1. Tallahassee, Fla.: Department of Health and Rehabilitative Services, Office of the Inspector General, Office of Evaluation and Management Review.

Freedman, Stephen, Jan Bryant, and George Cave. 1988. *New Jersey: Final Report on the Grant Diversion Project.* New York: Manpower Demonstration Research Corporation.

Friedlander, Daniel. 1988. *Subgroup Impacts and Performance Indicators for Selected Welfare Employment Programs.* New York: Manpower Demonstration Research Corporation.

Friedlander, Daniel, Gregory Hoerz, Janet Quint, and James Riccio. 1985a. *Arkansas: Final Report on the WORK Program in Two Counties.* New York: Manpower Demonstration Research Corporation.

Friedlander, Daniel, Gregory Hoerz, David Long, and Janet Quint. 1985b. *Maryland: Final Report on the Employment Initiatives Evaluation.* New York: Manpower Demonstration Research Corporation.

Friedlander, Daniel, Marjorie Erickson, Gayle Hamilton, and Virginia Knox. 1986. *West Virginia: Final Report on the Community Work Experience Demonstrations.* New York: Manpower Demonstration Research Corporation.

Friedlander, Daniel, Stephen Freedman, Gayle Hamilton, and Janet Quint. 1987. *Illinois: Final Report on Job Search and Work Experience in Cook County.* New York: Manpower Demonstration Research Corporation.

Garasky, Steven. 1990. "Analyzing the Effect of Massachusetts' ET Choices Program on the State's AFDC-Basic Caseload." *Evaluation Review,* 14 (December): 701–710.

Goldman, Barbara, Daniel Friedlander, and David Long. 1986. *California: Final Report on the San Diego Job Search and Work Experience Demonstration.* New York: Manpower Demonstration Research Corporation.

Greenberg, David H., and Michael Wiseman. 1991. "What Did the OBRA Demonstrations Do?" Discussion Paper, Institute for Research on Poverty, University of Wisconsin-Madison.

Hamilton, Gayle, and Daniel Friedlander. 1989. *Final Report on the Saturation Work Initiative Model in San Diego.* New York: Manpower Demonstration Research Corporation.

Haskins, Ron. 1989. "Congress Writes a Law: Research and Welfare Reform." Manuscript. Forthcoming in Wiseman, 1991.

Janzen, Frederick V., Jeffrey A. Bartlome, and Patrick M. Cunningham. 1987. "Emergency Welfare Work and Employment: An Independent

Evaluation of Utah's Emergency Work Program." Final report. Salt Lake City: Social Research Institute, Graduate School of Social Work, University of Utah.

Levy, Frank. 1978. "What Ronald Reagan Can Teach the United States about Welfare Reform." In *American Politics and Public Policy*, ed. Walter D. Burnham and Martha W. Weinberg. Cambridge, Mass.: MIT Press.

Lynn, Laurence E., Jr., and Mark D. Worthington. 1977. "Incremental Welfare Reform: A Strategy Whose Time Has Passed." *Public Policy*, 25 (Winter): 49–80.

Minnesota Department of Human Services. 1987. *The Community Work Experience Program in Minnesota*. St. Paul: Minnesota Department of Jobs and Training.

Munnell, Alicia H., ed. 1986. *Lessons from the Income Maintenance Experiments*. Boston: Federal Reserve Bank of Boston.

Nightingale, Demetra Smith, Douglas A. Wissoker, Lynn C. Burbridge, D. Lee Bawden, and Neal Jeffries. 1991. *Evaluation of the Massachusetts Employment and Training (ET) Program*. Washington, D.C.: Urban Institute Press.

North Carolina Department of Human Resources. 1985. *Final Assessment of the Community Work Experience Program Demonstration Project in North Carolina*. Raleigh, N.C.: Department of Human Resources, Division of Social Services, Planning and Information Section.

O'Neill, June. 1990. *Work and Welfare in Massachusetts: An Evaluation of the ET Program*. Boston: Pioneer Institute for Public Policy Research.

Oregon Department of Human Resources. 1988. *Section 1115, Demonstration Project Grant No. 11-P-98080-10-05: Final Progress Report*. Salem, Oreg.: Department of Human Resources, Adult and Family Services Division.

Pennsylvania Department of Public Welfare. 1986. *Evaluation of the Pennsylvania Community Work Experience Program*. Harrisburg: Pennsylvania Department of Public Welfare.

Plotnick, Robert D., and Russell M. Lidman. 1987. "Forecasting Welfare Caseloads: A Tool to Improve Budgeting." *Public Budgeting and Finance* (Autumn): 70–81.

Potomac Institute for Economic Research. 1988. *Impact of the Work Programs: A Long-Term Perspective*. Washington, D.C.: Potomac Institute for Economic Research.

Riccio, James, George Cave, Stephen Freedman, and Marilyn Price. 1986. *Virginia: Final Report on the Virginia Employment Services Program*. New York: Manpower Demonstration Research Corporation.

Riccio, James, Barbara Goldman, Gayle Hamilton, Karin Martinson, and Alan Orenstein. 1989. *The Greater Avenues for Independence (GAIN) Pro-*

gram: Early Implementation Experiences and Lessons. New York: Manpower Demonstration Research Corporation.

Sherwood, Kay E. 1984. *Arizona: Preliminary Management Lessons from the WIN Demonstration Program.* New York: Manpower Demonstration Research Corporation.

Szanton, Peter L. 1989. "'The Remarkable Quango': Knowledge, Politics and Welfare Reform." Manuscript. Forthcoming in Wiseman, 1991.

Washington State Department of Health and Social Services. 1983. *Report: Intensive Applicant Employment Services Evaluation.* Olympia: Washington State Department of Health and Social Services, Division of Administration and Personnel.

——— 1984. *Evaluation of the Community Work Experience Program.* Olympia: Washington State Department of Health and Social Services, Division of Administration and Personnel.

Wiseman, Michael, ed. 1991. "Research and Policy: A Symposium on the Family Support Act of 1088." *Journal of Policy Analysis and Management,* 10 (no. 4, October).

2 Designing an Evaluation of the Job Training Partnership Act

V. Joseph Hotz

Over the last 25 years, the federal government has funded a series of programs to improve the human capital of the nation's labor force. This effort began with the Manpower Development and Training Act (MDTA) of 1962, was modified and expanded under the Comprehensive Employment and Training Act (CETA) of 1973, and is currently authorized under the Job Training Partnership Act (JTPA) of 1982. While differing in their structure, content, and scope, all of these programs sought to increase the employment and earnings and reduce the dependence on public assistance of economically disadvantaged individuals. In order to assess the success of these programs, hundreds of evaluations of federally sponsored manpower training programs have been conducted. Unfortunately, despite this considerable body of research, no clear consensus exists as to whether these programs have achieved their stated goals. For example, after carefully reviewing a recent set of evaluations, Barnow (1987) concluded that "it is difficult to draw strong conclusions about how effective the CETA programs were at increasing the earnings of participants" (p. 159).

Virtually all of these evaluations of the impact of training on the trainees were based on quasi-experimental or nonexperimental designs. The nonexperimental approach to program evaluation compares the differences in post-program outcomes (for example, levels of employment and labor market earnings) of trainees and a comparison group consisting of individuals thought to be "similar" to the trainees except for not having received training. To achieve this comparability, a variety of matching and statistical adjustment procedures have been used to account for differences in both observed and unobserved characteristics of the two groups which might distort estimates of a training program's impact. Failure to adjust for these differences properly can lead to substantial bias, which is called selection bias.

The inconclusive findings of past training program evaluations led a number of researchers and experts in evaluation to call for the use of classical experiments when evaluating training programs. For example, Ashenfelter and Card (1985), on the basis of their own study of the impact of CETA on earnings, concluded that "randomized trials are necessary to reliably determine program effects." Experimental designs may mitigate the potential biases which can arise in nonexperimental evaluations by using random assignment to obtain their comparison group. In particular, individuals who have applied and been accepted into a program are randomly assigned out of the program and used as the control group for the purposes of evaluating the program. Properly implemented, an experimental design guarantees that differences in the post-training outcomes of trainees and control group members will produce unbiased estimates of program impacts.

Such calls for the use of experimental designs to evaluate the effectiveness of social programs are not unique to the training area. During discussions of the ways to reform the existing U.S. welfare system in the 1960s, researchers argued strongly for the implementation of "social experiments" to evaluate the likely impacts of alternative schemes for providing income support to the poor. Their arguments proved persuasive and gave rise to the Negative Income Tax Experiments conducted during the late 1960s and 1970s. Subsequent to these methodologically pathbreaking studies, social experiments have been conducted to evaluate policy innovations in a wide range of social policy areas, including housing, health insurance, and education.[1] In each case, the primary argument made for adopting experimental methods was to avoid the problem of selection bias that threatened the validity of estimates of the impacts of such programs.

As in the case of the advocacy of social experiments in the 1960s and 1970s, the call for an experimental design to evaluate training programs also has proved effective. Currently, the U.S. Department of Labor (DOL) is supporting a major evaluation which employs random assignment for evaluating JTPA.[2] The National JTPA Study is an ambitious evaluation project. It seeks to use experimental methods to conduct a

1. See Greenberg and Robins (1985) and Hausman and Wise (1985) for surveys of these experiments.
2. In addition, evaluations employing random assignment are being conducted (or designed) to evaluate the Food Stamp Employment and Training Program (FSETP) and the Job Opportunities and Basic Skills (JOBS) program.

nationally representative evaluation of a large-scale and diverse ongoing training system, randomly assigning more than 20,000 JTPA applicants to training and control groups in 16 locally administered sites. As described below, this application of random assignment broke new ground in the evaluation of social programs. In addition, the Study encompasses an effort that addresses the central question of whether nonexperimental evaluations can be designed to overcome problems of selection bias.

In this chapter I review the issues confronted in designing the National JTPA Study, discuss how these issues were dealt with, and assess the efficacy of the final design in evaluating the JTPA system and in resolving the inconclusiveness of past evaluations. While one must be cautious about generalizing from one case study, I attempt to draw some lessons from the experiences of designing the National JTPA Study which will, I hope, improve our ability to measure the effectiveness of a broad range of existing or prospective social programs.

The chapter is organized as follows. In the following section I review the history of past evaluations of subsidized employment and training programs and the conflicts they engendered which led the Department of Labor to commission the National JTPA Study. In the third section I discuss the generic differences involved in evaluating ongoing programs versus demonstration projects. The National JTPA Study represented one of the first attempts to use experimental methods to evaluate an operating large-scale social program as opposed to demonstration (or pilot) programs which seek to assess new policies or procedures for delivering social services, such as the use of a negative income tax scheme or housing vouchers, before they are adopted into law. In the fourth section I outline the particular features of the JTPA system which posed potential difficulties for implementation of an experimentally based evaluation design. In the next section I review the design of the experimental component of the Study, describing the problems that arose in implementing an experimental design and their solutions. In the sixth section I describe the second component of the JTPA Study, which will assess whether reliable procedures can be developed for choosing among alternative methods for nonexperimental evaluations. I review the proposed design and report on a pilot study by Heckman and Hotz (1989) which pretested some of the procedures to be used in this component of the National JTPA Study. In the final section I summarize the lessons learned from this exercise in evaluation design for conducting program evaluations in the 1990s.

Before proceeding, two caveats are in order. First, it is important to keep in mind that the National JTPA Study is not yet complete. The final enrollment of program participants in the Study was completed in late 1989; no data have yet been analyzed, and the final report of the Study is not scheduled for completion until late 1992. Nonetheless, some lessons from the experiences to date in designing the Study are informative. Second, the reader should be aware that I am not an impartial observer of the JTPA Study. I was involved in designing the nonexperimental component of this evaluation. Nonetheless, I have tried to be explicit in labeling opinions as my own when they are offered.

The Origins of the National JTPA Study

The National JTPA Study was heavily influenced by the history of previous evaluation efforts of training programs. While numerous evaluations of employment and training programs under the Manpower Development and Training Act were conducted during the late 1960s, the Department of Labor sought to establish an ongoing evaluation system to provide estimates of the impacts of programs under CETA shortly after its enactment in 1973. Central to this effort was the development of the Continuous Longitudinal Manpower Survey (CLMS), which provided a data base on participants in CETA programs. Starting in 1975, nationally representative random samples of CETA enrollees were drawn each quarter. Three types of data were compiled on members of these samples: (1) information on CETA activities[3] in which the enrollees subsequently participated was obtained from administrative records; (2) information on family and personal background was gathered in an interview conducted shortly after enrollment, while data on post-program labor market activity were gathered in two or three followup interviews; and (3) longitudinal data on pre- and post-enrollment earnings were obtained from the Social Security Administration and merged

---

3. CETA offered four basic program activities: (1) public service employment (PSE), which consisted of subsidized public sector jobs; (2) on-the-job training (OJT), which involved subsidized jobs in the private sector where the employer was reimbursed for the training costs incurred; (3) work experience (WE), which was similar to the PSE programs but was targeted at the most disadvantaged CETA participants; and (4) classroom training (CT), which provided classroom vocational training.

into the CLMS data base. While the CLMS data base provided useful information on the participation patterns of CETA enrollees, it was, by itself, considered inadequate for estimating the impact of the CETA programs on the post-enrollment earnings experiences of enrollees. To make such comparisons, the Department of Labor used data obtained on individuals from the annual March Current Population Surveys (CPS) together with data on those individuals' labor market earnings obtained from Social Security Administration records. The DOL contracted with Westat, Inc., both to manage this data base and to conduct nonexperimental evaluations of the impacts of CETA programs on earnings using this data.

The initial efforts by Westat to evaluate CETA with the CLMS/CPS matched data were not encouraging. The firm experienced problems in determining appropriate comparison groups with which to compare the post-enrollment experience of CETA enrollees. Based on its initial experiences, Westat concluded that "one simply cannot say at this time how comparable the comparison groups are to the participant groups in the absence of the CETA program" (Westat, 1982, p. 2). DOL and Westat continued their efforts to improve the quality of the data and the process for selecting comparison groups from the CPS data. In addition, DOL and the Congressional Budget Office commissioned several additional nonexperimental studies of CETA using the CLMS in order to determine whether methods could be found to estimate program impacts reliably.

Before the latter studies were completed, Congress undertook a major overhaul of the federal manpower training system. The elections of 1980 brought Ronald Reagan to the presidency and handed control of the U.S. Senate to the Republican party. A major retrenchment ensued with respect to federally funded social programs. CETA was an obvious target. At the time, much was made of documented cases of gross mismanagement in locally administered programs funded under CETA and of the cost of its public service employment program ($7 billion in 1978). In 1981, the job creation component of CETA was eliminated. In 1982, Congress completely eliminated CETA and enacted the Job Training Partnership Act.

The new act represented a substantial departure from CETA in terms of national employment and training policy. In particular, it (1) granted state governments more authority and responsibility for designing and operating training programs; (2) established a "contractual" relationship between the state-run programs and the federal government through a set of auditing and performance standards; (3) required states to establish a partnership with the private sector to forge a closer link between the needs of industry and the training activities provided by the local public-sector programs; (4) focused on training of the economically disadvantaged while eliminating the provision of income transfers and subsidized employment; and (5) established a retraining program for workers dislocated from their jobs as a result of structural changes in the U.S. economy. Congress also greatly reduced the level of spending on training under JTPA; the initial annual appropriation for JTPA was $3.6 billion. Finally, the Act explicitly directed the DOL "[to] evaluate the effectiveness of programs authorized under this act . . . [with respect to the effect of the Act on] increases in employment and earnings for participants, reduced income support costs, increased tax revenues, duration of training and employment situations, [provide] information on the post enrollment labor market experience of program participants for at least a year following their termination from such programs, and [provide] comparable information on other employees or trainees of participating employers" (JTPA, Section 454.[a]).

Pursuant to the mandate to evaluate the impact of JTPA on its participants, DOL began to develop a nonexperimental evaluation structure similar to that used for CETA. The CLMS was replaced by the Job Training Longitudinal Survey (JTLS), which consisted of longitudinal data derived from a two-tier random sampling of (1) local JTPA program units, called Service Delivery Areas (SDAs), and, within those units, of (2) program enrollees. Data similar to those contained in the CLMS were gathered for the enrollees.[4] In addition, the Department proposed a supplement to the CPS, called the Survey of History of Work (SHOW), which was to provide an extensive data base for the construction of comparison groups for estimating JTPA impacts. In the midst of this development phase, the commissioned nonexperimental studies of the CETA impact were completed and delivered to DOL. These studies showed a disturbingly wide range of estimates and found substantial sensitivity of impact estimates to alternative procedures for resolving the problem of selection bias.

---

4. One of the differences was that earnings data from Social Security records were not obtained for the sample members because of changes in the Social Security Administration's practices regarding the confidentiality of respondents.

In light of this evidence, late in 1984 DOL appointed a JTLS Technical Advisory Panel. Its purpose was to assess the general validity of the results of these studies and to evaluate alternative designs for collecting data with which to conduct mandated evaluations of JTPA. This panel, chaired by Ernst Stromsdorfer of Washington State University, spent the following year evaluating the available studies and consulting with other experts in the field of manpower training evaluation. It issued its recommendations in November 1985.

Most of the panel's report was devoted to the problem of selection bias in the nonexperimental CETA evaluations. To understand its consequences for nonexperimental evaluations, consider the task of evaluating the impact of a training program, such as those supported by CETA, on the post-program earnings of program participants. Nonexperimental evaluations estimate program impacts using data on program participants and a comparison group, where the latter group has not received training but, unlike an experimental control group, is not randomly selected from program participants. Because the comparison group was formed in this way, the post-program experiences of its members may be substantially different from what they would have been for the program participants if the latter group had not received the program's services.

The reason why differences are likely to exist is that participants in such programs typically self-select into programs. These individuals who are eligible for JTPA are not guaranteed services; participants will be screened by the program operators based on objective and subjective assessments of their appropriateness and likelihood of benefiting from the program. For example, the type of individual who applies for training programs is likely to have less education, on average, than those who do not apply, or program operators may choose to use low educational attainment as a criterion for selection in order to serve those who are more disadvantaged. Those seeking training, especially in training programs which do not provide a stipend (as is the case with JTPA), might also be highly motivated to obtain a job. To the extent that educational attainment and motivation affect earnings, those seeking training would not have had, on average, the same earnings in the absence of the program as those in the comparison group. In this case, the earnings of the comparison group do not equal, on average, what the earnings of trainees would have been if the latter group had not received training.

A variety of matching and statistical adjustment procedures have been

used in an attempt to adjust for discrepancies in observed and unobserved characteristics between trainees and candidate comparison group
members that generate the noncomparability between these two groups.
Failure to control for such discrepancies in nonexperimental evaluations
may lead to substantial bias in the estimate of program impacts; this bias
is selection bias. The essential problem with applying these statistical
adjustments in nonexperimental evaluations is that it is not clear, a priori, which one is appropriate, and the use of an inappropriate one may
exacerbate, rather than reduce, the pre-enrollment differences between
these two types of individuals. The latter problem was apparent in the
studies reviewed by the JTLS Research Advisory Panel. They found that
the resulting estimates differed widely, leading the Panel to conclude
that "no particular point estimate can be said to be the correct one"
(JTLS Research Advisory Panel, 1985, p. 10).

Even more disturbing were the findings of two independent studies
conducted by Robert LaLonde of the University of Chicago and by
Thomas Fraker and Rebecca Maynard of Mathematica Policy Research,
Inc. These studies addressed the question of whether one can use nonexperimental methods to replicate impact estimates obtained from experimental data. Each evaluated nonexperimental strategies for selecting comparison groups from existing data sources—such as the CPS and
the Panel Study of Income Dynamics (PSID)—and the use of alternative
nonexperimental statistical procedures for estimating the impact of
training. Both papers focused on the National Supported Work (NSW)
Demonstration Project. In the NSW demonstration, eligible individuals
were randomly assigned to a program consisting of job training and
counseling: one group (the experimentals) received the program "treatment," while members of the other group (the controls) were denied
access to the program. Therefore, experimentally based estimates of
training impacts could also be obtained for this program. In a joint
paper summarizing their respective studies, LaLonde and Maynard
(1987) reported that "the nonexperimental procedures may not accurately estimate the true program impacts. In particular, there does not
appear to be any formula [using nonexperimental methods] that researchers can confidently use to replicate the experimental results of
the Supported Work Program. In addition these studies suggest that
recently developed methods for constructing comparison groups are no
more likely (and arguably less likely) than the econometric procedures
to replicate the experimental estimates of the impact of training" (p.

121). Moreover, their "findings are further evidence that the current skepticism surrounding the results of nonexperimental evaluations is justified." In light of these findings, the JTLS Panel concluded:

> The recommendations of the panel are strongly conditioned by the judgment that it will not be possible to solve the problem of selection bias within the context of a quasi-experimental design such as the JTLS/SHOW; at least, not in a short enough time frame to meet Congress' need for valid information to guide policy. Even though many authors studying employment and training programs have recognized the selection problem, *no* such study using a quasi-experimental design can be said to have controlled adequately for selection bias. The panel does not intend to set forth a counsel of despair. Rather, it is concerned that the past evaluations of CETA have consumed, and the contemplated evaluations of JTPA will consume, millions of dollars and much valuable time. It would be extremely unfortunate if the analysis of the JTLS/SHOW design would yield the same ambiguous conclusions as has the analysis of the CLMS/CPS data base for CETA. (JTLS Research Advisory Panel, 1985, p. 21)

The Panel recommended that the JTLS/SHOW design be abandoned and that DOL conduct a classical randomized experiment to evaluate the impact of the JTPA system: "The most potentially fruitful solution to the problem of selection bias in any evaluation is the use of a classical randomized experiment. Here one has the greatest assurance that the program participants and the control group of program eligible individuals are on the average alike in every important sense except that one group has had the program treatment while the otherwise 'identical' group has not" (p. 15). The Panel's recommendation was based on the compelling nature of a randomized design. The average post-training earnings (or other outcomes of interest) of a control group, by design, provide an unbiased measure of what the trainees would have experienced if they had not received training. In this sense, randomization makes the counterfactual factual. The difference between the post-training earnings of experimental and control group members gives program impact estimates which do not suffer from selection bias.

While the Panel concluded that a randomized experimental design was needed to "generate answers that are usable for evaluating JTPA and for designing improvements in it" (p. 4), it also thought it was "prudent to continue development work on the econometric front; use of the quasi-experimental analysis design in the long run may be the only way one can regularly measure nationally representative program outcomes and be able to do this without having to deny program treatments to some" (pp. 4–5). Thus, its second primary recommendation was "to use these experimental results and the understanding of the selection process gained thereby to improve the effectiveness of quasi-experimental designs as a strategy for program evaluation. This approach should enable the implementation of some type of JTLS/SHOW design at a later date" (p. 15). This second recommendation was motivated by concerns about the difficulties and costs which the Panel foresaw in conducting evaluations of JTPA impacts with a randomized design. Such concerns were important in light of congressional pressures for DOL to provide annual assessments of the "effectiveness of [JTPA] programs authorized under the Act." Therefore, the Panel also advised that a complementary set of studies be undertaken in conjunction with the experiments in order to (1) improve our understanding of the processes by which members of the population eligible for JTPA services seek training and which characterize how JTPA operators select which of these applicants to serve, and (2) use the experiments to explore and benchmark the alternative nonexperimental methods to help improve future quasi-experimental efforts to evaluate the program.

The Department of Labor adopted the Panel's recommendations. In early 1986, it issued a Request for Proposals to implement and evaluate the Title IIA programs within JTPA[5] by randomly assigning up to 30,000 program applicants into treatment (services provided) and control (no services provided) groups in up to 20 local JTPA programs. These experiments were to be used to evaluate the net impacts of JTPA on earnings, employment, welfare dependency, and educational attainment for selected target groups and services provided and to improve the understanding of the JTPA selection process and the effectiveness of future quasi-experimental evaluations of the program. The proposed evaluation was ambitious. It sought to break new ground by implementing an experimentally based evaluation of program impacts for a large,

---

5. The Job Training Partnership Act authorizes services to be provided to eligible individuals within three categories. Title IIA, which entails the bulk of the funding under the Act, authorizes the provision of services on a year-round basis to economically disadvantaged adults and youths; Title IIB authorizes funding of summer programs for youths; and Title III authorizes funds that are targeted on dislocated workers. The National JTPA Study only evaluates Title IIA service provision.

ongoing program which would provide estimates which were both accurate (unbiased) within the sites studied (that is, have "internal validity") and which could be generalized to the national JTPA system (that is, have "external validity"). Furthermore, expanding on the innovative studies by LaLonde and Fraker and Maynard, it sought to use the experiments as a "testing ground" for nonexperimentally based methodologies. The Department issued two separate, competitively bid contracts. The first covered recruitment of sites, implementation of randomized assignment, and documentation (process analysis) of the structure and operation of the program in these sites. The second contract covered development of a research design, data collection, analysis of the experimental data, and assessment of quasi-experimental methods. The Department selected the Manpower Demonstration Research Corporation (MDRC), with Abt Associates as a subcontractor, to undertake the recruitment and implementation component. It selected Abt Associates, with MDRC, ICF, Inc., and the National Opinion Research Center (NORC) as subcontractors, to undertake the design, data collection, and analysis component.

Evaluating Demonstration Projects versus Existing Ongoing Programs

In his recent book on the role of social science research in government, Richard Nathan (1988) distinguishes between two types of evaluation research: demonstration research and evaluation research. Demonstration research is designed to test new programs and policy innovations implemented through a limited number of pilot or demonstration projects. The NIT experiments, the NSW Demonstration, and the other social experiments are examples. Evaluations of such projects do not always use experimental methods. Such evaluations involve the design and testing of a new program. These demonstration projects typically are implemented in a limited set of geographic sites and frequently require the establishment of a new administrative structure to run the new program or deliver the new set of services.

A key feature of demonstration projects is that they provide an easier rationale for the use of random assignment with its denial of services to members of a control group than is the case in other social contexts. In general, random assignment raises ethical and legal problems because of the potential that the denial of treatments may harm people or deny them something to which they are entitled, either legally or effectively. Demonstration projects minimize the problems associated with the denial because the treatment represents a service to which the population is not entitled. That is, the null treatment for controls in a demonstration project is the status quo.

Finally, demonstration research differs from evaluations of ongoing programs in terms of the goals of the research. Demonstration research typically has the more limited goal of determining whether a program *might* work. Such research focuses on questions of feasibility and the likely direction of impacts. Given this focus, demonstration research generally does not provide results which generalize to all potential program participants and to all possible states of nature in which the program might operate if it were adopted. Evaluation research, on the other hand, assesses the impacts of existing (ongoing) programs, such as the effect of the Head Start program on the educational attainment of low-income youths or the earnings of JTPA trainees.

There are at least three problems which arise (or are more difficult) in evaluating ongoing programs that do not arise (or are less difficult) in conducting demonstration research. The first problem is the inherent lack of control over the design of the program. The "treatments" are dictated by the program and frequently are not as neatly categorized as they can be in demonstration projects. The selection processes in an existing program may not be based on easily quantifiable criteria, and they may differ across program units or progam administrators. Such diversity complicates the analysis of the program's impact. More important, unlike demonstration studies, researchers in an existing program are generally not free to change the way the program operates. This is true because in evaluating an ongoing program, interest centers on how the program operates "as is." Typically those who commission evaluation research are interested in the impact of the program(s) which currently exist.

The second problem concerns establishing reliable information on the counterfactual state. Information on what behavior would be like if the program did not exist or if it had not provided services to a program participant is much more difficult to obtain.[6] This may be so because the

---

6. Consider, for example, evaluating what impact the availability of Social Security has on the work behavior of older workers. Virtually all citizens are eligible for Social Security

use of random assignment is generally difficult to implement. Program operators or public officials are likely to object to the denial of services to individuals who apply to a program, objecting that it is inappropriate to use individuals as human "guinea pigs." This reluctance is heightened when evaluations involve such substantial intrusions into the program as implementing an experimental design. As Nathan (1988) notes, this lack of cooperation stems from the inherent differences in objectives between those running an ongoing program and those trying to evaluate it. Program administrators are interested in providing services to individuals; they do not view their role as helping to facilitate evaluation of their program. Such administrators "may not want research to be conducted because they fear it would show a policy they favor to be ineffective or, if it works, to have results that fall short of what had been promised" (Nathan, 1988, pp. 123–124).

The third problem is that the questions being addressed in evaluations of ongoing programs are more difficult to answer relative to those for demonstration projects. Demonstration research seeks to address the question of what *might* happen if a new policy were to be implemented; such evaluations are "feasibility studies," determining whether something might work. To put it another way, demonstration projects provide an opportunity for rejecting the hypothesis that the policy innovation under consideration does not work or cannot be implemented under situations which provide a maximum amount of control and cooperation of the administrators and participants in the study. In contrast, in evaluations of existing programs the central question is: *does it work?* This question is inherently more demanding because it requires that an evaluation, conducted on a subset of the entire system (for example, on a subset of sites and/or participants), be valid for the units of the program under study, and also be generalizable to the program as a whole. That is, it is important that the results of such evaluations be representative; this requirement is typically less important in the evaluation of demonstrations.

These distinctive demands associated with the evaluation of ongoing programs were all, in fact, present in the National JTPA Study. They

---

and Medicare when they reach older ages; one cannot observe a situation in the United States where this program does not operate. Moreover, it is often difficult to conduct an experimental evaluation of an ongoing program, given the legal and ethical issues involved with making individuals assigned to the "no services" control status worse off.

proved to make the task of implementing a design for this study extremely difficult.

The JTPA System: Key Features and Their Challenges to Evaluation

At least three important aspects of the structure of the JTPA system distinguished it from other federal social programs and complicated its evaluation. First, the JTPA system is decentralized, with a diversity of organizational structures and objectives at the local level; second, the decision-making structure of local programs is complex; and third, the eligibility criteria for services are broad, and local programs are monitored and regulated by contractually based performance standards. I briefly describe each of these features of the system.[7]

Decentralization and Diversity

In establishing the JTPA system, Congress made a conscious attempt to reduce the federal government's role in the management and implementation of manpower training, transferring these responsibilities to the states. This change reflected the view that priorities for the training of disadvantaged Americans needed to be set at the local labor market level, enabling the program to meet the particular needs and unique features of a diverse set of labor market environments. Specifically, the Act gave authority to the governors to establish relatively independent local units or service delivery areas (SDAs), designed to correspond to existing labor markets. Within certain guidelines, these SDAs were given latitude in developing programs which reflected the local population and labor force needs and the training and manpower development resources available within these localized units. Based on early assessments, the states in fact did establish a diverse set of localized programs, often making dramatic changes relative to CETA in the delivery and composition of their programs. Today, over 600 separate SDAs make up the JTPA system. Local programs vary in the type and delivery of services, typically providing various mixes of job search assistance (JSA),

7. See also Doolittle and Traeger (1990) for a discussion of the role these issues played in designing the National JTPA Study.

classroom training (CT), and on-the-job training (OJT) services. Typically, the local SDAs contract with service providers (community colleges, specialized vocational training organizations, and local employers) to provide these services to JTPA program participants.

Multifaceted and Complex Governing Structure

Consistent with the desire to pass greater authority to the states and to establish a system of programs which would be responsive to localized manpower training needs, the Act established a governing structure in which authority and decision-making are shared by several different parties. The Act requires the establishment of a Private Industry Council (PIC) within each SDA to serve as a "board of directors" for the local program. The PICs are appointed by the governors and are required to include representatives from the private sector (which must constitute a majority of the PIC's membership), economic development agencies, labor and educational organizations, and community-based organizations. The predominance of representatives from the business community in these organizations represented a precedent-setting establishment of a public-private partnership in the governance of a social program and reflected Congress's desire to focus the nation's manpower training efforts on meeting localized manpower needs in private industry.[8] Each SDA also has a chief elected official (CEO) who shares power and policy-setting authority over the operation of the SDA with the PIC. These officials are intended to provide a direct voice for the SDA's local constituency in the operation of the program. The PICs and CEOs jointly select the administrative entity which runs the SDA program.

Who Is Served and the Role of Performance Standards

While the SDAs have substantial autonomy from the federal government and, to a lesser degree, from the state government, their performance in meeting the objectives of Title IIA of the Act is monitored and controlled by a set of enrollment and expenditure requirements and performance standards. The Act designates that the population eligible for JTPA Title IIA services are those individuals who belong to at least one

8. Along with the establishment of a partnership with private industry, the Act also eliminated provisions for public service employment available under CETA.

of the following groups: (1) AFDC recipients; (2) Food Stamp recipients; (3) members of households whose income in the six months prior to enrollment in the program is less than the OMB poverty level or 70 percent of the lower living standard income level, whichever is higher.[9] While JTPA does not entitle all who are eligible to be served, it specifies that the SDAs are to provide training services to those who can benefit from such services and who are most in need of them. In meeting these vague mandates, SDAs are also expected to provide "equitable services" among "substantial segments" of the eligible population. The Act also contains further requirements on who is served and how funds should be spent. In particular, each SDA is supposed to spend 40 percent of the funds it receives on eligible youths (those between the ages of 16 and 21). Failure to meet these goals can lead to reorganization of the SDA. Finally, the Act authorized the Secretary of Labor to set performance standards for SDAs to monitor whether they are meeting the goals of the Act. The Department of Labor issues standards which governors may adopt for their states or may adjust to take account of the unique features of the participant characteristics and local labor market conditions prevailing in their states. While states have elected to make such adjustments in the standards for their SDAs, standards have been implemented for the following types of outcomes: rates of job placement and welfare termination, wage rates of those placed, schooling or other training completion (for youths), and the program costs of participants who are placed. To provide an incentive for compliance with these standards, up to 6 percent of the funds provided to each state were to be allocated to SDAs depending on whether they exceeded their standards.[10] This use of incentive contracting is an important feature of the JTPA system, and initial investigations suggested that many SDAs took such standards quite seriously.

Implications of JTPA Program Features for Evaluation

The features of the JTPA system described above posed many problems for the design and implementation of the National JTPA Study. Given

---

9. The Act allows the SDAs to serve individuals who do not meet any of these criteria, but they must not exceed 6 percent of the participants served.

10. For a more detailed discussion of the implementation of performance standards in the JTPA system, see Chapter 10 in this volume.

the decentralized structure of the system and the degree of autonomy stipulated for the SDAs, the Department of Labor could not make the participation of SDAs in the Study mandatory; rather, MDRC was required to obtain voluntary participation on the part of SDAs in the experimental component of the Study. Furthermore, the complex governing arrangement of each SDA made recruitment of sites into the Study quite difficult, since many individuals at each site had to be "sold" on such participation. The lack of program uniformity across sites also presented serious challenges to designing the Study. The diversity of services (treatments) being provided made it difficult to define a set of standardized treatments which could be compared across SDAs; moreover, these differences across sites meant that characterizing the selection processes would be an essential but time-consuming task. Finally, since many SDAs handled applicant assessment and allocation to services in a decentralized manner,[11] the integrity of the random assignment was a potential problem. Thus, in addition to the problems previously encountered in designing experimentally based evaluations of demonstration programs such as the Negative Income Tax (NIT) Experiments, the National Supported Work Demonstration (NSW) Project, or the more recent state Work/Welfare Initiatives, the National JTPA Study encountered several new and potentially troublesome problems in implementing its evaluation.

Designing the Experimental Component of the National JTPA Study

While the goals set out by the Request for Proposal issued by the Department of Labor for the experimental component of the National JTPA Study were clear, what was less certain was the feasibility of achieving them. The design team confronted numerous problems in implementing the experimental evaluation sought by the Department;[12] some were

---

11. In many SDAs, especially in western states, the service providers actually handled the eligibility determination and assessment of appropriate services of JTPA applicants.

12. As noted earlier, the DOL contracts to conduct the National JTPA Study involve several different research organizations. While the design of the various components of the study was a collaborative effort, the primary responsibility for the design of the experimental component was that of research teams from MDRC and Abt Associates, while the evaluation of nonexperimental methods was the primary responsibility of researchers

satisfactorily resolved, some were not. In this section I summarize this experience.[13]

In designing an experimental evaluation of the JTPA system, the design team was confronted by the following issues or questions:

E-1. How should the sites (SDAs) in which to conduct the study be selected, and how could their participation be gained?

E-2. How could the intrusion on the operations of the SDAs be minimized while conducting the experiments?

E-3. At what stage in the program's processing of program applicants should random assignment be conducted?

E-4. What should be the allocation of participants between treatment groups and control status?

E-5. How long should controls be "embargoed," that is, denied access to JTPA services?

E-6. What should be the definition of "treatments" in the Study and, thus, what type of impact estimates would be provided?

E-7. How large should the treatment and control groups be to obtain estimates with statistical power?

While some of these issues had been encountered before in the demonstration projects which preceded the JTPA Study (for example, Questions E-5 through E-7), some represented uncharted territory. The design team for the Study developed an initial set of answers to these questions and then proceeded to try to implement them. In this study, implementation hinged crucially on being able to gain the cooperation of the SDAs constituting the JTPA system; thus, dealing with the second part of Question E-1 was the essential issue in the success of any particular set of design decisions. In what follows, I consider the initial set of answers the design team made to these questions, relate how well they "went over" with the SDAs, and indicate how the initial designs were modified to accommodate implementation.

at NORC and ICF, Inc. In addition, the Study had an Advisory Panel which provided input into the design development process. Finally, DOL, through the office of the Employment and Training Administration, exercised final approval over all design decisions.

13. For a detailed report on the implementation of the experimental design in the National JTPA Study, see Doolittle and Traeger (1990).

Question E-1: Site Selection and Gaining SDA Participation

The conflict in selecting sites in which to conduct the experimental evaluation was between representativeness and the likely willingness of SDAs to participate in a study involving random assignment. The evaluation sought to be a representative study of the JTPA system. The proper design for obtaining a representative sample of SDAs was to use a probabilistic sampling of the existing SDAs. At the same time, the design team anticipated that SDAs would resist participating in a study in which program participants were denied services on a random basis. Here, the obvious approach to site selection would be to recruit SDAs which were willing to participate in the experiment, a process which would severely compromise the ability to generalize from the experimental results to the entire JTPA system. Further confounding this trade-off was the fact that the Department of Labor could not require SDAs to participate in such a study.

The Department, in consultation with the JTPA Evaluation Advisory Panel and the contractors, agreed to try to select sites using probabilistic sampling. A stratified random sampling procedure was designed in which characteristics such as SDA size (number of participants in previous years), geographic region, and success in meeting performance standards were used to stratify the relevant universe of 425 SDAs into some 20 strata.[14] An ordered list of replacement SDAs within each category, selected in a random fashion, was also created. SDAs were randomly drawn within each stratum and approached by MDRC to seek their participation in the study, based on the initial design, which is explained below.

In August of 1986, MDRC began contacting this initial list of SDAs. Over the next five months more than 73 SDAs were contacted; by the end of that period none of the initial set of SDAs had agreed to participate,[15] and in 8 of the 20 categories MDRC had in fact contacted 4 or more SDAs for possible participation. Clearly, random site selection was not viable in the National JTPA Study. While many in the research team had anticipated this outcome, it was instructive to learn the reasons why SDAs refused to participate. Of the 228 SDAs which MDRC contacted to

14. The relevant universe consisted of those SDAs in the contiguous 48 states which had not exhibited serious administrative or legal problems.

15. In fact, 2 of the original 20 randomly selected SDAs did eventually agree to participate in the study.

determine their willingness to participate in the Study, over 62 percent cited the ethical or public-relations problems with random assignment and 54 percent cited the denial of services to controls as major reasons for not wanting to participate (Doolittle and Traeger, 1990, table 2.1). In addition, 48 percent of the SDAs contacted were concerned about the adverse effect on client recruitment goals of having to assign randomly a proportion of their participants to a control group, and 25 percent of the SDAs were concerned about the adverse effect of diverting applicants to a control group on their ability to attain their performance standards (Doolittle and Traeger, 1990, table 2.1). The latter concerns were especially important to SDAs in regions of the country experiencing reductions in local unemployment, many of which were having a harder time recruiting participants into their JTPA training programs.

After this initial experience, the Department, at the urging of the design team, abandoned the initial site selection design and opted for a more flexible site selection procedure that attempted to select SDAs "representing" the diversity of the program,[16] but, more important, that would yield adequate numbers of sites with which to conduct the Study. While this change in selection criteria eased the burden on MDRC's site recruitment effort, it still did not yield adequate samples. Finally, to facilitate site recruitment, the Department agreed to changes in other parts of the design (described below) which were motivated by the concerns about the implementation of random assignment and the size of the control group raised by the SDAs contacted in the initial rounds of recruitment. The design team also decided to reallocate resources from data collection and the component concerning evaluation of nonexperimental methods in order to provide greater up-front cash payments to SDAs for participating in the Study. In the initial design, SDAs were to be given a pre-negotiated lump-sum payment on the order of $40,000; in the end, the average payment received by an SDA included in the Study was $170,000, and some sites were authorized to receive as much as $300,000 to compensate for their participation.[17]

A total of 16 sites,[18] listed in Table 2.1, were recruited by September

16. In particular, MDRC continued to recruit sites according to the strata of the original site selection design, but no longer restricted itself to following the ordered list of sites and often entered into negotiations simultaneously with multiple SDAs within a stratum.

17. These figures were provided to me by Dr. Larry Orr of Abt Associates.

18. The SDA in Fresno, California, initially had agreed to participate, but its City Council voted to withdraw from the Study.

Table 2.1 Sample of SDAs in National JTPA Study

SDA[a]	1986 UE rate[b]	Percentage in poverty[c]	Population density[d]	Target sample	Actual sample
Capital Areas, MS (Jackson)	6.7	13.3	310	1,220	1,478
Concentrated Employment Program, MT (Butte)	7.7	7.5	10	825	683
Coosa Valley, GA (Rome)	5.7	11.2	80	1,800	1,840[e]
*Corp. for Employment and Training, NJ (Jersey City)	9.6	14.7	7,000	1,600	1,686[e]
Corpus Christi/Nueces County, TX (Corpus Christi)	10.4	13.4	320	1,500	1,609[e]
Crawford/Hancock/Marion/Wyandot Counties, OH (Marion)	10.0	7.2	120	1,150	1,154
East Central Iowa, IA (Cedar Rapids)	5.9	6.1	90	2,963	498
Greater Omaha, NE (Omaha)	5.6	6.6	520	1,600	1,362
Heartland, FL (Lakeland)	10.3	11.4	90	4,850	597
*JobWorks, IN (Fort Wayne)	6.0	5.9	160	3,600	3,608
Land of Ozarks, MO (Springfield)	5.9	10.1	70	2,000	1,202
Larimer County, CO (Fort Collins)	5.9	5.9	60	1,200	1,027
Macon/De Witt Counties, IL (Decatur)	11.3	7.8	150	750	471
Northwest Minnesota, MN (Thief River Falls)	10.0	11.1	10	550	560
Oakland, CA	8.7	8.7	6,300	1,065	1,072[e]
*Providence/Cranston, RI	4.6	9.0	4,630	1,750	1,759[e]

Source: Fred Doolittle and Linda Traeger, Implementing the National JTPA Study (Manpower Demonstration Research Corporation, 1990), tables 5.9, B.1. Copyright © 1989, 1990 by the Manpower Demonstration Research Corporation and used with its permission.

a. Name of SDA's largest city given in parentheses.

b. Unemployment rate for program year 1986.

c. Percentage of families below poverty level ($7,356 in 1979 for 2 children, 2 adult household).

d. Number of persons per square mile.

e. Some persons at this site were randomly assigned to the treatment or control group at a ratio higher than 2:1.

* Denotes SDA in which sample of eligible nonparticipants was drawn for use in evaluation of nonexperimental methods component of the Study.

1988, two years after the site recruitment effort began. In the various phases of the recruitment effort, the acceptance rate among SDAs contacted by MDRC never reached 10 percent. Site selection in this study thus proved incredibly difficult! In the end, the JTPA Study consists of a volunteer sample of SDAs. Moreover, despite initial indications that the characteristics of these sites—including their size, groups served, local labor market conditions, and so forth—appear not to differ significantly from the average characteristics of the universe of SDAs, the lack of a well-defined sampling frame for the resulting sites makes it difficult to generalize from this set of sites to the population as a whole.

Questions E-1 through E-6: Intrusion of the Study
into the Operations of the SDA and Implementation
of the Random Assignment Process

One of the design goals of the study was to evaluate existing SDA programs "as is" and to avoid altering the program when implementing random assignment. At the same time, the diversity of the programs, along with the concerns raised by SDAs, suggested that certain changes would need to be made in the programs in order to implement random assignment in a consistent fashion across all of the SDAs in the Study.[19] The design team considered a number of ways to implement random assignment based on information from the DOL regarding program operation at the SDA level. The typical SDA was thought to process applicants through its system in the following way. Individuals would apply to an SDA, either through its main office or, possibly, through vendors contracted by the SDA to supply services. An assessment would be made as to whether the applicant was eligible according to the criteria discussed earlier. If the applicant was found to be eligible, the program operators or vendors would conduct an assessment concerning the applicant's trainability and attempt to match her training needs to the types of training available. Based on this assessment, the program operators would either assign the person to some training activity (such as

19. In designing the Study, the design team began with little information about the structure of the SDAs because of the relative youth of the program (recall that the JTPA program was enacted in 1982). The initial assumptions about how particular SDAs were structured made by the design team were subject to error and were revised on the basis of information gathered by MDRC in its interviews of the SDA administrators during site recruitment.

classroom training, on-the-job training, or some form of job search assistance) or would indicate to the applicant that she could not be served by the JTPA program. At that point an applicant could be considered as a participant in the JTPA program and would be directed to report to the designated training activity.

Given this selection process, two alternative methods of random assignment (see Question E-3) were considered which differed in terms of the type of impact estimates which could be obtained. One option consisted of random assignment immediately after eligibility determination but before assessment, with eligible applicants randomly assigned to one of the available training activities. This option had the desirable feature of enabling researchers to estimate the differential impacts of alternative treatments. But such a design would intrude on the operation of the SDAs in important ways: it would circumvent the usual staff or vendor assessment process, thereby distorting the way SDAs typically operated, and it would likely exacerbate the problem of individuals assigned to a training activity who did not show up for the activity. For these reasons the design team strongly preferred a second option, which consisted of random assignment after the assessment phase, with individuals randomly assigned to receive the staff/vendor recommended activity or to be placed in a control group and denied any JTPA services. (This design is shown in Figure 2.1.) This was judged to be the least intrusive on the operations of the program and least likely to heighten the no-shows problem, since it did not entail assigning program participants to activities inappropriate to their needs (for example, assigning an adult in need of remedial reading training to an OJT slot). The primary disadvantage of this design was that it meant that differential impacts of the program could not be estimated experimentally. Initially, this option was selected.

In implementing this design for random assignment, the design team had to decide how to classify the JTPA training activities, that is, Question E-6. Based on their initial information and that from the operation of CETA programs, the design team anticipated that one of the following three activities would be offered to JTPA participants by the SDAs: on-the-job training (OJT), classroom training (CT), or job search assistance (JSA). Thus, the initial design consisted of these three treatments.

Finally, two additional issues related to the implementation of the random assignment design had to be resolved: the proportion of applicants assigned to the control group (Question E-4), and how long con-

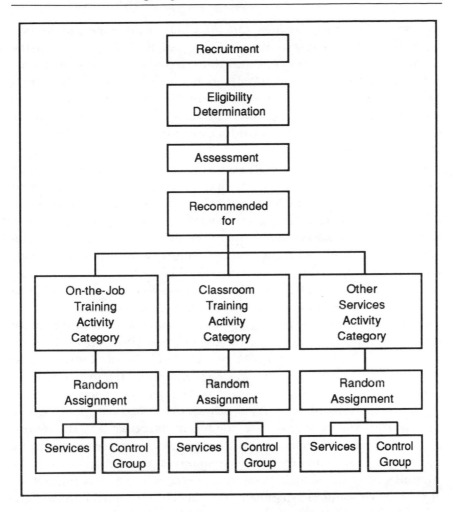

Figure 2.1. Random assignment model for the National JTPA Study. *Source:* Fred Doolittle and Linda Traeger, *Implementing the National JTPA Study* (Manpower Demonstration Research Corporation, 1990), Figure 1.1. Copyright © 1989, 1990 by the Manpower Demonstration Research Corporation and used with its permission.

trols would be denied services (Question E-5). With respect to the first issue, the initial design decision was to employ a 50–50 split in the random allocation of controls and those treated. With respect to the issue of the embargo from JTPA services on controls, it was initially decided that the embargo period should be 30 months, and that to minimize "treating" the controls, the JTPA staff should not provide members of the control group with any information about other (non-JTPA) training program options.

In the initial phase of the site recruitment process, MDRC presented this design to the SDAs as a description of how random assignment would be conducted. The SDAs did not react positively to implementation of the random assignment scheme; they were particularly concerned about the adverse effect that assigning one of every two applicants to the null-treatment, control status would have on their recruitment goals and their ability to meet their performance standards, and about the ethics of providing no assistance to the controls for a period of 30 months. Given the difficulties experienced in recruiting sites, the Department, at the urging of the design team, decided to make some alterations in its design of the random assignment procedures in an attempt to secure greater SDA cooperation. It made four changes: (1) the treatment-control split was changed from 1:1 to 2:1 and, in cases where SDAs were having severe recruitment problems, to 5:1 for temporary periods of time; (2) the SDAs were encouraged to expand their recruitment efforts to offset the loss of participants to the control group and were provided access to extensive assistance in designing recruitment and client retention techniques; (3) the embargo period on controls was reduced to 18 months after random assignment; and (4) at the time of random assignment, members of the control group were informed of alternative training programs for which they were eligible, although they were not provided specific referrals to these services. Even with these changes, which move the evaluation away from the goal of "as is" examinations, the success rate in site recruitment did not increase substantially.

The final design implementation also entailed a different taxonomy for program treatments than was initially planned. Based on MDRC's extensive interviews with the SDAs, it was learned that SDAs frequently used, or recommended that participants receive, a combination of services—often sequencing primary activities like classroom training (CT) with provision of information on job search techniques—and that

SDAs seldom provided only JSA services. Thus, in the final design, the following classification scheme was used to define treatments:

1. The *OJT Treatment,* with either OJT alone or OJT in combination with other services, but where OJT is the primary service, was the SDA staff/vendor service recommendation at assessment.
2. The *CT Treatment,* with either CT alone or CT in combination with other services, but where CT is the primary service, was the SDA staff/vendor service recommendation at assessment.
3. The *Other Services Treatment,* which was unrestricted and allowed for inclusion of all possible service recommendations.[20]

Question E-7: Sample Sizes and the Statistical Power of Alternative Types of Impact Estimates

An important element in the design of an evaluation study is the determination of the sample sizes needed to reject confidently the null hypothesis of no program impact or, equivalently, to detect an impact of some minimal magnitude with a given level of confidence. In the National JTPA Study, initial power calculations were conducted to determine whether the anticipated number of participants under various assumptions about the yield from site recruitment would be adequate to detect anticipated magnitudes for the alternative treatment-by-target-groups impact estimates for the various outcomes of interest. In fact, based on the total sample achieved (see Table 2.2), it would appear that the sizes provided adequate statistical power if impact analysis was conducted on samples which *pooled* all observations across the included SDAs. Estimating program impacts by treatment and by target group using this pooled sample would produce estimates that were externally valid for the entire JTPA system *if* the sites had been representative for the system as a whole. But, because the attempt to obtain the SDAs participating in the Study by random sampling methods was not successful, estimates of program impacts using the pooled sample of program participants and controls from the SDAs that volunteered for the Study will not have external validity. Such estimates will only be internally

---

20. The proportion of participants assigned to this catch-all category was capped at a negotiated rate which varied from 15 to 70 percent to reflect the pattern of services offered by the SDA in the past.

Table 2.2 Sample for the National JTPA Study by target group and treatment category

Target group	Treatment category			Total
	OJT	CT-OS	Other service	
Adult males	3,190	1,592	2,078	6,860
Adult females	2,672	3,417	1,980	8,069
Out-of-school youth	1,571	2,097	2,009	5,677
White	1,027	981	873	2,881
Minority	544	1,116	1,136	2,796
Total	7,433	7,106	6,067	20,606

Source: Fred Doolittle and Linda Traeger, *Implementing the National JTPA Study* (Manpower Demonstration Research Corporation, 1990), table 5.8. Copyright © 1989, 1990 by the Manpower Demonstration Research Corporation and used with its permission.

valid for the collection of SDAs who *volunteered* to participate in the Study. One cannot readily project these results beyond this collection, and concerns about the potentially select nature of the SDAs that volunteered cannot be easily dismissed, especially given the high rate of SDAs that refused. The need to alter the way SDAs operated (for instance, the provision of assistance in recruiting applicants) in order to gain their cooperation further clouds exactly what can be inferred from the experimental sample in this study. For these reasons, it is not clear what is gained from an experiment having this limited validity, given the legislated mandate for an evaluation of the entire JTPA system.

Given this situation, it would be desirable if the experimental results could be conducted site-by-site. Such analysis could have several benefits. First, it would enable one to use the separate sites as replication studies. Such replications would enable 16 separate assessments of the impacts of JTPA services on the target groups, which could be compared to determine whether such services consistently had a positive or negligible impact or whether there was substantial heterogeneity in program impacts across local SDAs. If the former outcome occurred, the results of the study would enable a somewhat stronger inference about the programs operating in the entire JTPA system to be made from the "preponderance of evidence" that the replications provided. If substantial heterogeneity were found, separate site-by-site analysis would enable the research team to explore more readily how different contextual situations affected the impacts of JTPA on its participants. In either case, analysis which is internally valid at the site level would help to mitigate the problems of generalizability arising from the lack of representativeness of the participating SDAs in this study.

Unfortunately, the sample sizes do not appear adequate to conduct site-by-site analysis separately for the various treatment/target groups. While econometric methods, such as analysis of variance or regression techniques, can be employed to attempt to investigate these issues, a priori claims for the generalizability of such analysis cannot be made because of the uncertainty that the level of aggregation (that is, which types of sites are pooled together) is appropriate. Moreover, there appears to be no easy solution to this problem because there was little that could have been done to obtain adequate samples on a site-by-site basis. Restricting the analysis to only large SDAs would not be representative of the overall system, and it would have been difficult to recruit such sites. Alternatively, asking sites to increase their enrollments to obtain adequate samples within SDAs would have altered the local programs even more and, given the difficulties in recruiting participants that many SDAs were experiencing over the period in which random assignment was conducted, probably would not have worked. Thus, compared to demonstration studies in which the ability of adjusting sample sizes usually is constrained by available funding, selecting sample sizes to achieve precision is inherently even less of an option in experimental evaluations if one seeks to conduct site-level analyses.

Designing an Evaluation of Nonexperimental Methods and the Selection Process for the National JTPA Study

As noted earlier, the JTLS Research Advisory Panel also recommended that the DOL study the use of nonexperimental methods to estimate the program's impact. To improve the Department's ability to use such methods in the future, the Panel recommended that analysis be conducted of the determinants of the selection processes that governed which eligibles applied for the program and which of the applicants were selected by the program for receipt of JTPA services. The design team was faced with several questions:

N-1. Which combinations of statistical procedures and evaluative criteria could be used to choose among alternative nonexperimental estimators in order to obtain *unbiased* estimates of program impact?

N-2. How should one exploit the availability of experimentally generated data in verifying these procedures?

N-3. Can one obtain reliable nonexperimental estimates (which answer Questions N-1 and N-2) using data from existing national surveys like the SIPP or the PSID to construct nonexperimental comparison groups, or does one need to gather site-specific samples on eligible non-participants (or nonparticipating program applicants)?

N-4. Are more detailed data on individual-level characteristics than are available from past evaluations needed in order to control adequately for differences between trainees and nonexperimentally generated comparison groups?

N-5. How does one assess how well such procedures will work?

In what follows, I describe the design decisions made for this component of the Study.

Questions N-1 through N-5: Designing Procedures for Choosing among Alternative Nonexperimental Estimators

The fundamental question concerning the application of nonexperimental methods is their reliability. As the JTLS Research Advisory Panel concluded in its report, this is an open question. Such estimates are threatened by selection bias, and any given nonexperimental estimator cannot be guaranteed, a priori, to eliminate such bias. The task in this component of the JTPA Study was to determine whether procedures could be found which would reduce this inherent uncertainty.

In designing this component of the Study, the primary aim was to ascertain whether an *objective procedure* can be used to find a consistent (unbiased) nonexperimental estimator of program impact. The design team decided to focus on a set of data-based, statistical procedures to select appropriate nonexperimental methods, to be applied to particular target groups, training programs, or types of SDAs considered in the National JTPA Study.

The logic behind the design team's approach was based on the following two observations about the use of nonexperimental methods for evaluation of program impacts. First, it is important to realize that different nonexperimental methods are based on different assumptions about the nature of the differences between program participants and members of comparison groups who did not receive training. For example, some methods are based on the assumption that selection bias can be eliminated by controlling for a set of individual-level observable characteristics, using regression analysis or matching techniques. Other procedures assume that there exist permanent, unobservable differences in the outcomes of individuals which influence their likelihood of selection into the program. In this latter case, pre-program and post-program measures of outcomes are needed in order to account statistically for such permanent components and to isolate the amount of the difference between the outcomes of participants and comparison-group members. These different nonexperimental methods, which differ in their assumptions, will tend to produce different impact estimates, even using the same data. This observation provides an explanation for the variability of estimates found in the studies cited earlier. Evidence of striking differences across nonexperimental methods merely confirms the existence of the underlying systematic differences between participants and comparison-group members.

The second observation, which follows from the first, is that the potential exists for subjecting some of these assumptions to "test" using data readily available in most nonexperimental contexts. Specifically, one can test whether a particular method (with its underlying assumptions) is able to eliminate the differences in the *pre-program* outcomes of program participants and comparison-group members. One might expect that application of methods based on inappropriate assumptions about the nature of the selection process would still leave disparities between the pre-program outcomes of such groups. In addition, since methods often impose "over-identifying" restrictions on the data, it is possible to test these restrictions, that is, to check the consistency of the implied structure of a particular method with the data.

Given these insights, procedures were designed for nonexperimental *method selection* that assess whether available nonexperimental methods "pass" a battery of such tests. Two types of tests were decided upon, using data on program participants (or their equivalent) and data for comparison groups measured prior to the time participants enter the program: *pre-program alignment tests* and *tests of implied model restrictions*.

The pre-program alignment tests are based on the following logic. If a candidate nonexperimental estimation method is appropriate (that is, if it would yield unbiased or statistically consistent estimates of program impact) when applied to post-program data on outcomes for program participants and nonparticipants from a nonexperimentally devised comparison group, applying that procedure to pre-enrollment data on these two groups should make the adjusted outcomes the same for the two groups. If the candidate method does not align these two sets of outcomes, that method is unlikely to yield unbiased estimates on post-program data.

It is important to note that pre-program alignment tests presume that the specification of model for pre-program outcomes is the same as that for the post-program outcomes, that is, the outcome process is "temporally stable." If this is not true, these tests are likely to be unreliable. In particular, lack of temporal stability in outcome processes raises the prospects of either nonexperimental estimators which "pass" the alignment tests on pre-program data but, in fact, do not eliminate the differences in latent outcomes of participants and the comparison group on post-program data, or methods which do not pass these tests but would eliminate these differences on post-program outcomes.

Tests of the implied restrictions underlying particular nonexperimental methods are based on the observation that many procedures to correct for selection entail more restrictions than are needed to identify program impacts with nonexperimental data. Such over-identifying restrictions generally can be tested with this same pre-program data. Consider, for example, the commonly used "fixed effect" estimator. It is based on the notion that the outcome for an individual can be expressed as a linear function of three components—the component characterized by measured regressors (the person's education, age, and so on), a random component reflecting transitory factors which are serially uncorrelated and uncorrelated with the included regressors, and an unmeasured component representing fixed, person-specific characteristics such as motivation.

If this is the true model and if an individual's decision to enter a training program depends *only* upon his or her "fixed" but unobserved characteristics, then a "first difference" estimation procedure with pre-enrollment *and* post-enrollment outcome measures[21] will be an appro-

21. To illustrate, note that for this model while the pre-enrollment levels of outcomes and post-enrollment outcomes *even if no training took place* would systematically differ between future trainees and members of a comparison group, comparing the *difference* between a pre-enrollment and the corresponding post-enrollment outcomes for trainees

priate estimator of the program impact. More important, for the purpose of testing, this model is over-identified. It implies that there should be no systematic relationship between the first differences in outcomes in *any* two pre-enrollment years for future trainees and comparison group members. Given three or more years of pre-enrollment data, this property of the fixed effect model can be tested. (See Heckman and Hotz, 1989, for such a test.)

Obviously, any procedures for selection of methods are only as good as their ability to identify methods that will produce unbiased estimates of training impacts and to eliminate methods that will not. To assess "success" in this regard, the design team decided to conduct a *validation analysis* of these method selection procedures. The National JTPA Study provides an unusual opportunity for conducting such a validation because of the availability of post-program data on the behavior of members of a control sample. Data on a control group provide a measure of what the post-program outcomes of JTPA participants would have been if they had not received JTPA services. In conducting a nonexperimental evaluation, one seeks methods which result in the nonexperimental comparison group's "mimicking" the experimental control group. Thus, to validate the procedures for choosing among nonexperimental estimators, an assessment can be made of the extent to which the nonexperimental methods not eliminated by these procedures result in little or no difference (in a statistical sense) between the post-program outcomes of controls and comparison-group members. A further validation of the method selection procedures will be conducted to determine whether methods eliminated by these procedures result in differences between the adjusted post-program outcomes of controls versus comparison-group members.

In order to assess the likely success of the proposed set of procedures for evaluating alternative nonexperimental methods, two members of the design team, James Heckman and I, conducted a pilot study of these procedures using data from the National Supported Work (NSW) Demonstration Project.[22] This was the same data set which LaLonde (1986) and Fraker and Maynard (1987) used in their investigations,

---

and for the comparison group members would yield consistent estimates of the average training effect.

22. See Heckman and Hotz (1989) and the accompanying discussions of this study by Paul Holland and Robert Moffitt.

which compared the ability of nonexperimental estimators to replicate the results of experimental methods. Using the same data as in the Fraker and Maynard study—namely, earnings data from Social Security Administration records for NSW trainees and controls and members of CPS comparison groups—for two of the targeted groups considered in the NSW Demonstration, high school dropouts and women on AFDC, we first compared NSW program impact estimates derived from the experimental data with those derived from a limited set of nonexperimental estimators.[23] This comparison, for both target groups, exhibited the same sensitivity across a limited set of the nonexperimental estimators as has been found in the previous literature cited by the JTLS Panel. In addition, many of the resulting estimates based on these estimators deviated significantly from the experimental estimates. Heckman and I then applied the types of tests described above to each of the two target groups, using pre-program data only, and rejected methods based on the P-Value Criterion used in classical hypothesis testing. For each group, these tests were able to generate rejections of a number of candidates for nonexperimental estimators. Moreover, when conducting the same type of validation tests to be used in the JTPA Study, we found that the *same* models were rejected,[24] and the estimators which were not rejected in pilot study produced exactly the *same* inference as was drawn from the experimental estimates.

This pilot study strongly suggests that the procedures proposed in the National JTPA Study can work. However, they are not conclusive for three reasons. First, the testing procedures which do not require the presence of experimental data for validation—namely, the tests of over-identification—cannot be guaranteed, a priori, to identify the correct model. The reason is that these procedures can only reject over-identifying restrictions; classes of models may be rejected by these tests even though just-identified versions of such estimators may be correct.[25] Data on controls from an experiment are needed to deal decisively with this latter case. Second, a closer examination of the results in Heckman's

23. Because only grouped SSA earnings data were available, Heckman and Hotz (1989) were limited to using nonexperimental estimators based on response models which were linear in Y and the regressor variables.

24. There was one minor exception to this, which, upon more careful examination, did not appear to be inconsistent with the general conclusion drawn here. See Heckman and Hotz (1989) for more on this point.

25. Robert Moffitt makes this point in his comment that is contained in Heckman and Hotz (1989).

and my paper reveals that for one of the target groups—high school dropouts—the point estimates derived from the experimental and non-rejected nonexperimental methods, respectively, are substantially different, even though they lead to the same statistical inference about the impact of the NSW program on post-training earnings. This similarity in inference is a result of the imprecision of the nonexperimental estimators, leading to an inability to reject the null hypothesis of no program impact. Further analysis is needed to determine the precision which can be achieved with nonexperimental methods relative to experimental methods. Third, given the skepticism about the use of nonexperimental methods for estimating the impacts of training, further replications of the informativeness of these tests will be needed to convince the evaluation community.

In conducting the assessment of procedures for choosing alternative nonexperimental estimators in the National JTPA Study, an important question concerns the type of data which will be used to form comparison groups. The original design of the Study called for a comparison group in 10 of the participating SDAs. Random samples were to be drawn of individuals who met the JTPA eligibility requirements but who, at the time of the baseline interview, had not participated in JTPA. This was called the ENP (Eligible Nonparticipant) Sample. A total of 7,500 observations were to be drawn from 10 SDAs. Comparable data were to be drawn on what was anticipated to be roughly the same number of controls in these 10 SDAs. (Originally, trainees were also to receive this extensive baseline interview, but the design team and DOL decided to concentrate resources on the controls in order to maximize the number of data points available for the proposed tests.) Unfortunately, these plans had to be scaled back. The costs of locating observations for the ENP sample proved extremely high. As a result, the ENP sampling and the detailed baseline interviewing of controls were conducted in only four SDAs (Fort Wayne, Providence/Cranston, Jersey City, and Corpus Christi/Nueces County). The resulting total samples will consist of approximately 3,400 controls and 3,400 members of the ENP sample.

Because gathering data within these sites on a comparison group turned out to be extremely expensive, the Department also requested that the analysis group assess the validity of using comparison groups drawn from existing national data sets. Thus, to answer Question N-3, the testing procedures described above will also be conducted using data from SIPP.

Conclusions: Designing Evaluations of Ongoing Programs

The National JTPA Study represents a new era in the conduct of evaluations of large-scale social programs. The Study seeks to conduct an experimental evaluation of a large, decentralized program; it also seeks to determine whether one can find reliable ways to cope with potential selection bias in such evaluations. Such goals were ambitious, probably overly so. It would be inappropriate to draw strong conclusions from this study about designing evaluations of all ongoing social programs. The National JTPA Study represents only one example of such an evaluation. Currently, experimental evaluations of ongoing programs, on a similar scale but under different circumstances, are being conducted[26] or are being planned.[27] Thus it is likely that in a few years a larger "sample" will be available from which to draw more reliable conclusions about the best way to conduct evaluations for such programs. Nonetheless, I shall offer some observations about what this one case study suggests about designing evaluations. I shall consider what I think is learned from this experience about designing both experimental evaluations and reliable nonexperimental evaluations for large, ongoing social programs.

Lessons for Experimental Evaluations

The experience of attempting to design and implement an experimental evaluation of the JTPA system is, I think, sobering. Clearly, despite significant efforts on the part of the designers of the Study, a design which guaranteed external validity was not achieved. Given the decentralized structure of the JTPA system, with a diverse set of programs and multiple decision-makers running the programs, it is not surprising that this failed. Will future evaluations of large-scale, ongoing programs be able to implement experimental designs which are nationally representative? I suspect so, if the conditions are right,[28] but the costs of

26. MDRC is conducting a major evaluation of the Greater Avenues to Independence (GAIN) training program within the California welfare system, and Abt Associates is conducting an evaluation of the Food Stamps Employment and Training Program (FSETP), both using experimental designs.

27. MDRC has recently been awarded a contract by HHS to evaluate the Job Opportunities and Basic Skills (JOBS) component of the Family Support Act of 1988.

28. Larry Orr of Abt Associates tells me that in implementing an evaluation of the Food Stamps Employment and Training Program, his firm was much more successful in

doing so are likely to be nontrivial. The JTPA experience suggests that seeking cooperation from agencies to implement random assignment and to deny benefits to eligible applicants is likely to be problematic politically. The recent experiences in the states of Texas and Florida, in which there was substantial negative local publicity about the use of (in Texas) and the planned use of (in Florida) random assignment to conduct studies of welfare initiatives, suggest that the potential for public relations problems is always present. This is likely to limit the willingness of programs administered at the local level to participate voluntarily in evaluations that deny benefits to individuals on a random basis. The National JTPA Study has not provided a counterexample to such concerns.

It is also unfortunate, but unavoidable, that the sample sizes within SDAs will not support site-by-site analysis. Because of the problems with generalizing the results of these experiments to the JTPA system as a whole, it would be beneficial if separate evaluations could be done at the disaggregate level. But, as noted earlier, this is simply not possible. The sizes of samples from individual SDAs are constrained by their capacity and by the extent of the demand for their services.

What about the internal validity of the experiments being conducted in the individual SDAs? Is not that at least being achieved? Clearly, the implementers have attempted to safeguard the integrity of random assignment within these local sites so that internal validity will be achieved. But I think the following analogy holds and provides further reasons for caution in interpreting the results from these experiments.

---

obtaining the participation of a representative sample of local program sites—only 20 percent of the randomly selected local programs refused to participate in the study—even though the evaluation used random assignment of participants to allocate the program's employment and training services. Although this experience provides a counterexample to that of the National JTPA Study, it is also important to note that FSETP differs in a number of ways from JTPA. The most important, I suspect, is that participation in employment and training services under the Food Stamps Program is *obligatory* for many food stamp recipients. Unless exempted, recipients are required to participate in such programs in order to maintain their eligibility for the food stamps. No such obligation exists in JTPA; individuals are not required to participate in its training programs in order to maintain their eligibility for any other types of subsidies. This difference in the structure may explain why site recruitment for evaluation purposes was so different across the two programs. In particular, it is quite likely that local FSETP administrators did not find the denial of these obligatory services to control group members to be ethically or politically undesirable; in fact, it is likely that they saw this as a wonderful opportunity to avoid having to adjudicate what some recipients surely find to be a punitive requirement.

It is always true that an estimator is unbiased for some population parameter; unfortunately, it is not always the one we want. So, too, the JTPA experiments will be internally valid, but perhaps not for the situation which policymakers want to know about.[29] As noted, one of the serious concerns in conducting evaluations of ongoing programs is how to keep the program "as is." Unfortunately, I think the JTPA experience suggests that this is not easy. In the face of performance standards, enrollment goals, and unanticipated improvements in local labor markets, the experiment had to assist local programs in increasing their recruitment to avoid shortfalls in program participation. Such efforts changed the pool of applicants in unknown ways. In addition, some adjustments had to be made in the ratio of controls to trainees in order to maintain the cooperation of local SDAs. This too changed the nature of the program in unknown ways. Thus, while individual SDA evaluations remain internally valid, they are estimates for programs that have been altered by the conduct of the experiment. One does not know if these changes *significantly* altered the existing programs, but the *ex ante* guarantee that random assignment is intended to obtain cannot be assured.

Despite this pessimistic assessment, I think that both policymakers and those interested in evaluation methodology will learn a great deal from the National JTPA Study. To understand my grounds for this conclusion, recall the reason these experiments were conducted: because we did not have an answer to the question of whether training programs for the economically disadvantaged actually improved the labor market experiences of the participants in these programs. The experiments, despite all of their problems with generalizability, will, I think, provide us with an answer to the feasibility question: "*Can* these programs improve the labor market prospects of the trained?" While this is not all that Congress would like to know, an answer to this narrower question will go a long way toward justifying the costs of implementing an experimental design in the National JTPA Study.

Lessons for Evaluating Nonexperimental Methods

What have we learned from the nonexperimental component of the JTPA Study? I do not think we have made much progress, at least not

29. See Chapter 5 in this volume for more on this issue and the limitations of conducting experimental evaluations of social programs.

yet. Restoring nonexperimental methods to a status of credibility (if they ever had such a status) will not be readily accomplished, given the intensity of the skepticism about their validity. The pilot study undertaken by Heckman and myself to assess procedures for choosing among alternative nonexperimental methods has met with some success. However, this success is inadequate to sway those who strongly favor experimental designs for social program evaluation. Yet I think the proposed strategy for selecting among alternative methods holds promise. More important, the National JTPA Study will provide another opportunity for narrowing our range of ignorance about the application of these methods. Properly executed, the experimental results will provide a benchmark against which to determine whether we can eliminate alternative nonexperimental methods based on systematic and empirically based criteria. This is an important and useful product from the National JTPA Study.

Finally, I recommend that future funders of evaluation research *require* nonexperimental investigations similar to that being undertaken in the National JTPA Study.[30] While experimental evaluations will get better in the future, the limitations and problems encountered in the JTPA Study suggest that nonexperimentally based evaluations have much to recommend them and are here to stay. Thus, it seems wise to try to make them better.

References

Ashenfelter, Orley, and David Card. 1985. "Using the Longitudinal Structure of Earnings to Estimate the Effect of Training Programs." *Review of Economics and Statistics*, 67: 648–660.

Barnow, Burt. 1987. "The Impact of CETA Programs on Earnings: A Review of the Literature." *Journal of Human Resources*, 22: 157–193.

Doolittle, Fred, and Linda Traeger. 1990. *Implementing the National JTPA Study*. New York: Manpower Demonstration Research Corporation.

Fraker, Thomas, and Rebecca Maynard. 1987. "The Adequacy of Comparison Group Designs for Evaluations of Employment-Related Programs." *Journal of Human Resources*, 22: 194–227.

---

30. According to Tom Cook of Northwestern University, such companion analysis is being undertaken in a study of the WIC program being conducted by Abt Associates.

Greenberg, David, and Philip Robins. 1985. "The Changing Role of Social
    Experiments in Policy Analysis." *Journal of Policy Analysis and Manage-
    ment,* 5 (no. 2, Summer): 340–362.

Hausman, Jerry, and David Wise, eds. 1985. *Social Experimentation.* Chicago:
    University of Chicago Press, for the National Bureau of Economic Re-
    search.

Heckman, James, and V. Joseph Hotz. 1989. "Choosing among Alternative
    Nonexperimental Methods for Estimating the Impact of Social Pro-
    grams: The Case of Manpower Training." *Journal of the American Statisti-
    cal Association,* 84 (no. 408): 862–874.

Job Training Longitudinal Survey Research Advisory Panel. 1985. *Recom-
    mendations of the Job Training Longitudinal Survey Research Advisory Panel.*
    Report prepared for the Office of Strategic Planning and Policy Devel-
    opment, Employment and Training Administration, U.S. Department
    of Labor. Washington, D.C.: U.S. Department of Labor.

LaLonde, Robert. 1986. "Evaluating the Econometric Evaluations of Train-
    ing Programs with Experimental Data." *American Economic Review,* 76:
    604–620.

LaLonde, Robert, and Rebecca Maynard. 1987. "How Precise Are Evalua-
    tions of Employment and Training Programs? Evidence from a Field
    Experiment." *Evaluation Review,* 11: 428–451.

Nathan, Richard. 1988. *Social Science in Government: Uses and Misuses.* New
    York: Basic Books.

Westat, Inc. 1982. "The Impact of CETA on 1978 Earnings: Participants in
    Selected Program Activities Who Entered CETA during FY 1976." In
    Continuous Longitudinal Manpower Survey, Net Impact Report, No. 1. Rock-
    ville, Md.: Westat, Inc.

3 The Role of Evaluation in State Welfare Reform Waiver Demonstrations

Michael E. Fishman and Daniel H. Weinberg

The Call for Welfare Reform

In his 1986 State of the Union Address, President Ronald Reagan drew attention to the problems of poverty and welfare in America:

> In the welfare culture, the breakdown of the family, the most basic support system, has reached crisis proportions—in female and child poverty, child abandonment, horrible crimes and deteriorating schools . . . I am charging the White House Domestic Council to present me by December 1, 1986, an evaluation of programs and a strategy for immediate action to meet the financial, educational, social, and safety concerns of poor families. I am talking about real and lasting emancipation, because the success of welfare should be judged by how many of its recipients become independent of welfare. (Office of the Press Secretary, The White House, 1986, pp. 4, 5)

The President's address reopened the welfare reform debate, which had been dormant since the late 1970s. Within the next year at least five major studies were issued; these included *Ladders Out of Poverty* (Meyer, 1986); "A New Social Contract—Rethinking the Nature and Purpose of Public Assistance" (New York State Task Force on Poverty and Welfare, 1986); "To Form a More Perfect Union" (Evans and Robb, 1985); "Investing in Poor Families and Their Children: A Matter of Commitment" (American Public Welfare Association and the National Council of State Human Service Administrators, 1986); and *The New Consensus on Family and Welfare* (Working Seminar on Family and American Welfare Policy, 1987). In direct response to the President's charge, the White House Domestic Policy Council charged a Low-Income Opportunity Working Group to conduct a study of welfare and poverty and prepare the requested report. The Working Group issued its initial report, entitled *Up from Dependency* (White House Domestic Policy Council, 1986).

Up from Dependency reviews the historic growth of federal public assistance programs and reviews the poverty trends over the past 25 years. It concludes that centralized welfare and lack of coordination contribute significantly to the persistence of poverty.

> With these failures in mind, the Working Group proposes a sharp change in direction in national welfare policy. For 50 years, welfare policy in this country has been inspired and implemented from the top down, from federal agencies and Congressional committees in Washington, D.C., to states, communities, and then to individuals. This strategy needs to be turned on its head. The Working Group is proposing that both policy ideas and implementation be allowed to percolate from the bottom up, *to the federal government from the individuals, communities, and states that have to live with these policies.* The federal government should first of all do nothing to add to the confusion of the current system by introducing more changes or "reforms" *until this country better knows what both relieves poverty and reduces dependency. Instead, the federal government should initiate a program of widespread, long-term experiments in welfare policy through state-sponsored and community-based demonstration projects.* (p. 3)

The call for a halt to national welfare "reform" efforts, to be replaced by state and community-based demonstrations, represented a marked departure from the approach taken by other welfare reform panels. With the exception of the Committee on Federalism report (Evans and Robb, 1985), the other welfare reform reports called for national reforms designed to improve the performance of the existing national welfare system. Examples of proposed reforms included strengthened Aid to Families with Dependent Children (AFDC) education, training, and work programs; mandatory AFDC-UP (Unemployed Parent) programs for two-parent families; national minimum AFDC benefit levels; increases in the Earned Income Tax Credit (EITC) in order to help the working poor; expanded health and day care services for poor families; and an increased minimum wage. Even the Committee on Federalism report called for an increased federal responsibility (for health and welfare programs), balanced by an increased state responsibility for education and social service programs.

It is against this backdrop that the Interagency Low-Income Opportunity Advisory Board was created by Executive Order on July 20, 1987.

The Interagency Low-Income Opportunity Advisory Board

Purpose and Membership

The purpose of the Board was to enhance coordination of federal public assistance programs and policies that cut across department lines and to create a focal point for intergovernmental coordination. During its first year in existence, the Board focused its efforts on encouraging the submission and review of state welfare reform demonstration proposals.

During 1987 and 1988, the Board was chaired by an Assistant to the President, Charles Hobbs, who worked in the White House Office of Policy Development (OPD). The Board included Assistant Secretary–level representatives of all the major federal domestic departments as well as the Office of Management and Budget (OMB).

Reflecting the programs covered by the proposed state welfare reform demonstrations, the key actors on the Board were the Chairman; three representatives from the Department of Health and Human Services (HHS)—the Assistant Secretary for Planning and Evaluation (ASPE), the Administrator of the Health Care Financing Administration (HCFA), and the Administrator of the Family Support Administration (FSA); the Assistant Secretary for Food and Consumer Services (head of Food and Nutrition Services, FNS) at the Department of Agriculture; and the Associate Director for Human Resources, Veterans, and Labor at OMB. While it was not unusual for other members to be present at meetings, they played a limited role in the Board's decision processes.

The Board was staffed by OPD personnel as well as by two detailees from HHS. The Secretary for the Board, who was on detail from FSA in HHS, coordinated the overall welfare reform demonstration review process. Specific OPD staff functioned as "state advocates" who encouraged states to submit demonstrations, followed their progress through the Board process, and lobbied departmental staff for favorable consideration. Staff from ASPE, FSA, HCFA, FNS, OMB, and OPD formed different federal working groups for each state demonstration proposal. (These, of course, tended to include many of the same people.)

Board Procedures

During the fall of 1987, the Board developed a set of formal review procedures to be followed in considering the political, legal, moral, and ethical aspects of the state proposals. The governors of the states could submit their requests for program waivers through the Board, or a federal agency could request that the Board coordinate waiver requests that had been submitted by states directly to the agency. A determination was made by the Chairman as to whether a particular demonstration and waiver request would be reviewed by the Board. Once the request was accepted for review, the state was offered the opportunity to make a presentation of how its proposed demonstration would meet needs and reduce dependency. The Board attempted to arrange a schedule that permitted agency consideration of waiver proposals to be completed within 90 days of the receipt of the state proposal. The Board then made recommendations to the Secretaries regarding waivers needed from programs under their jurisdiction (only they are empowered by law to grant the waivers).

The Board procedures outlined three criteria to be used in evaluating state welfare reform demonstration proposals.

1. Consistency with the policy goals contained in *Up from Dependency* adopted by the President.
2. Federal cost-neutrality:
   a. Where a potential for additional costs is identified, a method must be developed and agreed to by all parties for ensuring that the total federal costs of all affected programs each year under the demonstration will not be higher than they would have been in the absence of the demonstration.
   b. To determine what federal spending would have been in the absence of the demonstration, the preferred method is a simple random sample control group chosen from current cases and new applicants in the program populations affected by the demonstration.
   c. If for technical or other reasons this method cannot be used, alternative methods may be substituted. These alternative methods must provide a high degree of confidence that federal costs in each year of the demonstration will not exceed what they would have been in the absence of the demonstration.
3. There must be an evaluation designed to measure the net effects upon dependency and the cost effectiveness of the demonstration as a whole.
   a. For efficiency, randomly assigned control groups should be designed to serve the dual requirements of cost neutrality and evaluation.

b. If the use of this kind of experimental design is not feasible, other evaluation methods may be used. These alternative methods should be capable of isolating and measuring the net effects and costs of the demonstration.

Applications for waivers or demonstrations coordinated by the Board must in all cases meet the statutory and regulatory requirements of the respective agencies with authority to approve the requested waivers or demonstrations. The Chairman transmitted the Board's advice on a reviewed demonstration proposal and waiver requests to the departmental Secretaries who have authority to approve the requested waivers and demonstrations. The advice included the Board's view of whether the total program warranted demonstration as an attempt to improve the welfare system's performance. Where appropriate, the advice specified terms and conditions recommended by the Board. As its title indicates, the role of the Board was advisory, though in practice the formal Board recommendation was followed in all cases. This result was the outcome of extensive internal negotiations prior to the development of Board recommendations.

State Demonstration Proposals

From July 1987 through October 1988, 26 states submitted welfare reform demonstrations to the Board. Of these, 16 state demonstrations were approved and 10 were withdrawn or disapproved. While it is difficult to categorize the state demonstrations that were approved, they focused on the following areas:

- Cashing-out food stamps (4 states).
- New work programs for welfare recipients (6 states).
- Transition benefits for those leaving welfare with jobs (6 states).
- Learnfare approaches, that is, a requirement for school attendance (2 states).
- Entrepreneurship programs (2 states).
- Changes in the relationship between child support and AFDC (2 states).

The vast majority of the demonstration proposals were submitted by the summer of 1988. Only one of the proposals was officially received by the Board after the passage of the Family Support Act in September 1988. None has been received since the end of 1988 because states have been devoting their efforts to implementing the Act.[1]

Role of Evaluation

Alternative Roles

According to Rossi and Freeman (1982, p. 20), "Evaluation research is the systematic application of social research procedures in assessing the conceptualization and design, implementation, and utility of social intervention programs." In other words, evaluation should answer these questions: Did the waiver demonstrations have a measurable effect on the recipients, the community, or government budgets? Furthermore, if any effects are found, why did they occur?

Presumably, a state would not undertake a major effort to revise its welfare system without some expectation that the changes would (1) improve the well-being of recipients (such as increasing their disposable income or making them more self-sufficient), (2) provide some additional benefits to the community at large, while keeping costs under control (such as additional public services performed by recipients), or (3) reduce welfare costs. Of course, these benefits are not mutually exclusive. Indeed they may be in conflict, particularly in the short run.

---

1. The Family Support Act maintained the existing structure of Title IV of the Social Security Act, while providing for a number of significant reforms. The Act did the following: (1) Strengthened child support enforcement provisions related to paternity establishment, support guidelines, regular review of awards, and mandatory withholding. (2) Established the Job Opportunities and Basic Skills Training (JOBS) Program, which requires participation of able-bodied welfare recipients with children over age 3 (age 1 at state option) in education, training, or work activities while providing child care and support services necessary to their participation. JOBS also requires young mothers who are AFDC caseheads to stay in school or participate in some alternative educational activity. State costs are matched for both education/training and child care and support services. (3) Expanded Medicaid transition benefits to one year for AFDC recipients who left because of earnings and created a one-year child care transition benefit for these recipients. (4) Mandated that states provide at least six months of AFDC benefits each year to two-parent families which meet the provisions of the Unemployed Parent program. The Act did not include the broad waiver authority sought by the administration. However, it did include authority for numerous demonstration projects and studies which have been a major focus of federal effort since enactment.

For example, provision of additional job training may be intended to make a recipient more self-sufficient in the long run, but might entail additional short-run costs.

Finally, from the federal point of view, allowing state experimentation with multiple alternatives creates test laboratories for possible nation-wide changes at lower cost and lower risk. The potential adoption of localized changes nationwide increases the necessity for careful evalua-tion of the costs and outcomes of those changes.

Evaluation Methods

The four common methods used to evaluate social policy demonstra-tions are pre-post comparisons, structural modeling, quasi-experimental design, and social experimentation. Pre-post comparisons involve con-trasting the experiences of program participants with their pre-program circumstances. Structural modeling involves building an elaborate model of behavior, often predicated on economic decision-making, and predicting what would have happened in the absence of the demonstra-tion. This prediction is then compared to the actual outcomes for those experiencing the program changes, and an impact is inferred. Pre-post and structural modeling are attractive because neither is expensive to use, and already existing data collection systems can often be employed. However, both leave a high degree of uncertainty about measured out-comes, mainly because of the difficulties these methods have in account-ing for external factors.

In quasi-experimental design, a comparison group of individuals is identified, whether from a neighboring (similar) locality or from a na-tional data base, to serve as a "control" group to measure what would have happened in the absence of demonstration. Average outcomes (for example, change in earnings, employment rates, welfare benefits re-ceived) for the individuals in the treatment group (that is, those subject to the policy changes) are then compared directly to average outcomes for those in the comparison group. Structural modeling and quasi-experimental design often overlap in that these average outcomes are usually corrected econometrically through structural modeling for pre-existing differences in the two groups.

The reliability of quasi-experimental design can be improved substan-tially by randomly assigning locations to experimental or control status, with careful control for external factors that might affect outcomes through pre-selection matching. Unfortunately, there is a major problem with quasi-experimental evaluations.

> Those who enter employment and training programs may do so for a variety of economic reasons and non-economic reasons. However, the decision to enter a program is a result of systematic differences between those who enroll and those who do not, *even if* both groups have the same *observable* demographic characteristics and economic histories before enrollment . . . This problem has been called the problem of selection or selection bias. Econometricians have been working to solve the problem of selection mostly by trying to better understand the program enrollment decision, which in turn will help provide an understanding of how those legally-eligible persons who are and are not enrolled in the program differ from one another. (Stromsdorfer et al., 1985, p. 4)

The preferred alternative to quasi-experimental design is random assignment, that is, true experimental design:

> An alternative strategy for determining which individuals are sufficiently similar so that outcomes can be compared is to conduct an experiment in which program-eligible individuals are assigned randomly to the program. If this random assignment is not compromised by either the eligible individuals or the program managers, program participants will not differ statistically in any systematic or unmeasured way from those who do not enroll in the program. (More precisely, there will be differences, but the expected value of those statistical differences will be zero.) Such experiments require the withholding of services from some program-eligible individuals on a random basis. This is a difficult proposition to implement, but, if successful, this random assignment will yield valid direct estimates of net program impact. (pp. 3–4)

While random assignment is the most sensitive technique for detecting small impacts, it is important to note that even experimental evaluations suffer from problems. Although it is true that families or individuals randomly assigned to the experimental and control groups will not differ in terms of their observed characteristics, differences in their unobserved characteristics could lead to differential attrition from the experimental and control groups and consequently to invalid impact estimates. For this reason, such evaluations often model the attrition process in an attempt to correct for potential bias.[2] Indeed, the structural modeling that is used to correct for bias can often rival that used for quasi-experimental evaluation.

Use of a quasi-experimental design could be less expensive, and pre-post and structural models could be substantially less expensive (both economically and politically), than implementing a randomized social experiment. In addition, Heckman and Hotz (1989) have argued that nonexperimental methods can accurately estimate the effects of demonstrations, though others disagree (for example, Burtless and Orr, 1986; Fraker and Maynard, 1987). Finally, it may be true that the design of certain demonstrations precludes the use of an experimental design. This may be the result of statute, or it may occur if outreach efforts are an integral part of the demonstration and control group members cannot be excluded. There is, however, general agreement among evaluators that experimental designs provide the most reliable estimates of the net impact of social policy demonstrations, particularly those which include employment and training programs.

State and Federal Evaluation Preferences

The evaluation preferences of the states and the various federal agencies involved in the demonstrations varied greatly. The state evaluation preferences are best captured by looking at their initial evaluation proposals to the Board. The 26 states that submitted proposals had the following preferences:

- Experimental designs (6 states).
- Quasi-experimental designs with randomly matched offices (1 state).
- Non-equivalent comparison group designs (7 states).
- Pre-post designs (12 states).

2. See the papers in Hausman and Wise (1985) for further discussion. Also, neither experimental evaluations nor comparison group studies can correct for displacement effects (for example, jobs going to program participants instead of otherwise qualified nonparticipants) in determining the cost effectiveness of the interventions. In addition, use of income taxes to pay for transfer programs may have a marginal effect on reducing overall work incentives (through the return from a job) and thus total work hours in the economy.

Table 3.1 Evaluation transition matrix

| | FINAL OUTCOME | | | | | |
| | Demonstrations Approved | | | | | |
Proposed design[a]	Experimental	Random matched sites	Non-equivalent comparison group	Pre-post	Withdrew	TOTAL
Experimental	4				2	6
Random matched sites					1	1
Non-equivalent comparison groups		1	2	1	3	7
Pre-post (structural modeling)	4	3	1		4	12
TOTAL	8	4	3	1	10	26

Note: Matrix reflects the most rigorous design either approved or submitted when multiple designs were involved.
a. As of February 1990.

By comparison, the final evaluation designs of the 16 approved states were:

- Experimental designs (5 states).
- Quasi-experimental with randomly matched offices (4 states).
- Combination of experimental and quasi-experimental (3 states).
- Non-equivalent comparison group designs (3 states in which 2 demonstrations had extremely small sample sizes).
- Pre-post (1 state with an extremely small sample size).

The Evaluation Transition Matrix (Table 3.1) makes it clear that negotiations between the federal agencies and states resulted in substantial movement toward more rigorous evaluation designs. On its face, this may not seem to be a terribly remarkable finding. The Board's procedures called for a sound impact study and listed experimental design as the preferred evaluation methodology.

However, these waiver demonstration proposals were considered in a highly political context. The state proposals were often the governor's highly touted plans for reducing welfare rolls. In many cases they were partially implemented by the states before coming to the Board. In other cases the states insisted on statewide implementation, which made rigorous evaluation difficult, if not impossible. In two cases, the states had obtained federal statutory authority from Congress for operation of the demonstrations. In addition, the White House was actively encouraging governors to submit proposals in order to bolster its policy of promoting state experimentation and decentralization of the federal welfare system.

It is enlightening to examine the evaluation designs proposed by states that were not approved and the reasons why they withdrew. Their evaluation designs were as follows:

- Experimental designs (2 states; 1 state withdrew because of passage of the Family Support Act, and 1 because of demonstration design difficulties).
- Random matched offices design (1 state that withdrew for a combination of reasons, including evaluation costs).
- Non-equivalent comparison group or pre-post designs (7 states, 5 of which encountered difficulty with the Board's evaluation criteria and 2 which withdrew after passage of the Act).

Thus it is clear that despite strong state preferences for less rigorous designs and significant political pressure from both states and the White House, approval of a state's demonstration request was related to its willingness to adopt a fairly rigorous evaluation design. Where did the federal pressure for rigorous impact evaluation arise? What factors contributed to the strong role of evaluation design in the demonstration approval process?

The ground rules for state experimentation in *Up from Dependency* called for broad state flexibility in program design as long as impacts could be measured and federal cost neutrality assured. The proposals of the first two states considered by the Board (New Jersey and Wisconsin) were approved prior to the development of the Board procedures. As the New Jersey case study that follows makes clear, the early experience with state proposals created strong tensions among multiple federal objectives. The prime directive from the White House was state flexibility. However, state proposals often pushed hard against two other important federal objectives: containing federal costs and maintaining consistency with the welfare policy agenda of the Reagan administration. That agenda in its early years had succeeded in tightening program eligibility and reporting requirements and placing increasing emphasis on work obligations. These policy concerns were important to administration officials not only because they had fought hard battles with the Democratic Congress to enact these changes, but also because they were then at the core of the welfare reform debate in the 100th Congress.

Not surprisingly, all of the state welfare reform proposals had substantial potential to increase costs. Potential cost increases generally fell into two categories. First, there were proposals which asked for federal financial participation (FFP) for services which the federal government did not normally match. Examples of such services were one-year Medicaid and child care transition benefits for those leaving welfare, and education and training costs which went beyond existing work programs for welfare recipients. Second, and more difficult to specify, were program rule changes in AFDC or Food Stamps which had the potential to increase caseloads and benefits. Examples of these included proposals to liberalize AFDC benefit reduction rates, proposals to align AFDC and Food Stamp eligibility requirements by adopting the more liberal of the two, as well as proposals in the first category which had potential to draw recipients into programs, keep them there longer, or encourage them to return sooner. Many of these same proposals also involved rollbacks of earlier changes in program eligibility requirements.

The cost pressure created by the state proposals, particularly costs that were the result of AFDC, Food Stamp, and Medicaid caseload increases, drove OMB, HHS, and FNS in search of methods for protecting federal cost neutrality. States invariably presented cost projections which showed overall demonstration savings despite the costs of additional services and the probable impact of eligibility liberalizations. Rather than argue over whose cost projections were correct, the federal agencies agreed to require states to provide a reliable method for determining federal costs year-by-year in the absence of the demonstration. The method most preferred by staff of the federal agencies was the use of an experimental evaluation design. Such a randomly selected control group could provide a basis not only for measuring the impact of the demonstration on the treatment group, but also as a cost neutrality counterfactual.

Since the staff evaluation experts were knowledgeable about the evaluation literature, they were aware of the controversy between experimental and non-experimental techniques. Nevertheless, they placed great weight on two facts. First, the Department of Labor had appointed a blue-ribbon panel to recommend an evaluation strategy for the Job Training Partnership Act (JTPA) programs, and they had chosen random assignment (Stromsdorfer et al., 1985). Second, the Manpower Demonstration Research Corporation had recently completed a series of evaluations of AFDC work programs using random assignment as the main methodology, and the results were persuasive both technically and politically.

Rigorous impact design also made HHS more comfortable in granting waivers to states for policies that were not consistent with Administration AFDC or Medicaid policy. Sound impact designs would help ensure that claims of program effectiveness would be supported by reliable evaluation results. This was also a major concern for OMB. HHS officials were relatively comfortable in allowing states to test program changes that went counter to Administration policy. AFDC and Medicaid are state-federal partnerships in which funding is shared and states have flexibility in program design. Thus, it is plausible that an evaluation result which affirmed the effectiveness of a state policy which was inconsistent with Administration policy could be managed by making that policy a state option.

FNS found its position more difficult here. Food Stamps is a federally funded national program with uniform eligibility requirements and benefit levels. Any change that was permitted under waivers opened the possibility of changes in the entire program. Thus, FNS insisted on strong evaluation designs (all five of the approved demonstrations that included Food Stamp waivers had either experimental or randomly-matched-offices designs). Indeed, under some circumstances FNS refused to approve waiver requests despite sound evaluation designs.

It is clear that evaluation was a critical factor in the approval of state welfare reform waiver demonstrations. With few exceptions, agreement on evaluation design assured approval of the demonstration proposal. (In addition, states and the federal government retained the right to reopen negotiations, or to opt out of the demonstration, should economic or other conditions change significantly.) Rigorous evaluation designs provided a sound basis for assuring federal cost neutrality and for allaying federal agency policy concerns. The White House staff supported sound designs when they encouraged agency and OMB approval.

In many cases, however, states were either unwilling or unable to satisfy federal evaluation requirements specified by federal staff. This often led to high-level debate among senior officials in the White House, the Department of Agriculture, and HHS. It is not our purpose to report on those debates. However, it may encourage evaluators to know that consideration of these demonstrations provided numerous opportunities for the states and federal evaluation staff to discuss the strengths and weaknesses of various evaluation designs with high-level federal officials. The Evaluation Scorecard (Table 3.2) as well as the case studies that follow reflect the outcome of those discussions.

Case Studies

New Jersey

The first state to reach agreement with the Interagency Low-Income Opportunity Advisory Board was New Jersey. The New Jersey demonstration proposal, REACH (Realizing Economic ACHievement), requires all non-exempt adult recipients (that is, all adults with no child under 6) to participate in employment-related activities. Additional day care, extended transitional Medicaid benefits, and targeting of JTPA and child support enforcement resources as well as case management are included in the program. Implementation plans called for phasing counties into the program over a two-year period.

New Jersey proposed an evaluation strategy in August 1987 that consisted of (1) an impact evaluation, (2) a cost-effectiveness analysis, and (3) a process evaluation. The state explicitly excluded random assignment as an evaluation technique because (they argued) the mandatory nature of the program and considerations of equity prevented it. They proposed to identify program impacts by forecasting the expected size and characteristics of the dependent population in the absence of REACH based on historical, pre-REACH data and comparative data from New Jersey counties not yet implementing REACH.

The federal government was wary of accepting New Jersey's design because (1) caseload models are a notoriously inaccurate basis for assessing impact, (2) pre-REACH data cannot account for changes in economic and environmental conditions, and (3) phased non-random implementation of REACH could not ensure unbiased comparisons with other counties. Nevertheless, faced with a legal opinion that New Jersey law required that extended Medicaid transition benefits be offered to all program participants, the federal government proposed in September 1987 a quasi-experimental design in which data would be collected on cases in counties implementing the reforms (the treatment group) and in counties not implementing the reforms (the matched comparison group), where the selection of counties from matched pairs to be in each group was random. To supplement this "matched comparison sample," the federal officials also proposed collecting data on the prior experience in these counties.

The state rejected random selection of counties, wanting, for political reasons, to stick with the phased implementation originally proposed. After eleventh-hour negotiations, a four-part evaluation was agreed to: (1) an implementation and process analysis; (2) an impact analysis using non-random quasi-experimental design; (3) a cost-effectiveness analysis; and (4) an in-depth (ethnographic) analysis. The implementation and process analysis was designed to let evaluators know what went on in each county during the phased implementation, that is, to provide the context for the evaluation.

The impact analysis would consist of two complementary approaches: comparison of outcomes for those in the counties implementing REACH early with (1) a group in matched comparison counties and (2) a "prior experience" sample in the same counties sampled two years before implementation. Outcomes for early REACH participants would be compared to outcomes for non-participants in matched counties in the same time period. Estimates of the impact of REACH from that approach

Table 3.2 Evaluation scorecard

State[a]	Design proposal	Design accepted
New Jersey	Pre-post/Structural	Non-equivalent comparison group and structural
Wisconsin	Pre-post	Random assignment and structural
Washington	Non-equivalent comparison group	Random matched offices
New Hampshire	Pre-post	Withdrew
New York	Random assignment	Random assignment
Ohio	Pre-post	Random assignment and random matched counties
West Virginia	Non-equivalent comparison group	Pre-post
North Carolina	Pre-post/Interrupted time series	Random assignment
Georgia	Pre-post/Structural	Random matched counties
Alabama	Pre-post	Random matched counties
Arizona	Random assignment	Withdrew
Illinois	Pre-post	Random assignment and random matched counties
Colorado	Random assignment	Withdrew
South Carolina	Pre-post/Non-equivalent comparison group	Pending
California (San Diego)[b]	Survey of participant satisfaction	Random matched offices
New Mexico	Random matched counties	Withdrew
Iowa	Random assignment/ Structural/Pre-post	Random assignment
Kansas	Pre-post/Non-equivalent comparison group	Withdrew
Pennsylvania[c]	Non-equivalent comparison group	Non-equivalent comparison group
Wyoming[d]	Non-equivalent comparison group	Non-equivalent comparison group
Maryland	Random assignment	Random assignment

Table 3.2 (cont.)

State[a]	Design proposal	Design accepted
Maine	Pre-post	Withdrew
Utah	Non-equivalent compar-ison group	Withdrew
Tennessee	Pre-post	Withdrew
Nebraska	Structural/Pre-post	Withdrew
Texas	Random assignment	Random assignment

a. Demonstration sites listed in rough order of application to the Board.

b. California was approved by FNS outside of the Board because it did not meet the criterion of reducing welfare dependency.

c. Pennsylvania withdrew after final agreement on terms and conditions.

d. Wyoming was approved by FSA outside the Board because it was not possible for the demonstration to be cost-neutral.

would be supplemented by estimates of changes over time (two years) within the treatment counties compared to changes in the comparison counties. This dual approach was intended to capture (to the extent possible) both any special characteristics of the treatment counties that may affect outcomes and the effects of changes in economic conditions. Because of the non-random selection of counties, there may be a bias implicit in these comparisons.

The cost-effectiveness analysis was designed to compare the costs and benefits of REACH from the perspective of the participants and the government (at the federal, state, and local levels). The in-depth study would collect qualitative information through the use of focus group discussions on the impact of the program on the attitudes and behaviors of program participants.

The evaluation design for New Jersey did not provide a control group to be used for cost control, so an alternative had to be developed. New Jersey wanted to be able to use savings generated by REACH to finance the increased Medicaid coverage (and any other costs), while the federal government wanted to ensure that it did not incur any additional costs as a result of the demonstration. It was agreed that an AFDC caseload model based on a regression model would be developed to estimate what the AFDC, Food Stamp, and Medicaid costs of the AFDC caseload would have been in the absence of REACH. Separate econometric time-series models of the determinants of the AFDC-Basic and AFDC-UP caseloads were developed, based on statewide demographic, economic, and program-related data through the third quarter of 1987 (Barnow, 1988). As each quarter passes thereafter (and data become available), an estimate of the counterfactual caseload can be computed and savings can be credited to New Jersey on the basis of the actual caseload that quarter. Provision was made to trigger either credit for the savings or federal reimbursement for extra costs based on caseload fluctuations larger than one standard error of estimate, sustained over several quarters. Clearly, the models' errors of estimate may cumulate over time and allow the counterfactual estimate of the AFDC caseload to deteriorate in quality, so provision was made for ad hoc model adjustment should obvious deficiencies surface. Such ad hoc adjustment would indeed become necessary after implementation of the Family Support Act of 1988. (Additional savings are also credited for additional child support collections made on behalf of those remaining on the rolls.)

The outcome in New Jersey was dictated by both political and time pressures, exacerbated by the inexperience of both Board and agency personnel, since New Jersey was the first waiver demonstration considered. Because the final evaluation and cost control designs were less than satisfactory, the Board agreed that, subject to adequate sample sizes, states in the future would need to estimate costs in the absence of the demonstration on the basis of either a random assignment control group or some type of randomly matched comparison group.

New York

New York proposed implementing the Child Assistance Program (CAP), a program designed to reinforce the idea that both custodial and noncustodial parents are responsible for the support of their children. CAP is very similar to the Child Support Assurance System proposed for Wisconsin (see Nichols-Casebolt, Garfinkel, and Wong, 1985) and authorized in the federal Child Support Amendments of 1984. The New York State Legislature authorized a test, and the state applied for a waiver to operate and evaluate its program. Statutory authority for the federal government to waive any requirement in Title IV of the Social Security Act in order for New York to implement CAP was provided in the Omnibus Budget Reconciliation Act of 1987. The key goals of CAP are to (1) encourage participants to obtain court orders for child support; (2) provide greater incentives for participants to increase work effort; and (3) supplement income when child support payments received combined with earnings leave household income below a minimum standard.

To be eligible to participate in CAP, a custodial parent must be a current AFDC recipient, possess a support order, and voluntarily request a transfer to CAP. The incentives to transfer to CAP are several: less stringent reporting requirements, no assets test, increased retention of earnings (90 percent up to the poverty level and 33 percent above), Food Stamp benefits paid as cash, financial assistance for child care, Medicaid including a four-month transition benefit, and job-related assistance (available to both AFDC and CAP recipients).

The state was quite interested in determining the impact of this program on the beneficiaries and on state costs. They proposed a two-part design. In four social-services districts in the state, the program would be made available to all AFDC recipients, and program operators would be allowed to implement the program as they saw fit. In three or four other districts, the program would be operated on an experimental, random assignment basis. In Part I (the "saturation" districts), the natural experiment would give the state information mainly about participation rates and marketing strategies. The experimental group of districts would permit an examination of the program's impact on subgroups—for example, those with support orders and a job, those with a job but no support order, those with a support order but no job, and those with neither a job nor a support order—and provide a rigorous estimate of program costs and savings.

Since the state's proposed research design met the federal government's requirements for an adequate evaluation, negotiations focused on developing a cost-control methodology for the saturation districts and on identifying appropriate outcome measures and independent variables. The state and the federal government were able to agree on an evaluation consisting of an implementation and participation study (to be conducted primarily in the saturation districts) and an impact study (to be conducted in the experimental districts). Also included in the evaluation in the experimental districts is an evaluation of the effect of the Food Stamp cash-out.

The fact that the state was proposing a demonstration substantially similar to a previously proposed program that had been the subject of much prior debate and the fact that the state proposed a true experimental design to examine impact made negotiations relatively easy and straightforward. Indeed, evaluation of program participation, impossible with a random assignment design, was made possible by the addition of saturation counties. In effect, because the initial proposal met the federal government's requirement for adequate evaluation and cost control, concerns were limited to the saturation counties, and the final outcome was quite satisfactory to both sides.

Ohio

Ohio proposed a three-part Transitions to Independence Program for AFDC recipients:

- An extension of the mandatory work and training programs (Ohio's Fair Work program) from the then-current 29 counties to all 88 counties in Ohio.
- Incentives (increased earnings disregarded in calculating AFDC benefits plus one year transitional Medicaid and child care) and support services (counseling and job assessment) to increase the voluntary participation of mothers with young children (under 6) in work and training programs.
- A requirement that teenage parents who have not graduated from high school participate in an educational program (those attending would get an incentive payment of $62 per month, those who did not would suffer a like reduction in benefits).

All programs also involved additional child care for the children of participants. Ohio officials predicted that these programs, phased in over three years, would result in a 10 percent reduction in the AFDC caseload.

Ohio proposed a "cross-sectional time series research design" to examine the impacts of both the mandatory and voluntary work programs. This design involved data collected both before and after program implementation. The educational component for teenage parents, Project Learn, would be evaluated by a pretest-posttest design. In its waiver proposal, the state did express a willingness to work with federal officials in investigating the feasibility of using random assignment, though it expressed reservations because of equity problems, potential contamination effects, and administrative difficulties.

The federal government was interested in pursuing a true experimental design strategy for both cost-control and evaluation purposes wherever possible and proposed this to the state. In the 59 counties that had not already implemented the mandatory work program, the state agreed to an experimental design. However, they initially opposed an experimental design for the voluntary program and Project Learn. With respect to the voluntary program, they were concerned with issues of administrative complexity, discrimination in the provision of day care services (they were worried about caseworkers being unwilling to withhold child care services from the control group), and confusion among recipients because of the voluntary nature of the program (since incentives need to be advertised to make people volunteer, they felt confusion would arise because not all volunteers would be eligible). Their main objection to an experimental design in Project Learn was that it would be viewed as inequitable that some teenage mothers would be "punished" (have their grant reduced) for not attending school while others would not be. They were also worried about educators "covering up" for those in the control group to avoid the loss of welfare benefits.

Further negotiations ensued. The state agreed to carry out a process and implementation study, an impact study, and a benefit-cost study, mostly along the lines suggested by federal officials. The evaluation of the effects of the mandatory work program would be based on random assignment, with 10 percent of the mandatory caseload assigned to a control group. The state also agreed to a random assignment design for evaluating Project Learn, with 5 percent of the caseload assigned to a control group. (Later negotiations restricted the evaluation to 12 counties, with 20 percent of the sample assigned to the control group in four of the counties.)

The design for the voluntary program was different. Ohio agreed to a random selection of counties by matched pairs, after clustering into affinity groups on the basis of observable characteristics. Five pairs of counties were selected to serve as the basis for the evaluation; half were randomly chosen to implement the program (the treatment group) and half to maintain the current AFDC program services (the control group). Montgomery (Dayton) and Cuyahoga (Cleveland) counties were excluded from this process, the former because it definitely wanted to implement the program, the latter because the state saw no way to ensure implementation in the near future. To demonstrate their commitment to the voluntary program, Montgomery County officials agreed to a random assignment design for the program in their county, with 50 percent of the caseload in the control group.

The negotiations between Ohio and the federal government have to be considered a success. The key fact leading to this success was the state's early and strong commitment to sound research design in order to determine definitively the impacts of the demonstrations. The state showed flexibility in accepting true experimental design for cost control and evaluation for part of its proposed program, and the federal government showed flexibility in accepting a randomized quasi-experimental design based on randomly matched sites for the rest of its program. By realizing each other's constraints—that AFDC is a county-administered program in Ohio and that strict cost control and sound evaluation were necessary from the federal perspective—the negotiations were carried out cooperatively rather than adversarially.

North Carolina

North Carolina proposed to experiment with the provision of child care in one county, Mecklenburg, containing the city of Charlotte. By providing employment-contingent assured child care services for preschool-age children in families receiving AFDC, the state hoped to assess the role of child care in leading to increased parental employment and consequent reduction of welfare costs. One key feature of the five-year demonstration would be recycling—as welfare costs are reduced, the savings would be allocated to providing more child care services.

The proposed evaluation design involved an "Equivalent Time-Samples Design"—an artificial reduction in available slots midway through the demonstration—coupled with a "Nonequivalent Control Group Design"—a comparison to three other counties. In Phase I, 500 additional day care slots would be made available to eligible AFDC recipients, phased in during months 7–9. These slots would be phased out in months 19–21. Phase II, beginning nine months later, would see the reintroduction of the 500 day care slots.

Federal officials felt that the proposed research design was unnecessarily complex, especially because it provided no reliable method for determining what would have happened in the absence of the demonstration—some AFDC families leave the program with earnings even in the absence of a child care guarantee. The federal government argued that because the link between day care availability and increased employment had not been established by existing research, a rigorous design to test this important and policy-relevant linkage was vital. Particular concerns involved substitution between types of care, the effects of an artificial expansion and contraction on the supply side of the child care market, and the relevance of the cross-county comparison given the lack of control over their day care services. The main suggestions made were to focus on a smaller target group and use random assignment.

After considering these points, North Carolina proposed to scale back their demonstration to one year and use a classical experimental design to test the program. The evaluation design included random assignment of a minimum of 260 AFDC applicants and recipients each to control and experimental groups. The treatment is a guarantee of a child care slot for children between 1 and 5 years of age when recipients secure full-time employment. (The control group can apply for child care slots using normal procedures.) In addition, the analysis would include an investigation of the employment experience of AFDC recipients using time-series analysis, an interview with a random sample of participants, focus group interviews, and a benefit-cost analysis.

The refusal of the federal government to pay for demonstration costs prospectively or to credit as savings 100 percent of all reductions in welfare benefits for recipients leaving welfare with a full-time job forced the state to address the inadequacy of its initial methodology to determine the amount of those savings. The state opted for a smaller demonstration, funded entirely under existing program authorities. In order to get the federal government to pay 50 percent of the cost of the demonstration evaluation, the state accepted random assignment as the evaluation methodology. In this state, it is clear that cost issues motivated the adoption of this methodology.

Kansas

The Kansas demonstration (Kanwork) proposed requiring participation of mothers with children aged 3 and older in a job preparation, training, and education program. In addition, the child care disregard would be increased from $160 to $200 per month per child, and six months of transitional child care and one year of transitional medical services would be provided to participants who lost cash assistance because of earned income. To preserve the family unit, two-parent General Assistance families not qualified for UP would also be eligible for these transitional services.

The state proposed to operate and had begun implementing the program in four preselected counties. To evaluate its employment and training and its transitional child care and Medicaid programs, the state proposed comparing outcomes to expected caseloads projected through a statistical model. In addition, the state planned to compare outcomes in the four preselected demonstration counties to four matched comparison counties and to the remaining non-demonstration counties in the state. Although the state had not implemented the program statewide and was willing to use matched counties for evaluation and cost control, the preselection of counties for implementation of the demonstration introduced significant bias into the evaluation design.

The federal agencies offered the state the option of employing either an experimental design with random selection of treatment and control group participants or a randomly matched county design. Kansas found neither alternative acceptable and withdrew, citing the inability to reach agreement with the federal agencies as the reason for withdrawing their proposal.

Conclusions

We feel that the Interagency Low-Income Opportunity Advisory Board's focus on evaluation was one key to a successful waiver demonstration program. The marriage of evaluation and cost control greatly strengthened the role of evaluation in the demonstration approval process. By demonstrating that a good evaluation methodology could serve as the mechanism for cost control, federal staff were able to ensure that (in most cases) program analysts and policymakers learned the impacts of these demonstrations. One should not be overly optimistic about this result; federal evaluation preferences of staff were often overridden by political realities (for example, in New Jersey). Nevertheless, a number of states (New York and Ohio are good examples) were pleased that good evaluation design was part of the approval process.

In our opinion, the net effect of the federal focus on evaluation was positive. Excluding states whose demonstrations were small, of the remaining 12 waiver demonstrations approved, 11 had a solid impact design for at least a major demonstration component. A secondary but also important impact was the fostering of high-level debates in the federal government as a whole and within individual executive departments on the role and value of evaluation. Unfortunately, most of the political appointees who benefited from these debates have moved on, but the legacy of this innovative approach for welfare program demonstrations continues.

For example, the Family Support Act of 1988 included explicit recognition of the desirability of evaluating the new JOBS program with an experimental design. To be sure, much of the impetus for the inclusion of legislative language must be credited to the recent series of experimental evaluations carried out by the Manpower Demonstration Research Corporation. While the process used for waiver demonstration approval is unlikely to be used for JOBS, we feel that acceptance of both the necessity for evaluation and the desirability of an experimental design by the states and by federal actors was facilitated by the recent debates.

Evaluation played different roles and had different priorities in different federal departments. The evaluation was of differing importance to the three major agency players in the process—OMB, HHS, and FNS. In the mid-1980s, control of federal costs was critical to OMB, which viewed evaluation as the mechanism for enforcing fiscal restraint. In fairness, OMB staff were also concerned about policy development and supported strong evaluation as a means of discerning valid and invalid claims of program impacts. In contrast, both at the staff and the political levels, FNS was much more persistent in advocating the most rigorous evaluation possible in order to identify program effects accurately. Since Food Stamps is a national program, program officials were reluctant to examine policies counter to Administration policy. Further, strong congressional oversight has made Agriculture officials reluctant to approve demonstrations without credible evaluations. Thus, all states which received Food Stamp waivers adopted rigorous evaluation designs.

HHS was less strongly committed to good evaluation than FNS, reflecting the separate interests of the several divisions involved—FSA, HCFA, and ASPE. In contrast to Food Stamps, AFDC and Medicaid are programs which provide for significant diversity among the states. FSA has a long history of granting waivers to test state innovation, and often these waivers have not been accompanied by rigorous evaluation requirements. HCFA's interest in the welfare reform demonstrations was limited, despite the fact that Medicaid is now the largest federal means-tested transfer program (funded at $40 billion in FY 1990). HCFA has focused more of its recent attentions on the Medicare program (funded at $105 billion in FY 1990).

ASPE was committed to good evaluation at both the staff and political level. Nevertheless, as a staff division rather than a division with program responsibilities, ASPE could only try to influence the process. If it was successful in moving the process within HHS toward better evaluation, that success was a function of both its institutional history of sponsoring good evaluations (for example, the Seattle-Denver Income Maintenance Experiment) and its good working relationship with FSA staff. By working cooperatively with the agency responsible for the program at the center of most state proposals (AFDC) and by providing substantial evaluation expertise, ASPE was able to exert significant influence on the entire Board approval process.

The White House OPD staff, in general, were concerned about evaluation only insofar as it facilitated approval of state demonstration proposals. The Board Chairman was concerned primarily with promoting state flexibility and often acted as an advocate on the states' behalf when evaluation became a barrier to demonstration approval.

What general conclusion do we draw from this activity? In summary:

- States will sometimes accept rigorous evaluation design, but this usually requires strong federal direction.
- Evaluation matters, but not as much as cost control (unless it is in the legislation).
- Staff preferences matter, but not as much as politics (or political appointees).
- State preferences tend to dominate in the political arena when state programs are involved (AFDC and Medicaid), but federal preferences dominate in the political arena when federal programs are involved (Food Stamps).

We should note that state preferences for knowledge (good evaluation) can in cases dominate state preferences for political gain through program implementation (as was demonstrated in New York and Ohio).

Evaluation played multiple roles in the waiver demonstration process—knowledge building, policy development, cost neutrality—and was used both to facilitate and to block demonstration approval within the context of other forces. Of course, there's many a slip between design and implementation, but the evident good faith that was established between the states and the federal government as a result of this process can go a long way toward resolving future conflicts cooperatively. We have every reason to believe that evaluation will continue to play an important and valuable role in welfare reform in the 1990s.

References

American Public Welfare Association and the National Council of State Human Service Administrators. 1986. "Investing in Poor Families and Their Children: A Matter of Commitment." Issued by APWA, Washington, D.C.

Barnow, Burt S. 1988. "Estimating the New Jersey AFDC Caseload." Final report submitted to the Office of the Assistant Secretary for Planning and Evaluation, U.S. Department of Health and Human Services, by ICF Incorporated, Fairfax, Va., February.

Burtless, Gary, and Larry Orr. 1986. "Are Classical Experiments Needed for Manpower Policy?" *Journal of Human Resources,* 21 (no. 4, Fall): 606–639.

Evans, Daniel J., and Charles S. Robb. 1985. "To Form a More Perfect Union: The Report of the Committee on Federalism and National Purpose." Issued by the committee, Washington, D.C.

Fraker, Thomas, and Rebecca Maynard. 1987. "The Adequacy of Comparison Group Designs for Evaluations of Employment-Related Programs." *Journal of Human Resources,* 22 (no. 2, Spring): 194–227.

Hausman, Jerry A., and David A. Wise, eds. 1985. *Social Experimentation.* Chicago: University of Chicago Press, for the National Bureau of Economic Research.

Heckman, James J., and V. Joseph Hotz. 1989. "Choosing among Alternative Nonexperimental Methods for Estimating the Impact of Social Programs: The Case of Manpower Training." *Journal of the American Statistical Association,* 84 (no. 408, December): 862–874.

Meyer, Jack A., ed. 1986. *Ladders out of Poverty: A Report of the Project on the Welfare of Families.* Washington, D.C.: American Horizons Foundation.

New York State Task Force on Poverty and Welfare. 1986. "A New Social Contract—Rethinking the Nature and Purpose of Public Assistance." Albany, N.Y., December.

Nichols-Casebolt, Anne, Irwin Garfinkel, and Patrick Wong. 1985. "Reforming Wisconsin's Child Support System." Discussion Paper No.

793-85, Institute for Research on Poverty, University of Wisconsin-Madison.

Office of the Press Secretary, the White House. 1986. "Address by the President on the State of the Union." Washington, D.C., mimeo., February 4.

Rossi, Peter H., and Howard E. Freeman. 1982. *Evaluation: A Systematic Approach.* 2d ed. Beverly Hills, Calif.: Sage Publications.

Stromsdorfer, Ernst, Robert Boruch, Howard Bloom, Judith Gueron, and Frank Stafford. 1985. "Recommendations of the Job Training Longitudinal Survey Research Advisory Panel." Report to the Employment and Training Administration, U.S. Department of Labor, Washington, D.C.

White House Domestic Policy Council, Low Income Opportunity Working Group. 1986. *Up from Dependency: A New National Public Assistance Strategy.* Washington, D.C.: Executive Office of the President.

Working Seminar on Family and American Welfare Policy. 1987. *The New Consensus on Family and Welfare.* Washington, D.C.: American Enterprise Institute.

4 Are High-Cost Services More Effective than Low-Cost Services?

Daniel Friedlander and Judith M. Gueron

Part I: Overview

The Family Support Act of 1988 (FSA) expresses a vision of the responsibilities of parents and government for the well-being of recipients of Aid to Families with Dependent Children (AFDC). The message is straightforward: Parents—both fathers and mothers—should be the primary supporters of their children, and public assistance should be coupled with encouragement, assistance, and requirements aimed at moving families from welfare to self-support. FSA, through its centerpiece, the Job Opportunities and Basic Skills Training (JOBS) Program, calls on welfare recipients to take jobs or participate in employment-directed services; it calls on government to provide services and incentives to assist them in finding employment.

JOBS allows states substantial flexibility in designing welfare-to-work programs. The legislation does not establish a uniform federal "program," but rather sets up a structure for funding individual state initiatives. Using enhanced federal matching rates, this structure creates incentives intended to reorient programs toward (1) reaching women with younger children, (2) targeting more difficult-to-serve people, (3) involving a greater share of the AFDC caseload, and (4) providing basic education and other intensive activities in addition to services that emphasize immediate job entry and are usually lower-cost.

Although JOBS offers some new funding, the experience of the 1980s suggests that in no state will the resources be sufficient to provide education or training to everyone in the greatly expanded mandatory caseload.[1] State JOBS administrators, operating within fixed budgets, face a

---

1. Under the Work Incentive (WIN) Program, JOBS' predecessor, AFDC women with

difficult choice among the following: (1) operating a low-cost program for a large proportion of the expanded caseload; (2) targeting more intensive, higher-cost services on a smaller, more narrowly defined group and leaving the rest unserved; or (3) operating low-cost components for certain large groups and higher-cost components for other, much smaller groups. Choosing to expand participation in higher-cost services will clearly require trade-offs. In assessing these trade-offs, states would benefit from information on the relative effectiveness of low-cost versus higher-cost services.

"Effectiveness" means different things to different people. Choices between providing intensive services and achieving high rates of program participation or coverage are often conditioned by different views of a program's objectives. Some advocates of reform, focusing on the goal of reducing poverty, have argued that education and training are necessary to provide people on welfare with the skills they need to raise their earnings enough to make significant improvements in their and their family's standard of living. Others, emphasizing the importance of reducing welfare receipt, have advocated programs that require participation for as many people as possible and provide lower-cost services emphasizing job entry, rather than more expensive and longer-term education or training.

Researchers have tended to focus on dollars rather than general quality of life or participant attitudes and have defined effectiveness as the ability of a program to increase unsubsidized employment and earnings and decrease welfare receipt and welfare expenditures. Grossman, Maynard, and Roberts (1985), in a comparative analysis of several programs, found higher-cost services much more effective in raising earnings, with effects on welfare receipt less clear.[2] In a comprehensive review of ex-

---

no children under age 6 were required to participate. Under JOBS, the age cutoff is lowered to 3 years, and to age 1 at state option.

2. Grossman, Maynard, and Roberts found that "job-search assistance programs, which tend to be short-term and low cost, can be expected to have small and persistent impacts on employment and earnings, but lead to only very small and relatively short-lived reductions in welfare receipt. In contrast, the longer and more costly employment and training services seem to have sizeable, lasting impacts on earnings ($600 to $1,000 per year), while the estimated impacts on welfare dependence are more ambiguous, ranging from sizeable reductions for two of the three programs to no long-term effects for the third" (p. 12). For a similar assessment, see also the earlier study of Grossman and Mirsky (1985), especially pp. 20, 25–26. Moffitt (1987) cautiously reaches a similar conclusion: "Taken together, these evaluations show that positive earnings gains are possible from training and workfare programs. There are suggestions that earnings gains are positively related to the strength of the training elements" (p. 58).

perimental and nonexperimental studies, Burtless (1989) pointed to the many uncertainties embedded in comparisons of programs, but noted that "the largest gains in participant earnings were typically observed in the most expensive programs" (p. 128). At the same time, he concluded, the costs of achieving these large gains may be prohibitive.[3]

Until recently, most of the empirical evidence on program effectiveness has come from nonexperimental studies of the Work Incentive (WIN) Program, Comprehensive Employment and Training Act (CETA) programs, and a small number of demonstration projects. But selection bias, which undermines the creation of an appropriate comparison group, has made reliable estimates of overall impacts from these data elusive, and comparisons of components within programs have likewise been suspect.[4]

Social experiments based on randomly assigning eligible people to treatment and control status can avoid selection biases affecting internal validity. Recently, a number of rigorous experimental studies of welfare-to-work programs have been completed. The programs used different approaches to increase the employment of single parents on AFDC (mostly women). All of these experiments were originally designed only to determine whether particular kinds of intervention would be feasible and effective, and they have provided clear answers to this first-order question. But the availability of the series of studies has invited cross-program comparisons aimed at determining the relative effectiveness of alternative approaches.

Our goal in this chapter is to examine what those experiments reveal about the relative effectiveness of low-cost and higher-cost services and combinations of services in the context of JOBS. In our view, this question cannot be answered definitively at this time. While the completed studies included almost 68,000 people, for the purpose of this chapter

3. Burtless concluded: "Nearly all of the most successful programs have been quite expensive, costing about $10,000 per participant. While it is possible to conceive of a reform that might cost this much, it is hard to believe that this level of resources would be invested in very many welfare mothers" (p. 138).

4. For analyses questioning the reliability of nonexperimental methods, see LaLonde (1986); Dickinson, Johnson, and West (1987); Fraker and Maynard (1987); and LaLonde and Maynard (1987). Nonexperimental methods have also been called into question by a panel convened by the National Academy of Sciences (Betsey, Hollister, and Papageorgiou, 1985) and an advisory panel to the U.S. Department of Labor (Job Training Longitudinal Survey Research Advisory Panel, 1985). Heckman, Hotz, and Dabos (1987) and Heckman and Hotz (1989), however, argue that applying proper specification tests can lead to adequate nonexperimental estimates.

they represent 13 observations of programs that differ in many interrelated dimensions in addition to cost. There are also limits to their relevance for JOBS administrators: They were conducted in a pre-FSA environment, when work incentives and supports were more limited, and did not assess some of the main innovations in services and targeting included in the legislation. As a result, although we analyze the available evidence, the goal is not to recommend particular JOBS strategies but to clarify the open questions for research. Our general message is one of caution. JOBS administrators will be making program design decisions in an environment of substantial uncertainty about the effects of different approaches. At the end of this analysis, we discuss the types of future experiments that, when combined with studies now in progress, should provide more conclusive answers.

We begin in Part II by discussing the uncontrolled variables that make cross-study comparisons difficult and may obscure the true relationship between cost and impact. The most critical source of noncomparability is that some studies evaluate welfare-to-work delivery *systems* (which we call "broad-coverage" programs), while others assess individual *components* within these systems (which we call "selective-voluntary" demonstrations or programs). Associated with this distinction are differences in targeting, screening, and selection; participation rates; and scale. In addition, even within these two categories, there is substantial variation in the programs and local conditions.

In examining these issues, it is important to keep in mind that the JOBS legislation places new emphasis on a particular type of potentially high-intensity service: basic skills education. The higher-cost programs evaluated to date have provided primarily subsidized employment and on-the-job training. While some studies are under way, there are no comparable completed evaluations of basic skills education, and specifically not of education offered in the context of a mandatory welfare-to-work program. Nor is it clear how frequently education, as implemented under JOBS, will be a relatively high-intensity or low-intensity activity.

Beyond this, to some extent the discussion simplifies the analysis of program costs. First, while the chapter focuses on employment-directed services (job search, work experience, education, and training), Part II notes that other factors (for example, the extent of case management, assessment, monitoring, and support services) will also have an influence on average cost. Second, these different cost factors do not always compete for the same budget dollars. Although all states will face a JOBS budget constraint, some services must be paid for directly with JOBS funds while others may be accessed through other delivery systems. The legislation's emphasis on coordination across the welfare, training, and education systems means that, within bounds, the budget constraint is not independent of the service strategy.

In Part III we examine the results of the completed experiments, keeping in mind the issues raised in Part II. As a framework for our analysis, we compare services along four dimensions of effectiveness: average impact per sample member, aggregate impact (the total sum of earnings impacts or welfare savings for all individuals exposed to a program), savings for government budgets net of program cost, and effect on income and poverty. When we look at average impact per experimental sample member, we find some evidence that increasing the cost and intensity of services increases the effects on earnings; the results for AFDC payments are less clear. When we account for costs, the picture changes: Within a fixed budget, providing higher-cost services for some enrollees implies denying lower-cost services to many, which our analysis suggests may decrease aggregate program impact. Further, from the government budget perspective, lower-cost services usually pay for themselves; higher-cost services, even when they have larger average impacts, have not always paid for themselves, and, when they do, require more years to break even.

The results for the average, aggregate, and budgetary impacts may leave people unsatisfied. First, these ways of viewing program effects all deal in estimates that pertain to the entire group of program enrollees, but policymakers and administrators may be interested in what lies behind the average numbers. In particular, JOBS points specifically to long-term and potential long-term AFDC recipients as key target groups, and we therefore look separately at the effects of low-cost and higher-cost services on the most disadvantaged program enrollees. Also, the findings suggest that the measured average impacts are really driven by much larger changes for a relatively small number of people, suggesting the importance of looking beyond averages to the distribution of earnings gains. Second, the fact that these studies follow people for at most three years is a critical limitation: Higher-cost programs are designed to invest more in the short run in anticipation of greater future results, and the JOBS legislation specifically seeks to reduce long-term dependency. Moreover, the impacts of lower-cost services, although tending to persist through the available follow-up period, may begin to fade eventually.

We discuss evidence about impacts on household income and poverty in the last section of Part III and find it to be the least complete. The existing experimental research indicates that both the lowest-cost and the highest-cost programs can have lasting effects. However, the low-cost programs often lead to low-paying jobs. Higher-cost services have been shown to increase wage rates or weekly hours of work, but effects on these aspects of "job quality" have not been explored thoroughly.

Overall, while the existing experimental studies leave administrators with some uncertainty in making JOBS design choices, this research suggests that they may have to balance competing objectives in choosing among the three strategies outlined at the beginning of this chapter. The evidence suggests that a program that provides primarily low-cost services (as long as they are above a certain threshold level of intensity) to as many people as possible may have the greatest *aggregate* impact on earnings or welfare payments within a given budget. Using the same resources to serve fewer people with higher-cost components may produce lower aggregate effects but may help those served achieve earnings above a certain level. While some administrators may opt for the low-cost services strategy, others may prefer targeting fewer people, especially if it can be shown that this approach would result in a long-term, marked improvement in the lives of people likely to be long-term welfare recipients. Pressure to meet both objectives—cost effectiveness and target group effectiveness—suggests the value of the third choice: a combination of low-cost and higher-cost services in a system designed for both broad coverage and careful targeting.

While this analysis reflects our conclusions from the available studies, because of the issues raised in Part II they remain more hypotheses than firm lessons. As should by now be clear, our general view is that there is not sufficient evidence at this time to answer with confidence the question in the chapter title. Given the importance of this issue, it is critical to refine our understanding further. The existing research leaves important gaps in our knowledge, especially with regard to the effects of higher-cost services, and particularly when such services are provided for the more disadvantaged. These gaps cannot be filled without new studies more consciously directed at higher-cost services in large-scale programs.

In Part IV we draw conclusions from the completed studies and point to two priority areas for future experimental research: (1) evaluations of programs that provide basic education, occupational skills training, and other human capital development services for substantial numbers of potential long-term welfare recipients, and (2) tests that directly compare the relative effectiveness of different service strategies for similar groups of people within the same community. These latter "differential impact" studies, if successfully implemented, could more definitively confirm or disprove conclusions based on evaluations of programs implemented in different localities, with different goals and services, and for different target groups.

Part II: The Comparability of Empirical Estimates

The main objective of each experimental study examined in this chapter was to determine, as accurately as possible, whether a particular approach was feasible, had an impact, and was cost-effective. The use of controlled experiments gives us confidence about the findings for each program. The diversity of programs represented in these studies makes a convincing case that several different approaches can be effective under a variety of circumstances. But diversity across studies makes it difficult to use these experiments to answer questions about the *relative* (that is, differential) cost and effectiveness of alternative service sequences.

The 13 studies discussed here fall naturally into two categories: nine of them were of systems that provided one or more employment or training activities directed at assisting people in moving from welfare to work (broad-coverage programs); the other four were of particular activities or components that were among the many services offered within the local welfare-to-work systems (selective-voluntary demonstrations or programs).

We begin by discussing three factors that determine the effectiveness of both categories of welfare-to-work programs: (1) the nature and intensity of program treatment and implementation—which determine program cost; (2) the local environment—the context in which the program is implemented; and (3) target group characteristics—the composition of the population singled out for service. These factors vary across studies within categories and between them, complicating comparisons. Next we discuss how the two major categories of studies differ in terms of the voluntariness, selectivity, coverage, and scale of the programs. We also begin the explanation, elaborated on in the following section, of why these differences, combined with resulting differences in participation rates and experimental design, make it inappropriate to compare average impact results across these two types of studies. These differences lead us to discuss the results of each category separately and to introduce measures that go beyond the average impacts.

Noncomparabilities in Services, Environment, and Target Groups

Table 4.1 shows the completed experimental studies of welfare-to-work programs for single-parent AFDC recipients, grouped by their basic structure (broad-coverage versus selective-voluntary) and, within that, their average net cost per member of the treatment (experimental) group.[5]

These studies differed, first, in *program treatment,* which includes cost, program objectives, type and sequencing of services, whether participation was voluntary or required as a condition of receiving welfare benefits, the degree to which any mandate was enforced, provision of support services, and the extent of case management and monitoring. Service mix and structure differed across the programs, but included one or more of the following kinds of activities: job search assistance, unpaid work experience, direct placement, wage subsidies for on-the-job training, basic and remedial education, and occupational skills training. By and large, program cost was directly related to the kind of service offered: job search and work experience were the main activities for programs representing the lower end of the cost spectrum; higher-cost programs offered training and wage subsidies.

Costs varied across the 13 programs, with particular noncomparabilities across the two categories of studies. The reason for this is that the generally higher costs for the four selective-voluntary programs reflect, in part, the inclusion of subsidized wages that may have led directly to offsetting AFDC savings. There are particular problems in comparing other programs' costs to those for Supported Work. The inflation of Supported Work's costs from mid-1970 to 1985 dollars may have produced some distortion. Furthermore, not only did Supported Work spend the most on participants' wages, but it also incurred substantial

5. Net cost is defined in the first note to Table 4.1. See Gueron and Pauly (1991) for a description of the other experimental studies currently under way, for further discussion of the basic distinction between broad-coverage and selective-voluntary programs and for further detail on the estimation of program costs.

expenses that were subsequently offset by revenues received from the sale of goods and services generated by Supported Work projects, thus reducing the net budget cost below the figure shown in Table 4.1.

As indicated in the table, the highest-cost programs were Supported Work ($18,000 per experimental, in 1985 dollars) and Homemaker–Home Health Aide training ($9,500 per experimental, with a cross-site range of $6,000 to $12,500 per experimental). Both of these provided subsidized employment and training, and their cost included substantial amounts for wages paid to participants ($8,500 per experimental in Supported Work and $3,800 in the Homemaker–Home Health Aide Demonstrations; see Table 4.1). Next were a middle group of programs with costs of $800 to $2,000 per experimental. These included two voluntary on-the-job training (OJT) programs, consisting of placement and a wage subsidy, in Maine and New Jersey. Also in this cost range were two multi-component, mandatory approaches: the Baltimore Options program, which offered a range of services and permitted some choice by enrollees; and the San Diego Saturation Work Initiative Model (SWIM), which rigorously enforced participation in a sequence of job search, followed by unpaid work experience, followed by education and training. The lower-cost programs included the two Louisville tests of job search; the job search and unpaid work experience programs in Cook County (Chicago), Arkansas, Virginia, and San Diego I (the program that preceded SWIM); and the West Virginia test of unpaid, unlimited-duration work experience.

Of the broad-coverage programs, only two—Baltimore and SWIM—made an effort to increase participation in education as part of an overall mix of activities, which still relied mainly on lower-cost services. None of the selective-voluntary demonstrations tested education. The absence of impact estimates specific to education is a serious gap in knowledge. Compared to Supported Work, Homemaker–Home Health Aide training, and wage subsidies, education is much less directed toward short-term labor market outcomes and is far more amenable to large-scale application. Therefore, it may not be appropriate to generalize about high-cost services on the basis of the completed high-cost demonstrations. The lack of impact results for education poses a critical problem in projecting the relative effectiveness of low-cost and high-cost services as they are likely to be implemented in many state JOBS programs in the 1990s.

Table 4.1 AFDC welfare-to-work programs: Characteristics, costs, and impacts

Program (ordered by increasing net cost)	Program activities and study characteristics	Coverage/ mandatoriness	Net cost per experimental (in dollars)	Outcome	Annual impacts for all years of follow-up	
					Experimental-control difference (in dollars)	Percentage change over control group level
		BROAD-COVERAGE PROGRAMS				
Arkansas WORK Program	Sequence of group job search and (for a few) unpaid work experience; low-grant state; highly disadvantaged population; evaluation began in 1983	Mandatory; targeted AFDC applicants and recipients with children 3 or older; few sanctions; 38% ever participated in job search or work experience during 9-month follow-up	118	Earnings		
				Year 1	167**	33
				Year 2	223	23
				Year 3	337**	31
				AFDC payments		
				Year 1	−145***	−13
				Year 2	−190***	−19
				Year 3	−168***	−18
Louisville WIN Laboratory Experiment—Individual Job Search (Louisville I)	Individual job search; low-grant state; evaluation began in 1978	Mandatory and voluntary; targeted AFDC applicants and recipients with children of any age; 55% ever participated in individual job search during 8-month follow-up	136[a]	Earnings		
				Year 1	289**[b]	18
				Year 2	456**[b]	20
				Year 3	435**[b]	18
				AFDC payments		
				Year 1	−75*[b]	−3
				Year 2	−164**[b]	−8
				Year 3	−184**[b]	−10

Program	Program description	Targeting and participation	Sample size	Outcome		
Cook County WIN Demonstration	Sequence of individual job search and un-paid work experience; program provided little direct assistance, mainly monitored and sanctioned those who did not participate; medium-grant state; highly disadvantaged population; evaluation began in 1985	Mandatory; targeted AFDC applicants and recipients with children 6 or older; many sanctions; 39% ever participated in any activity during 9-month follow-up	157	Earnings Year 1 AFDC payments Year 1	10 −40	1 −1
Louisville WIN Laboratory Experiment—Group Job Search (Louisville II)	Group job search; low-grant state; evaluation began in 1980	Mandatory and volun-tary; targeted AFDC applicants and recipients with children of any age; 65% ever partici-pated in group job search during 6-month follow-up	230[a]	Earnings Year 1 AFDC payments Year 1	464**[c] −40[c]	43 −2
West Virginia Com-munity Work Expe-rience Program (CWEP)	Open-ended unpaid work experience; rural labor market with very high un-employment; low-grant state; highly disadvantaged pop-ulation; evaluation began in 1983	Mandatory; targeted AFDC applicants and recipients with children 6 or older; few sanctions; 24% ever participated in work experience during 9-month follow-up	260	Earnings Year 1 AFDC payments Year 1	16 0	4 0

Table 4.1 (cont.)

Program (ordered by increasing net cost)	Program activities and study characteristics	Coverage/ mandatoriness	Net cost per experimental (in dollars)	Outcome	Annual impacts for all years of follow-up	
					Experimental-control difference (in dollars)	Percentage change over control group level
Virginia Employment Services Program (ESP)	Sequence of individual or group job search, unpaid work experience, and some education or job skills training (but only slightly more than controls received on their own); medium-grant state; disadvantaged population; evaluation began in 1983	Mandatory; targeted AFDC applicants and recipients with children 6 or older; few sanctions; 58% ever participated in any activity during 9-month follow-up	430	Earnings		
				Year 1	69	5
				Year 2	280**	14
				Year 3	268*	11
				AFDC payments		
				Year 1	−69	−3
				Year 2	−36	−2
				Year 3	−111**	−9
San Diego I (Employment Preparation Program/ Experimental Work Experience Program [EPP/EWEP])	Sequence of group job search and unpaid work experience; substantial program assistance provided; high-grant state; less disadvantaged population; evaluation began in 1982	Mandatory; targeted AFDC applicants with children 6 or older; many sanctions; 46% ever participated in job search or work experience during 9-month follow-up	636	Earnings		
				Year 1	443***	23
				AFDC payments		
				Year 1	−226***	−8

Program	Description	Sample size	Measure	Impact	%
San Diego Saturation Work Initiative Model (SWIM)	Sequence of group job search, unpaid work experience, and education and job skills training; high participation and ongoing participation requirement; high-grant state; less disadvantaged population; evaluation began in 1985	919	Earnings		
			Year 1	352***	21
			Year 2	658***	29
			AFDC payments		
			Year 1	−407***	−8
			Year 2	−553***	−14
Baltimore Options Program	Choice of services, including individual or group job search, education, job skills training, unpaid work experience, and on-the-job training; program constrained to serve 1,000 enrollees per year; medium-grant state; less disadvantaged population; evaluation began in 1982	933	Earnings		
			Year 1	140	10
			Year 2	401***	17
			Year 3	511***	17
			AFDC payments		
			Year 1	2	0
			Year 2	−34	−2
			Year 3	−31	−2

Table 4.1 (cont.)

Program (ordered by increasing net cost)	Program activities and study characteristics	Coverage/ mandatoriness	Net cost per experimental (in dollars)	Outcome	Annual impacts for all years of follow-up	
					Experimental- control difference (in dollars)	Percentage change over control group level
SELECTIVE-VOLUNTARY PROGRAMS						

New Jersey On-the-Job Training (OJT) Program	Subsidized on-the-job training; enrollees quite disadvantaged in terms of prior welfare receipt and recent work histories, but had relatively high levels of GED attainment; medium-grant state; evaluation began in 1984	Voluntary; targeted selected AFDC recipients over 18 with children of any age; 40% participated in employment with OJT (84% ever participated in any WIN or JTPA activity) during 12-month follow-up	787 [439][d]	Earnings
				  Year 1
				  Year 2
				AFDC payments
				  Year 1
				  Year 2
					N/A[e]
					591*[e]
					
					−190**[e]
					−238*
						N/A
						14
						
						−6
						−11

Maine On-the-Job Training (OJT) Program	Sequence of employability training, unpaid work experience, and subsidized on-the-job training; enrollees quite disadvantaged in terms of prior welfare receipt and recent work histories, but had relatively high levels of GED attainment; medium-grant state; evaluation began in 1983	Voluntary; targeted selected unemployed AFDC recipients on rolls for at least prior 6 months, with children of any age; 90% ever participated in any activity during 12-month follow-up	2,019 [1,635][d]	Earnings
				  Year 1
				  Year 2
				  Year 3
				AFDC payments
				  Year 1
				  Year 2
				  Year 3
					104
					871**
					941*[f]
					
					64
					29
					80[f]
						8
						38
						34
						
						2
						1
						4

Program	Description	Cost		
AFDC Homemaker–Home Health Aide Demonstrations	Job skills training and subsidized employment program; varied population; low-, medium-, and high-grant states; evaluation began in 1983	9,505 (5,957–12,457 across states) [5,384]d		
			Earnings	
			Year 1	2,026g	N/A
			Year 2	1,347g	N/A
			Year 3	1,121g	N/A
			AFDC and Food Stamp benefits	
			Year 1	−696g	N/A
			Year 2	−855g	N/A
			Year 3	−343g	N/A
National Supported Work Demonstration	Structured, paid work experience; targeted extremely disadvantaged AFDC recipients; low-, medium-, and high-grant states; evaluation began in 1976	17,981a [9,447]d,h		
			Earnings	
			Year 1	6,402***i	327
			Year 2	1,368***i	36
			Year 3	1,076***i	23
			AFDC payments	
			Year 1	−2,200**i	−39
			Year 2	−1,165***i	−26
			Year 3	−401**i	−10

Source: As published in *From Welfare to Work*, by Judith M. Gueron and Edward Pauly, © 1991 by the Manpower Demonstration Research Corporation, published by the Russell Sage Foundation and used with its permission.

Notes: The cost estimates reported in this table are the net costs of these programs. These include all expenditures incurred specifically for the programs under study by the operating agency, plus any expenditures for services by other organizations for services that were an essential part of the program treatment, minus costs to the operating agency or other organizations of serving members of the control groups. Net costs and annual impacts are in nominal dollars except where noted.

a. The net cost is adjusted to 1985 dollars.

b. The impact is adjusted to 1985 dollars. Year 1 begins with the quarter of random assignment. The annual earnings impact for year 3 is based on three quarters of follow-up. The annual AFDC payments impact for year 3 is based on one quarter of follow-up. The annual AFDC payments impact for year 3 is based on three quarters of follow-up. Statistical significance was not calculated for year 3. However, since the quarterly impacts are statistically significant, the annual impacts are assumed also to be significant.

Table 4.1 (cont.)

c. The impact is adjusted to 1985 dollars. The annual earnings impact is based on two quarters of follow-up. Statistical significance was not calculated. However, since the quarterly impacts are statistically significant, the annual impact is assumed also to be significant. The annual AFDC payments impact is based on four quarters of follow-up.

d. The bracketed figure excludes wage subsidy payments for participants, whereas the other figure includes them.

e. A year 1 earnings impact is not available in New Jersey for the same sample as the year 2 impact and is therefore not shown. The annual earnings impact for year 2 is based on three quarters of follow-up. Statistical significance was not calculated for year 2. However, since the earnings impact for quarters 5–7 is statistically significant, the annual impact is assumed also to be significant. Similarly, the quarterly AFDC payments impacts for quarters 2, 3, and 4 of year 1 are statistically significant, so the annual impact is assumed also to be significant.

f. Annual earnings and AFDC payments impacts for year 3 are based on three quarters of follow-up. Statistical significance was not calculated for year 3. However, since the quarterly earnings impacts are statistically significant, the annual earnings impact is assumed also to be significant.

g. Cross-state annual impacts are estimated from state-specific impacts, so statistical significance and experimental and control group means are not available. Year 1 is defined by the original researchers as the number of months from random assignment until the typical experimental left subsidized employment. Year 2 is defined as the 12-month period following the time when the typical experimental left subsidized employment. Year 3 is based on all months in the follow-up period after year 2. Average annual impacts for each year were calculated by multiplying the average monthly impacts for that period by 12. Total earnings of the experimental group include both demonstration and non-demonstration earnings. Since the Homemaker–Home Health Aide Demonstrations offered up to a year of subsidized paid employment, earnings and consequently reduced AFDC and Food Stamp benefits during the first two years partly reflect wages earned in the program, and not post-program impacts. In year 2, there were statistically significant gains in monthly earnings in all seven states and welfare savings in six. In year 3, there were significant gains in monthly earnings in five of the seven states and welfare savings in four.

h. Supported Work projects generated revenues of $4,352 per experimental (in 1985 dollars), which offset part of the cost reported here.

i. The impact is adjusted to 1985 dollars. Since Supported Work offered up to 18 months of subsidized paid employment, earnings and consequently reduced AFDC payments during the first two years partly reflect wages earned in the program, and not post-program impacts. The annual earnings and AFDC payments impacts for year 3 are based on quarter 9, the last quarter for which there are common follow-up data for all recipients who responded to the final survey. AFDC payments impacts include impacts on General Assistance, Supplemental Security Income, and other unspecified cash welfare.

* Denotes statistical significance at the 10 percent level; ** at the 5 percent level; and *** at the 1 percent level.

Other factors may also affect the relationship between cost and impact under JOBS. The JOBS program not only encourages the provision of education, but also is likely to affect the extent and nature of other activities that draw on program resources, namely, assessment, case management, monitoring, child care, and other support services. In addition, through its emphasis on coordination across delivery systems, the JOBS legislation encourages states to use existing institutions (for example, schools and community colleges) and tap into other funding streams. This can affect the real cost of particular services. It can also mean that, within limits, all JOBS activities are not competing under the same budget constraint. While these factors will be of obvious importance to JOBS administrators, in this chapter we generally simplify the discussion and assume that costs reflect mainly employment-directed services and that administrators face fixed budget constraints rather than some opportunity for leveraging other systems' resources.

Second, the studies differed in *local environment*. This constellation of factors—labor market conditions, AFDC grant levels, and the number, capacity, and quality of community training institutions—determined the level of disadvantagedness of the program population and the likelihood that potential enrollees would find a job or training without special program assistance. For example, in Arkansas, AFDC grant levels were among the lowest in the nation, which means that heads of families who chose to apply for or receive AFDC probably had few other options. In fact, the rates of employment, even among controls, were considerably below those observed in most other studies. In Baltimore, with AFDC grant levels near the national median, 40 percent of controls were employed by the end of three years, compared to only 18 percent for Arkansas. At the same time, however, the low grant levels in Arkansas meant that virtually any full-time job would produce earnings high enough to close an AFDC case. Thus, any employment impacts might more readily translate into welfare reductions than in states with higher AFDC benefit levels.

Third, the studies differed in *target group characteristics*. Studies have shown the AFDC population to be quite heterogeneous in its probability of employment and length of future welfare receipt (Bane and Ellwood, 1983; Ellwood, 1986), and it seems reasonable that program impact will vary with the dependency level of the target group. Evidence indicates that impacts do increase with dependency, although the increase may not apply to the most disadvantaged groups (see Friedlander, 1988).

The differences in targeting strategies among the evaluated programs, therefore, constitute another obstacle to ready comparison.

For example, the San Diego I program worked only with AFDC applicants, a generally less disadvantaged group than AFDC recipients. Thus, even among controls, more than 35 percent were employed within a year of random assignment and more than half had already left the AFDC system. Other low-cost programs served a cross section of the mandatory caseload, including first-time AFDC applicants, applicants with previous welfare spells, and long-term current recipients. Employment rates were therefore lower, and welfare receipt rates greater, in those samples. Thus SWIM, implemented in the same county as the San Diego I experiment, nevertheless showed only a quarter of the control group employed by the end of a year, and three-quarters still on AFDC. Supported Work, which was more narrowly targeted, enrolled only long-term welfare recipients with weak recent employment histories. The sample averaged 8.6 years of prior AFDC receipt, and 65 percent of the control group were still on AFDC at the end of three years of follow-up.[6]

Further complicating matters is the fact that most of the programs targeted mothers with school-age children, but several included a substantial number of women with younger children. Also, as discussed below, selectivity and screening by some programs led to noncomparabilities across samples. Such differences may result in impact differences that obscure the influence of service cost and intensity. Moreover, the fact that the earlier evaluations focused on women with older children—rather than the women with younger children and young custodial parents newly targeted in JOBS—means that the findings from past studies may not be relevant to the expanded JOBS population.

Noncomparabilities in Program Structure

The major difficulty in comparing results across studies stems from differences in the way low-cost and higher-cost services have been structured and evaluated. High-cost services have usually been tested as demonstration projects with voluntary participation and limited, sometimes

---

6. The first figure is from Hollister and Maynard (1984), p. 97; the second is from Grossman, Maynard, and Roberts (1985), p. 72, and was estimated for a subsample of the early enrollees with longer follow-up than the bulk of the sample.

selective, enrollment. In contrast, lower-cost services have been tested in the context of broad-coverage programs, aimed at large segments of the eligible caseload, usually with mandatory participation and no selection. Also broad in coverage were those programs that combined a primarily low-cost approach with higher-cost components for some enrollees (for example, San Diego SWIM and Baltimore).

Table 4.1 therefore includes into two main analytic categories:

- *Broad-coverage programs,* which, as with state JOBS initiatives, are intended to reach the wide range of AFDC-eligibles, usually including those who are not likely to seek services on their own.[7] These programs are service delivery systems that include individual service components as well as administrative activities such as an intake and assessment process.
- *Selective-voluntary demonstrations of specific components,* with limited enrollment, which encourage but do not require participation by a subset of the AFDC population.[8] The services tested are not a "system" but a small-scale component or potential component of a much larger system that, as described above, contains a range of activities. In this sense, they can be viewed as subsets of broad-coverage programs. These demonstrations can be "selective" in two ways: eligible people select whether to enroll, and program operators may select among eligible applicants.

This distinction is fundamental to understanding why neither the impact nor the cost estimates for these two categories are directly comparable—and why different experimental research designs were used to address different questions. One example—discussed at length in the following section—may help to explain this. Impact studies of

7. The distinction between broad-coverage programs and selective-voluntary demonstrations (or programs) is not strictly a distinction between mandatoriness and voluntariness. The two classes differ instead in the degree to which they try to involve a representative cross section of the eligible caseload. Some broad-coverage programs have encouraged but not required participation (for example, Massachusetts' ET Choices program). However, these have not been experimentally evaluated and thus are not included in Table 4.1 or discussed in this chapter.

8. Studies of this type of program have only included those that are voluntary; hence, they are referred to in this chapter as "selective-voluntary" demonstrations (or programs) of specific service components. However, it is possible for such components to be implemented with mandatory participation requirements.

broad-coverage, mandatory programs ask the question: "What is the impact of the entire system?" In broad-coverage programs, large numbers of eligible clients go through intake, orientation, and specific service components, but there is typically a dropoff at each step, significantly reducing the participation rate in the actual service components. This dropoff occurs for a variety of reasons, including normal welfare caseload dynamics, deterrence of nonparticipants, and temporary or permanent deferrals owing to illness, child care problems, or part-time or full-time employment. The experimental design for broad-coverage programs therefore typically places the point of random assignment earlier in the system flow in order to capture the system's full effects. Thus, costs—as well as impacts—are spread across a large number of individuals, only some of whom enter, or are affected by, specific service components.

In contrast, impact studies of selective-voluntary demonstrations ask the question: "What is the impact of one specific service component?" From a system perspective, smaller numbers of individuals reach this stage, but those who do are much more likely to participate in the service. Consequently, to measure the impact of the service on likely participants, the research design places the point of random assignment as close to the service as possible. Hence, cost per experimental and impacts per experimental will tend to be higher because they are concentrated on a smaller number of individuals, most of whom participate in the service.

Table 4.1 includes four selective-voluntary demonstrations. In order of increasing cost per experimental, they are New Jersey, Maine, the Homemaker–Home Health Aide Demonstrations, and Supported Work.[9] The four selective-voluntary programs had relatively high per-experimental costs because they tested the more intensive services and their services were used by a relatively large share of the experimental groups.

By design, these programs usually had specific eligibility criteria and served individuals who were motivated to seek out and participate in services. For example, for Supported Work—which sought to enroll very disadvantaged people and did not screen out eligible applicants—it

9. A number of other studies of selective-voluntary programs are in progress, for example, the Minority Female Single Parent (MFSP) Demonstration (see Gordon and Burghardt, 1990) and the JOBSTART Demonstration (see Auspos et al., 1989). See also Gueron and Pauly (1991).

has been estimated that, on the basis of objective targeting criteria alone, at most only 17 percent of AFDC recipients would qualify (Hollister and Maynard, 1984, p. 96). Supported Work thus operated as one possible referral for certain welfare recipients within the WIN system in the demonstration cities. In Homemaker–Home Health Aide training, statistics on trainee recruitment indicate that fewer than 3 percent of all AFDC recipients contacted applied for training, and fewer than 2 percent were accepted into the research sample (Cella, 1987, pp. 32–34). In New Jersey and especially in Maine, selective screening by program staff was an integral part of program intake into this component of the WIN system.[10]

The nine broad-coverage programs included in Table 4.1, in order of increasing cost per experimental, are Arkansas, Louisville I, Cook County, Louisville II, West Virginia, Virginia, San Diego I, San Diego SWIM, and Baltimore. The common feature of these broad-coverage programs, which distinguishes them from the selective-voluntary programs, is that they were highly inclusive, within the bounds of their scale and target population.[11] Instead of serving small numbers of self-selected or staff-screened volunteers, they attempted—through a participation requirement, enforced to varying degrees—to reach everyone in a target population defined by specified *objective* eligibility criteria. For example, San Diego SWIM operated in only two offices in the county and targeted only individuals with school-age children. But the program had no screening or selection criteria: all applicants for and recipients

---

10. The case of Maine is of some interest. There, objective eligibility criteria limited enrollment to single heads of household who had been receiving AFDC for six consecutive months and who were not employed at the time of enrollment. But staff were also instructed to screen out women with low literacy levels and eligible women who had child care, transportation, health, or other problems that could interfere with their participation. In addition, staff imposed informal screening criteria and sought to enroll only the most motivated people, those with high school diplomas, and those whose job goals were commensurate with their current skills. See Auspos, Cave, and Long (1988), pp. 4–5.

11. In several other respects, these programs differed from one another. Six were localized in a county or urban area, with some (for example, Baltimore) of limited scale, while the Arkansas, Virginia, and West Virginia programs operated over many or all counties in a state. In contrast to the other seven, the two Louisville demonstrations were both voluntary and mandatory. For mothers with children under age 6 (that is, those outside the traditional mandatory category), participation was voluntary. Mothers with no children under age 6 could choose either to remain in the regular WIN program or to be randomly assigned for the special demonstration program. After they made their choice, however, their compliance was mandatory, although monetary sanctions were not imposed.

of AFDC in the defined target areas and target group were required to enroll. (SWIM and the other broad-coverage programs in effect replaced the WIN system in these locations.)

The two classes of program also differed in scale. For example, SWIM, even though it operated in only a portion of San Diego, enrolled more than 10,000 AFDC applicants and recipients (excluding controls) during the two years of its operation.[12] Cook County enrolled nearly 8,000 experimentals in only six months. Arkansas, Virginia, and West Virginia enrolled all mandatory welfare recipients statewide or in large areas of the state, although the samples selected for study were much smaller. The other broad-coverage programs were also either large in scale or prototypes that could be expanded to larger scale.

In contrast, Supported Work, which was tested for AFDC recipients in seven sites (including such large cities as New York, Chicago, and Newark), enrolled only 1,620 welfare sample members, about half of whom were controls and therefore were not part of the program. The placement/wage subsidy demonstrations in Maine and New Jersey, although large for that kind of treatment, worked with a total of only 297 and 814 AFDC recipients, respectively (that is, the number of experimentals), even though outreach covered large portions of each state and, for New Jersey, involved such large cities as Newark.

Under JOBS, many more AFDC recipients may be judged to be in need of intensive services than the small numbers who were part of the selective-voluntary demonstrations. It is important for the future to determine the maximum scale at which higher-cost services can effectively and efficiently be delivered. From the selective-voluntary studies, it is unclear whether the specific services tested could be significantly expanded and whether they would have the same results if they were.

Some, but not all, of the evaluations of the broad-coverage programs have explicitly addressed the issue of scale. Unfortunately, projections from this set of evaluations are limited somewhat by the fact that we have no examples of broad-coverage programs making extensive use of education or other higher-cost services. Nor can we separately estimate the differential impact of low-cost and higher-cost components with the data that exist for the few broad-coverage evaluations in which some higher-cost services were part of the program model.

---

12. Only a randomly selected subsample of all enrollees was included in the research sample.

Implications of Program Structure for Experimental Design

The differences in local environment, service mix, and targeting outlined previously suggest caution in making comparisons among studies within the two categories of programs. Even greater caution is needed in comparing *across* classifications because of the implications for experimental design that follow from the distinction between selective-voluntary and broad-coverage programs, especially when the latter are mandatory. In this case, even when studies of both use random assignment, the research designs and thus the interpretation of results will be fundamentally different, reflecting the disparity in goals and structure of the programs.

Selective-voluntary programs are intended to have their impact only on individuals who actually participate in program services. For experimental evaluations of such programs, random assignment is most appropriately located *after* program enrollment and, ideally, just at the point where participation in services is about to begin.[13] There will thus be few dropouts between random assignment and the start of participation. Moreover, the samples will consist of volunteers who *want* to participate and who will make some effort to do so. In some cases, as in the Maine demonstration, program staff may intensively screen prospective participants for "suitability" and motivation before random assignment. For these reasons, impacts will be estimated for experimental groups with very high, perhaps nearly universal, participation rates.

This is a very different kind of study, and a very different research design, from the typical evaluation of broad-coverage, mandatory programs. These mandatory programs are designed to have impacts not only on participants—that is, individuals who actually spend time in education, training, job search, or work experience—but also on individuals who do *not* participate. Such programs are, in fact, specifically set up to affect the behavior of nonparticipants by imposing monetary penalties—sanctions—on those who do not cooperate with program directives. In addition, part of the impact of mandatory programs may arise because individuals find jobs or otherwise leave welfare precisely to avoid having to participate, the so-called *deterrence effect*.

This important difference between broad-coverage and selective-

13. Random assignment at that point is most appropriate to estimating the impact of program services; earlier random assignment would facilitate generalization to the broader caseload.

voluntary programs has led to some confusion in terminology. In broad-coverage programs, one is "in" the program if one is subject to its mandate. Thus, "being in the program" is *not* the same as "being a participant," but "being in the program" is what counts for impact estimation. Analyses of selective-voluntary services ordinarily do not look for impacts on nonparticipants because almost no program effort is focused on them. But broad-coverage programs devote considerable resources to working with nonparticipants (for example, through monitoring, counseling, and imposing sanctions), and the effects of that effort must be included in the overall program impact.

The intent to produce impacts on nonparticipants requires that studies of mandatory programs, if they are to capture the full program effect, must estimate impacts across the entire caseload that is actually subject to the participation mandate. In order to bring into the research sample all persons who might be affected by the program, random assignment should occur at or near the point where individuals are *first told about* or *enrolled in* the program rather than at the start of actual participation.[14] Thus, for example, the research sample may include not only persons receiving AFDC but also program-eligible applicants for AFDC, many of whom will never complete their applications or have a grant approved. The sample will therefore include many people who will leave the welfare system quickly through the normal process of turnover, without participating in the program and for reasons unrelated to it. Consequently, studies of broad-coverage programs typically yield participation rates within the experimental group—with participation defined as actual receipt of employment services such as job search assistance or training and not simply registration with the program or attendance at "orientation"—of about 50 percent or lower.[15]

Thus, different experimental designs and participation rates result from the fact that broad-coverage, mandatory programs seek to change the behavior of nonparticipants, while selective-voluntary programs do not. Evaluations of broad-coverage, mandatory programs thus provide

14. Random assignment, even at this early point, would not, however, capture general equilibrium effects such as increased or decreased rates of application for welfare.
15. Participation rates for the programs under consideration illustrate the differences between selective-voluntary demonstrations and broad-coverage programs. For the four selective-voluntary demonstrations, 84 to 97 percent of experimentals began program activities. In contrast, participation rates for the experimental groups in the broad-coverage studies ranged from about 40 to 65 percent. (See Table 4.1.)

estimates of the effectiveness of a system (that is, a combination of services, requirements, and monitoring) on a diverse group of people in the caseload subject to the participation requirement; evaluations of selective-voluntary demonstrations provide estimates of the effectiveness of a component of the system (that is, a specific service or group of services) for a subset of the caseload who volunteer for and usually actually participate in services.

As a result, comparisons of studies of selective-voluntary services with those of broad-coverage, mandatory programs must be made with care, even when both use experimental designs. Three precautions must be observed. First, because broad-coverage, mandatory programs may have impacts for nonparticipants, the average impact per sample member must be stated on a per-experimental basis rather than a per-participant basis. Indeed, the concept of "impact per participant," though it has an obvious and crucial policy significance for the selective-voluntary studies, has less meaning for the broad-coverage, mandatory studies.

Second, allowance must be made for the differences in participation rates and in the total number of enrollees. Within an experimental group, nonparticipants are usually expected to have smaller impacts, on average, than participants. Thus, even if the actual *participants* in broad-coverage programs experience impacts as large as those in selective-voluntary programs, the lower rate of participation for the former will reduce the average impact measured on a *per-experimental* basis. As a result, the impact per experimental may be greater in a selective-voluntary demonstration (or program) merely because a higher proportion of experimentals participate in services.[16] On the other hand, a broad-coverage evaluation will generally have a much larger experimental group—many times larger, in fact. As a consequence, the *aggregate* impact for the broad-coverage program could be larger even if the impact per experimental were smaller. Our analysis will explicitly take into account the distinction between individual and aggregate impacts.

Third, the differences in recruitment and targeting must be taken

16. An example may help to illustrate this point. If we assume *no* impact on the nonparticipants, then a participation rate of 50 percent for a broad-coverage program would imply that the impact per participant would be twice the impact per experimental. In Table 4.1, this extreme assumption of no impact on nonparticipants would imply that the magnitude of impact per participant for some of the broad-coverage programs would approach the magnitude of impact per participant for such selective-voluntary demonstrations as Homemaker–Home Health Aide and Maine.

into account. For selective-voluntary programs, the voluntarism on the part of participants and screening on the part of staff mean that participants will be neither representative of the larger target groups from which they were drawn, nor typical of the cross section of the eligible caseload enrolled in broad-coverage programs. In general, people in these studies will be more motivated and more likely to use program services, both of which factors may increase or decrease program impacts.[17]

In addition, some services that are offered on a voluntary basis or are selective may, by their nature, be quite difficult to expand. For example, there may be limits to how many on-the-job training slots can be created. Also, there may be only a small number of AFDC recipients who would be interested in participating in the particular service or who would pass the screening criteria. Making participation mandatory as a device to help increase coverage could be self-defeating if it changed the character of the services and their impact. The higher-cost services that have been rigorously tested may not, in fact, be suitable for large-scale implementation. Instead, as previously noted, they may be appropriate as relatively small components of large-scale programs.

The variety of differences between broad-coverage and selective-voluntary programs discussed in this section make direct comparisons of "average impact per experimental" across the two kinds of study problematic. To account for research design differences and to facilitate comparisons, we will develop impact measures that supplement average impact by adjusting for cost: impact per dollar outlay and savings net of cost. We will also examine differences in the quality of impacts (for example, differences in impact on hourly wage rates). Nevertheless, broad-coverage and selective-voluntary programs will be handled separately for much of this chapter. The various questions about effectiveness will, in many cases, be asked in two parts: First, among the broad-coverage evaluations, were those with a higher per-experimental cost more effective than those with a lower cost? Second, do the selective-voluntary demonstrations provide additional evidence about the effectiveness of higher-cost components?

---

17. These factors, since they relate to controls as well as experimentals, may have either positive or negative effects on the ability of programs to achieve impacts: more motivated individuals may be more prone to help themselves, with or without program assistance, or to seek out alternative services on their own, thus lowering the potential for program impact.

Part III: Findings on Relative Effectiveness

In assessing low-cost and higher-cost programs and program components, administrators and legislators may ask four questions: Which have larger average impacts per enrollee? Which produce larger aggregate impacts on the caseload per dollar spent? Which create greater savings for government budgets? Which have larger effects on household income or poverty? This section examines the experimental results as they apply to each of these questions.[18] In the light of funding constraints, we do not find that one approach can best meet all goals. Instead, the data suggest trade-offs, with the relative advantage of either approach dependent on which program goals have priority. The differences across studies discussed in the previous section provide the context for this discussion, qualifying the character of the conclusions.

For each program, Table 4.1 shows estimates of net costs and of impacts on earnings and AFDC payments. Impact estimates are the difference between average outcomes for experimentals and controls and are shown for each available year of follow-up. Our discussion will focus mainly on the final year of follow-up for each experiment, since it best represents the program's longer-term effects. This choice is particularly appropriate for the selective-voluntary programs: During year 1, and to a lesser extent during year 2, the earnings impacts of these programs include wage subsidies paid to employers by the program or wage payments made directly from the program to the participant.

True to the experimental designs, all sample members have been included in the averages. Thus, the behavior of both program participants and nonparticipants is included in the average for an experimental group. Likewise, estimates of average earnings include zeros for sample members who were not employed, and average AFDC payments include zeros for sample members who were no longer receiving AFDC.

All estimates are given in evaluation year dollars, except for Supported Work and the two Louisville experiments, which have been converted to 1985 dollars to permit comparisons with the more recent stud-

---

18. These questions address only some of the goals that may be set for welfare employment programs. For example, some administrators maintain that literacy gained through remedial education will not only improve earnings but also foster such benefits as improved parenting, reduced social isolation, and more active citizenship. Proponents of workfare argue that working in return for the AFDC grant can increase self-esteem and reinforce society's work ethic.

ies. *Relative gains*—that is, the percentage of improvement in earnings compared to the control average and the percentage of saving in welfare payments—are also shown, in the last column of Table 4.1. The costs shown in the table are not the gross costs[19] but *net* costs, the difference in average cost per experimental and average cost per control, with all sample members included in the calculations.[20]

For most of the following discussion, we, like other researchers, deal with impacts that are averages across a large number of individuals. But such averages probably give a misleading impression of how these programs affect individual behavior. An impact of $300 in average annual earnings, for example, may seem to suggest that a program raised the earnings of most sample members by about $300. In fact, impacts on employment rates (not reported in this chapter) suggest that it is more likely that only a small proportion of program enrollees actually change their employment behavior. For example, an earnings increase of $300 per experimental in a job search program is probably concentrated among 5 to 10 percent of experimentals.[21] The annual earnings gains for many of these individuals may be several thousand dollars, especially for those who would not have worked without the program but who secure stable employment with its assistance. A similar situation exists for welfare impacts: Reductions of several thousand dollars can occur for the small number of long-term recipients who are induced the leave the rolls, with only minimal effects for the other program enrollees.

19. Gross cost per experimental is the average cost of all program services and administrative activities (such as registration and assessment) involving members of the experimental group. This cost includes all expenditures by the administering agency—on program service components, support services, allowances, and administration—and the costs to other agencies of providing education and training that are integral parts of the program treatment. A gross cost can also be calculated for controls. Net program cost is the difference between these two gross costs. Where controls obtain few services, gross and net costs will be similar. Where controls obtain more services, however, gross and net costs may be quite different. For example, gross costs in Arkansas were $122 per experimental, compared to $118 for net costs. In contrast, in SWIM, gross costs per experimental were $1,545, compared to $919 for net costs. Many state JOBS budgets are likely to have resources per targeted case that fall within this range of $100 to $1,500 in gross costs. See Gueron and Pauly (1991), Appendix A.

20. Cost per control was close to zero where controls received very little service. For several of the experiments, however, controls did participate in services, not in the experimental program directly but through other providers.

21. Maximum quarterly impacts on employment rates fall within this range.

Average Impacts: Broad-Coverage Programs

Broad-coverage programs will be considered first. As a visual aid, Figures 4.1 and 4.2 plot final-year earnings gains and welfare savings per experimental against net cost per experimental, using the estimates in Table 4.1.

Earnings Impacts. Seven of the nine broad-coverage studies found earnings gains that held up through the end of the follow-up period, ranging in the final year from about $250 to $650 per experimental—increases of 10 to 40 percent relative to control group means. The details of the individual programs, discussed below, suggest that this variation was at least partly related to differences in program services and to cost and intensity of effort. But they also highlight the complexities involved in making cross-study comparisons and the uncertainty that remains.

The two programs with no earnings impact—Cook County and West Virginia—were among the least costly. The Cook County program attempted to reach all mandatory individuals on one of the nation's largest urban caseloads. Since supplemental or demonstration funding was not obtained, this meant that expenditures were only about $160 per experimental sample member. Program staff, with average caseloads of about 300, spent more of their time than did staff in the other experiments on administrative and monitoring functions and less on actual services. In West Virginia, the rural labor market and very high unemployment rate strongly conditioned the expectations of program planners. With little hope that the local labor market could provide jobs, they offered unpaid work experience as the program's only activity, and no formal job search activity was included.

Three other programs with costs in the $100 to $250 bracket did achieve impacts. These were the Arkansas and the two Louisville programs. Their earnings impacts in the final year ran from just over $300 to almost $500 per experimental. All three programs focused on job search activities, although a limited number of enrollees in Arkansas participated in unpaid work experience. Louisville I tested individual job search assistance, while Arkansas and Louisville II used a group format for job search, which is generally considered more intensive. The participation rate among experimentals was substantially higher in both Louisville studies compared with Arkansas, which may account for their somewhat larger earnings effects. On the other hand, annual im-

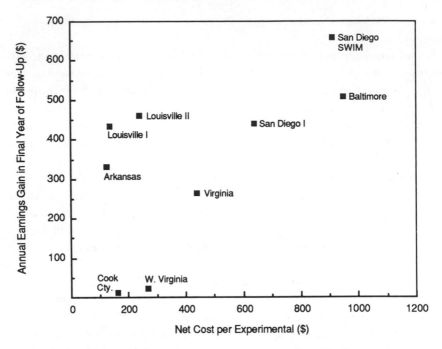

Figure 4.1. Broad-coverage programs: relationship between earnings impact and net cost. *Source:* Table 4.1.

pact estimates for Louisville II are calculated from only two quarters of follow-up, which makes them more uncertain and possibly overstated.

Virginia and San Diego I make up the middle step of the cost distribution for broad-coverage programs; both used unpaid work experience as well as job search.[22] The Virginia earnings impacts of $268 were less than in some lower-cost programs, possibly reflecting the reliance on individual job search for a major share of participation. San Diego I used the more intensive group format for job search. Its earnings impact, an increase of $443, was the same as that of the most successful lower-cost programs.

Baltimore and San Diego SWIM had the highest per-experimental costs and represented the greatest intensity of effort. Both offered mostly low-cost activities but also incorporated some higher-cost ser-

---

22. The Virginia program also referred some enrollees to outside providers for education and training, but controls engaged in similar activities on their own initiative to almost the same degree.

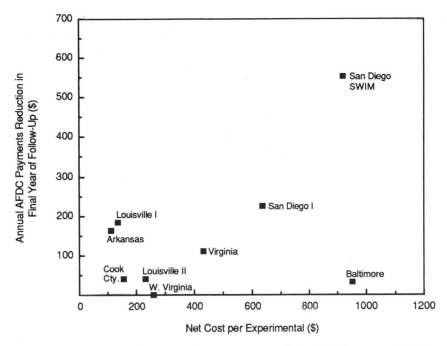

Figure 4.2. Broad-coverage programs: relationship between AFDC payments impact and net cost. *Source:* Table 4.1.

vices, including education and training. Baltimore achieved earnings gains of $511 and SWIM of $658. These were the largest earnings impacts among the broad-coverage programs, but the difference between these and the much less expensive Arkansas and Louisville programs was not as large as might be expected on the basis of cost differences.

To some extent, differences in caseloads, local conditions, administrative capacity, and other factors may affect the comparison. Both Arkansas and Kentucky were low-grant states; Maryland was near the median; California was a high-grant state. Low-cost job search may produce greater employment effects in a low-grant state because almost any earnings opportunities it generates will exceed the income from AFDC. The fact that all three successful low-cost programs were in low-grant states may cloud the true relationship between cost and impact. (In addition, lower staff salaries in these states may imply greater real program resources than in low-cost programs in areas such as Chicago.)

Other differences may also affect the comparison. In terms of administrative capacity, the San Diego social services department had a reputation for unusual expertise, and the Baltimore Office of Manpower Resources—which ran Options—was among the most experienced and highly regarded CETA/JTPA operators in the country. Further, for SWIM, it is not clear how much of the strong impacts came from the program services and how much from other unique features of that saturation experiment, in particular its effort to enforce an ongoing participation requirement.

In addition, the Arkansas and two Louisville programs were the only ones that targeted substantial numbers of women with preschool-age children, and this could have influenced net impact. Finally, inflation of the Louisville estimates to 1985 dollars does not take into account erosion of the real minimum wage and real AFDC benefits over time. The actual earnings obtained if these programs had been run in 1985 might have been somewhat lower than the inflated figures.

It might seem that a comparison between San Diego I and SWIM would avoid some of these biases. Because both experiments were mandatory and were run in the same city by most of the same management team, the influence of some confounding factors might be lower than for other cross-study comparisons. Table 4.1 suggests that in going from the earlier to the later program, the increase in cost of 44 percent (from $636 to $919) was associated with a roughly equivalent increase in earnings impact of 49 percent ($443 to $658). This would seem to imply a rather high rate of increase of impact with cost. Unfortunately, the strength of this comparison is considerably reduced because of differences in the populations covered. San Diego I worked only with AFDC applicants—a less disadvantaged group—and covered all areas of the county, whereas SWIM recruited only from the inner-city welfare offices and enrolled all AFDC recipients as well as new applicants.[23]

In sum, we are left with a sense that increased service intensity increased earnings impact, but we are still in doubt about the strength of that relationship.

AFDC Impacts. Earnings impacts are produced directly by a program through job entry. Welfare impacts are produced only indirectly

23. It is useful to compare the San Diego I results with those only for SWIM applicants. Net costs and earnings impacts were not much different for applicants between the two demonstrations. However, partly because of differences in labor market conditions, SWIM applicants were substantially more welfare-dependent than those in San Diego I. Some 53 percent of SWIM applicant controls were still on AFDC at the sixth quarter of follow-up, compared to only 36 percent for San Diego I.

through a complex interaction of job entry, future AFDC spell length in the absence of job entry, and the often state-specific regulations and administrative practices governing the relationship between earnings and continued welfare receipt. Reductions in welfare receipt were found less often than were gains in earnings. Some programs that produced earnings gains—Baltimore and Louisville II—produced virtually no change in average AFDC payments. Among the others, welfare impacts tended to be smaller, in dollar terms, than the corresponding impacts on earnings.

As shown in Figure 4.2, costs and welfare impacts appear to have no obvious relationship. One of the higher-cost programs, SWIM, also had the largest AFDC savings, but the other, Baltimore, had none. Arkansas, at the bottom of the cost distribution, achieved dollar AFDC savings that exceeded those of most other programs, and, as a percentage of average control group receipts, they were the largest. Louisville I also achieved relatively large welfare reductions at low cost. The welfare effects for these two programs may reflect the states' low AFDC grant levels, since even a relatively small amount of earnings would be enough for case closure.

Factors other than cost or intensity of service may play important roles in producing welfare impacts. The case of Baltimore is particularly interesting in this regard, since it achieved one of the largest increases in earnings but without translating these gains into reductions in welfare. Researchers ruled out administrative error as a major explanation. Individuals with earnings did, for the most part, leave welfare. But many of those who experienced greater earnings as a result of the program would have left welfare in a short time anyway.[24] Thus, although their AFDC grants were terminated, this did not constitute a change from what would have happened without the program. Earnings gains for groups of enrollees who would have left welfare shortly even without assistance will therefore show up as an earnings impact without a corresponding welfare impact.

In addition—and this point pertains to almost all programs—the impact on earnings for an individual may be larger than the amount needed to make that individual ineligible for AFDC and larger than the amount of the AFDC grant that was received. For such an individual,

---

24. It was found that a substantial share of earnings impacts accrued to subgroups in which a high proportion of both experimentals *and* controls left welfare in a short time.

the welfare saving will be small in comparison to the earnings gain. Also, any welfare savings for some experimentals in Baltimore may have been canceled out by increases in the welfare receipt of other experimentals. These others would have been individuals induced to remain on AFDC in order to participate or continue participating in the program when they normally would have left the rolls.

Finally, the rate at which a program applied monetary sanctions was not necessarily associated with welfare savings. It is true that the Baltimore program, although mandatory, achieved participation through persuasion rather than through monetary sanctions[25] and permitted enrollees some choice among activities. However, Louisville I—and, as we will see, New Jersey, Homemaker–Home Health Aide training, and Supported Work—did not sanction and did achieve welfare savings.

Sanctioning may have contributed to welfare savings for some programs. The direct effect of grant reduction through sanctioning should, however, be distinguished from the overall effects of vigorous enforcement of program requirements, which may prompt some people to participate who would not otherwise do so and others to leave the rolls. San Diego SWIM is an example of the welfare reductions that can be achieved with a "hard-nosed" approach. In contrast to Baltimore, SWIM activities were arranged in a fixed sequence, which enrollees could bypass only by substituting a self-arranged education or training activity. Eleven percent of experimentals were sanctioned for failure to comply with some program directive, one of the highest sanctioning rates in these studies.

The direct monetary grant reductions resulting from sanctions were probably not responsible for the bulk of welfare savings. Most of the savings in SWIM were achieved because more experimentals than controls left the AFDC rolls. Thus, services that increase employment and bring about AFDC case closure may be more instrumental in producing sustained welfare reductions for programs than sanctions, which are temporary and reduce the grant only partially.

Average Impacts: Selective-Voluntary Demonstrations

As noted earlier, the selective-voluntary demonstrations had the highest costs per experimental. The lowest costs in this group were for the

25. Reviewing a sample of case histories in Baltimore, researchers could not find a single instance of actual grant reduction from a sanction.

New Jersey wage subsidy experiment. At $787 per experimental, this program cost somewhat less than the maximum observed for the broad-coverage programs. The New Jersey program also represented the least intensive of the selective-voluntary treatments. It included a placement effort and wage subsidy, but no training was provided directly by the program agency, and fewer than half of the experimentals were placed in OJT positions. Maine, which offered work preparation and unpaid work experience positions prior to the subsidized private sector placement, cost about $2,000 per experimental. Homemaker–Home Health Aide training cost from about $6,000 to $12,500 per experimental across the seven states, and Supported Work cost nearly $18,000 per experimental. Both provided actual training to participants and paid wages for work performed by participants as part of the training effort. Thus, as with the broad-coverage programs, increasing cost is a rough index of increasing intensity of employment preparation and training. (As indicated in Table 4.1, subsidized wages were included in the costs of all four programs and were particularly high for Supported Work and the Homemaker–Home Health Aide Demonstrations. This creates difficulties in comparing the costs of the four selective-voluntary programs with those of the broad-coverage programs.)

Earnings Impacts. Earnings impacts among the selective-voluntary demonstrations appear to have increased with cost. New Jersey, the least costly of the selective-voluntary programs, raised average earnings by $591 per year. Maine yielded an increase of $941 in average annual earnings. Homemaker–Home Health Aide training produced mixed results across its seven sites, with some showing only small effects, but average gains in annual earnings were nevertheless about $1,100. Earnings gains from Supported Work were about $1,400 in the second year of follow-up and $1,100 in the third year, although the latter annualized figure is calculated from only one quarter of data.[26]

---

26. Like all the other impact estimates in Table 4.1, except those for Homemaker–Home Health Aide training, the Supported Work earnings gains and welfare reductions are based on a sample consistent for all years of follow-up. In the original Supported Work study, this was not the case. Impacts for the first 18 months of follow-up were based on the maximum sample of 1,351 individuals. Data for many of these individuals were not available beyond 18 months, and impacts for the 19- to 27-month period were estimated using only an early cohort of 620 enrollees (MDRC, 1980, p. 59). A subsequent set of impact estimates (Grossman, Maynard, and Roberts, 1985, p. 71)—used in this chapter, with an adjustment to 1985 dollars—incorporated more observations at the end of follow-up, which were available from a final survey wave. For example, 1,069 sample

On the face of it, results for the selective-voluntary demonstrations appear to show a positive relationship between amount spent per experimental and average earnings impact per experimental—a relationship that was evidenced in the broad-coverage programs. The maximum earnings impacts for the broad-coverage programs were in the range of $500 to $650 per year for the most expensive systems. For a similar cost per experimental, New Jersey achieved a similar result, and the demonstrations with higher average costs showed larger average earnings impacts. This apparent continuity of the cost-impact relationship across both the broad-coverage and the selective-voluntary programs may be deceptive, however, given the discussion in Part II.

AFDC Impacts. Three of the four selective-voluntary programs achieved welfare savings. New Jersey reduced AFDC payments by $238 per experimental in the last year of follow-up, and Homemaker–Home Health Aide training saved $343 per experimental on average across sites. Savings for Supported Work were about $1,200 in the second year of follow-up and about $400 in the third year, although, as with earnings, that annualized figure is calculated from only one quarter of data.

Maine was the one selective-voluntary demonstration that did not have an impact on AFDC, despite its large earnings impact. The issues discussed in connection with Baltimore may have been at work in Maine. In addition, extensive pre-enrollment screening in Maine produced a sample that was less likely to stay on welfare than their predominantly long welfare histories might have suggested. In fact, among controls, half were off AFDC within two and a half years of the date of random assignment, even without the program's assistance.

In addition, in Maine the program consisted of a sequence of three distinct activities: preliminary training in job-seeking and job-holding, unpaid work experience, and actual placement into subsidized employment and training in the private sector. The length of this sequence, and the attractiveness with which the final placement may have been viewed by participants, may have increased welfare stays for some.[27]

---

members were used for the 25- to 27-month follow-up period, the last period with data for this full sample. As indicated earlier for Louisville, inflation to 1985 dollars may overstate the actual impacts that would have been achieved had the demonstration been run in the 1980s.

27. Finally, Maine was one of a small number of states where the AFDC standard of need exceeded the maximum grant and where the standard of need was used to determine supplemental grants to working recipients. As a result, the amount by which grants were reduced when someone went to work was lowered, and work incentives were increased.

These observations suggest important operational lessons. If administrators target more costly services to longer-term welfare recipients with the goal of obtaining welfare savings, this goal may be defeated by intensive screening for "employability," "motivation," or other characteristics heralding imminent departure from the welfare rolls. Also, a rich service offering may lengthen some welfare spells, possibly offsetting the overall welfare savings expected from the higher-cost intervention. Finally, the additional "waiting time" for complex and intensive service sequences will be greater than for simple job search, and, by its nature, intensive training will take longer to complete.

Trade-offs: Broad-Coverage versus Selective-Voluntary Programs

The evidence from broad-coverage experiments (reviewed earlier) suggests that, although even low-cost programs can produce sustained earnings gains, adding higher-cost components appears to increase average earnings impacts. The relationship between average cost and average welfare savings is less clear. The results for selective-voluntary demonstrations point in the same direction.

The discussion of average impacts has provided only some of the information of interest to those assessing the relative merits of low-cost and higher-cost services. We now turn to the questions of aggregate impact, savings for government budgets, and effects on poverty. The first two of these aspects of program impact provide ways of looking at effectiveness that take account of the differential cost of providing intensive services, thereby facilitating the comparison across the two categories of studies. The evidence presented tends to favor broad coverage with low- to moderate-cost services compared to a more narrow enrollment approach emphasizing higher-cost services.

However, aggregate impacts and budgetary savings are similar to average impacts in that all three look at estimates for an entire group of enrollees or eligibles. When we begin to look behind the overall impacts at differences in impact across subgroups and at effects on individual families, potential advantages of high-cost services again emerge. We therefore next examine the trade-off between achieving broad coverage through lower-cost services and targeting key disadvantaged subgroups with higher-cost services.

The question of effects on individual families brings us to a discussion of impacts on household income and poverty. From this perspective, a given overall impact may be viewed very differently depending on whether it results from some people getting earnings above the poverty line or a larger number being helped to find jobs that provide them with much lower earnings. Job quality, the duration of earnings impacts, and other outcomes affecting living standards also assume importance. The net result of this discussion is to suggest some potential trade-offs and to point to important questions for experimental research in the 1990s.

Aggregate Impacts. Higher-cost services may have greater *average* impact per enrollee, but low-cost services may produce larger *aggregate* program impacts simply because they can be made available to a much larger number of individuals for the same total cost. Program administrators, operating within generally fixed budgets, may want to know whether allocating a significant portion of their budget to higher-cost services for a relatively small proportion of program enrollees will increase or decrease the *total* amount of earnings gains and welfare savings.

This can be conceptualized as the amount of impact obtained from a one-dollar investment—a figure calculated by dividing Table 4.1's impact estimate (using the last follow-up year) by the cost estimate.[28] Omitting West Virginia and Cook County, the earnings impact/cost ratios are lowest for the programs with the highest per-experimental cost. Each dollar invested produced a gain of 47 cents in Maine, 12 cents in Homemaker–Home Health Aide training, and 6 cents in Supported Work. In contrast, programs costing in the middle range (that is, Virginia, San Diego I, SWIM, Baltimore, and New Jersey) all have impact/cost ratios between about 50 and 75 cents on the dollar for annual earnings. The low-cost Arkansas program and both Louisville programs yielded two dollars or more on the dollar. Thus, on this measure, cost effectiveness appears to decrease from low-cost to higher-cost systems, apparently because the addition of higher-cost components as enrichments to the basic job search and work experience model encounters decreasing returns.

On the welfare side, Homemaker–Home Health Aide training had reductions in AFDC payments for the last follow-up year of 4 cents per dollar of cost, and Supported Work had reductions of 2 cents. Maine

28. These ratios could also be calculated on the basis of the present value of earnings gains or welfare savings. Because of limited follow-up, however, most of the present value will derive from a projection of the final year's impact, yielding parallel results.

and Baltimore had no welfare effects. In Virginia, San Diego I, SWIM, and New Jersey, a dollar yielded from about 25 to 60 cents in annual payment reductions. In Louisville I and Arkansas, this ratio was over a dollar. Louisville II had no welfare effects. Thus, as with earnings, the addition of higher-cost components to a system may meet with decreasing returns.

These results have two implications, the importance of which depends on how much an administrator values increasing aggregate impact versus, for example, assuring that earnings for those served increase by more than a small amount, or successfully reaching long-term recipients. First, the results imply that a program operator whose resources are not even sufficient to provide job search and other low-cost services to all program-eligibles may well reduce total program impact by diverting funds to higher-cost services for some enrollees: impacts per enrollee served would be larger, but the total number of enrollees served would have to be dramatically reduced. For example, enrolling one person in a wage subsidy program costing the same as Maine's would mean reducing enrollment by nearly five individuals in broad-coverage job search costing the same as in the Virginia program. As a result of the shift, the operator would then obtain a $941 aggregate impact (third year, Maine), but would lose about $1,260 (third year, Virginia, multiplied by the shift in enrollment). The aggregate impact of the program would decrease by the difference of more than $300.

Second, program operators who have more than enough resources to provide job search assistance and other low-cost services to all eligibles may face decreasing returns in allocating additional funds to some kinds of higher-cost services. How much returns might decrease is uncertain. Evidence from the broad-coverage programs is ambiguous, given the confounding site differences. Evidence from the selective-voluntary demonstrations suggests that, in achieving aggregate impacts, the most intensive kinds of training may be relatively inefficient, at least in the forms tested. However, they may be better at producing high average impacts.

As previously mentioned, however, the relevance of both of these implications to JOBS' administrators is not clear, since the high-cost programs evaluated to date provided very little education. This represents a major unknown and could substantially revise these trade-offs. Also, as noted later, the evidence on who benefits from different services further complicates the trade-off. More fundamentally, because of the noncomparabilities raised in Part II, this analysis of aggregate impacts is subject to the same uncertainties as that of average impacts: the cross-study comparisons raise questions more than they provide definite answers.

Savings for Government Budgets. Policymakers also wish to know whether the impacts of a program produce reductions in expenditures that exceed the program cost. From this perspective, most of the dollar costs of welfare-to-work programs are the costs of delivering services, including operating expenses and allowances (and sometimes wages) paid to participants, less the costs that would normally be incurred for enrollees in the absence of the program. The measurable benefits are largely composed of savings in public assistance outlays (AFDC, Medicaid, and Food Stamps), reductions in other social service costs, and increased taxes (from increased earnings). Impacts on AFDC payments were essential in producing returns to government budgets that offset costs. Thus, for Maine and Baltimore, which had no welfare savings, the programs cost more than they saved.

Estimates of net budgetary benefits reinforce the conclusions reached in the discussion of aggregate impacts. Of the nine broad-coverage programs, seven at least broke even or produced positive returns to government budgets within five years of enrolling a group of welfare recipients.[29] For both the least and most costly of these programs, welfare savings and other fiscal effects were sufficient to offset costs.

The services studied in selective-voluntary demonstrations differed from the job search and work experience of the lower-cost broad-coverage programs in making an explicit up-front investment in anticipation of slower, but larger, eventual returns. For these four demonstrations, only the least costly (New Jersey) produced net benefits for

29. Formal benefit-cost estimates, in which impacts were projected to five years after random assignment, were made for all the broad-coverage programs except the two Louisville programs. Calculations from the published impact tables for the Louisville programs indicate that both would have broken even in the short run. The two programs that did not at least break even were Baltimore and West Virginia.

An alternative frame of reference for estimating benefits and costs—often referred to as the "taxpayer perspective"—differs from the budget perspective discussed here by including as a benefit the value of the work produced by participants in work experience activities. This somewhat broader perspective does not fundamentally change the story presented here, but it does shift Baltimore to the break-even point and provides taxpayers in West Virginia with a positive net present value. Within this taxpayer perspective, the Maine and Homemaker–Home Health Aide demonstrations also come closer to breaking even.

government budgets in the short run. As indicated above, Maine did not break even. Homemaker–Home Health Aide training, even with its welfare savings, fell short, by a wide margin, of making back its relatively high costs. Supported Work was projected to pass the break-even point eventually. Producing returns for government budgets from the most intensive training activities was therefore less certain and required a longer investment horizon.

Coverage versus Targeting. The discussion of aggregate impacts and net budgetary benefits showed the advantages of broad coverage. But the discussion did not distinguish among different groups of AFDC recipients. As noted earlier, there are wide differences in the expected duration of welfare receipt within the AFDC population. Most AFDC families spend a relatively short time on the rolls. But at any given time, most of those on welfare are in the midst of long spells. Achieving impacts on long-term and potential long-term recipient groups could therefore have a relatively large impact on AFDC caseloads and costs. For this reason, program impacts on these groups are particularly important, as reflected in the specifically stated goal of the JOBS legislation to reduce long-term dependence on AFDC.

Subgroup results for welfare savings differed from subgroup results for earnings gains. The evaluations of broad-coverage programs have produced evidence that *welfare reductions* are, in fact, obtained largely for long-term recipients.[30] Among groups *most* at risk of extended time on the rolls, however, the low- to moderate-cost programs may have difficulty producing sustained *earnings gains.* Thus, for example, earnings gains have not been found consistently for clients who combine poor work experience with long welfare history and other barriers to employment. This suggests that for individuals whose overall level of disadvantagedness is greater than some threshold level, low-cost services may be ineffective in raising earnings.

Careful targeting of intensive services to long-term welfare groups may be a way to economize on program resources while increasing the rate of success for very disadvantaged program enrollees. By addressing skills deficits, the higher-cost services might increase the ratio of earnings gains to welfare reductions for the most disadvantaged while still yielding the AFDC savings expected for these groups. If these two effects

---

30. For a more complete analysis of subgroup impacts in five broad-coverage programs, see Friedlander (1988).

can be demonstrated, higher-cost services may be regarded not as substitutes for job search and work experience but as specific targeting devices embedded in larger programs that rely on lower-cost services to achieve broad coverage.

An important question for future research is whether more intensive services, especially education, can work for disadvantaged subgroups more effectively than low-cost ones, as it is hoped. The targeting plan of Supported Work may serve as a prototype for future studies. This demonstration focused exclusively on long-term AFDC recipients with weak recent work records. The large earnings impacts found for this group, which averaged more than 8.5 years on the rolls, give the demonstration special significance. Similar results on a larger scale would support targeting as an optimal intervention strategy and increase projections of the overall impact of welfare-to-work programs.

With these considerations in mind, results from the SWIM demonstration take on added significance (see Hamilton and Friedlander, 1989). SWIM did make some assignments to education and also used a targeting plan for those assignments.[31] For *recipients* (a group that is, overall, more disadvantaged than AFDC *applicants* and that made up about 60 percent of the SWIM caseload) during the second year of follow-up, earnings impacts averaged $889 per experimental (50 percent more than controls' earnings) and welfare savings were $608 (13 percent less than controls' average grants). In this case, a broad-coverage, relatively large-scale program achieved impacts on the more dependent half of the caseload of a magnitude comparable to the impacts of the much smaller selective demonstrations, despite all the factors outlined earlier (for example, lower participation and the inclusion of nonparticipants in the estimates) that reduce average impacts in these studies. Moreover, it achieved these impacts at moderate cost, with net savings for government budgets and an increase in one measure of income—namely, earnings gains less reductions in welfare payments—for recipient enroll-

31. Education was assigned *after* a program enrollee had completed an initial job search component and had completed an unpaid work assignment without obtaining employment. This fixed sequence of activities was a targeting plan in that it encouraged those who could to find work or otherwise leave welfare during the low-cost, up-front activities, before the higher-cost activity was assigned. SWIM also permitted enrollees who were pursuing their education when they entered the program to fulfill their program participation requirement by continuing in those courses, provided the courses met certain criteria.

ees.[32] This result suggests the importance of determining whether these impacts can be replicated. The study of other large-scale programs that place even greater emphasis on education and training for long-term AFDC recipients is also a high priority for future experimental research.

Impact on Household Income and Poverty. The fourth and final question concerns the relative impact of low-cost and higher-cost services on income and poverty. Impacts on poverty depend largely on the magnitude of average earnings gains and the degree to which they are taxed away by offsetting reductions in welfare payments. One must also look behind the average impacts to the quality of employment that program graduates obtain.

Job search and other low-cost services are not expected to increase earning power, so even when participants find jobs they may mostly be low-paying, without opportunity for future growth and the kind of on-the-job skill investment that promotes retention. For a training program to get a family out of poverty through the earnings of the enrollee, it must lead to full-time jobs that pay far better than the minimum wage, and the jobs must be stable and long-lasting.[33] Investment in education and training is generally expected to have greater effect than lower-cost services on wages, hours, and employment stability.

The findings on wages and hours are suggestive but far from conclusive. In part, the uncertainty stems from the fact that only Supported Work and Homemaker–Home Health Aide training carried out followup surveys that could collect wage data. All the other experiments relied primarily on earnings records reported through local Unemployment Insurance systems, and these give only the total amount earned during a quarter. Nevertheless, even without the ability to separate out impacts on wage rates, weekly hours, and weeks worked, a partial picture has emerged from the completed studies. For the broad-coverage programs, the estimated increases in average earnings came about largely through increases in the number of individuals who worked rather than through increases in the amount they earned while employed.[34] Results reported

32. It is unclear which features of SWIM accounted for these results: its continuous and strictly enforced participation requirement, the particular service sequence, the extensive experience of program staff, or other characteristics of the environment and caseload.

33. Ellwood (1988) calculates that a representative single mother with two children would require a full-time job at nearly $6 per hour to exceed poverty line income, figuring in reductions in AFDC and Food Stamps, the Earned Income Tax Credit, and child care expenses during work hours (pp. 138–139).

34. In Arkansas, Virginia, SWIM, and the two Louisville programs, increases in employ-

for the two most costly broad-coverage programs did indicate statistically significant increases in the percentage of experimentals earning
$5,000 or more a year: in Baltimore, there was a 3.8 percentage point
gain in the share of experimentals earning more than $6,000 per year;
in SWIM, there was a 4.6 percentage point increase in the share of
applicants and recipients earning $5,000 or more per year and a 3.2
percentage point increase in the share of recipients earning $10,000 or
more per year (Friedlander, 1987; Hamilton and Friedlander, 1989).
Only the results for Baltimore suggested increases in hourly wages or
weekly hours among employed persons, however.

Findings from the selective-voluntary demonstrations suggest that
higher-cost activities usually increase the earnings of employed persons
somewhat. For example, the Maine wage subsidy program produced
earnings gains three-quarters of which were attributed to higher wages
or weekly hours for employed experimentals rather than to an increase
in employment. The corresponding figure for New Jersey was even
greater.[35] For the Homemaker–Home Health Aide experiments, however, sites with earnings gains got them largely from increases in employment. Some gains in wage rates were found, but not uniformly
across states and not always in the states with earnings gains.[36] The most
complete analysis of this issue has been performed for Supported Work.
For this demonstration, it has been estimated that wage increases ac-

---

ment accounted for more than 80 percent of the total earnings increase in the last observed
follow-up year; in San Diego and Baltimore the same figure was about two-thirds. These
estimates were obtained by comparing the ratio "impact on employment/control employment rate" with the ratio "impact on earnings/control mean earnings" in the same period.

35. Auspos, Cave, and Long (1988), p. xx. Only 7 percent of the earnings gain came
from jobs found by persons who would not have worked. Another 19 percent was associated with an increase in the number of quarters in which employment was reported.
Three-quarters of the earnings impact therefore stemmed from a combination of higher
wages or longer weekly work hours. Analogous calculations were performed for New
Jersey on the portion of the sample for whom data are available into the second follow-up
year. These show quite similar amounts of employment for experimentals and controls,
making almost 90 percent of the earnings impact attributable to greater earnings per
quarter employed for experimentals. See Freedman, Bryant, and Cave (1988), p. xxii, for
the data that went into these calculations.

36. Increases in employment rates of over 10 percentage points for non-demonstration
jobs were found in four of the seven states for "post-demonstration year 2," which corre-
sponds approximately to the third year of follow-up starting from random assignment.
These four states were among the five states with earnings gains in that year. Only two
of the states with earnings increases showed an increase in wage rates of trainees employed
in non-demonstration work. See Enns, Bell, and Flanagan (1987), table III.5, p. 48; table
III.3, p. 44; and table III.8, p. 53.

counted for 42 percent of the total long-term increase in earnings, and an increase in hours accounted for another 18 percent (Masters, 1981, p. 616). It is important to add, however, that even in Supported Work, the dollar amount of the wage increase was not large.[37]

The issue of job stability and the persistence of earnings and welfare impacts has not been resolved either. The data do show that experimental-control differences in earnings for Maine and Supported Work were still continuing at least into the third year from the date of enrollment, and that the same is likely to be true for Homemaker–Home Health Aide training. But, surprisingly, all the low- and moderate-cost programs that produced earnings gains (and have two to three years of follow-up available) also show that those impacts hold up over the same interval.[38] Among programs that achieved welfare savings, these impacts also appear to persist for low-cost as well as higher-cost programs. Without longer follow-up it is still an open issue whether high-cost interventions produce longer-lasting impacts.

Family living standards and well-being depend on factors other than earnings and welfare income. For example, working may entail new expenses, such as day care and transportation. Work by a single parent may also have broader effects on the family. Some of these may be positive, such as those stemming from the parents' increased self-confidence and self-esteem; others may be negative, for example, if working increases family stress. In general, little is known about the actual impact of welfare-to-work programs on these outcomes.

Some people view a program's effect on poverty as its paramount justification. There is evidence that some of the programs studied increased income, but there is little evidence that they reduced the prevalence of poverty. Even Supported Work, with its large earnings impact, produced only a small and not statistically significant reduction in the number of experimental families living below the poverty line. In this, as in some other programs, earnings gains were substantially offset by welfare savings (see MDRC, 1980, p. 71). In sum, while prior expecta-

37. Wages rose about 12 percent, from $3.69 to $4.12, in current dollars (Masters, 1981, p. 616).

38. Earnings impacts lasted at least into the third year in Arkansas, Virginia, and Louisville II, as well as in Baltimore. Only two years of data are available for SWIM, but earnings gains there appear likely to continue at least into the third year. The longer-term results for New Jersey are not yet known, and extended follow-up data for San Diego I and Louisville II are not available. The Chicago and West Virginia experiments showed no earnings effects to begin with. Whether even longer follow-up would reveal differences between high-cost and low-cost programs is, of course, uncertain.

tions and some evidence suggest that higher-cost services can have a greater impact on income, by affecting job quality and stability, collectively the studies suggest that welfare-to-work programs for AFDC single parents may have to be complemented by other policy tools (for example, an increase in the minimum wage or Earned Income Tax Credit and increased child support collections) to reach the goal of not only reducing welfare receipt but also reducing poverty.

At this time, the uncertainties remaining from prior experiments constitute an important gap in knowledge of effects on income and poverty. Experimental studies of the JOBS programs of the 1990s can close this gap by collecting information about job quality—hourly wages, weekly hours, medical insurance and other fringe benefits, specific on-the-job training, and promotion possibilities—and by observing sample members for a longer follow-up period (at least five years). Given the high cost of the follow-up surveys needed to obtain information about job characteristics, such surveys cannot be part of all experimental studies. But priority for survey resources should go to studies of programs emphasizing higher-cost services.

Part IV: Conclusions and an Agenda for Future Research

Limited resources will force program planners to choose among three broad approaches in designing their JOBS system: operating a large-scale program providing relatively low-cost services; operating a small-scale program providing higher-cost services; using a mixed approach, with low-cost components for certain groups and higher-cost services for others. The studies completed to date do not provide definitive answers on whether introducing more expensive services, particularly those encouraged in the JOBS legislation, will increase program effectiveness. They do, however, suggest that the choice among these three options may not be clear-cut: each may be superior in achieving a different set of objectives. While the results of the research can help in assessing the trade-offs, allocation of resources may ultimately be guided largely by the relative importance planners assign to competing program goals.

The completed experimental research has provided information on a number of questions, but on others there is still considerable uncertainty. Table 4.2 summarizes what the key trade-offs between low-cost

Table 4.2 Low-cost and higher-cost services: Trade-offs, knowledge gaps, and strategies for field experiments

Issue	Low-cost services	Higher-cost services	Research strategy
Coverage versus targeting	Feasible for large-scale implementation	Subsidized structured work experience and training probably only feasible as smaller program components. Education may be feasible for wider use in large-scale programs	Study localities that intend heavy use of education in broad-coverage programs. Examine participation rates and constraints on participation
	May reach large numbers with available resources	Budget constraints will limit number served. JOBS targeting criteria and local priority-group schemes must be validated by confirming that services are effective for those groups	Plan experimental design to allow adequate samples for estimates of impacts for relevant target groups. Test alternative standards of performance to ensure that they do not establish incentives to focus on groups with small expected impacts
	Inconsistent earnings gains for the most disadvantaged owing to a possible threshold effect	Potentially greater impacts on the most disadvantaged	Study sites with policy of working with disadvantaged enrollees and plan for impact estimates for those groups

Table 4.2 (cont.)

Issue	Low-cost services	Higher-cost services	Research strategy
Potential diseconomies	Possible dilution of service content in seeking broad coverage with inadequate resources	Monitoring service quality and participant completion of education and training courses may be costly	On-site observation of service quality and collection of data on receipt of degrees or certificates from schools and training providers
Short-term impacts	Rapid job entry	Education may delay job entry	Compare short-term impacts. Differential impact designs particularly useful
Quality of impacts	Increase employment but not earnings of employed persons	Results suggest some increase in wage rates, hours of work, and job stability	Confirm by collecting survey data on job quality and other outcomes where possible. Differential impact designs particularly useful
Duration of impacts	Impacts persist through 2–3 years of follow-up and probably longer	Impacts persist through 2–3 years of follow-up and probably longer. Unknown whether they last longer than those for low-cost services	Track earnings and welfare receipt for at least 5 years. Differential impact designs particularly useful

AFDC impacts and taxpayer savings	Welfare reductions commensurate with generally modest expenditures. Greater impact per dollar of program cost implies larger aggregate caseload impact from a given outlay. Taxpayers usually break even or reap net saving in the short run	The most expensive services appear to break even in the long run, but evidence is incomplete	Track earnings and welfare receipt for at least 5 years
	Most welfare impacts come from longer-term recipients, but low-cost services may not achieve full potential impact with these groups	May increase welfare impacts for long-term recipients	Study sites with policy of working with long-term recipient groups and plan for impact estimates for those groups
Poverty impacts	Greater earnings impact per dollar of program cost implies larger aggregate earnings increase from a given budget, but few enrollees enter higher-bracket earnings	Some enrollees enter higher-bracket earnings, but evidence is incomplete	Examine impacts on earnings brackets. Supplement with estimates of impact on family formation and various sources of income (e.g., health insurance, Food Stamps, Unemployment Compensation) from survey where possible

and higher-cost services are believed to be, where the major uncertainties remain, and how experimental research can confirm and add to our knowledge.

The low- to moderate-cost, broad-coverage programs discussed in this chapter have shown clear impacts on earnings and to a lesser extent on welfare receipt, although effects on neither have been dramatic. The selective-voluntary programs also showed positive results. When we look across all the broad-coverage studies, the average impacts suggest that the programs that include some more expensive components seem to produce the largest earnings gains. For welfare savings, the results were less clear. When costs are considered, however, we find that the lower-cost programs produced larger *aggregate* impacts for a given budget and yielded quicker and more consistent budgetary savings for taxpayers than the programs that focused on more costly activities.

However, striving for broad coverage with lower-cost services also entails risks. The Cook County experience suggests that there may be a point beyond which resources are spread so thin in an effort to cover a large caseload that the content of services is excessively diluted, undercutting the chance for any program impact. In addition, when we look beyond the aggregate numbers and average impacts to the effects on individuals, we find that low-cost programs have failed to achieve some policy objectives. Employed graduates of low-cost programs, despite their demonstrated earnings increases, for the most part remain at levels of earnings below the poverty line. Moreover, low-cost services do not appear consistently to produce earnings gains for the most disadvantaged. For these groups, low-cost services may be hampered by a threshold effect. Partly for this reason, low-cost services cannot be expected to bring about radical changes in work behavior and welfare receipt for the AFDC caseload.

Higher-cost services may better achieve some of these goals. The selective-voluntary demonstrations examined in this chapter produced relatively large earnings gains and welfare savings per experimental. Higher-cost services show greater ability to improve job quality and to raise a family's earnings above a minimum target level. They may also produce earnings increases for the most disadvantaged welfare recipients. The cost of this greater individual effectiveness is a great reduction in the number of individuals who can be served. In the selective-voluntary demonstrations, impact per program dollar spent tended to be relatively low, implying that a given budget allotment would produce larger aggregate impacts if it were used to provide low-cost services to many rather than higher-cost services to a relative few.

At the very heart of the issue of service intensity is the presumption that the capacity of low-cost services to produce *more* total job entries will be offset by the capacity of higher-cost services to lead to *better*, more stable jobs. Unfortunately, evidence that high-cost services improve wage rates and other aspects of job quality is incomplete, and the length of follow-up available from the concluded experiments is insufficient to judge whether, as commonly supposed, the impacts of high-cost services last longer.

We have noted many uncertainties in making comparisons across studies, uncertainties stemming from differences in services offered, enrollee characteristics, local conditions, and research designs. In addition, there may be limits on the extent to which the higher-cost services tested in the selective-voluntary demonstrations can be expanded and still achieve the same results. Further, it is not known whether the results discussed in this chapter would hold up for women with younger children—a group that is required to participate in the JOBS program. But, if the pattern of results suggested here holds generally for higher-cost components of large-scale programs, then planners in all but quite richly endowed programs may face a choice between, on the one hand, maximizing aggregate impacts on earnings and welfare savings and, on the other, focusing on obtaining greater increases in the living standards of a relatively small number of AFDC recipients. One route to reducing the starkness of this trade-off is to adopt a mixed strategy—in effect, the third option outlined at the beginning of this chapter—using a JOBS system that combines a broad-coverage, low-cost approach with carefully targeted higher cost components.

A critical unknown facing administrators using this calculus is the effect of providing education for persons with poor basic skills in the context of broad-coverage systems. In many localities, the existence of community colleges and other institutions may make education the intensive service most feasibly provided to substantial numbers of enrollees, and may limit its cost. Expanded use of education is encouraged under the JOBS legislation, but hard knowledge about the feasibility, cost, and effectiveness of education in large-scale welfare-to-work programs is lacking. We are, in effect, in a position with respect to education similar to the one we were in ten years ago for low-cost services: the basic questions have yet to be addressed rigorously.

As shown in Table 4.2, two kinds of field experiments can help fill the gaps in knowledge. First, we need *net* impact and cost estimates for broad-coverage programs that provide higher-cost activities—education and occupational skills training, but also more intensive case management and assessment—for significant numbers of individuals in long-term and potential long-term AFDC subgroups, especially those key subgroups named in the JOBS legislation.[39] Such experiments would be similar to those broad-coverage evaluations examined in this chapter in that they would compare a JOBS program experimental group to a non-JOBS control group.

Second, given the various competing explanations that inevitably arise when comparing results across locations and studies, it will be important to implement well-designed *differential* impact studies, in which sample members in the same location are randomly assigned to different service approaches within a JOBS program. Such studies can be used for head-to-head tests of high-intensity human capital investment approaches featuring education and training compared with (1) low-intensity approaches featuring job search and placement, or (2) high-intensity approaches stressing participation in the labor force. The results will be important in confirming and refining—with rigor and for key subgroups—conclusions drawn from comparisons across a larger and more varied group of new impact studies.[40]

39. In order to avoid a reduction in federal matching rates, states must spend at least 55 percent of JOBS monies on families with the following characteristics: the family received AFDC in 36 of the preceding 60 months; the custodial parent is under age 24 and has no high school diploma or equivalent or has had little or no work in the preceding year; the youngest child is within two years of ineligibility for AFDC. JOBS prescribes education (with some exceptions) for custodial parents under age 20 who have not finished high school, regardless of the age of their children. Education may also be the prescribed service for adults age 20 or older who do not have a high school diploma and fall below a basic literacy level, although states may choose to provide other services for this group.

40. Among the studies discussed in this chapter, there were three differential impact designs. The most successful was in San Diego I, where the full program sequence of job search followed by unpaid work experience was compared not only to a control group but also to a second experimental group offered only job search. It was found that the work activity added 16 percent to net operating cost but more than doubled earnings impact and increased short-term welfare savings by more than 40 percent. Researchers urged caution in generalizing this result because all of the effect was observed for a portion of the sample enrolled during a weak but rapidly improving labor market (Goldman, Friedlander, and Long, 1986, p. 64). In Cook County, a three-group design similar to the San Diego design was utilized. The full program produced only a small net impact, however, so there was no measurable differential effect. In Virginia, a second experimental

If this research agenda is to be pursued, the experiments must have certain other features. First, the budget for experimental field research will best be spent not in studying a random, representative selection of local programs, but in examining a set of mature programs that assign a significant number of enrollees from the key subgroups to the higher-cost services of interest.[41] Second, to interpret the impact estimates, data will be needed both on the extent and duration of participation in education and training (for controls as well as experimentals) and on the quality of those services. Without such data, it would be impossible to confirm that higher-cost services have been given a fair test. Similarly, obtaining some test data measuring academic achievement would be essential in determining whether the education component had achieved its intermediate goal of improving basic skills.

Third, since some of the most important expectations regarding higher-cost services concern durability and quality of impacts, it will be important to follow sample members longer (that is, for five years or more) than has been the rule in previous studies and, wherever possible, to collect data on wage rates, work hours, fringe benefits, on-the-job training and promotion opportunities, and other aspects of job quality.[42]

Several field experiments along these lines are already under way or being planned.[43] Complementing these existing studies is the major evaluation of JOBS, recently funded by the U.S. Department of Health and Human Services. This ten-site study is being specifically designed to

---

group was created to estimate the differential impact of education and training services. Many members of the second experimental group entered education and training on their own through community providers outside the program, wiping out the expected activity differential. This surprising degree of self-initiated activity, although an important finding that influenced later work, made moot the differential impact computation.

41. The number should be large enough to provide both substantively and statistically meaningful impact estimates. This restriction on kind of site is another way of saying that it is of greater interest to address a specific set of hypotheses about welfare-to-work programs than to estimate the national impact on the JOBS provisions of the Family Support Act. This agenda for experimental research would be designed to help improve JOBS programs in the future, not to determine how well JOBS as a whole worked in the past. Other kinds of research need not necessarily be bound by these same objectives.

42. Most of the experiments discussed in this chapter obtained earnings data from state Unemployment Insurance reporting systems, which do not normally record hourly wage rates, weekly hours, or other job characteristics. Surveys, a much more expensive method of data collection, are required to obtain such information.

43. See Gueron and Pauly (1991) for a summary of the design and results to date from studies in progress.

address the unanswered questions about the effectiveness of higher-cost services identified in this chapter, as well as other key open issues.

The studies examined in this chapter constitute "round one" in the experimental evaluation of welfare-to-work programs. Apart from their substantive findings, these studies have demonstrated that large-scale experimental field testing is feasible under certain conditions and can make significant contributions to the formulation of policy. But experimentation is difficult: Success hinges critically on sustained collaboration among policymakers, researchers, and local program administrators and interest groups. Care must therefore be taken to see that future experiments answer well the most pressing policy questions. Of the many issues facing welfare-to-work programs in the 1990s, determining the relative effectiveness of higher-cost services is not only one of the most important but also one that is well suited to investigation with the experimental method. Providing rigorous information on this issue should be a priority of "round two" of experimental studies.

References

Auspos, Patricia, George Cave, and David Long. 1988. *Maine: Final Report on the Training Opportunities in the Private Sector Program.* New York: Manpower Demonstration Research Corporation, April.

Auspos, Patricia, George Cave, Fred Doolittle, and Gregory Hoerz. 1989. *Implementing JOBSTART: A Demonstration for School Dropouts in the JTPA System.* New York: Manpower Demonstration Research Corporation, June.

Bane, Mary Jo, and David T. Ellwood. 1983. "The Dynamics of Dependence: The Routes to Self-Sufficiency." Cambridge, Mass.: Urban Systems Engineering, Inc., June.

Betsey, Charles L., Robinson G. Hollister, and Mary R. Papageorgiou, eds. 1985. *Youth Employment and Training Programs: The YEDPA Years.* Washington, D.C.: National Academy Press.

Burtless, Gary. 1989. "The Effect of Reform on Employment, Earnings, and Income." In *Welfare Policy for the 1990s,* ed. Phoebe H. Cottingham and David T. Ellwood. Cambridge, Mass.: Harvard University Press.

Cella, Margot. *Operational Costs of Demonstration Activities.* 1987. Cambridge, Mass.: Abt Associates, Inc., December.

Dickinson, Katherine P., Terry R. Johnson, and Richard W. West. 1987.

"An Analysis of the Sensitivity of Quasi-Experimental Net Impact Estimates of CETA Programs." *Evaluation Review*, 11 (no. 4, August):
452–472.

Ellwood, David T. 1986. *Targeting "Would-Be" Long-Term Recipients of AFDC*.
Princeton, N.J.: Mathematica Policy Research, Inc., January.

———. 1988. *Poor Support: Poverty in the American Family*. New York: Basic
Books.

Enns, John H., Stephen H. Bell, and Kathleen L. Flanagan. 1987. *Trainee
Employment and Earnings*. Cambridge, Mass.: Abt Associates, Inc., December.

Fraker, Thomas, and Rebecca Maynard. 1987. "The Adequacy of Comparison Group Designs for Evaluations of Employment-Related Programs."
Journal of Human Resources, 22 (no. 2, Spring): 194–227.

Freedman, Stephen, Jan Bryant, and George Cave. 1988. *New Jersey: Final
Report on the Grant Diversion Project*. New York: Manpower Demonstration Research Corporation, November.

Friedlander, Daniel. 1987. *Maryland: Supplemental Report on the Baltimore
Options Program*. New York: Manpower Demonstration Research Corporation, October.

———. 1988. *Subgroup Impacts and Performance Indicators for Selected Welfare
Employment Programs*. New York: Manpower Demonstration Research
Corporation, August.

Goldman, Barbara, Daniel Friedlander, and David Long. 1986. *Final Report
on the San Diego Job Search and Work Experience Demonstration*. New York:
Manpower Demonstration Research Corporation, February.

Gordon, Anne, and John Burghardt. 1990. *The Minority Female Single Parent
Demonstration: Report on Short-Term Economic Impacts*. New York: Rocke-
feller Foundation.

Grossman, Jean, Rebecca A. Maynard, and Judith Roberts. 1985. *Reanalysis
of the Effects of Selected Employment and Training Programs for Welfare
Recipients*. Princeton, N.J.: Mathematica Policy Research, Inc., October.

Grossman, Jean Baldwin, and Audrey Mirsky. 1985. *A Survey of Recent Programs Designed to Reduce Long-Term Welfare Dependency*. Princeton, N.J.:
Mathematica Policy Research, Inc., April.

Gueron, Judith M., and Edward Pauly. 1991. *From Welfare to Work*. New
York: Russell Sage Foundation.

Hamilton, Gayle, and Daniel Friedlander. 1989. *Final Report on the Saturation
Work Initiative Model in San Diego*. New York: Manpower Demonstration
Research Corporation, November.

Heckman, James J., and V. Joseph Hotz. 1989. "Choosing among Alternative Nonexperimental Methods for Estimating the Impact of Social Pro-

grams: The Case of Manpower Training." *Journal of the American Statistical Association,* 84 (no. 408, December): 862–874.

Heckman, James J., V. Joseph Hotz, and Marcelo Dabos. 1987. "Do We Need Experimental Data to Evaluate the Impact of Manpower Training on Earnings?" *Evaluation Review,* 11 (no. 4, August): 395–427.

Hollister, Robinson G., Jr., and Rebecca A. Maynard. 1984. "The Impacts of Supported Work on AFDC Recipients." In *The National Supported Work Demonstration,* ed. Robinson G. Hollister, Jr., Peter Kemper, and Rebecca A. Maynard. Madison: University of Wisconsin Press.

Job Training Longitudinal Survey Research Advisory Panel. 1985. *Recommendations of the Job Training Longitudinal Survey Research Advisory Panel.* Report prepared for the Office of Strategic Planning and Policy Development, Employment and Training Administration, U.S. Department of Labor. Washington, D.C.: U.S. Department of Labor.

LaLonde, Robert J. 1986. "Evaluating the Econometric Evaluations of Training Programs with Experimental Data." *American Economic Review,* 76 (no. 4, September): 604–620.

LaLonde, Robert J., and Rebecca Maynard. 1987. "How Precise Are Evaluations of Employment and Training Programs? Evidence from a Field Experiment." *Evaluation Review,* 11 (no. 4, August): 428–451.

Manpower Demonstration Research Corporation. 1980. *Summary and Findings of the National Supported Work Demonstration.* Cambridge, Mass.: Ballinger.

Masters, Stanley. 1981. "The Effects of Supported Work on the Earnings and Transfer Payments of Its AFDC Target Group." *Journal of Human Resources,* 16 (no. 4, Fall): 600–636.

Moffitt, Robert. 1987. "Work and the U.S. Welfare System: A Review." Report prepared for the U.S. Department of Health and Human Services, Office of the Assistant Secretary for Planning and Evaluation, Washington, D.C., October.

PART II

The Design of Evaluations

5 Randomization and Social Policy Evaluation

James J. Heckman

In this chapter I consider the benefits and limitations of *randomized* social experimentation as a tool for evaluating social programs.[1] The argument for social experimentation is by now familiar. Available cross-section and time-series data often possess insufficient variability in critical explanatory variables to enable analysts to develop convincing estimates of the impacts of social programs on target outcome variables. By collecting data to induce more variation in the explanatory variables, more precise estimates of policy impacts are possible. In addition, controlled variation in explanatory variables can make endogenous variables exogenous; that is, it can induce independent variation in observed variables relative to unobserved variables. Social experiments induce variation by controlling the way data are collected. Randomization is one way to induce extra variation, but it is by no means the only way or even necessarily the best way to achieve the desired variation.

The original case for social experimentation took as its point of departure the Haavelmo (1944)–Marschak (1953)–Tinbergen (1956) social planning paradigm. Social science knowledge was thought to be sufficiently advanced to be able to identify basic behavioral relationships which, when estimated, could be used to evaluate the impacts of a whole host of social programs, none of which had actually been implemented at the time of the evaluation. The "structural equation" approach to social policy evaluation promised to enable analysts to simulate a wide array of counterfactuals that could be the basis for "optimal" social poli-

1. Throughout this chapter I refrain from restating familiar arguments about the limitations of social experiments and focus on a problem not treated in the literature on this topic. See Cook and Campbell (1979), the papers in Hausman and Wise (1985a), and the other chapters in this volume for statements on problems of attrition, spillover effects, and so forth.

cymaking. The goal of social experimentation as envisioned by Conlisk and Watts (1969) and Conlisk (1973) was to develop better estimates of the structural equations needed to perform the simulation of counterfactuals.

The original proponents of the experimental method in economics focused on the inability of cross-section studies of labor supply to isolate "income" and "substitution" effects needed to estimate the impact of negative income taxes (NIT) on labor supply. Experiments were designed to induce greater variation in wages and incomes across individuals to afford better estimation of critical policy parameters. The original goal of these experiments was not to evaluate a specific set of NIT programs but to estimate parameters that could be used to assess the impacts of those and many other possible programs.

As the NIT experiments were implemented, their administrators began to expect less from them. Attention focused on evaluations of specific treatment effects actually in place. (See Cain, 1975.) Extrapolation from and interpolation between the estimated treatment effects took the place of counterfactual policy simulations based on estimated structural parameters as the method of choice for evaluating proposed programs not actually implemented. (See Hausman and Wise, 1985b.)

The recent case for randomized social experiments represents a dramatic retreat from the ambitious program of "optimal" social policy analysis that was never fully embraced by most economists and was not embraced at all by other social scientists. Considerable skepticism has recently been expressed about the value of econometric or statistical methods for estimating the impacts of specific social programs or the parameters of "structural" equations required to simulate social programs not yet in place. Influential studies by LaLonde (1986) and Fraker and Maynard (1987) have convinced many that econometric and statistical methods are incapable of estimating true program impacts from nonrandomized data.

Recent advocates of social experiments are more modest in their ambitions than were the original proponents. They propose to use randomization to evaluate programs actually in place (whether ongoing programs or pilot "demonstration" projects) and to avoid invoking the litany of often unconvincing assumptions that underlie "structural" or "econometric" or "statistical" approaches to program evaluation.[2] Their

---

2. In an early contribution Orcutt and Orcutt (1968) suggest this use of social experiments.

case for randomization is powerfully simple and convincing: randomly assign persons to a program and compare target responses of participants to those of randomized-out nonparticipants. The mean difference between participants and randomized-out nonparticipants is defined to be the effect of the program. Pursuit of "deep structural" parameters is abandoned. No elaborate statistical adjustments or arbitrary assumptions about functional forms of estimating equations are required to estimate the parameter of interest using randomized data. No complicated estimation strategy is required. Everyone understands means. Randomization ensures that there is no selection bias among participants, that is, there is no selection into or out of the program on the basis of outcomes for the randomized sample.

Proponents of randomized social experiments implicitly make an important assumption: that randomization does not alter the program being studied. For certain evaluation problems and for certain behavioral models this assumption is either valid or innocuous. For other problems and models it is not. A major conclusion of this study is that advocates of randomization have overstated their case for having avoided arbitrary assumptions. Evaluation by randomization makes implicit behavioral assumptions that in certain contexts are quite strong. Bias induced by randomization is a real possibility. And there is indirect evidence that it is an important phenomenon.

In addition, advocates of randomization implicitly assume that certain mean differences in outcomes are invariably the objects of interest in performing an evaluation. In fact, there are many parameters of potential interest, only some of which can be cast into a mean-difference framework. Experimental methods *cannot* estimate median differences without invoking stronger assumptions than are required to recover means. The parameters of interest may not be defined by a hypothetical randomization, and randomized data may not be ideal for estimating these parameters.

Advocates of randomization are often silent on an important practical matter. Many social programs are multistage in nature. At what stage should randomization occur: at the enrollment, assignment to treatment, promotion, review of performance, or placement stage? The answer to this question reveals a contradiction in the case for randomized experiments. In order to use simple methods (that is, mean differences between participants and nonparticipants) to evaluate the effects of the various stages of a multistage program, it is necessary to randomize at each stage. Such multistage randomization has never been implemented, probably because it would drastically alter the program being evaluated. But if only one randomization can be conducted, an evaluation of all stages of a multistage program entails use of the very controversial nonexperimental methodology sought to be avoided in the recent case for social experimentation.

The purpose of this chapter is to clarify the arguments for and against randomized social experiments. In order to focus the discussion, I first present a prototypical social program and consider what features of the program are of interest to policy evaluators. In the second section I discuss the difficulties that arise in determining program features of interest. A precise statement of the evaluation problem is given. In the following section I state the case for simple randomization; then I consider the implicit behavioral assumptions that underlie the case and the conditions under which they hold. I also discuss what can and cannot be learned from a randomized social experiment even under ideal conditions. The case for social experiments assumes that certain means are of paramount interest. Experiments are much less effective in recovering medians or more general features of distributions. In the fourth section I present some indirect evidence on the validity of these assumptions for the case of a recent evaluation of the Job Training Partnership Act (JTPA). I also consider some parallel studies of their validity in the randomized clinical trials literature in medicine. In the fifth section I discuss the issue of choosing the appropriate stage at which one should randomize in a multistage program. In the sixth section I discuss the tension between the new and the old cases for social experimentation. The final section summarizes the argument.

Questions of Interest in Evaluating a Prototypical Social Program

The prototype considered here is a manpower training program similar to the JTPA program described by Hotz in Chapter 2 of this volume. The prototypical program offers a menu of training options to potential trainees. Specific job-related skills may be learned as well as general skills (such as reading, writing, and arithmetic). Remedial general training may precede specific training. Job placement may be offered as a separate service independently of any skill acquisition or after completion of such an activity. Some specific skill programs entail working for an employer at a subsidized wage (that is, on-the-job training).

Individuals who receive training proceed through the following steps: they (1) apply; (2) are accepted; (3) are placed in a specific training sequence; (4) are reviewed; (5) are certified in a skill; and (6) are placed with an employer. For trainees receiving on-the-job training, steps (3)–(6) are combined, although trainees may be periodically reviewed during their training period. Individuals may drop out or be rejected at each stage.

Training centers are paid by the U.S. government on the basis of the quality of the placement of their trainees. Quality is measured in part by the wages received over a specified period of time after trainees complete their training program (for example, six months). Managers thus have an incentive to train persons who are likely to attain high-quality placements and who can achieve that status at low cost to the center. Trainees receive compensation (subsidies) while in the program. Training centers recruit trainees through a variety of promotional schemes.

There are many questions of interest to program evaluators. The question that receives the most attention is the effect of training on the trained:

Q-1. What is the effect of training on the trained?

This is the "bottom line" stressed in many evaluations. When the costs of a program are subtracted from the answer to Q-1, and returns are appropriately discounted, the net benefit of the program is produced for a fixed group of trainees.

But there are many other questions that are also of potential interest to program evaluators, such as:

Q-2. What is the effect of training on randomly assigned trainees?

The answer to Q-2 would be of great interest if training were mandated for an entire population, as in workfare programs that force welfare recipients to take training. Another question of interest concerns application decisions:

Q-3. What is the effect of subsidies (and/or advertising, and/or local labor market conditions, and/or family income, and/or race, sex) on application decisions?

There are many other questions of potential interest, such as:

Q-4. What are the effects of center performance standards, profit rates, local labor market structure, and governmental monitoring on training center acceptance of applicant decisions and placement in specific programs?

Q-5. What are the effects of family background, center profit rates, subsidies, and local labor market conditions on the decision to drop out from a program and the length of time taken to complete the program?

Q-6. What are the effects of labor market conditions, subsidies, profit rates, and so forth on placement rates and wage and hour levels attained at placement?

Q-7. What is the cost of training a worker in the various possible ways?

Answers to all of these questions and refinements of them are of potential interest to policymakers. The central evaluation problem is how to obtain convincing answers to them.

The Evaluation Problem

To characterize the essential features of the evaluation problem, it is helpful to concentrate on only a few of the questions listed above. I focus attention on questions Q-1 and Q-2 and a combination of the ingredients in questions Q-3 and Q-4:

Q-3′. What are the effects of the variables listed in Q-3 and Q-4 on application and enrollment of individuals?

To simplify the analysis I assume throughout the discussion in this section that there is only one type of treatment administered by the program, so determining assignment to treatment is not an issue. I assume that there is no attrition from the program and that length of participation in the program is fixed. These assumptions would be true if, for example, the ideal program occurs at a single instant in time and gives every participant the same "dose," although the response to the dose may differ across people. I also assume absence of any interdependence among units resulting from common, site-specific unobservables or feedback effects.[3]

This chapter does not focus exclusively or even mainly on "structural estimation" because it is not advocated in the recent literature on social experiments and because a discussion of that topic raises additional issues that are not germane here. Structural approaches require specification of a common set of characteristics and a model of program participation and outcomes to describe all programs of potential interest. They require estimating responses to variations in characteristics that describe programs not yet put in place. This in turn requires specification and measurement of a common set of characteristics that underlie such programs.

The prototypical structural approach is well illustrated in the early work on estimating labor supply responses to negative income tax programs. Those programs operated by changing the wage level and income level of potential participants. Invoking the neoclassical theory of labor supply, if one can determine the response of labor supply to changes in wages and income levels (the "substitution" and "income" effects, respectively), one can also determine who would participate in a program (see, for example, Ashenfelter, 1983). Thus from a common set of parameters one can simulate the effect of *all possible* NIT programs on labor supply.

It is for this reason that early advocates of social experiments sought to design experiments that would give maximal sample independent variation in wage and income levels across subjects so that precise estimates of wage and income effects could be obtained. Cain and Watts (1973) argued that in cross-section data, wages and income were sufficiently highly correlated and the variability in sample incomes was sufficiently small that it was difficult, if not impossible, to estimate separate wage and income effects on labor supply.

The structural approach is very appealing when it is credible. It focuses on essential aspects of responses to programs. But its use in practice requires invoking strong behavioral assumptions in order to place diverse programs on a common basis. In addition, it requires that the common characteristics of programs are able to be measured. Both the

---

3. This is Rubin's "SUTVA" assumption. See Holland (1986). It is widely invoked in the literature in econometrics and statistics even though it is often patently false. See Chapter 7 of the present volume for a discussion of this problem.

measurement problems and the behavioral assumptions required in the structural approach raise issues outside the scope of this chapter. I confine most of my attention to the practical—and still very difficult— problem of evaluating the effect of existing programs and the responses to changes in parameters of these programs that might affect program participation.

A Model of Program Evaluation

To be more specific, define variable $D = 1$ if a person participates in a hypothetical program; $D = 0$ otherwise. If a person participates, she/ he receives outcome Y_1; otherwise she/he receives Y_0. Thus the observed outcome Y is:

(1) $Y = Y_1$ if $D = 1$,

       $Y = Y_0$ if $D = 0$.

A crucial feature of the evaluation problem is that we do not observe the same person in both states. This is called the "problem of causal inference" by some statisticians (see, for example, Holland, 1986). Let Y_1 and Y_0 be determined by X_1 and X_0 respectively. Presumably X_1 includes relevant aspects of the training received by trainees. X_0 and X_1 may contain background and local labor market variables. We write functions relating those variables to Y_0 and Y_1 respectively:

(2a) $Y_1 = g_1(X_1)$,

(2b) $Y_0 = g_0(X_0)$.

In terms of more familiar linear equations, (2a) and (2b) may be specialized to

(2a)' $Y_1 = X_1\beta_1$

and

(2b)' $Y_0 = X_0\beta_0$

respectively.

Let Z be variables determining program participation. If

(3) $Z \in \Psi, D = 1$; $Z \notin \Psi, D = 0$,

where Ψ is a set of possible Z values. If persons have characteristics that lie in set Ψ, they participate in the program; otherwise they do not. Included among the Z are characteristics of persons and their labor market opportunities as well as characteristics of the training sites selecting applicants. In order to economize on symbols, I represent the entire collection of explanatory variables by $C = (X_0, X_1, Z)$. If some variable in C does not appear in X_1 or X_0, its coefficient or associated derivative in g_1 or g_0 is set to zero for all values of the variable.

If one could observe all of the components of C for each person in a sample, one might still not be able to determine g_1, g_0 and Ψ. The available samples might not contain sufficient variation in the components of these vectors to trace out g_0, g_1 or to identify set Ψ. Recall that it was a "multicollinearity" problem (in income and wage variables needed to determine labor supply equations) and a lack of sample variation in income that partly motivated the original proponents of social experiments in economics.

Assuming sufficient variability in the components of the explanatory variables, one can utilize data on participants to determine g_1, on nonparticipants to determine g_0, and the combined sample to determine Ψ. With knowledge of these functions and sets, one can readily answer evaluation problems Q-1, Q-2, and Q-3' (provided that the support of the X_1, X_0, and Z variables in the sample covers the support of these variables in the target populations of interest). It would thus be possible to construct Y_1 and Y_0 for each person and to estimate the gross gain to participation for *each* participant or for each person in the sample. In this way questions Q-1 and Q-2 can be fully answered. From knowledge of Ψ it is possible to answer fully question Q-3' for each person.

As a practical matter, analysts do not observe all of the components of C. The unobserved components of these outcome and enrollment functions are a major source of evaluation problems. It is these missing components that motivate treating Y_1, Y_0 and D as random variables, conditional on the available information. This intrinsic randomness rules out a strategy of determining Y_1 and Y_0 for each person. Instead, a statistical approach is adopted that focuses on estimating the joint distribution of Y_1, Y_0, D conditional on the available information or some features of it.

Let subscript a denote available information. Thus C_a contains the variables *available* to the analyst thought to be legitimate for determining Y_1, Y_0 and D. These variables may consist of some components of C as well as proxies for the missing components.

The joint distribution of Y_1, Y_0, D given $C_a = c_a$ is

(4) $F(y_0, y_1, d|c_a) = \Pr(Y_0 \leq y_0, Y_1 \leq y_1, D = d|C_a = c_a),$

where I follow convention by denoting random variables by uppercase letters and their realization by lowercase letters. If (4) can be determined, and the distribution of C_a is known, it is possible to answer questions Q-1, Q-2 and Q-3′ in the following sense: one can determine population distributions of Y_0, Y_1 and the population *distribution* of the gross gain from program participation,

$$\Delta = Y_1 - Y_0,$$

and one can write out the probability of the event $D = 1$ given Z_a.

The Parameters of Interest in Program Evaluation

We can answer Q-1 in the sense of determining

$$F(y_0, y_1|D = 1, c_a)$$

and hence

$$F(\delta|D = 1, c_a)$$

(the distribution of the effect of treatment on the treated, where δ is the lowercase version of Δ). One can answer Q-2 by determining

(5) $F(y_0, y_1|c_a),$

which can be produced from (4) and the distribution of the explanatory variables by elementary probability operations. In this sense one can determine the gains from randomly moving a person from one distribution, $F(y_0|c_a)$, to another, $F(y_1|c_a)$. The answer to Q-3′ can be achieved by computing from (4) the probability of participation:

$$\Pr(D = 1|c_a) = F(d|c_a).$$

In practice, comparisons of means occupy most of the attention in the literature, although medians, or other quantiles, are also of interest. Much of the literature *defines* the answer to Q-1 as

(6) $E(\Delta|D = 1, c_a) = E(Y_1 - Y_0|D = 1, c_a)$

and the answer to Q-2 as

(7) $E(\Delta|c_a) = E(Y_1 - Y_0|c_a),$

although in principle knowledge of the full distribution of Δ, or some other feature besides the mean (for example, the median), might be desirable.

Even if the means in (6) and (7) were zero, it is of interest to know what fraction of participants or of the population would benefit from a program. This would require knowledge of $F(\delta|D = 1, c_a)$ or $F(\delta|c_a)$ respectively. In order to ascertain the existence of "cream skimming" (defined in one version of that concept as the phenomenon that training sites select the best people into a program—those with high values of Y_0 and Y_1), it is necessary to know the correlation or stochastic dependence between Y_1 and Y_0. This would require knowledge of features of

$$F(y_1, y_0|D = 1, c_a)$$

or $F(y_1, y_0|c_a)$

other than the means of Y_1 and Y_0. To answer many questions, knowledge of mean differences is inadequate or incomplete.

Determining the joint distribution (4) is a difficult problem. In the next section I show that randomized social experiments of the sort proposed in the recent literature do not produce data sufficient for this task.

The data routinely produced from social program records enable analysts to determine

$$F(y_1|D = 1, c_a),$$

the distribution of outcomes for participants, and

$$F(y_0|D = 0, c_a),$$

the distribution of outcomes for nonparticipants, and they are some-times sufficiently rich to determine

$$\Pr(D = 1|c_a) = F(d|c_a),$$

the probability of participation. But unless further information is available, these pieces of information do not suffice to determine (4). By virtue of (1), there are no data on both components of (Y_1, Y_0) for the same person. In general, for the same values of $C_a = c_a$,

(8a) $F(y_0|D = 1, c_a) \neq F(y_0|D = 0, c_a)$

and

(8b) $F(y_1|D = 1, c_a) \neq F(y_1|D = 0, c_a),$

which gives rise to the problem of selection bias in the outcome distributions. The more common statement of the selection problem is in terms of means:

(9a) $E(\Delta|D = 1, c_a) \neq E(Y_1|D = 1, c_a) - E(Y_0|D = 0, c_a),$

(9b) $E(\Delta|c_a) \neq E(Y_1|c_a) - E(Y_0|c_a),$

that is, persons who participate in a program are different people from persons who do not participate in the sense that the mean outcomes of participants in the nonparticipation state would be different from those of nonparticipants even after adjusting for C_a.

Many methods have been proposed for solving the selection problem either for means or for entire distributions. Heckman and Honoré (1990), Heckman and Robb (1985, 1986), Heckman (1990a,b), and Manski (1991) offer alternative comprehensive treatments of the various approaches to this problem in econometrics and statistics. Some untestable a priori assumption must be invoked to recover the missing components of the distribution. Constructing these counterfactuals inevitably generates controversy.[4]

---

4. Manski (1991) has shown that it is sometimes possible to bound $E(\Delta|D = 1, c_a)$ and $E(\Delta|c_a)$ even if they cannot be determined exactly.

LaLonde (1986) and Fraker and Maynard (1987) have argued that these controversies are of more than academic interest. In influential work analyzing randomized experimental data using nonexperimental methods, these authors produce a wide array of estimates of impacts of the same program using different nonexperimental methods. They claim that there is no way to choose among competing nonexperimental estimators.

Heckman and Hotz (1989) reanalyze their data and demonstrate that their claims are greatly exaggerated. Neither set of authors performed model specification tests. When such tests are performed, they eliminate all but the nonexperimental models that reproduce the inference obtained by experimental methods.

There is, nonetheless, a kernel of truth in the criticism of LaLonde (1986) and Fraker and Maynard (1987). Each test proposed by Heckman and Hotz (1989) has its limitations. Tests of overidentifying features of a model can be rendered worthless by changing the model to a just-identified form. Tests that check if nonexperimental selection bias methods adjust for pre-program differences in outcome measures have no power against the alternative hypothesis that selection occurs on post-program differences between participants and nonparticipants that are stochastically independent of pre-program differences but are not themselves outcomes of the program (Heckman, 1990b).

All nonexperimental methods are based on some maintained, untestable assumption. The great source of appeal of randomized experiments is that they appear to require no assumptions. In the next section I demonstrate that the case for randomized evaluations rests on unstated assumptions about the problem of interest, the number of stages in a program, and the response of agents to randomization. These assumptions are different from and not arguably better than the assumptions maintained in the nonexperimental econometrics and statistics literature.

The Case for and against Randomized Social Experiments

The case for randomized social experiments is almost always stated within the context of obtaining answers to questions Q-1 and Q-2—the "causal problem" as defined by statisticians. (See Fisher, 1935; Cox, 1958; Rubin, 1978; and Holland, 1986.) From this vantage point, the participation equation that answers Q-3' is a "nuisance function" that may give rise to a selection problem. Simple randomization makes treatment status statistically independent of (Y_1, Y_0, C).

To state the case for randomization most clearly, it is useful to introduce a variable A indicating actual participation in a program:

$$A = 1 \quad \text{if a person participates}$$

$$= 0 \quad \text{otherwise}$$

and separate it from variable D indicating who would have participated in a program in a nonexperimental regime. Let D^* denote a variable indicating if an agent is at risk for randomization (that is, if the agent applied and was accepted in a regime of random selection):

$$D^* = 1 \quad \text{if a person is at risk for randomization}$$

$$= 0 \quad \text{otherwise.}$$

In the standard approach, randomization is implemented at a stage when D^* is revealed. Given $D^* = 1$, A is assumed independent of (Y_0, Y_1, C), so

$$F(y_0, y_1, c, a \mid D^* = 1) = F(y_0, y_1, c \mid D^* = 1)F(a \mid D^* = 1).$$

More elaborate randomization schemes might be implemented but are rarely proposed.

Changing the program enrollment process by randomly denying access to individuals who apply and are deemed suitable for a program may make the distribution of D^* different from D. Such randomization alters the information set of potential applicants and program administrators unless neither is informed about the possibility of randomization—an unlikely event for an ongoing program or for one-shot programs in many countries such as the United States where full disclosure of program operating rules is required by law. Even if it were possible to surprise potential trainees, it would not be possible to surprise training centers administering the program. (Recall that D^* is the outcome of joint decisions by potential trainees and training centers.) The conditioning set determining D^* differs from that of D by the inclusion of the probability of selection ($p = \Pr(A = 1)$), that is, it includes the effect of randomization on agent and center choices.

Proponents of randomization invoke the assumption that

AS-1 $\Pr(D = 1|c) = \Pr(D^* = 1|c, p)$

or assume that it is "practically" true.[5]

There are many reasons to suspect the validity of this assumption. If individuals who might have enrolled in a nonrandomized regime make plans anticipating enrollment in training, adding uncertainty at the acceptance stage may alter their decision to apply or to undertake activities complementary to training. Risk-averse persons will tend to be eliminated from the program. Even if randomization raises agent utility,[6] behavior will be altered. If training centers must randomize after a screening process, it might be necessary for them to screen more persons in order to reach their performance goals, and this may result in lowered trainee quality. Degradation in the quality of applicants might arise even if slots in a program are rationed. Randomization may solve rationing problems in an equitable way if there is a queue for entrance into the program, but it also may alter the composition of the trainee pool.

Assumption AS-1 is entirely natural in the context of agricultural and biological experimentation in which the Fisher model of randomized experiments was originally developed. However, the Fisher model is a potentially misleading paradigm for social science. Humans act purposively, and their behavior is likely to be altered by introducing randomization into their choice environment. The Fisher model may be ideal for the study of fertilizer treatments on crop yields. Plots of ground do not respond to anticipated treatments of fertilizer, nor can they excuse themselves from being treated. Commercial manufacturers of fertilizer can be excluded from selecting favorable plots of ground in an agricultural experimental setting in a way that training center managers cannot be excluded from selecting favorable trainees in a social science setting.

If AS-1 is true,

(10a) $F(y_1, c|A = 1) = F(y_1, c|D^* = 1) = F(y_1, c|D = 1),$

5. Failure of this assumption is an instance of the Lucas critique (1981) applied to social experimentation. It is also an instance of a "Hawthorne" effect. See Cook and Campbell (1979).

6. This can arise even if agents are risk-averse by convexifying a nonconvex problem. See Arnott and Stiglitz (1988).

(10b) $F(y_0, c|A = 0) = F(y_0, c|D^* = 1) = F(y_0, c|D = 1)$,

(11) $E(Y_1|A = 1) - E(Y_0|A = 0) = E(\Delta|D = 1)$.

Simple mean difference estimators between participants and randomized-out nonparticipants answer question Q-1 stated in terms of means, at least for large samples. The distribution of explanatory variables C is the same in samples conditioned on A. The samples conditioned on $A = 1$ and $A = 0$ are thus balanced.

In this sense, randomized data are "ideal." People untrained in statistics—such as politicians and program administrators—understand means, and no elaborate statistical adjustments or functional form assumptions about a model are imposed on the data. Moreover, (11) *may* be true even if AS-1 is false.

This is so for the widely used dummy endogenous variable model (Heckman, 1978). For that case,

(12) $Y_1 = \alpha + Y_0$.

This model is termed the "fixed treatment effect for all units model" in the statistics literature. (See Cox, 1958.) That model writes

$$Y_1 = g_1(x_1) = \alpha + g_0(x_0) = \alpha + Y_0,$$

so the effect of treatment is the *same* for everyone. In terms of the linear regression model of (2a)′ and (2b)′, this model can be written as $X_1\beta_1 = \alpha + X_0\beta_0$. Even if AS-1 is false, (11) is true because

$$E(Y_1|A = 1) - E(Y_0|A = 0)$$

$$= E(\alpha + Y_0|A = 1) - E(Y_0|A = 0)$$

$$= \alpha + E(Y_0|D^* = 1) - E(Y_0|D^* = 1)$$

$$= \alpha$$

$$= E(\Delta|D = 1)$$

$$= E(\Delta).$$

The dummy endogenous variable model is widely used in applied work. Reliance on this model strengthens the popular case for randomization. Questions 1 and 2 have the same answer in this model, and randomization provides a convincing way to answer both.

The requirement of treatment outcome homogeneity can be weakened and (11) can still be justified if AS-1 is false. Suppose there is a random response model (sometimes called a random effects model)

(13a) $Y_1 = Y_0 + (\alpha + \Xi)$,

where Ξ is an individual's idiosyncratic response to treatment after taking out a common response α and

(13b) $E(\Xi|D^* = 1) = 0$,

then (11) remains true. If potential trainees and training centers do not know the trainees' gain from the program in advance of their enrollment in the program, and they use α in place of $\alpha + \Xi$ in making participation decisions, then (11) is still satisfied. Thus even if responses to treatments are heterogeneous, the simple mean-difference estimator obtained from experimental data may still answer the mean-difference version of question 1.

It is important to note how limited are the data obtained from an "ideal" social experiment (that is, one that satisfies AS-1). Without invoking additional assumptions, one cannot estimate the distribution of Δ conditional or unconditional on $D = 1$. One cannot estimate the median of Δ nor can one determine the empirical importance of "cream-skimming" (the stochastic dependence between Y_0 and Y_1) from the data. One cannot estimate $E(\Delta)$. Both experimental and nonexperimental data are still plagued by the fundamental problem that one cannot observe Y_0 and Y_1 for the same person. Randomized experimental data of the type proposed in the literature only facilitate simple estimation of one parameter,

$$E(\Delta|D = 1, c).$$

Assumptions must be imposed to produce additional parameters of interest even from ideal experimental data. Answers to most of the questions listed in the first section still require statistical procedures with their attendant controversial assumptions.

If assumption AS-1 is not satisfied, the final equalities in (10a) and (10b) are not satisfied, and in general

$$E(Y_1|A = 1) - E(Y_0|A = 0) \neq E(\Delta|D = 1).$$

Moreover, the data produced by the experiment will not enable analysts to assess the determinants of participation in a nonrandomized regime because the application and enrollment decision processes will have been altered by randomization; that is,

$$\Pr(D = 1|c) \neq \Pr(D^* = 1|c, p)$$

unless $p = 1$. Thus experimentation will not produce data to answer question Q-3' unless randomization is a permanent feature of the program being evaluated.

In the general case in which agent response to programs is heterogenous ($\Xi \neq 0$) and agents anticipate this heterogeneity (more precisely, Ξ is not stochastically independent of D), assumption AS-1 plays a crucial role in justifying randomized social experiments. While AS-1 is entirely noncontroversial in some areas of science—such as in agricultural experimentation where the original Fisher model was developed—it is more problematic in social settings. It may produce clear answers to the wrong question and may produce data that cannot be used to answer crucial evaluation questions, even when question Q-1 can be clearly answered.

Evidence on Randomization Bias

Violations of assumption AS-1 in general make the evidence from randomized social experiments unreliable. How important is this theoretical possibility in practice? Surprisingly, very little is known about the answer to this question for the social experiments conducted in economics. This is so because, except for one program, randomized social experimentation has only been implemented on "pilot projects" or "demonstration projects" designed to evaluate new programs without precedent. The possibility of disruption by randomization cannot be confirmed or denied on data from these experiments. In the one ongoing program evaluated by randomization, participation was compulsory for the target population (Doolittle and Traeger, 1990). Hence randomization did not affect applicant pools or assessments of applicant eligibility by program administrators.

Fortunately there is some information on this question, although it is indirect. In response to the wide variability in estimates of the impact of manpower programs derived from nonexperimental estimators by LaLonde (1986) and Fraker and Maynard (1987), the U.S. Department of Labor financed a large-scale experimental evaluation of the ongoing large-scale Job Training Partnership Act (JTPA), which is the main vehicle for providing government training in the United States. Randomization evaluation was implemented in a variety of sites. The organization implementing this experiment—the Manpower Demonstration Research Corporation (MDRC)—has been an ardent and effective advocate for the use of randomization as a means of evaluating social programs.

A recent report by this organization (Doolittle and Traeger, 1990) gives some indirect information from which it is possible to do a crude revealed preference analysis.[7] Job training in the United States is organized through geographically decentralized centers. These centers receive incentive payments for placing unemployed persons and persons on welfare in "high-paying" jobs. The participation of centers in the experiment was not compulsory. Funds were set aside to compensate job centers for the administrative costs of participating in the experiment. The funds set aside range from 5 percent to 10 percent of the total operating cost of the centers.

In attempting to enroll geographically dispersed sites, MDRC experienced a training center refusal rate in excess of 90 percent. The reasons for refusal to participate are given in Table 5.1. (The reasons stated there are not mutually exclusive.) Leading the list are ethical and public relations objections to randomization. Major fears (items 2 and 3) were expressed about the effects of randomization on the quality of the applicant pool, which would impede the profitability of the training centers. By randomizing, the centers had to widen the available pool of persons deemed eligible, and there was great concern about the effects of this widening on applicant quality—precisely the behavior ruled out by assumption AS-1. In attempting to entice centers to participate, MDRC had to reduce the randomized rejection probability from ½ to as low as ⅙ for certain centers. The resulting reduction in the size of the control

---

7. Hotz (in Chapter 2 of this volume) also summarizes their discussion.

Table 5.1 Percentage of local JTPA agencies citing specific concerns about participating in the experiment

Concern	Percentage of training centers citing the concern
1. Ethical and public relations implications of:	
a. Random assignment in social programs	61.8
b. Denial of services to controls	54.4
2. Potential negative effect of creation of a control group on achievement of client recruitment goals	47.8
3. Potential negative impact on performance standards	25.4
4. Implementation of the study when service providers do intake	21.1
5. Objections of service providers to the study	17.5
6. Potential staff administrative burden	16.2
7. Possible lack of support by elected officials	15.8
8. Legality of random assignment and possible grievances	14.5
9. Procedures for providing controls with referrals to other services	14.0
10. Special recruitment problems for out-of-school youth	10.5
Sample size	228

Source: Based on responses of 228 local JTPA agencies contacted about possible participation in the National JTPA Study. From Fred Doolittle and Linda Traeger, *Implementing the National JTPA Study* (Manpower Demonstration Research Corporation, 1990). Copyright © 1989, 1990 by the Manpower Demonstration Research Corporation and used with its permission.

Notes: Concerns noted by fewer than 5 percent of the training centers are not listed. Percentages may add to more than 100.0 because training centers could raise more than one concern.

sample impairs the power of statistical tests designed to test the null hypothesis of no program effect. Compensation was expanded sevenfold in order to get any centers to participate in the experiment. The MDRC analysts conclude:

> Implementing a complex random assignment research design in an ongoing program providing a variety of services does inevitably change its operation in some ways . . . The most likely difference arising from

a random assignment field study of program impacts . . . is a change in the mix of clients served. Expanded recruitment efforts, needed to generate the control group, draw in additional applicants who are not identical to the people previously served. A second likely change is that the treatment categories may somewhat restrict program staff's flexibility to change service recommendations. (Doolittle and Traeger, 1990, p. 121)

These authors go on to note that "some [training centers] because of severe recruitment problems or up-front services cannot implement the type of random assignment model needed to answer the various impact questions without major changes in procedures" (p. 123).

This evidence is indirect. Training centers may offer these arguments only as a means of avoiding administrative scrutiny, and there may be no "real" effect of randomization. In a short while data will be available to determine if, in the training centers that did participate in the randomized experiments, center performance declined during the period when randomization was used, or if the mix of trainees in the centers was altered. During the experiment conducted at Corpus Christi, Texas, center administrators successfully petitioned the governor of Texas for a waiver of its performance standards on the ground that the experiment disrupted center operations. Self-selection likely guarantees that participant sites are the least likely sites to suffer disruption. Such selective participation in the experiment calls into question the validity of the experimental estimates as a statement about the JTPA system as a whole. At least the data can be used to provide a lower-bound estimate of the impact of disruption.

Randomization is also controversial in clinical trials analysis in medicine, which is sometimes held up as a paragon for empirical social science (Ashenfelter and Card, 1985). The ethical problem raised by the manpower training centers of denying equally qualified persons access to training has its counterpart in the application of randomized clinical trials. For example, Joseph Palaca, writing in *Science* (1989), notes that AIDS patients denied potentially life-saving drugs took steps to undo random assignment. Patients had the pills they were taking tested to see if they were getting a placebo or an unsatisfactory treatment, and were likely to drop out of the experiment in either case or to seek more effective medication, or both. In the MDRC experiment, in some sites qualified trainees found alternative avenues for securing exactly the same training presented by the same subcontractors by using other methods of financial support.

Writing in the *Journal of the American Medical Association,* Kramer and Shapiro (1984, p. 2739) note that subjects in drug trials were less likely to participate in randomized trials than in nonexperimental studies. They discuss one study of drugs administered to children afflicted with a disease. The study had two components. The nonexperimental phase of the study had a 4 percent refusal rate, while 34 percent of a subsample of the same parents refused to participate in a randomized subtrial, although the treatments were equally nonthreatening.

These authors cite evidence suggesting that non-response to randomization is selective. In a study of treatment of adults for cirrhosis, no effect of the treatment was found for participants in a randomized trial. But the death rates for those randomized out of the treatment were substantially lower than among those individuals who refused to participate in the experiment, despite the fact that both groups were administered the same alternative treatment.

This evidence qualifies the case for randomized social experimentation. Where feasible, it may alter the program being studied. For many social programs it is not a feasible tool for evaluation.

At What Stage Should Randomization Be Implemented?

Thus far I have deliberately abstracted from the multistage feature of most social programs. In this section I briefly consider the issue of the choice of the stage in a multistage program at which randomization should be implemented.

In principle, randomization could be performed to evaluate outcomes at each stage. The fact that such multiple randomization has never been performed likely indicates that it would exacerbate the problem of randomization bias discussed in the two previous sections. Assuming the absence of randomization bias, if only one randomization is to be performed, at what stage should it be placed? One obvious answer is at the stage where it is least disruptive, although that stage is not so easy to determine in the absence of considerable information about the process being studied. If randomization is performed at one stage, nonexperimental "econometric" or "statistical" estimators are required to evaluate outcomes attributable to participation at all other stages. This accounts for the sometimes very complicated (Ham and LaLonde, 1989) or controversial (Cain and Wissoker, 1990; Hannan and Tuma, 1990) analyses of randomized experimental data that have appeared in the recent literature.

Moreover, for some of the questions posed at the beginning of the chapter, it is not obvious that randomization is the method of choice for securing convincing answers. Many of the questions listed there concern the response of trainees and training centers to variations in constraints. While enhanced variation in explanatory variables (in a sense made precise by Conlisk, 1973) facilitates estimation of response functions, there is no reason why randomized allocations are desirable or optimal for this purpose.

Thus if we seek to enhance our knowledge of how family income determines program participation, it is not obvious that randomly allocated allotments of family income supplements are a cost-effective or optimal substitute for nonexperimental optimal sample design strategies that oversample family incomes at the extremes of the eligible population.[8] If we seek to enhance our knowledge about how local labor market conditions affect enrollment, retention, and training-center acceptance and placement decisions, variation across training sites in these conditions would be desirable. It is not obvious that randomization is the best way to secure this variation.

Randomization in eligibility for the program has been proposed as an alternative to randomization at enrollment. This is sometimes deemed to be a more acceptable randomization point because it avoids the application and screening costs that are incurred when accepted individuals are randomized out of a program. Since the randomization is performed outside of the training center, it prevents the center from bearing the political costs of denying eligible persons the right to participate in the program. For this reason, it is thought to be less disruptive than randomization performed at some other stage.

If eligibility is randomly assigned in the population with probability q and such assignment does not affect the decision to participate in the program among the eligibles, a simple mean difference comparison between treated and untreated persons is *less* biased for $E(\Delta|D = 1)$ than what would be produced from a mean difference comparison between treated and untreated samples without randomized eligibility. In general, the simple mean difference estimator will still be biased. Thus if $p = \Pr(D = 1)$ and e denotes eligibility, and $\Pr(e = 1) = q$,

---

8. This remark assumes a linear model. For optimal designs in nonlinear models see, for example, Silvey (1980).

$$E(Y_1|D = 1, e = 1) - E(Y_0|e = 0)$$

$$= E(Y_1|D = 1)$$

$$- \left\{ E(Y_0|D = 1) \frac{p(1 - q)}{p(1 - q) + 1 - p} + E(Y_0|D = 0) \frac{(1 - p)}{p(1 - q) + 1 - p} \right\}$$

$$= E(Y_1 - Y_0|D = 1)$$

$$+ \frac{(1 - p)}{p(1 - q) + 1 - p} \left\{ E(Y_0|D = 1) - E(Y_0|D = 0) \right\}$$

$$= E(\Delta|D = 1)$$

$$+ \frac{(1 - p)}{p(1 - q) + 1 - p} \left\{ E(Y_0|D = 1) - E(Y_0|D = 0) \right\},$$

so the bias is smaller in absolute value than would be obtained in nonrandomized data:

$$E(Y_1|D = 1) - E(Y_0|D = 0)$$

$$= E(\Delta|D = 1) + \{E(Y_0|D = 1) - E(Y_0|D = 0)\}$$

so long as $0 < q < 1$ (assuming $0 < p < 1$). The intuition is clear: because some potential participants have been made ineligible, the nonparticipant population now includes some persons whose mean outcomes are the same as what participant outcomes would have been if they did not participate.

The Tension between the Case for Social Experiments as a Substitute for Behavioral Models and Social Experiments as a Supplementary Source of Information

There is an intellectual tension between the optimal experimental design point of view and the simple mean difference point of view toward social experiments. The older optimal experimental design point of view stresses explicit models and the use of experiments to recover parameters of behavioral or "structural" models. The simple randomization point of view seeks to bypass models and produces—under certain conditions—a clean answer to a central question (Q-1): does the program work for participants? The two points of view can be reconciled if one is agnostic about the prior information at the disposal of analysts to design experiments. (See Savage, 1972.) However, the benefits of randomization are less apparent when the goal is to recover trainee participation and continuation functions than if it is to recover the distribution of program outcome measures.

The potential conflict between the objectives of experimentation as a means of obtaining better estimates of a behavioral model and experimentation as a method for producing simple estimators of mean program impacts comes out forcefully when we consider using data from randomized experiments to estimate a behavioral model. To focus on main points, consider a program with two stages. $D_1 = 1$ if a person completes stage one; $= 0$ otherwise. $D_2 = 1$ if a person completes stage two; $= 0$ otherwise. Suppose that outcome Y can be written in the following form:

$$(14) \quad Y = \theta_0 + \theta_1 D_1 + \theta_2 D_1 D_2 + U.$$

The statistical problem is that D_1 and D_2 are stochastically dependent on U because unobservables in the outcome equation help determine D_1 and D_2. Randomizing at stage one makes D_1 independent of U. It does not guarantee that $D_1 D_2$ is stochastically independent of U.

The simple mean-difference estimator, comparing outcomes of stage one completers with outcomes of those randomized out, estimates, in large samples,

$$E(Y|D_1 = 1) - E(Y|D_1 = 0) = \theta_1 + \theta_2 E(D_2|D_1 = 1).$$

In order to estimate θ_2 or θ_1, to estimate marginal effects of program completion at each stage, it is necessary to find an instrumental variable for $D_1 D_2$.

Randomization on one coordinate only eliminates the need for one instrument to achieve this task. The appropriate stage at which the randomization should be implemented is an open question. The trade-off between randomization as a source of instrumental variables and better nonexperimental sample design remains to be investigated. The optimal design of an experiment to estimate the parameters of (14) in general would not entail simple randomization at one stage. The data generated as a by-product of a one-shot randomization are only ideal for the estimation of models like (14) in the limited sense of requiring one less instrumental variable to consistently estimate θ_1 or θ_2, although this is a real benefit.

Summary

This chapter critically examines the recent case for randomized social experimentation as a method for evaluating social programs. The method produces convincing answers to certain policy questions under certain assumptions about the behavior of agents and the questions of interest to program evaluators.

The method is ideal for evaluating social programs if attention focuses on estimating the *mean* effect of treatment on outcomes of the treated and if one of the following set of assumptions holds:

AS-1   There is no effect of randomization on participation decisions;

or

AS-2   If there is an effect of randomization on participation decisions, either (a) the effect of treatment is the same for all participants or (b) if agents differ in their response to treatments, their idiosyncratic responses to treatment do not influence their participation decisions.

If attention focuses on other features of social programs such as the determinants of participation, rejection, or continuation decisions, randomized data possess no comparative advantage over stratified nonrandomized data. Even if AS-1 is true, experimental data cannot be used to investigate the *distribution* of program outcomes or its median without invoking additional "statistical" or "econometric" assumptions. In a multistage program, randomized experimental data produce a "clean" (mean-difference) estimator of program impact only for outcomes defined conditional on the stage(s) where randomization is implemented.

Statistical methods with their accompanying assumptions must still be used to evaluate outcomes at other stages and marginal outcomes for each stage.

Under assumptions that ensure that it produces valid answers, the randomized experimental method bypasses the need to specify elaborate behavioral models. However, this makes experimental evidence an inflexible vehicle for predicting outcomes in environments different from those used to conduct the experiment. Interpolation and extrapolation replace model-based forecasting. However, such curve-fitting procedures may produce more convincing forecasts than ones produced from a controversial behavioral model.

Assumption AS-1 is not controversial in the context of randomized agricultural experimentation. This was the setting in which the Fisher model of experiments (1935) was developed. This model is the intellectual foundation for the recent case for social experiments. AS-1 is more controversial in the context of randomized social experiments and is controversial even in the context of randomized clinical trials in medicine. Human agents may respond to randomization, and these responses potentially threaten the reliability of experimental evidence. The evidence on randomization bias presented earlier calls into question the validity of AS-1.

If that assumption is not valid, and if program participants respond differently to common treatments and those differences at least partly determine program participation decisions (so that AS-2 is false), experimental methods do not even estimate the mean effect of treatment on the treated. In this case, randomized experimental methods answer the wrong question unless randomization is a permanent feature of the social program being evaluated. Data from randomized experiments cannot be used to estimate program participation, enrollment, and continuation equations for ongoing programs.

References

Arnott, Richard, and Joseph Stiglitz. 1988. "Randomization with Asymmetric Information." *Rand Journal of Economics,* 19 (Autumn): 344–362.

Ashenfelter, Orley. 1983. "Determining Participation in Income-Tested Programs." *Journal of the American Statistical Association,* 78 (September): 517–525.

Ashenfelter, Orley, and David Card. 1985. "Using the Longitudinal Structure of Earnings to Estimate the Effect of Training Programs." *Review of Economics and Statistics*, 67: 648–660.

Cain, Glen. 1975. "Regression and Selection Models to Improve Nonexperimental Comparisons." In *Evaluation and Experiment*, ed. C. A. Bennett and A. A. Lumadaine. New York: Academic Press.

Cain, Glen, and Harold Watts. 1973. "Summary and Overview." In *Income Maintenance and Labor Supply*, ed. Cain and Watts. Chicago: Markham.

Cain, Glen, and Douglas Wissoker. 1990. "A Reanalysis of Marital Stability in the Seattle-Denver Income Maintenance Experiment." *American Journal of Sociology*, 95 (March): 1235–1269.

Conlisk, John. 1973. "Choice of Response Functional Form in Designing Subsidy Experiments." *Econometrica*, 41: 643–656.

Conlisk, John, and Harold Watts. 1969. "A Model for Optimizing Experimental Designs for Estimating Response Surfaces." *American Statistical Association Proceedings, Social Statistics Section*, pp. 150–156.

Cook, Thomas, and Donald Campbell. 1979. *Quasi-Experimentation: Design and Analysis Issues for Field Settings*. Chicago: Rand McNally.

Cox, David R. 1958. *Planning of Experiments*. New York: John Wiley.

Doolittle, Fred C., and Linda Traeger. 1990. *Implementation of the National JTPA Study*. New York: Manpower Demonstration Research Corporation.

Fisher, Ronald A. 1935. *The Design of Experiments*. London: Oliver and Boyd.

Fraker, Thomas, and Rebecca Maynard. 1987. "The Adequacy of Comparison Group Designs for Evaluations of Employment-Related Programs." *Journal of Human Resources*, 22: 194–227.

Haavelmo, Trygve. 1944. "The Probability Approach in Econometrics." *Econometrica*, 12 (Supplement, July).

Ham, John, and Robert LaLonde. 1989. "Estimating the Effect of Training on the Incidence and Duration of Unemployment: Evidence on Disadvantaged Women from Experimental Data." Manuscript, University of Chicago, Graduate School of Business.

Hannan, Michael, and Nancy B. Tuma. 1990. "A Reassessment of the Effect of Income on Marital Dissolution in the Seattle-Denver Experiment." *American Journal of Sociology*, 95: 1270–1298.

Hausman, Jerry, and David Wise, eds. 1985a. *Social Experimentation*. Chicago: University of Chicago Press, for the National Bureau of Economic Research.

—— 1985b. "Technical Problems in Social Experimentation: Cost versus Ease of Analysis." In *Social Experimentation*, ed. Hausman and Wise.

Chicago: University of Chicago Press, for the National Bureau of Economic Research.

Heckman, James J. 1978. "Dummy Endogenous Variables in a Simultaneous Equations System." *Econometrica*, 46 (July): 931–961.

——— 1990a. "Varieties of Selection Bias." *American Economic Review*, 80 (May): 313–318.

——— 1990b. "Alternative Approaches to the Evaluation of Social Programs: Econometric and Experimental Methods." Invited lecture delivered at the World Congress of the Econometric Society, Barcelona, Spain, August.

Heckman, James J., and Richard R. Robb. 1985. "Alternative Methods for Evaluating the Impact of Interventions." In *Longitudinal Analysis of Labor Market Data*, ed. Heckman and Burton Singer. New York: Cambridge University Press.

——— 1986. "Alternative Methods for Evaluating the Impact of Interventions: An Overview." *Journal of Econometrics*, 30: 238–269.

Heckman, James, and V. Joseph Hotz. 1989. "Choosing among Alternative Nonexperimental Methods for Estimating the Impact of Social Programs: The Case of Manpower Training." *Journal of the American Statistical Association*, 84 (December): 862–874.

Heckman, James, and Bo Honoré. 1990. "The Empirical Content of the Roy Model." *Econometrica*, 58 (September): 849–891.

Holland, Paul W. 1986. "Statistics and Causal Inference." *Journal of the American Statistical Association*, 81 (December): 945–960.

Kramer, Michael S., and Stanley Shapiro. 1984. "Scientific Challenges in the Application of Randomized Trials." *Journal of the American Medical Association*, 252 (November 16): 2739–2745.

LaLonde, Robert. 1986. "Evaluating the Econometric Evaluations of Training Programs with Experimental Data." *American Economic Review*, 76: 604–620.

Lucas, Robert E. 1981. "Econometric Policy Evaluation: A Critique." In Lucas, *Studies in Business Cycle Theory*. Cambridge, Mass.: MIT Press.

Manski, Charles F. 1991. "The Selection Problem." In *Advances in Econometrics: Proceedings of the Sixth World Congress of Econometrics*, ed. Christopher Sims. New York: Cambridge University Press.

Marschak, Jacob. 1953. "Economic Measurements for Policy and Prediction." In *Studies in Econometric Method*, ed. William C. Hood and T. C. Koopmans. Cowles Commission Monograph 13. New York: John Wiley.

Orcutt, Guy, and Alice Orcutt. 1968. "Experiments for Income Maintenance Policies." *American Economic Review*, 58 (September): 754–772.

Palaca, Joseph. 1989. "AIDS Drug Trials Enter New Age." *Science Magazine*, October 6, pp. 19–21.

Rubin, Donald B. 1978. "Bayesian Inference for Causal Effects: The Role of Randomization." *Annals of Statistics*, 6: 34–58.

Savage, L. J. 1972. *Foundations of Statistics Inference*. New York: John Wiley.

Silvey, S. D. 1980. *Optimal Design*. London: Chapman Hall.

Tinbergen, Jan. 1956. *Economic Policy Principles and Design*. Amsterdam: North-Holland.

6   Evaluation Methods for
Program Entry Effects

Robert Moffitt

Most program interventions are intended to change the characteristics of the recipients on a program, to change the caseload of the program, or both. In the case of welfare programs, most of the major interventions of policy interest over the past twenty years, both those that have been implemented as well as those that have only been proposed or tested, have been aimed at the twin goals of increasing the labor supply and earnings of welfare recipients and of the low-income population in general, and reducing welfare caseloads. However, most of the designs of program evaluations, both those using experimental methods and those using nonexperimental methods, have focused considerably more attention on the former goal than on the latter. Evaluations of a negative income tax, for example, were primarily concerned with the effects of such a program on labor supply. Evaluations of training programs for welfare recipients, to take another example, have as their primary focus the estimation of the effects of such programs on the earnings and employment of trainees. The excessive focus on earnings and labor supply effects has led to a surprising, indeed disturbing, lack of attention to effects on program entry. While considerable attention has been paid to program effects on exit rates from welfare, estimation of the effects of a program intervention on the caseload requires the estimation of effects on the program entry rate as well as the exit rate; both together determine the caseload effect. Entry effects may be particularly important in the long run, for such effects may develop gradually as the eligible population becomes aware of the program change put in place by the intervention.

The evaluation of the effect of an intervention on program entry, or on the caseload as a whole, requires very different methods than an evaluation of its effects on earnings or labor supply. Most evaluation designs for the estimation of earnings and labor supply effects are based on an examination of individuals who are on the welfare rolls; this is natural since the treatments under consideration (training, for example) can only be received by those who are welfare recipients. However, such an approach precludes the estimation of entry effects, for such estimation requires an examination of the extent to which those off the rolls go onto them in greater or lesser numbers than was the case prior to the intervention.

It is also possible that the earnings and labor supply effects estimated with conventional designs are themselves adversely affected by the neglect of attention to program entry. For example, if program entry rates increase as a result of an intervention, and if those who newly enter the rolls have systematically different earnings and labor supply effects than those initially on the rolls, the final average earnings and labor supply effects will be altered. In addition, if a conventional design is used to study the effect of an intervention on program exit rates—by examining the rate at which those on the rolls move off them—the estimates so obtained may also be contaminated by program entry effects. If, again, program entry increases and if those who enter the rolls have different exit rates than those initially on the rolls, final program exit rates will be altered. In both of these cases, proper estimation of earnings, labor supply, and exit-rate effects cannot be obtained in the first place without proper attention to entry-rate effects.

This chapter discusses evaluation methods for the estimation of the effects of interventions on program entry. Methods for the evaluation of such effects pose special difficulties and require attention to several features of design that are quite different from those that usually generate attention. In the following section, the general issues involved are illustrated by a review of several major past evaluations of the impacts of interventions in the Aid to Families with Dependent Children (AFDC) program. The subsequent section discusses possible evaluation designs for the estimation of entry effects. The bearing of these issues on the estimation of earnings effects is the subject of the next section. A summary and conclusions appear in the final section.

Past Evaluations of Welfare Interventions

Over the past twenty years there have been several major evaluations of actual interventions in the AFDC program and of proposed interventions in welfare programs in general. These include (1) one set of experiments of the work-incentive effects of benefit-reduction rates on labor supply, the income maintenance experiments; (2) two sets of evaluations of the major pieces of AFDC legislation prior to 1988, the 1967 Amendments to the Social Security Act and the 1981 Omnibus Budget Reconciliation Act (OBRA); and (3) one set of evaluations of the work and training programs spawned by the OBRA legislation, best exemplified by the experimental evaluations conducted by the Manpower Demonstration Research Corporation (MDRC).[1] In addition, evaluations are currently under way or in the planning stage for the most important recent piece of AFDC legislation, the Family Support Act of 1988.

Despite the high quality of many of these evaluations in numerous respects, not a single one has addressed the issue of entry effects.

Income Maintenance Experiments. The income maintenance experiments were tests of the effect of a negative income tax on labor supply; they were conducted in four different locations during the 1960s and 1970s (for reviews see Moffitt and Kehrer, 1981; SRI International, 1983). The explicit aim of the experiments was to estimate the effect of lowering the benefit-reduction rate on work incentives, although implicitly it was understood that the public goal behind such an intervention was to lower the caseload as well. The experiments were conducted by randomly assigning members of the low-income population in the different areas to experimental and control groups, the former to receive the negative income tax with its lower benefit-reduction rate and the latter to receive only the then-existing set of welfare benefits.

The experimental design reflected a lack of interest not only in entry-rate effects but in participation-rate effects in general. Specifically, in all of the evaluations the members of the experimental group were not permitted not to receive payments to which they were financially entitled. To maintain compliance with the rules of the experiment and to avoid being terminated from the experiment by the program operators for noncompliance, all families were required to submit income report forms on a monthly basis. If the income of the family was sufficiently low to warrant a payment, a check was automatically issued. A family not wishing to participate had only the option of attrition, in which case no further information on its status would be collected by the survey

---

1. There have been many other evaluations of AFDC and other interventions; these are only those that are best known. See Chapter 1 in this volume by Greenberg and Wiseman for a survey of others following OBRA, and see Moffitt (forthcoming) for a survey of other training evaluations such as Supported Work.

staff. Consequently, it was not possible in the income maintenance experiments to estimate the participation rate in a negative income tax, much less how that participation rate would be decomposed into exit and entry rates.[2]

It is also possible that the experimental labor supply estimates were affected by this defect of the design. In a program instituted on a national level, participation among eligibles would not be required and would certainly be less than 100 percent. Consequently, some of those receiving payments in the experiments, whose labor supply was therefore affected, would probably not participate in a nationally implemented program. If it were the case that such nonparticipants had systematically different responses to the experiment than did those who would participate in a national program—for example, if they had stronger desires to work off the rolls and hence had lower responses to the negative income tax—the average labor supply effect estimated in the experiments would not be a correct estimate of that which would obtain in a national program.

If the experiments had considered designs that would permit the estimation of participation-rate effects, a fundamental dilemma would have appeared which arises in virtually all experimental evaluations, including those discussed below (for example, the welfare employment evaluations conducted by MDRC). If an experiment had been constructed to permit estimation of the participation rate, the randomization would have had to be conducted on the eligible population—as opposed to only participants—and the members of the experimental group would have had to be permitted not to receive benefits (that is, the treatment would be only the offer of benefits, not their receipt). Unfortunately, this would permit an "experimental" estimate only of the effect of the intervention on the combined labor supply of participants and nonparticipants in the experimental group; an experimental estimate of the labor supply effect on only those who participated in the program would not be obtainable.[3] On the other hand, if randomization

---

2. Families were permitted to move above the break-even level and retain enrollment in the experiment, but they were not permitted to move off the program while below break-even. In the control group, on the other hand, many women below the AFDC break-even did not participate in AFDC, a characteristic common to most AFDC-eligible populations (see, for example, Moffitt, forthcoming).

3. If it could be safely assumed that the labor supply levels of nonparticipating experimentals were unaffected by the treatment, an estimate of the labor supply effect for participating experimentals alone could be obtained. But this is an extra assumption that

were conducted only on recipients, the self-selection problems discussed previously would arise.

1967 Social Security Act Amendments. The 1967 amendments to the Social Security Act contained a number of provisions; one of the most prominent was the lowering of the nominal benefit-reduction rate in the AFDC program from 100 percent to 67 percent, a provision intended to provide work incentives similar to those of a negative income tax. Evaluation methodology was at a very early stage of development in the late 1960s and early 1970s, and hence only a few evaluations were conducted of the amendments, without the benefits of later methodological developments.

Appel (1972) and Smith (1974) examined aggregate data on the employment rates of welfare recipients in one state, Michigan, before and after the amendments. The object was to determine whether the employment of recipients was increased by the lowering of the benefit-reduction rate. Unfortunately, such a methodology is seriously flawed because the caseload after the amendments may have included new entrants who came onto the rolls to take advantage of the ability to work while on AFDC. Those new entrants may, for example, have been working the same amount while off AFDC and may have come onto the rolls simply to collect benefits.[4] Clearly the use of aggregate data does not permit the elimination of such compositional effects. A later study by Bell and Bushe (1975) used individual microdata, but only from a series of independent cross sections of the AFDC caseload conducted during the late 1960s and early 1970s. Again, the comparison of work-effort levels of recipients before and after the amendments in the successive waves of the microdata was contaminated by changes in composition and entry onto the rolls by workers. These studies show that it is panel data, not microdata per se, that are necessary to estimate entry effects in this type of analysis.

OBRA Evaluations. The 1981 OBRA legislation had a number of important features, but the major change in the AFDC benefit formula was the reinstitution of a nominal 100 percent benefit-reduction rate on

---

does not follow from the randomization itself, and must be justified independently of the randomization. Indeed, in some evaluations the assumption is obviously unwarranted.

4. This type of movement has been extensively discussed in the context of a negative income tax, for a lowering of the benefit-reduction rate is now known to create work disincentives through its attraction of new entrants at the same time that it creates work incentives for those initially on the rolls. See Levy (1979) and Moffitt (forthcoming).

earnings (at least after four months of work). An important question was whether this change would induce reductions in work effort among AFDC recipients, many of whom were working at the time of the legislation and could retain eligibility for benefits only if they stopped working.

Of the several evaluations of the legislation that were conducted, perhaps the best was that carried out by the Research Triangle Institute (RTI, 1983). The RTI design was based on a before-and-after examination of two cohorts. The first cohort was a nationally representative sample of AFDC recipients who were on the rolls just prior to the implementation of the OBRA legislation. The second (comparison) cohort was a similarly representative sample of AFDC recipients on the rolls one year prior to the first cohort. Both cohorts were followed over time, and their recipiency and work status were examined one year later to determine what percentage of recipients had left the rolls permanently and what percentage were still on the rolls but had moved from work to nonwork. The estimates of the OBRA effect on both the exit rate and the move-to-nonwork rate were based on a comparison of those rates in the "OBRA" cohort to those in the "pre-OBRA" cohort.

Although there are many issues surrounding this nonexperimental design, for present purposes the most important is its failure to permit the estimation of entry-rate effects of the legislation. Such effects should be expected to be present, for just as the 1967 amendments may have drawn new entrants onto the rolls who wished to work, the OBRA legislation should have been expected to discourage potential recipients who wished to work from joining the rolls. Just as the RTI design permitted the comparison of the exit rate in the OBRA cohort to a presumably "normal" exit rate in a pre-OBRA cohort, there should have been a comparison of the entry rate into AFDC in the OBRA period with a "normal" entry rate measured in the pre-OBRA period. That comparison could have been partially accomplished by the enrollment of replenishment samples each month to both the OBRA and pre-OBRA cohorts, as discussed later in this chapter. In any case, the RTI design thus did not permit the estimation of entry-rate effects nor, therefore, the net effects of the legislation on the AFDC caseload.[5]

MDRC Work-Welfare Experiments. The MDRC work-welfare experiments are reviewed in some detail by Greenberg and Wiseman in Chap-

---

5. For more detailed reviews of the OBRA evaluations, see Hutchens (1986) and Moffitt (1984, 1985).

ter 1 of this volume (see the references therein). The experiments were designed to evaluate the effects of welfare employment programs in eight different sites around the country. The programs were authorized by the 1981 OBRA legislation and provided various forms of job search, training, or work experience to AFDC and AFDC-UP recipients. The major goal of the evaluations was to estimate the effect of the various programs on the earnings of recipients, but effects on the exit rate from AFDC and the reentry rate onto the rolls ("recidivism") were also examined. The evaluation design was based on a randomization of individuals into experimental and control status, with experimentals receiving the new program and controls generally receiving existing services. However, the point of randomization varied across sites. In some, the randomization was conducted at the point of application for AFDC; in others, it was conducted at the point of certification of eligibility for AFDC, after some applicants had voluntarily dropped out of consideration or had been denied eligibility. In yet others, it was conducted at the point of reevaluation of eligibility, at the point of transition to mandatory program eligibility status, or after intensive recruitment for the program (see Greenberg and Wiseman, Chapter 1 of this volume.)[6]

Although the MDRC work-welfare experiments were admirably designed in many respects, they were little better than the prior evaluations discussed thus far in their provision for the estimation of entry effects. The randomization—at whichever point—was conducted only on AFDC applicants or recipients, and therefore no direct estimate of entry effects could be obtained. The estimates of effects on recidivism provided some information on reentry among those initially on the rolls, but it obviously did not provide information on entry-rate effects for those not on the rolls at the time of the experiment. Moreover, it is possible that exit-rate and recidivism effects in a national program would be different from those estimated in the experiment. If, for example, a national implementation of one of the programs tested were to increase the entry

6. In addition to creating some difficulties in interpreting the results across experiments, these differences in the points of randomization raise difficulties similar to those that would arise in income maintenance experiments that enroll eligibles rather than participants. For example, estimates of earnings effects for the subsample of an experimental group that actually receives and completes training are not possible without conducting an essentially nonexperimental analysis of differences in earnings within the experimental group. Note as well that the zero-effect assumption discussed in note 3 is unlikely to hold here. These issues are also discussed by Greenberg and Wiseman.

rate, and if the new entrants had systematically different exit and recidivism rates than did those initially on the rolls, the long-run effects on such rates would be different from those estimated in the experiment. Likewise, as discussed previously for other evaluations, the earnings effects estimated in the MDRC experiments might be quite different from those that would obtain in a national program if the entry rate were to change and if those who were to enter (or not enter) a national program had systematically different earnings responses to training than did the recipients on the rolls during the experiments.

It is worth noting that the entry, exit, and net caseload effects of welfare employment programs of the types tested in the MDRC experiments are not predictable a priori and can only be determined by direct evaluation. The net effect is likely to be determined by the interplay of two separate forces.[7] On the one hand, the effect of such programs on the AFDC entry rate would depend on the net present value of the training or other employment opportunity to the recipient, taking into account the changes in current and future benefits, earnings, and work effort associated with the program. If that net present value were positive, the AFDC entry rate would tend to increase and the exit rate would tend to decrease; if it were negative, the opposite would tend to occur.[8] On the other hand, the positive earnings impact of the training itself would work to decrease future entry and increase exit, thus working in the opposite direction. That the net effect of these forces cannot be known without analysis serves to underscore the importance of estimating entry effects as a part of any complete evaluation of welfare employment programs.

Family Support Act of 1988. Evaluations of the Family Support Act have not been completed at this writing. However, the major components of the Act have a clear potential for entry-rate effects. The JOBS component of the Act, which mandates the implementation of certain types of welfare employment programs in all state AFDC programs, should affect entry rates and the caseload in a manner similar in type, though obviously not necessarily in magnitude, to those just discussed for welfare employment programs in general. As before, an estimate of these entry effects is required in order to obtain an estimate of the effect of the

---

7. I have discussed these issues in more detail previously (Moffitt, forthcoming).

8. Greenberg and Wiseman (Chapter 1 in this volume) report several negative net present values in the MDRC experiments.

JOBS program on the long-run AFDC caseload. Two other components of the legislation that may induce entry effects are those mandating transitional child-care and Medicaid coverage for up to 12 months after leaving the AFDC rolls. As discussed elsewhere (Moffitt and Wolfe, 1990), Medicaid extensions have the potential to induce entry onto the rolls because they make the program more attractive to potential recipients. Child-care extensions have the same possible effects. The magnitude of these entry effects would certainly be affected by the magnitude of the benefits made available in the extensions, the fraction of recipients receiving them, and, as a timing issue, how quickly knowledge of these extensions would percolate through low-income communities. Thus estimation of entry effects should permit an assessment of the time pattern of response as well as its short-run magnitude.

Evaluation Methods for Program Entry Effects

General Considerations

A formal mathematical model of entry onto and exit from the rolls of a welfare program is outlined in Moffitt (1990). That model is not necessary to an understanding of the discussion that follows but does provide a mathematical framework for it.

There are three significant implications of the model for the evaluation of program entry effects of an intervention. First, the decision-making process on the part of an eligible individual is made on the basis of the same factors that affect the process for decisions regarding program exit—namely, relative incomes, benefits, and other factors that are different on welfare and off welfare. This obvious conclusion is nevertheless important because it provides a prima facie case that program effects on exit and on entry will be correlated in sign, if not in magnitude. To hypothesize, for example, that an intervention such as a welfare employment program may affect exit but not entry requires hypothesizing that individuals do not follow the same decision-making process when deciding whether to go onto welfare as they do when deciding whether to go off. Or, to take another example, if Medicaid and child-care extensions are important enough to affect AFDC recipients' relative valuations of staying on versus going off AFDC, it should be expected that they will also be important enough to affect potential recipients' relative valuations of going on versus staying off. If such extensions are so minor compared to the other factors determining relative valuations that they do not significantly affect entry decisions, they are unlikely to be sufficiently important to affect exit decisions as well.

Second, the evaluation of the effects of interventions on exit rates—at least those interventions that affect the individual only while on welfare—can be conducted by examining either the effects of the offer of an employment program while on the rolls, or the effects of actual receipt of services from such a program; but the evaluation of the effects of such interventions on entry rates can be conducted only by examining the effects of an offer of an employment program should the individual choose to go on welfare.[9] This has important implications for the types of evaluations that must be conducted to estimate entry effects.

Third, if entry effects are present, the short-run and long-run effects of an intervention are almost certain to be different. An intervention that causes individuals either to enter the rolls in greater numbers or to decline to apply for welfare in greater numbers will affect the types of individuals who end up on the welfare rolls. This, in turn, may affect future exit rates and earnings impacts. Moreover, it should be expected that entry rates will change over time as the intervention remains in place, not only because knowledge of it will become more widespread but also because the program will be in place for potential recipients at earlier points in their lifetimes. When an intervention is first introduced, both existing recipients and nonrecipients will have already made many decisions on the basis of the program during their lifetimes prior to the intervention. Existing nonrecipients, for example, may have already made a considerable commitment to working while off welfare for several years and therefore may not find it advantageous at a late stage to consider entering AFDC even if it offers an attractive training opportunity. But women just reaching maturity, or just entering their first spell as a head of household, with little work experience or AFDC history, may find such an opportunity more attractive. When those women reach the same age as the older nonrecipients were at the time of the intervention, they may have higher stocks of human capital and higher wages. In the long run, obviously, all women will have matured with the intervention in place over their entire lifetimes.[10] Thus the immediate effects of an intervention may be quite different from the long-run effects.

9. Of course, the employment program may be mandatory if an individual is on welfare, but the welfare participation decision itself will always be voluntary.

10. Perhaps more obviously, existing recipients at the time of the intervention who have been on welfare for many years may have suffered considerable declines in their

Evaluation with Experimental Methods

Evaluations using experimental methods have a powerful attraction for program evaluation in general. Experiments have the twin advantages of providing a treatment variable that is assured to be at least conditionally independent of the unobservables in the sample, and of permitting the investigator to manipulate the treatment so as to be able to examine program variation that may not have naturally occurred in ongoing programs. Despite these advantages, however, experimental designs are less advantageously placed for the estimation of program entry effects than for the estimation of other outcomes. As noted earlier, experimental evaluation of program entry requires randomization of the offer, rather than the receipt, of program services within a sample of the eligible population—since the individual has to be on welfare to receive services—and it is unlikely that this will be feasible in a conventional experimental design where randomization takes place within sites but across individuals. Because the spread of knowledge within community-wide information networks is likely to be an important intervening variable in the program entry mechanism, individualized offers of treatments are unlikely to replicate adequately the program environment that would obtain in a permanent community-wide program.

Randomization across sites is therefore the only mechanism by which experimental methods are likely to generate adequate estimates of program entry effects—and, therefore, adequate estimates of net participation and caseload effects.[11] The difficulties with such saturation experiments are all of a practical rather than a theoretical nature. In saturation experiments the nature of the treatment is difficult to control and to standardize across sites; costs are likely to be very high; cooperation from local agencies may differ across sites in a way that generates selection bias; and, most important, it is generally quite difficult to obtain the sample sizes necessary for adequate statistical power of the treatment impact estimates. These and other difficulties with saturation-site designs have often been discussed in the literature (for example, by Orr,

labor force skills, but those women who are recipients some time after the intervention will have already had exposure to training programs and therefore may have higher skill levels.

11. Of course, the offer may be quite different to different groups of individuals within a site. For example, potential recipients with children greater than or less than 3 years of age will face different "offers" from the JOBS program. But differences in the entry-rate responses between such groups cannot be separated from the effects of children themselves.

1988; see also Chapter 7 in this volume by Garfinkel, Manski, and Michalopoulos). The sample-size problem is particularly important, and it is made worse if the experimental design calls for stratification by type of area, as it often does. Unfortunately, the number of relatively large urban areas in the United States is finite and small.[12]

The problem of sample size is often addressed by sampling a relatively small number of areas but selecting pairs of sites matched on a set of observable site characteristics. Unfortunately, although matching procedures in general and paired-site matching procedures specifically have advantages in improving statistical efficiency and the precision of the estimates obtained in the evaluation, the sample sizes are still typically quite small and far less than required for adequate statistical power. It would be preferable, for example, to match many sites on each set of observable characteristics, not just two sites per set, but this is rarely feasible.

An additional difficulty with experimental estimation of program entry effects is the problem of limited experimental duration, which is discussed extensively in the literature on the income-maintenance and other large-scale social experiments in the 1970s. Long-run program entry effects are likely to be estimable only if the experiment is allowed to operate for a considerable period of time, thereby permitting knowledge of the change in the program to percolate through the eligible population and allowing the types of individuals who are on and off the rolls to change, as noted previously. Most experiments are not in place for sufficiently long periods for this to occur, even if the duration of the experiment were made part of the treatment design. Indeed, this is a case where estimated program entry effects are more likely to be accurate in the evaluation of an ongoing, permanent program than in the evaluation of one that is new and temporary.

---

12. For example, assuming equal numbers of treatment and control sites, the sample size of each necessary for a given power of the estimate of a difference in means is $2(\sigma t/\alpha)^2$, where σ is the standard deviation of the outcome variable, t is the level of t-statistic (power) desired, and α is the size of treatment impact to be detected. To take the case of earnings, if the desired t-statistic is 2, the expected treatment impact is $1,000 annually—about the maximum obtained in the MDRC work/welfare experiments—and σ is, for example, $3,000, the necessary sample size is 72, or 144 for the treatment and control sites combined. If σ were much lower, say $1,000, a combined sample of 16 sites would be necessary. This exceeds the number of sites in virtually all past saturation experiments that have been implemented.

Evaluation with Nonexperimental Methods

Evaluation of entry effects with nonexperimental methods will in most cases require that there be natural variation in program services ("natural experiments").[13] Since the evaluation of entry effects requires variation in the offer, rather than the receipt, of services, this implies once again that cross-site or geographic differences are likely to be the major sources of such natural variation. It is well known that the major difficulty with such variation is that it may not be independent of other factors determining the outcome—in this case, entry rates. The valid estimation of treatment effects in nonexperimental analyses therefore requires, at minimum, "more" data than does estimation in experimental analyses because these other factors must be measured (see Moffitt, 1990, for a mathematical formulation). Natural variation is more likely to be dependent on variations in welfare histories of the populations, welfare benefit levels and other welfare characteristics, labor market characteristics, and the socioeconomic characteristics of the populations across the sites. At best, suitably exogenous variation in treatment characteristics across sites will be available only conditional on these types of variables, and therefore they must be measured and controlled in the analysis for valid impact estimates to be obtained. Such data collection generates an extra cost of nonexperimental methods relative to experimental methods, although one that is unlikely to outweigh the cost of operating experiments in as large a number of sites as could be analyzed nonexperimentally.[14] However, it remains the case that in many nonexperimental analyses the requisite data on welfare histories of the populations in different sites, for example, have not been collected, a sign that there must be significant costs involved. In addition, at worst, even significant data collection and control for site variables may not be sufficient to absorb all the unobservables on which cross-site treatment variation is dependent.[15]

---

13. Longitudinal data can in some circumstances also serve this function. See Heckman and Robb (1985a, 1985b), Heckman and Hotz (1989), and Moffitt (1991).

14. An important determinant of the costs of operating saturation experiments is the extent to which the program costs themselves are borne by the experimental funders or the sites. In the case of ongoing programs, the sites themselves are surely to pay for much of the cost, although their compliance in the experiment may require heavy subsidy. See Chapter 2 by Hotz in this volume for a discussion of the JTPA experience in this regard.

15. The relative data demands of experimental and nonexperimental analyses have been discussed previously in Moffitt (1991). That paper also summarizes the arguments

An additional cost of estimating entry effects, whether experimentally or nonexperimentally, is the cost of collection of data on nonrecipients themselves. Obviously the direct calculation of entry rates requires samples from that group. Unfortunately, household surveys in a large number of sites, particularly surveys that collect the detailed histories necessary for adequate nonexperimental control, are difficult and costly. This is in contrast to data collection for recipients, for whom administrative data will provide much, though not all, of the desired information. To be sure, large surveys are not necessarily required, for the sampling rate of the nonrecipient population need not be as high as that of the recipient population.[16] In addition, in some cases it may be possible to utilize information on nonrecipients from publicly available data sets such as the Current Population Survey (CPS), the Survey of Income and Program Participation (SIPP), and similar household surveys, possibly matched to administrative records from the Social Security and AFDC systems. However, in many cases the sample sizes in such data sets will be too small for reliable estimation, particularly if the population under study is highly restricted. An additional disadvantage of these data sets is that they do not contain as detailed information on participation histories as could be obtained with a new household survey, although an advantage is that they are available historically—new household surveys that attempt to capture characteristics of past states of nonrecipiency are unlikely to be reliable. In addition, sole use of such publicly available data sets for program evaluation invariably leads to delay in the analysis, a disadvantage from the policymakers' point of view.

Analysis with Program Data Only. In light of the potential expense and difficulty of collecting information on the nonrecipient population, it is worth considering the possibility of evaluating entry effects with administrative data from the welfare system alone. Many evaluations rely heavily if not exclusively on such administrative data, a prominent example being the RTI OBRA evaluation discussed previously. Some evaluations also supplement the administrative data with household survey informa-

---

of Heckman and Hotz (1989) regarding the methods that can be used to ascertain when "enough" variables are available to warrant confidence in nonexperimental treatment-effect estimates.

16. The literature on choice-based sampling has demonstrated that different sampling rates of such populations can even improve statistical efficiency and can, in any case, be adjusted for in the analysis of the data. See Manski and Lerman (1977), Manski and McFadden (1981), Cosslett (1981), and, more recently, Imbens (1990).

tion on the recipients while they are still on the rolls or after they have left them. In any event, none of the major evaluations using administrative data have attempted the estimation of entry effects, and therefore it is not clear that such data can be used for that purpose.

Fortunately, administrative data can be used to address the estimation of entry effects by making use of data on new entrants to the welfare rolls. Subsequent to an intervention that varies across sites, variations in the numbers of new entrants across those sites will reflect, in part, any entry-rate effects that may have been induced by the intervention. However, variations in the numbers of new entrants may also reflect variations in the size of the eligible population. Nevertheless, treating that size as an unobservable leads directly to a consideration of whether the variation in treatment is independent of that unobservable, possibly after conditioning on a set of observables that are correlated with that size. In the lucky circumstance that treatment variation is independent of that size, variations in the numbers of new entrants across sites will permit valid estimates of entry effects. It is more probable, of course, that conditioning on additional variables will be required. One source of such variables will usually be aggregate data on population and other site characteristics available from published or unpublished governmental data bases. But another obvious source of such variables will be past values of the size of the welfare caseload and of new entrants into that caseload. A simple control for prior size of caseload is sufficient to standardize roughly for cross-site variation in numbers of new entrants by size of the population, and additional historical series on caseload sizes can be used to control for variations in growth rates of the caseload. Time-series data on the numbers of new entrants, either alone or as a percentage of the caseload, should provide additional leverage in controlling for the unobservables determining post-treatment variation in numbers of new entrants. In the final analysis the issue will be whether controlling for such observables leaves the conditional treatment variation independent of the remaining unobservables affecting post-intervention entry.[17]

The use of historical administrative information on caseload and entry sizes involves the same type of analysis as that generally conducted in studies of "caseload modeling." Caseload modeling has been con-

---

17. This procedure is exactly analogous to the type of procedure that must be followed with individual data in any nonexperimental analysis.

ducted for many years (see Lyon et al., 1975, for an early example) and has been used for a few recent program evaluations—see Chapter 1 in this volume by Greenberg and Wiseman, the studies discussed in Chapter 3 by Fishman and Weinberg, or the recent evaluation of the Massachusetts ET program by O'Neill (1990). However, it is the exception rather than the rule in these evaluations that entry, rather than caseload size per se, is the focus of the analysis.

The experience with caseload modeling has not been very favorable to date, for estimated caseload models are often found to be unreliable, nonrobust, and sensitive to specification. It is not clear whether this instability is a result of estimation with data from only one city or one state, as most caseload models have been, or a result of the inherent loss of information involved in the use of aggregate data.

The latter difficulty can be surmounted by replacing the traditional method of caseload modeling with an analysis of individual microdata drawn from the administrative records of the welfare system. Samples of records drawn from the records of all the sites in the analysis, and drawn for several periods in the past and into the future, would furnish information on individual characteristics that has been lacking in traditional caseload models. Moreover, collection of individual welfare histories from administrative records would permit an individual-specific analysis of entry (and exit) that is not possible with aggregate data.[18]

To date, the only evaluation effort to use a similar approach to this is the RTI OBRA evaluation, which used administrative information on the welfare experiences of two cohorts of recipients, one pre-OBRA and one post-OBRA, both of whose experiences were followed over a one-year period through administrative records. As noted previously, the evaluation failed to examine entry effects, but this could be remedied by collecting data on new entrants, or what are sometimes called "replenishment" samples. In addition, a complete analysis of this type would require two other significant extensions of the OBRA evaluation frame. First, more extensive histories on the welfare recipients should be collected, because one-year histories are unlikely to furnish sufficient control to guarantee conditional exogeneity of the typical treatment variables that are available. Second, more than two cohorts will in general be required to control for time-varying effects. Indeed, ideally a periodic sample of new entrants in every month or every few months

18. Use of microdata does not mean that the aggregate data must be ignored; the aggregate information can still be used in conjunction with the microdata. See Lancaster and Imbens (1989) for an econometric discussion of this issue.

for several periods prior to and subsequent to the intervention should be collected, with each cohort of new entrants then followed through the administrative records for the duration of the study.[19] One of the additional products that could be constructed from such a data base would be a sample of "ever on" individuals, namely, a sample of those members of a particular eligible population who were ever on welfare in the past. This sample could implicitly serve as a proxy for the unobservable discussed at the beginning of this section, namely, the population of eligibles from which new entrants are drawn.

Obtaining Adequate Cross-Sectional Treatment Variation. It is worth noting in conclusion to this discussion of nonexperimental methods for estimating entry effects that it is particularly important for all nonexperimental evaluations, both those on entry and those on exit, and both those with representative-population samples and those with administrative data only, for the data collection effort to include a detailed characterization of the treatment offered in each site. Such a characterization is generally obtained in fair detail in experimental studies because the analysts are more directly involved in the administration of the treatment, but a similar level of detailed characterization is generally missing from nonexperimental studies. The RTI evaluation, for example, was significantly hampered by the lack of any cross-sectional treatment variation whatsoever, even though the implementation of the OBRA rules did vary across the states; the RTI evaluation therefore relied solely on a time-series, before-and-after method of inference. Other evaluations (including randomized experiments) sometimes include a process analysis, but its results are rarely as integrated into the impact analysis as is necessary. This issue will be particularly important in any nonexperimental evaluation efforts conducted for the effects of the Family Support Act, for that act permits considerable cross-sectional variation in both the types of programs offered under the JOBS legislation and the character of the Medicaid and child-care extensions offered in each area.

Entry Effects and the Evaluation of Earnings Impacts

As noted earlier in the review of past evaluations, the neglect of entry effects in past evaluation efforts could have a deleterious effect on the earnings impacts estimated in those studies as well. The conditions un-

19. Supplementing these data with administrative information on earnings would add significant power to the analysis as well.

der which a problem will arise are demonstrated in formal terms in Moffitt (1990), but the intuition for the results given there is not difficult to obtain.

There are three conditions that must hold for a problem to arise. The first is that the effect of the treatment on earnings must vary across different individuals. This is a rather plausible eventuality, for different individuals no doubt differ in their past skill levels and therefore in their ability to take advantage of the training and other opportunities offered by welfare employment programs, for example. Indeed, discussions of "creaming," "targeting," and differential impact of employment programs for the more disadvantaged and the less disadvantaged implicitly presume that treatment impacts do vary across individuals.

The second condition is that an individual's likelihood of being on welfare is correlated with his or her ability to gain from the treatment. It is also quite plausible that this might be the case, for if the individual's ability to gain from the program is correlated with her underlying employability, for example, it will certainly be related to her probability of being on AFDC in the first place because that probability will be highly related to employability.

The third condition is that the evaluation is conducted by examining only those on welfare at the time of the intervention. As noted in the review of past evaluations, this has been the case for most experimental and nonexperimental evaluations.

If these three conditions hold, a problem will arise in the estimation of earnings effects because the estimated magnitude of those effects will change if the participation rate does, and that participation rate will change if there are entry effects in response to the intervention. The magnitude of estimated earnings effects will be dependent on the magnitude of the participation rate because individuals with a higher probability of participating in AFDC have different treatment responses, as discussed in the second condition above. Thus, for example, if an intervention involving a successful employment program draws new individuals onto the rolls and if, for illustration, those new entrants have higher labor force skills and are more employable than those on the rolls at the time of the intervention, then the average earnings impact of the program among those on the rolls after the intervention will presumably gradually rise. If those newly entering the rolls have lower levels of skills than those initially on, the opposite would result.[20]

20. Here it is implicitly assumed that the earnings impact of the employment program is positively correlated with the level of skills and employability. This is not obvious; the

A simple means of addressing this problem is to build into the design of the evaluation a means by which the dependence of mean estimated treatment responses in different sites on the participation rate can be explicitly estimated. Either by stratifying the sample on the initial participation rate or by examining participation-rate variations that naturally occur in the sample as part of the analysis, an evaluation with sufficient numbers of sites would permit the correlation of site-specific earnings effects and participation rates. Then, once an analysis of entry has been conducted and estimates of the effect of the intervention on participation rates have been obtained, the change in the mean earnings effect can also be estimated.

Conclusions

The neglect of program entry considerations is one of the most striking characteristics of the majority of program evaluations in the area of welfare and training. Yet, as stressed in this chapter, a careful consideration of program entry effects is required to properly estimate long-run effects on the caseload, on the costs of the program, and, possibly, on earnings and labor supply as well. The evaluation of entry effects, as well as the more general evaluation of long-run effects on program participation, requires somewhat different methods than does the evaluation of effects on program exit or on earnings conditional upon program participation. Although experimental methods are still feasible, they require randomization across sites rather than across individuals and are subject to limited-duration problems. Consequently, the relative advantage of experimental methods is considerably reduced for the estimation of entry and participation-rate effects. Nonexperimental analyses, even those which use administrative data only, are more likely to be feasible for such estimation.

Why the study of entry effects has been so extensively neglected in the program evaluation literature is not completely clear. It is possible that the experimental paradigm, which serves as a conceptual model for most evaluations including those conducted with nonexperimental methods, has focused attention away from the study of entry rate ef-

---

reverse may be the case, for example. If so, the direction of change in mean treatment effect magnitudes will be reversed. The point is the same; indeed, this serves to demonstrate the importance of estimating these effects to determine the direction of the bias.

fects. Because conventional experimental methods are not particularly well suited for the analysis of entry, they do not lead analysts ordinarily to consider entry effects at the time of evaluation design.

It is also worth stressing that experimental methods may of course still have a comparative advantage in addressing other outcomes such as exit and earnings impacts, although there is considerable disagreement in the literature even on this issue. But presuming that there are cases where the powerful advantages of experimental methods can be exploited, there is still a strong case for the supplementation of those methods with nonexperimental analyses of entry. It is quite possible that a combined experimental-nonexperimental analysis could provide treatment-effect estimates that complement each other, and could produce net impact estimates that are considerably stronger than the sum of the parts that could be obtained from either type of evaluation conducted individually.

References

Appel, Gary Louis. 1972. "Effects of a Financial Incentive on AFDC Employment: Michigan's Experience between July 1969 and 1970." Minneapolis: Institute for Interdisciplinary Studies. Photocopy.

Bell, Winifred, and Dennis M. Bushe. 1975. *Neglecting the Many, Helping the Few: The Impact of the 1967 AFDC Work Incentives.* New York: Center for Studies in Income Maintenance Policy.

Bjorklund, Anders. 1988. "What Experiments Are Needed for Manpower Policy?" *Journal of Human Resources,* 23 (Spring): 267–277.

Bjorklund, Anders, and Robert Moffitt. 1987. "Estimation of Wage Gains and Welfare Gains in Self-Selection Models." *Review of Economics and Statistics* 69 (February): 42–49.

Cosslett, Stephen. 1981. "Efficient Estimation of Discrete Choice Models." In *Structural Analysis of Discrete Choice Models,* ed. Charles F. Manski and Daniel McFadden. Cambridge, Mass.: MIT Press.

Goldberger, Arthur. 1972a. "Selection Bias in Evaluating Treatment Effects: Some Formal Illustrations." Discussion Paper 123-72, Institute for Research on Poverty, University of Wisconsin–Madison.

———— 1972b. "Selection Bias in Evaluating Treatment Effects: The Case of Interaction." Discussion Paper 129-72, Institute for Research on Poverty, University of Wisconsin–Madison.

Heckman, James, and V. Joseph Hotz. 1989. "Choosing among Alternative Nonexperimental Methods for Estimating the Impact of Social Programs: The Case of Manpower Training." *Journal of the American Statistical Association*, 84 (December): 862–874.

Heckman, James J., and Richard Robb. 1985a. "Alternative Methods for Evaluating the Impact of Interventions: An Overview." *Journal of Econometrics*, 30 (October/November): 239–267.

———— 1985b. "Alternative Methods for Evaluating the Impact of Interventions." In *Longitudinal Analysis of Labor Market Data*, ed. James Heckman and Burton Singer. Cambridge: Cambridge University Press.

Hutchens, Robert. 1986. "The Effects of the Omnibus Budget Reconciliation Act of 1981 on AFDC Recipients: A Review of Studies." In *Research in Labor Economics*, ed. Ronald Ehrenberg. Vol. 8, Pt. B. Greenwich, Conn.: JAI Press.

Imbens, Guido. 1990. "An Efficient Method of Moments Estimator for Discrete Choice Models with Choice-Based Sampling." Discussion Paper 9009, Department of Economics, Tilburg University, The Netherlands.

Lancaster, Tony, and Guido Imbens. 1989. "Uses of Marginal Information in Econometrics." Manuscript, Department of Economics, Brown University. Photocopy.

Levy, Frank. 1979. "The Labor Supply of Female Heads, or, AFDC Work Incentives Don't Work Too Well." *Journal of Human Resources*, 14 (Winter): 76–97.

Lyon, David W., C. Peter Rydell, and Mark Menchik. 1975. "Welfare Policy Research for New York City: Findings on the Dynamics of Dependency." Paper P-5565, Rand Corporation, Santa Monica, Calif.

Manski, Charles F., and Steven Lerman. 1977. "The Estimation of Choice Probabilities from Choice-Based Samples." *Econometrica*, 45 (November): 1977–1988.

Manski, Charles, and Daniel McFadden. 1981. "Alternative Estimators and Sample Designs for Discrete Choice Analysis." In *Structural Analysis of Discrete Data with Econometric Applications*, ed. Manski and McFadden. Cambridge, Mass.: MIT Press.

Moffitt, Robert. 1984. "Assessing the Effects of the 1981 Federal AFDC Legislation on the Work Effort of Women Heading Households: A Framework for Analysis and the Evidence to Date." Discussion Paper 742A-84, Institute for Research on Poverty, University of Wisconsin–Madison.

———— 1985. "Evaluating the Effects of Changes in AFDC: Methodological Issues and Challenges." *Journal of Policy Analysis and Management*, 4 (Summer): 537–553.

———— 1989. "Comment on Heckman and Hotz." *Journal of the American Statistical Association*, 84 (December): 877–878.

———— 1990. "Issues in the Estimation of the Impact of an Intervention on Welfare Participation and Earnings." Mimeographed, Brown University.

———— 1991. "Program Evaluation with Nonexperimental Data." *Evaluation Review*, 15 (June): 291–314.

———— Forthcoming. "Incentive Effects of the U.S. Welfare System: A Review." *Journal of Economic Literature*.

Moffitt, Robert, and Kenneth Kehrer. 1981. "The Effect of Tax and Transfer Programs on Labor Supply: The Evidence from the Income Maintenance Experiments." In *Research in Labor Economics*. ed. Ronald Ehrenberg. Greenwich, Conn.: JAI Press.

Moffitt, Robert, and Barbara Wolfe. 1990. "The Effects of Medicaid on AFDC Participation and Labor Supply." Special Report 49, Institute for Research on Poverty, University of Wisconsin–Madison.

O'Neill, June. 1990. *Work and Welfare in Massachusetts: An Evaluation of the ET Program*. Boston: Pioneer Institute for Public Policy Research. Photocopy.

Orr, Larry. 1988. "Choosing between Macroexperiments and Microexperiments." In *Social Experimentation*, ed. Jerry Hausman and David Wise. Chicago: University of Chicago Press, for the National Bureau of Economic Research.

Rangarajan, Anuradha. 1989. "The Effect of the AFDC Program on Human Capital Accumulation." Ph.D. diss., Department of Economics, Brown University.

Research Triangle Institute. 1983. "Final Report: Evaluation of the 1981 AFDC Amendments." Research Triangle Institute, Research Triangle Park, North Carolina. Photocopy.

Smith, Vernon. 1974. "Welfare Work Incentives: The Earnings Exemption and Its Impact upon AFDC Employment, Earnings, and Program Cost." Michigan Department of Social Services, Lansing. Photocopy.

SRI International. 1983. *Final Report of the Seattle-Denver Income Maintenance Experiment:* Vol. 1. *Design and Results*. Menlo Park, Calif.: SRI International.

7   Micro Experiments and Macro Effects

Irwin Garfinkel, Charles F. Manski,
and Charles Michalopoulos

In recent years, the belief that micro experimentation is the best way to evaluate social policy changes has become widespread in both the academic and policy worlds. Academic proponents of randomized micro experiments cite the ability to compare experimental and control groups without having to resort to statistical or behavioral models as the overriding advantage of experimentation. (See Ashenfelter, 1987; LaLonde, 1984; LaLonde and Maynard, 1987.) This argument has persuaded policymakers to require that new social programs be evaluated by micro experiments. Chapter 3 in this volume describes the efforts of the federal Interagency Low Income Opportunity Advisory Board during 1987 and 1988 to persuade states to evaluate experimentally their new work and training programs targeted at AFDC recipients. The Family Support Act of 1988 goes beyond urging by requiring that its JOBS component be evaluated by micro experiment.

Consensus on the preferred design of evaluations nevertheless remains elusive. Ethicists challenge the moral appropriateness of experimentation under certain conditions. Some economists argue that less expensive nonexperimental micro-evaluation designs might provide comparable estimates of program impacts. (See, for example, Heckman, Hotz, and Dabos, 1987.) Economists also point out that micro experiments misrepresent or ignore the effects of policy changes on program entry. (See Chapters 5 and 6 in this volume.) Even proponents of experiments recognize that biases can arise out of systematic, unplanned differences between experimental and control groups. Burtless and Orr (1986), for example, mention nonresponse, limited duration, the voluntary nature of participation, and Hawthorne effects as sources of potential bias in classical experiments.[1]

---

1. Hawthorne effects are behavioral changes that are induced by the process of observation rather than by the treatment under evaluation.

This chapter challenges micro experimentation from a different perspective: micro experiments inherently cannot capture the macro or community feedback effects of a real social policy change. The first section summarizes the all-too-sparse literature on macro effects. The second section illustrates the potential importance of macro effects and the corresponding deficiency of micro experimentation through a case study of a new child support assurance system, and the third section extends the discussion to income maintenance programs and work and training programs.

The discussion in the second and third sections is more speculative than we would like. We suspect that macro effects are often substantial and that, correspondingly, the policy impacts measured by micro-experimental evaluations are often seriously biased. But the only way to determine the magnitude of macro effects is to measure them, something that has not been done. In the final section we consider alternative evaluation approaches that might provide information on macro effects.

Macro Effects: A Review

The term "macro effects" embraces a wide spectrum of phenomena. We call attention to four here: market-equilibrium effects, information-diffusion effects, social-interaction effects, and norm-formation effects. Of these effects, the first two are uncontroversial and therefore are discussed only briefly. We devote the most space to norm formation, which is the most contentious idea.

Market-Equilibrium Effects

Perhaps the most widely recognized macro deficiency of a micro experiment is its inability to detect the changes in labor market equilibrium that might follow the introduction of a full-scale work or training program. For example, a job-counseling experiment conducted in a labor market with inelastic labor demand may detect positive employment effects on experimental subjects but would miss the associated "job displacement" effect, that is, the reduction in the employment opportunities available to other individuals in the community.

Information-Diffusion Effects

A second macro effect misrepresented by a micro experiment is the information-diffusion process by which potential participants learn that a new program exists and form impressions of its characteristics. Individuals presumably obtain much of their information by word of mouth, learning from the experiences of others. (See, for example, Lerman and Manski, 1982; Manski, 1990.) In an experimental setting, where a new program is available to only a small subset of the community, diffusion of information about the program may be slow. The diffusion process is likely to be more rapid when the policy is implemented in a comprehensive fashion.

Social-Interaction Effects

Various social scientists have proposed models of nonmarket social interaction which suggest that a small exogenous impetus can yield a large social effect. Two notable examples are Gunnar Myrdal's principle of cumulation and Thomas Schelling's tipping model.

Although Myrdal's exposition of the principle of cumulation was written in 1944, it remains of interest today. Myrdal suggests that social phenomena may not be well characterized by the stable equilibrium ideas that dominate economic thinking. He speculates that the interaction among individuals may be so intense that the economy, and society as a whole, are better described by unstable equilibria with complex dynamics. The idea behind the principle of cumulation is that a push on any of the dimensions of a society—such as the economy—will have effects on other dimensions of the same society. Myrdal's application of the principle to racial discrimination in the South provides an excellent example of the process: "If . . . the Negro plane of living should be lowered, this will—other things being equal—in its turn increase white prejudice. Such an increase in white prejudice has the effect of pressing down still further the Negro plane of living, which again will increase prejudice, and so on, by mutual interaction between the two variables, *ad infinitum*. A cumulative process is thus set in motion which can have final effects quite out of proportion to the magnitude of the original push" (1944, p. 1066).

In Myrdal's model, a change in one facet of a society has a cumulative effect because the various dimensions of society affect one another. In contrast, Schelling (1971, 1972, 1973) presents a model in which decisions of individuals along one societal dimension are affected by previous decisions of other individuals along the same dimension. Schelling's tipping model (1971, 1972) attempts to explain de facto housing segregation. Here individuals have preferences which make them unwilling to live in neighborhoods in which the percentage of residents of other races is above some threshold level. Using simulations, Schelling demonstrates that extreme segregation can result even when residents are only slightly averse to the presence of neighbors of other races. Suppose that housing patterns are in equilibrium, but that a nonwhite person moves into a predominantly white neighborhood. If all residents of the neighborhood are tolerant, then the equilibrium is stable. However, if some residents are averse to other races, they may move. Their movement results in an increase in the proportion of nonwhites in the neighborhood. This secondary effect on the racial composition of the neighborhood may induce more residents to leave. If this process continues, extreme segregation may result.[2]

In general, a micro experiment will misrepresent the Myrdal and Schelling types of social-interaction effects that would prevail when a program is implemented in a comprehensive fashion. The prevailing practice in micro experimentation has, in fact, been to ignore such effects entirely. Social-interaction effects imply that the introduction of a program not only directly affects the behavior of the target population but also indirectly affects the behavior of the general population. But the practice has been to monitor only the behavior of the target population.

Norm-Formation Effects

Information-diffusion effects and the social-interaction effects described by Myrdal and Schelling pose specific nonmarket channels, or externalities, by which each individual's behavior depends in part on the behavior of other individuals. The idea that the behavior of individ-

---

2. Schelling (1973) presents a model of binary choice with externality. In this model, the choices of individuals affect the payoffs for other individuals. Although it may be optimal for all to choose one way when everyone else chooses that way, unanimity may not be Pareto-efficient. If enough individuals make the opposite choice, then everyone may be better off than when all made the same choice.

uals is mutually dependent is perhaps carried furthest in the social psychological literature on norms.

Stripped to its basics, the idea is that an individual's valuation of a given behavior increases with the fraction of the population who engage in that behavior. Suppose that implementation of a new program generates an exogenous change in the behavior of a target population. If behavior is norm-dependent, this begins a feedback process wherein the exogenous change in behavior induces other members of the community to change their behavior, and this in turn reinforces the change in behavior of the program's original target population. In general, a micro experiment will underestimate the norm-formation effect that would be found if the program were implemented universally.

The notion that individual preference may depend in part on norms, which are themselves endogenous, has generally been dismissed by economists but does seem to have some empirical foundation. Given the contentiousness of this view, we review aspects of the relevant literature here.

Lamm and Myers (1978) summarize empirical findings on the phenomenon of group-induced polarization of ideas and actions. They cite research indicating that group discussion of ideas can solidify an individual's beliefs in the prevailing attitude. Related research indicates that individuals are often persuaded to change or suppress opinions—even strongly held opinions—if enough peers express the opposing point of view.

Studies by psychologists also suggest that imitation is an important mechanism by which groups influence individual behavior. West (1981) cites several relevant experimental findings. For example, Asch (1952) conducted experiments in which subjects were shown a line and three comparison lines and were asked to indicate which comparison line was the same length as the original line. The subject was then placed in a group with seven "stooges," each of whom was instructed to respond incorrectly. In the group setting, 33 percent of the subjects confirmed the incorrect answer of the stooges, while a control group, answering in isolation, responded incorrectly only 7 percent of the time. Crutchfield (1968) describes similar experiments in which experimental subjects, who were exposed to uniform group sentiment, expressed different opinions from those of the control subjects, who responded in isolation. (See also Kiesler, 1969.)

If we accept the premise that individual behavior is affected by norms, then strong potential consequences follow. Granovetter (1978) applied a model of norm formation to explain the discontinuous nature of riot behavior, and Crane (1988) adapted this model to general delinquent behavior. In these models, individual decisions to participate in riots or other delinquent acts depend in part on the proportion of the relevant group who are already delinquent. Individuals vary in their threshold levels: some individuals will commit delinquent acts even if few others do so, whereas others will not become delinquent even if delinquency is prevalent in the population. Much in the manner of Schelling's tipping model, Granovetter and Crane demonstrate that a small change in the distribution of thresholds can turn a peaceful crowd into a rioting one or a peaceful neighborhood into a crime-infested one.

We should note that concern with norm formation is not entirely foreign to the literature on social experimentation. Harris (1985), arguing for randomized macro experimentation, recognizes that micro experiments underestimate the effects of social interactions among individuals. He asserts that "changes in life-style are likely to involve social learning, the diffusion of information, the changing of norms, and other phenomena that render individuals' responses interdependent" (p. 154). Earlier, in a discussion of the income maintenance experiments, Kurz and Spiegelman (1973) expressed concern that the responses of isolated individuals to the negative income tax would provide an inappropriate forecast of society's response if the program were implemented broadly. In a research memo, they asserted, "An argument in favor of saturation experimentation is that individual conduct is conditioned by social norms which either discourage or reinforce him" (p. 18).

Potential Macro Effects of Child Support

This section begins by describing the child support system in effect through the 1980s and a proposed child support assurance system (CSAS). Next we take total child support payments as the key outcome variable and argue that the effects of CSAS on child support payments would, for several reasons, be misestimated by a micro-experimental evaluation of CSAS. The direction of bias would probably be to underestimate the change in payments. We also speculate that a CSAS micro experiment would underestimate the resulting decreases in poverty and welfare dependence.

The Child Support System in the Past and a Proposed New System

By child support, we mean the transfer of income to a resident parent of a child who has a living nonresident parent. Transfers paid for by the nonresident parent are referred to as private child support, while those paid for by the government are referred to as public child support. Assessments in the 1970s and 1980s of the U.S. child support system—composed of 50 different state systems and innumerable different county systems—indicated that this system condoned parental irresponsibility and contributed to the poverty and welfare dependence of single mothers and their children. In 1978, only 60 percent of women with an eligible child had a child support award (U.S. Bureau of the Census, 1987). Among unmarried mothers, only about one in ten had a child support award. Among the 60 percent of mothers with awards, only half received the full amount due and over a quarter received nothing. One estimate of the ability of nonresident parents to pay child support concluded that, according to guidelines adopted by states, nonresident fathers should have been paying about four times the amount they were paying (Garfinkel and Oellerich, 1989).

The failure of the system to ensure that nonresident parents paid child support contributed to the impoverishment of children and shifted the burden of their support to the public sector. Nearly half of all children living in female-headed households were poor and on welfare.[3] If these families had received all the private child support to which they were entitled under the prevailing child support standards, both the poverty gap and the costs of AFDC to the U.S. Treasury would have been reduced by about 25 percent (Oellerich, Garfinkel, and Robins, 1989). Finally, because they had little education and experience, and would have had child care expenses if they did work, a large proportion of mothers receiving AFDC could not earn enough to lift their family out of poverty even if they worked full time (Sawhill, 1976).

To rectify these shortcomings of the child support system, a group of researchers at the Institute for Research on Poverty at the University of Wisconsin–Madison, in conjunction with civil servants in the Wisconsin Office of Child Support Enforcement, developed a proposal for a new child support assurance system (CSAS) (Garfinkel and Melli, 1982). The philosophical premise underlying CSAS is that parents are responsible for sharing income with their children, and government is responsible

---

3. See U.S. Bureau of the Census (1982, table 11). For the proportion dependent on welfare, see Garfinkel and McLanahan (1986, p. 138).

for assuring that children who live apart from their parents receive the share to which they are entitled.

The three major components of CSAS are a child support standard, routine income withholding, and an assured child support benefit. The share of income, or child support obligation, is determined by a simple legislated standard. Child support payments are routinely withheld from wages and other sources of income. The child's custodian receives either what the nonresident parent pays or an assured child support benefit, whichever is higher.

The Effects of CSAS on Child Support Payments

Total child support payments are the product of the proportion of eligible children with awards, the level of awards, and the proportion of awards paid. That is,

(1)   CS = % with awards × award level × % paid.

To simplify the discussion, we shall assume that mothers get residential custody of children and that fathers are the nonresident parents; in fact, introduction of CSAS might alter custody arrangements, an impact which would further strengthen the arguments made here. Also for simplicity, we assume that mothers know the award level and that awards are paid either in full or not at all.

Economic reasoning predicts that the decision of a mother to seek a child support award should depend on the value of having an award, which in turn depends upon the level of the award, the probability that an award will be paid, and the level of the publicly assured child support benefit, which is available only to those who have awards. (The decision to seek an award should also depend on the costs of seeking an award, which depend in turn on the father's resistance to the award. We ignore this resistance to simplify the exposition here; it is discussed in a later section.) Sociological theorizing about norms suggests that the mother's propensity to seek a child support award will also depend upon the norms in the community. Putting economic and sociological thinking together suggests that

(2)   % with awards = f(award level, % paid, assured benefit, norms).

Exactly what norms are and how they influence behavior are the subjects of debate.[4] We abstract from the details of this debate and simply
assume that the norm in period t with regard to seeking a child support
award increases with the proportion of eligible mothers in previous periods who actually had awards. That is,

(3) $\text{Norm}_t = f(\% \text{ with awards}_{t-1}, \% \text{ with awards}_{t-2}, \ldots)$.

Thus, entering norms makes the model dynamic.

To complete the specification, we note that the level of child support
awards will depend on the child support standards that are adopted.
That is,

(4) $\text{Award level} = f(\text{child support standards})$.

Similarly, the proportion of awards paid will depend upon how effectively the government collects child support payments. That is,

(5) $\% \text{ paid} = f(\text{govt. efficacy})$.

Equations (1) through (5) provide a simple framework for considering
the changes in child support payments that would result from implementation of a child support assurance system. Previous research suggests that the child support standard in CSAS will increase award levels
(Oellerich, Garfinkel, and Robins, 1989). Experience with wage withholding, as well as some research, suggests that routine withholding of
child support obligations will increase the proportion of awards paid
(Garfinkel and Klawitter, 1990). These impacts of CSAS, in combination
with the increased security provided by the assured benefit, suggest that
implementation of CSAS would increase the proportion of mothers who
seek child support awards.

The direct impact of CSAS could, in principle, be learned from a
micro-experimental evaluation of CSAS. However, the direct impact
might also change norms with regard to securing child support awards,
thereby yielding an additional indirect impact. This macro effect cannot
be learned from a micro experiment. In what follows, we consider this
and other problems of micro experimentation in some detail.

4. Some theoretical models of norm formation in sociology and economics include
Opp (1979, 1982), Demsetz (1967), Akerlof (1980), and Axelrod (1986).

The Problems of a Micro Experiment

What would a micro-experimental evaluation of CSAS look like? If we follow the practice in recent micro experiments, a sample of mothers potentially eligible for child support would be chosen in a few cities. Half of them would be provided CSAS, and half would be provided the previously existing child support system. Within a period of one to two years, the samples of experimentals and controls would have been enrolled. The experiment would continue for one to five years. If there were an interest in long-run effects, a small subsample of the experimental group—randomly chosen, of course—would be eligible for the experimental program for eighteen years.[5] The discussion that follows describes potential shortcomings of such an experimental design.

1. *The Duration Problem*

Nearly all micro experiments last only a few years. Metcalf (1977) analyzes the problem of inferring long-run micro effects from short-run micro experiments. Our concern about short duration is different. The usual short duration of micro experiments truncates the entry effects and the dynamic macro feedback effects described below.

2. *The Entry Problem*

Our description of a micro experiment did not specify how the sample of mothers would be selected. One possibility is to randomly assign mothers who come to court to obtain a divorce or separation or to establish paternity. The problem with this selection procedure, however, is that a large proportion of mothers with children born out of wedlock never enter the courts. Similarly, a substantial proportion of separated mothers do not enter the court system. Increases in award levels, payment rates, and the assured benefit all work to increase incentives to obtain a child support award. If the sample is drawn only from those already in the system, the micro experiment will miss the effects of CSAS on entry into the system.

Another possible point of random assignment is among women receiving Aid to Families with Dependent Children (AFDC). A fairly large proportion of mothers with children born out of wedlock receive AFDC benefits. Randomization of AFDC cases presents a better method of detecting the effects of CSAS on the entry of AFDC mothers into the court

---

5. Eighteen years would appear to be the maximum period for eligibility because CSAS is relevant only until the child reaches age 18.

system. Of course, effects among those who are neither in the court system nor receiving AFDC will still be missed.

Even if we succeed in randomizing among eligible mothers, the entry problem disappears only if CSAS has no effects on divorce, out-of-wedlock births, and child custody decisions. To assess these effects, a micro experiment would have to randomize over the entire population of potential parents. It is difficult to conceive of a practical method of randomizing over the entire population of potential parents other than to randomize by site—that is, to conduct a macro experiment.

3. *The Information-Diffusion Problem*

Even if an appropriate point of randomization can be found, the stimulus in the micro experiment is likely to differ from the stimulus that would be received in a real program. In the micro experiment, the experimenter explains the advantages of the new system to the mother in the experimental group; at that point she can choose to enter the program. This stimulus may be repeated periodically. For the small group that is eligible for eighteen years, the stimulus could be repeated every year.

In the real world, mothers are likely to find out about the new system from friends and relatives who experience the improvements of the system. A micro experiment, by its nature, precludes learning from the experiences of others. We speculate that whereas information diffusion would make the real-world stimulus grow stronger over time, the salience of the micro-experimental stimulus would be likely to diminish over time. Unfortunately, because we know so little about how the stimuli in micro experiments compare to the stimuli in real programs, we can do no more than speculate about this.[6]

4. *The Problem of Detecting Norm-Formation Effects*

a. *Norms and the experimental subjects.* A micro experiment, in which only the experimentals and controls are observed, precludes estimation of the effects of individual changes in behavior on social norms. If, as hypothesized, an individual's valuation of a given behavior does increase with the fraction of the population who engage in that behavior, then each additional mother who secures a child support award increases the normative value of securing awards. In the next period, the increase in the normative value of securing awards leads to a further increase in the number of mothers who choose to secure awards. Where this process

6. See Knudsen et al. (1977) for a discussion.

stops depends on the specific relationship between micro behavior and norms. The social change induced by a micro experiment might be close to or much smaller than the change induced by a real shift in policy.

b. *Norms and other actors in the community.* So far we have discussed the influence of norms only on the behavior of mothers. Norms may also influence the resistance of fathers. The mother's decision to seek a child support award will depend on the costs as well as the benefits of seeking an award, and the costs will depend upon the resistance of fathers. The effects of the provisions of CSAS are asymmetrical on resident and nonresident parents. The asymmetry arises from the fact that, under CSAS, government weighs in heavily on the side of the resident parent and the children. It follows that CSAS may induce some resistance on the part of fathers. To the extent that fathers' resistance is an individualistic behavior, a micro experiment can capture its influence. But the evidence of collective behavior on the part of nonresident fathers seems too strong to ignore. Fathers' rights groups have sprung up all over the country. It is conceivable that these groups will succeed in rolling back some of the initial increases in award levels achieved by CSAS.

On the other hand, fathers' resistance to child support awards may decrease in the long run as a result of changes in norms. The father's resistance to establishing paternity and to a child support award may depend upon how common paternity establishment is among his friends and relatives. Thus an initial increase in the proportion of fathers with child support obligations could set off a dynamic process that results in a larger ultimate increase. Once again, a micro experiment cannot capture this effect.

c. *Normative effects on earnings and welfare use.* Microeconomic theory predicts that CSAS will decrease the labor supply of mothers who would otherwise not have been on AFDC and increase the labor supply of those who would have been on AFDC in the absence of CSAS.[7] We focus on mothers who, in the absence of CSAS, would have been AFDC recipients. CSAS promotes work among this group because it has both a lower guarantee and a lower tax rate.[8] A micro experiment can capture this initial effect.

---

7. CSAS increases the income of resident parents, which in turn leads to a decrease in labor supply. See Garfinkel et al. (1990).

8. The lower guarantee applies to Wisconsin and the nation as a whole. In some states, however, a national assured benefit would exceed the current level of AFDC.

But the initial decline in welfare use decreases the proportion of single mothers who are AFDC recipients. If mothers' decisions concerning welfare depend upon how common welfare use is, the initial decline in welfare use is reinforced by a macro feedback effect. That is, as the proportion of mothers dependent on AFDC declines, the acceptability of being a welfare recipient may decrease and the stigma of AFDC increase.[9] Once again, it is impossible to say how big the initial micro effect will be relative to the long-run total effect. All that is certain is that the micro experiment cannot capture this macro effect.

5. *The Civil Servant Morale Problem*

There is another way in which a micro experiment might misestimate the effects of CSAS on earnings and welfare use. This reason is more speculative, but should not be dismissed out of hand. As AFDC caseloads begin to shrink, the morale of the civil servants who run our public assistance systems may increase. There is probably no more dispirited group of public servants in the country. A decline in caseloads brought about by an improvement in conditions outside of welfare may improve the morale of caseworkers, middle-level bureaucrats, and even the top civil servants for two reasons: it will reduce their feeling of being overwhelmed by the number of cases they have to deal with, and it will also make them feel successful in both increasing economic well-being and decreasing dependence on AFDC. Improvements in morale in turn could lead to greater efforts on the part of civil servants to promote the economic well-being and independence of poor mothers. A micro experiment cannot tell us anything about this morale effect.

Macro Effects in Income Maintenance Programs and Work and Training Programs

In the previous section we examined in some detail the possible effects of a child support assurance system and argued that a micro experiment would be likely to yield biased estimates of these effects. In this section we briefly consider the difficulties that arise in experimental evaluations of two other kinds of social programs: income maintenance programs and work and training programs.

---

9. See Moffitt (1983) for a model of the effects of stigma on welfare use.

Income Maintenance Programs

During the 1960s and 1970s four different income maintenance experiments were conducted. A principal interest in these experiments was to learn the effect of negative income tax (NIT) programs on the labor supply of beneficiaries.

Suppose that individual labor supply behavior is a function not only of income and prices but also of the behavior of others. Then the results of the income maintenance experiments are biased because they cannot measure norm-formation effects. That is, the decrease in the labor supply of prime-age men that results directly from the economic disincentives of an NIT weakens the norm of full-time, full-year work for men by reducing the percentage of them who actually fulfill that norm. It follows that the ultimate labor supply effect of the program is stronger than that measured by the micro NIT experiment.

Is there any evidence to suggest that norms are an important determinant of individual labor supply behavior? We think so. The income and substitution elasticities of labor supply for prime-age able-bodied men are much lower than those of married women and of men of college age and retirement age.[10] It is plausible that the difference is due to differences in norms with respect to full-time work. Prime-age, able-bodied men are expected to work full time for the full year, whereas the other groups have more socially acceptable alternatives to market work—keeping house and raising children, going to school, and being retired. It may be the case that the other groups show greater response to economic incentives because norms give them more options.

Work and Training Programs

At least two kinds of macro effects may result from work and training programs. One—the so-called displacement effect—has received a great deal of attention and has led the government to sponsor a matched-site evaluation.[11]

10. See Pencavel (1986) and Killingsworth and Heckman (1986). Both of these articles present elasticities from a number of studies. While estimates of uncompensated wage elasticities for men range from −0.29 to 0.14, nearly half of the estimated elasticities for women are greater than 0.50. See Masters and Garfinkel (1977) for an estimation of elasticities for both men and women that uses common data.

11. The Youth Incentive Entitlement Pilot Projects (YIEPP) were conducted in Baltimore, Cincinnati, Denver, and rural Mississippi with comparison sites in Louisville, Cleveland, Phoenix, and rural Mississippi. For an overview, see Gueron (1984).

The displacement effect is easiest to understand in the context of a work program. A new job created by the government may be at the expense of another job. When an unemployed person is paid to repaint buildings that have not been painted in years, a professional painter may lose future work. A micro-experimental test of a work program will overstate the effects of the program because it cannot capture displacement effects. The micro-experimental evaluation measures the effects on individual experimental subjects; it does not capture the effects on individuals outside the purview of the experiment. On the other hand, a macro experiment, with communities rather than individuals the focus of study, can capture displacement effects.

Training programs may also suffer from displacement effects. The simplest, but most extreme, argument is that training does not lead to an improvement in productivity but merely provides credentials that alter individuals' order in the job queue. If so, a micro experiment might find differences between the earnings of the experimental and control groups even if there are no social benefits to training. A less extreme argument is that the short-run difference in earnings between the experimental and control groups overstates the long-run effects on productivity because of ordinary supply and demand responses of markets.

The discussions in the two previous sections suggest a second macro effect of work and training programs, one implying that a micro experiment may underestimate the benefits of such programs. If work and training programs succeed in increasing the work and productivity of individuals in the community, then these programs may also lead to a change in norms with respect to work and training. This might set off the kind of reinforcing process we have described earlier. We can only conjecture about the magnitude of such a feedback effect.

Measuring Macro Effects

We believe that the various macro effects discussed in this chapter may well be important consequences of many social policy changes. The arguments presented here seem to us forceful enough to shift the burden of proof to advocates of micro experiments: they must show that the macro effects of the program under evaluation are likely to be small.

Given the long history of concern with displacement, information diffusion, social interaction, and norm formation, we find it frustrating that those who carry out evaluations continue to act as if macro effects are negligible or, at most, treat them as unquantifiable caveats to be placed on the findings from micro-experimental analyses. Progress will be made in understanding the magnitude and nature of macro effects only if we obtain appropriate data and apply suitable modes of analysis.

How, in fact, can we measure macro effects? To conclude this chapter, we pose four alternatives. None of these is problem-free; nevertheless, they all warrant consideration.

Macro Experimentation

In theory, macro experimentation would seem to provide the most effective means of data collection. Ideally, the unit of analysis in a macro experiment is a closed system, one in which entry and exit are impossible. In practice, a macro experiment usually refers to an experiment in which the unit of analysis is a local site, perhaps a city or county. Some randomly selected sites are designated as experimentals, and the policy is implemented comprehensively in these sites; other randomly selected sites are designated as controls.[12]

Macro experiments can be difficult to implement. Harris (1985) observes that randomization of sites is problematic if communities must be voluntary participants in an experiment. Harris also notes that, given the high cost of administering experiments over entire communities, there are likely to be few sites in a macro experiment. As a result, it may be difficult to distinguish experimental effects from pre-experimental idiosyncrasies and from extraneous events that occur during the experiment (for example, a plant closing).[13]

12. Local sites obviously are not closed systems, so migration into or away from experimental communities can be a problem in macro experimentation. The experimental intervention may promote immigration to take advantage of the new benefit being offered. For example, the availability of CSAS in one Wisconsin county might provoke a single mother residing in a neighboring county without CSAS to relocate. Experimentally induced migration could provide biased estimates of the national costs. Burtless and Orr (1986) and Harris (1985) observe that micro experiments are also subject to experimentally induced migration. It is likely, however, that the migration bias arising from a micro experiment will be less severe than the migration bias from a macro experiment. In a macro experiment, individuals can move from the control to the experimental group and vice versa, while in a micro experiment, attrition is a problem only if there are differences in attrition between the control and experimental groups.

13. In a comment on Harris, Orr (1985) adds that, given a limited number of sites, the researcher must have a very specific experiment in mind. In contrast, in a micro experiment many different treatments can be applied to different sections of the experimental group.

Some situations do lend themselves to macro experimental evaluation. In particular, states frequently decide to implement new programs even when they have insufficient funds to implement the programs universally. The usual solution to this difficulty is to randomly select individuals who will be allowed to participate in the program. A valid alternative is to randomly select communities or counties in which the program will be implemented. For example, if the state determines that its funds allow only half of eligible individuals to participate in the program, then it can hold a lottery in which the program is implemented in the winning counties. If counties within a state are sufficiently similar, this strategy will allow evaluation of the effects of the program at the aggregate level.

Phased-in Experimentation

An alternative is an experimental design that combines aspects of both micro and macro experimentation. The experiment could start with two matched communities, one assigned as a control and one as an experimental community. The eventual goal would be saturation of the experimental program in the experimental community. If saturation is gradual, then micro-experimental evaluation could occur within the context of the macro experiment. At the beginning of the experiment, half of the individuals potentially eligible for the program might be assigned randomly to a control group; the other half would constitute the initial experimental group. Several years later, the control group would be further subdivided, half of that half remaining in the control group and half being placed in a second experimental group. Several years after this subdivision, complete saturation could be effected.

The gradual saturation of the experimental community permits the collection of enough data to conduct a micro-experimental evaluation. A comparison of the responses of the original experimental group to those of the group that is phased in later could provide information regarding macro effects. After saturation, the experimental and control communities could be compared again. If the differences between the first and second experimental groups and those between the experimental and control communities could be explained solely by responses predicted by the initial micro experiment, this would be evidence that macro effects were absent. On the other hand, if the differences could not be explained in this manner, then one would have a measure of the net magnitude of the macro effects.

Micro Experimentation with Cluster Sampling

Some kinds of macro effects, particularly social interaction and norm-formation effects, might be measured by conducting a micro experiment and observing the behavior of persons who live in the vicinity of persons participating in the experiment as experimentals and controls. In the absence of macro effects, the behavior of those sampled persons living near experimentals should not vary systematically from the behavior of those who live near controls. If macro effects do exist, one may in principle detect them in the differential behavior of the two sets of sampled persons when the experiment is under way. It is not clear, however, whether the differences would be substantial enough for them to be detected in practice.

Analysis of Natural Variation

An obvious alternative to any kind of randomized experiment is to observe natural variation in policy across political jurisdictions. This method is already commonly used to study micro effects because it avoids much of the expense of experimental evaluation. It can readily be applied to the study of macro effects as well.

Analysis of natural variation sometimes seeks to mimic experimental conditions by matching sites that are observationally similar before the policy intervention and then attributing later differences to the change in policy. In the absence of matching, the evaluator must bring to bear prior knowledge that permits him to distinguish the impacts of differences between communities from the impacts induced by variations in policy.

References

Akerlof, George. 1980. "A Theory of Social Custom, of Which Unemployment May Be One Consequence." *Quarterly Journal of Economics*, 94 (no. 4): 749–775.

Asch, Solomon E. 1952. *Social Psychology*. Englewood Cliffs, N.J.: Prentice-Hall.

Ashenfelter, Orley. 1987. "The Case for Evaluating Training Programs with Randomized Trials." *Economics of Education Review*, 6 (no. 4): 333–338.

Axelrod, Robert. 1986. "An Evolutionary Approach to Norms." *American Political Science Review,* 80 (no. 4): 1095–1111.

Burtless, Gary, and Larry L. Orr. 1986. "Are Classical Experiments Needed for Manpower Policy?" *Journal of Human Resources,* 21 (no. 4): 606–639.

Crane, Jonathan. 1988. "An Epidemic Model of Social Problems in Ghettos." Manuscript, Center for Health and Human Resources Policy, John F. Kennedy School of Government, Cambridge, Mass.

Crutchfield, Richard S. 1968. "Conformity and Character." *American Psychologist,* 10: 191–198.

Demsetz, H. 1967. *Toward a Theory of Property Rights,* reprinted in *The Economics of Property Rights,* ed. E. Furobotn and S. Pejovich. Cambridge, Mass.: Ballinger, 1974.

Garfinkel, Irwin, and Marieka Klawitter. 1990. "The Effect of Routine Withholding of Child Support Collections." *Journal of Policy Analysis and Management,* 9 (no. 2): 155–177.

Garfinkel, Irwin, and Sara McLanahan. 1986. *Single Mothers and Their Children: A New American Dilemma.* Washington, D.C.: Urban Institute Press.

Garfinkel, Irwin, and Marygold Melli. 1982. *Child Support: Weaknesses of the Old and Features of a Proposed New System.* Special Report 32, Institute for Research on Poverty, University of Wisconsin–Madison. Report prepared for the Division of Economic Assistance, Wisconsin Department of Health and Social Services, Madison, Wisconsin.

Garfinkel, Irwin, and Donald Oellerich. 1989. "Noncustodial Fathers' Ability to Pay Child Support." *Demography,* 26 (no. 1): 219–233.

Garfinkel, Irwin, Philip Robins, Patrick Wong, and Daniel Meyer. 1990. "The Wisconsin Child Support Assurance System: Estimated Effects on Poverty, Labor Supply, and Costs." *Journal of Human Resources,* 25: 1–31.

Granovetter, Mark. 1978. "Threshold Models of Collective Behavior." *American Journal of Sociology,* 83 (no. 6): 1420–1443.

Gueron, Judith. 1984. *Lessons from a Job Guarantee: The Youth Incentive Entitlement Pilot Projects.* New York: Manpower Demonstration Research Corporation.

Harris, Jeffrey E. 1985. "Macroexperiments versus Microexperiments for Health Policy." In *Social Experimentation,* ed. Jerry A. Hausman and David A. Wise. Chicago: University of Chicago Press.

Heckman, James J., V. Joseph Hotz, and Marcelo Dabos. 1987. "Do We Need Experimental Data to Evaluate the Impact of Manpower Training on Earnings?" *Evaluation Review,* 11 (no. 4): 395–427.

Kiesler, Charles A. 1969. "Group Pressure and Conformity." In *Experimental Social Psychology,* ed. Judson Mills. London: Macmillan.

Killingsworth, Mark R., and James J. Heckman. 1986. "Female Labor Supply." In *Handbook of Labor Economics*, vol. 1, ed. Orley Ashenfelter and Richard Layard. Amsterdam: North-Holland.

Knudsen, Jon Helge, John Mamer, Robert A. Scott, and Arnold R. Shore. 1977. "Information Levels and Labor Response." In *The New Jersey Income-Maintenance Experiment*. Vol. 2. *Labor Supply Responses*, ed. Harold W. Watts and Albert Rees. New York: Academic Press.

Kurz, Mordecai, and R. G. Spiegelman. 1973. "Social Experimentation: A New Tool in Economics and Policy Research." Research Memorandum 22, Stanford Research Institute, Menlo Park, Calif.

LaLonde, Robert. 1984. "Evaluating the Econometric Evaluations of Training Programs with Experimental Data." *American Economic Review,* 76 (no. 4): 604–620.

LaLonde, Robert, and Rebecca Maynard. 1987. "How Precise Are Evaluations of Employment and Training Programs: Evidence from a Field Experiment." *Evaluation Review,* 11 (no. 4): 428–451.

Lamm, Helmut, and David G. Myers. 1978. "Group-Induced Polarization of Attitudes and Behavior." *Advances in Experimental Social Psychology,* 11: 145–195.

Lerman, Steven, and Charles F. Manski. 1982. "A Model of the Effect of Information Diffusion on Travel Demand." *Transportation Science,* 16 (no. 2): 171–191.

Manski, Charles F. 1990. "Dynamic Choice in a Social Setting." Social Systems Research Institute Paper 9003, University of Wisconsin–Madison.

Masters, Stanley, and Irwin Garfinkel. 1977. *Estimating the Labor Supply Effects of Income-Maintenance Alternatives.* New York: Academic Press.

Metcalf, Charles E. 1977. "Predicting the Effects of Permanent Programs from a Limited Duration Experiment." In *The New Jersey Income-Maintenance Experiments*. Vol. 3. *Expenditures, Health, and Social Behavior, and the Quality of the Evidence*, ed. Harold W. Watts and Albert Rees. New York: Academic Press.

Moffitt, Robert. 1983. "An Economic Model of Welfare Stigma." *American Economic Review,* 73 (no. 5): 1023–1035.

Myrdal, Gunnar. 1944. *An American Dilemma.* New York: Harper and Row.

Oellerich, Donald, Irwin Garfinkel, and Philip Robins. 1989. "Private Child Support: Current and Potential Impacts." Discussion Paper No. 888-89, Institute for Research on Poverty, University of Wisconsin–Madison.

Opp, Karl-Dieter. 1979. "The Emergence of Effects of Social Norms: A Confrontation of Some Hypotheses of Sociology and Economics." *Kyklos,* 32 (no. 4): 775–801.

———— 1982. "The Evolutionary Emergence of Norms." *British Journal of Social Psychology*, 21: 139–149.

Orr, Lawrence L. 1985. "Comment: Choosing between Macroexperiments and Microexperiments." In *Social Experimentation*, ed. Jerry A. Hausman and David A. Wise. Chicago: University of Chicago Press.

Pencavel, John. 1986. "Labor Supply of Men." In *Handbook of Labor Economics*, vol. 1, ed. Orley Ashenfelter and Richard Layard. Amsterdam: North-Holland.

Sawhill, Isabel. 1976. "Discrimination and Poverty among Women Who Head Families." *Signs*, 2: 201–211.

Schelling, Thomas. 1971. "Dynamic Models of Segregation." *Journal of Mathematical Sociology*, 1: 143–186.

———— 1972. "A Process of Residential Segregation: Neighborhood Tipping." In *Racial Discrimination in Economic Life*, ed. A. Pascal. Lexington, Mass.: D.C. Heath.

———— 1973. "Hockey Helmets, Concealed Weapons, and Daylight Saving: A Study of Binary Choices with Externalities." *Journal of Conflict Resolution*, 17: 381–428.

U.S. Bureau of the Census. 1982. *Characteristics of the Population below the Poverty Level: 1980*. Current Population Reports, Series P-60, No. 133. Washington, D.C.: U.S. Government Printing Office.

———— 1987. *Child Support and Alimony: 1985*. Current Population Reports, Series P-23, No. 152. Washington, D.C.: U.S. Government Printing Office.

West, Charles K. 1981. *The Social and Psychological Distortion of Information*. Chicago: Nelson-Hall.

PART III

Institutional Behavior

8 The Effects of Performance Standards on State and Local Programs

Burt S. Barnow

The Family Support Act (FSA), which was passed in October 1988, made a number of changes in the nation's Aid to Families with Dependent Children (AFDC) program.[1] In addition to establishing transitional child care and Medicaid programs for AFDC recipients, the FSA called for a new training program, the Job Opportunities and Basic Skills Training (JOBS) program, to replace the Work Incentive (WIN) program and WIN demonstration programs in all states by October 1990.

The JOBS program is authorized to provide academic and vocational training, work experience, and supportive services to AFDC recipients to assist them in becoming economically self-sufficient. States must provide educational activities, vocational classroom training, job readiness activities, job development, and job placement. States must also provide at least two of the following activities: group and individual job search, on-the-job training, work supplementation, and community work experience.[2]

Section 203 of the Family Support Act requires the Secretary of Health and Human Services to develop performance standards for the JOBS program based, in part, on the Secretary's evaluations of JOBS and the initial state evaluations. The Secretary is required to make recommendations on performance standards by October 1, 1993. The Act states that the performance standards are to provide specific measures of outcomes and are to be based on the degree of success that may be reasonably expected of states in helping individuals to increase earnings,

1. The FSA also modified the child support system in the United States for AFDC children and others.
2. In work supplementation, states use AFDC funds to partially subsidize jobs for AFDC recipients. Community work experience programs (CWEP) require grant recipients to perform unpaid work as a condition of receiving their grant.

achieve self-sufficiency, and reduce welfare dependency.[3] This chapter discusses the issues that should be considered in developing performance standards for the JOBS program. In the first section I define the concept of performance management as it relates to employment and training programs; in the following section I discuss the objectives and behavior of state and local governments. The third section provides a discussion of how performance is measured and rewarded under training programs, particularly the Job Training Partnership Act (JTPA) Title II-A program for economically disadvantaged youth and adults. In the final section I discuss how these lessons might be applied to the JOBS program.

Performance Management in Employment and Training Programs

Definition

I shall define the term "performance management" in the context of employment and training programs to refer to a system whereby programs are systematically judged against specified objectives. A formal performance management system is generally characterized by the following elements:

- *Performance measure(s).* An obvious requirement of a performance management system is the use of one or more measures of how well the entities being judged are performing. As discussed below, the types of measures that are used may vary, but they should be related to what is expected of the program.
- *Method of setting the standards.* For each measure, specific standards of acceptable performance must be established. The standards can be based on statutory requirements, goals of the manager, performance of similar programs, or on a relative basis (that is, so that a certain proportion of the programs being judged are expected to achieve satisfactory performance). Note that performance standards can be set arbitrarily rather than being based on a specific rationale. To be most useful, the standards should be set rationally and developed in a manner understood by the programs that will be judged.

3. The Act further specifies that the performance is not to be measured solely by levels of activity or participation.

In addition, the standards can be set to take account of factors that vary among the programs being judged, so that all programs are not expected to meet the same standards.

• *Rewards and sanctions.* Performance management systems usually include some method of rewarding programs that meet or exceed the standards and sanctioning programs that fail to meet the standards. The rewards and sanctions may be monetary in nature, may involve loss of the right to operate programs, or may simply involve receiving praise or criticism.

Note that performance management is not synonymous with achieving economic efficiency. As I will discuss further, government programs often have other goals, particularly regarding equity. In addition, performance management systems may be concerned with concepts such as managerial efficiency and due process as well as the ultimate outcomes. Performance management can (and should) be used to make program managers accountable for what takes place in their programs.

Performance management should also be distinguished from evaluation. Programs can be evaluated in terms of their impacts on an occasional or one-shot basis, but performance management is an ongoing feature that continuously provides feedback to the program managers and the agencies and organizations responsible for monitoring the programs. Thus, while evaluations often include one or more years of post-program follow-up, performance management systems must rely on shorter post-program periods to provide reasonably quick feedback.

While evaluations answer the question "What is the impact of the program?" performance management systems generally seek answers to simpler outcome and process questions that are associated with the goals of the program; the issue is more one of accountability than impact. Finally, evaluations of human service programs are generally costly and require the use of comparison or control groups to identify what would have occurred in the absence of the program. Performance management systems are generally less intrusive, but they then must sacrifice including impact measures.

Performance management is not unique to the public sector, but the intrinsic nature of public enterprises such as training programs makes them difficult to monitor in the manner used by the private sector. The key difference, of course, is that the output for a government program is not sold—there is no "bottom line" that can be monitored.

Rationale for a Performance Management System

In addition to the legal requirements to establish performance management systems for programs such as JOBS, the Job Training Partnership Act (JTPA), and the Food Stamp Employment and Training Program, there are at least three rationales for establishing such systems for government programs.

Identifying Poor Performers and Taking Corrective Actions. Even if all programs have the best of intentions, there is likely to be a range in the performance across programs. Some administrators may be less able than others, some may inadvertently use the wrong training techniques or choose the wrong curricula, and some may simply not work as hard as others. Whatever the reason, performance management, if properly used, can help to identify the poor performers.

Once identification has taken place, actions can be taken to improve performance. Milder actions include technical assistance and counseling, while more extreme measures include termination of managers and reducing funding for the program.

Identifying and Rewarding Good Performers. Identifying the programs with good performance is important, just as firms try to identify and reward good employees. If good performers do not receive any additional recognition or compensation, they may lose the incentive to continue performing well. In addition, efforts can be made to determine why the above-average performers do well so that their techniques can be replicated in other sites.

Modifying the Objective Function of Programs. Will state and local programs receiving grants from the federal government automatically have the same objectives as the federal government? As I have argued elsewhere, state and local programs may be interested in maximizing the number of people served by their programs rather than the gains that accrue.[4] In addition, most government-sponsored training programs contract out training activities rather than provide the training themselves. Political pressures may result in awarding contracts to organizations with the most political influence rather than those who will provide the best services at the best cost. Niskanen (1971) has developed a theory of bureaucratic behavior, and he concludes that bureaucrats will often not act in the best interest of their constituents.[5]

---

4. See Barnow (1979).

5. Niskanen's basic model assumes that bureaucrats will seek to maximize their budgets. In a federal-state grant program where the budget is determined by formula, alternative objectives must be considered.

Given that grantees often do not share the same objectives as their funders, a performance management system can influence the behavior of state and local programs through appropriate rewards and sanctions. Rewards such as increased budgets, recognition, and increased programmatic flexibility and sanctions such as reduced funding or termination of the program can exert strong influence on state and local programs.

Types of Performance Measures in Employment and Training Programs

Economists and policy officials have struggled with the issues of defining, measuring, and rewarding performance in public sector programs for years. The term "performance," as used by policy and program officials, does not necessarily correspond to any single economic concept. Performance may refer to gross or net program outputs or outcomes, the value of gross or net outcomes, and factor inputs or process variables. A program can, of course, use more than one type of performance measure. In this section the use of these alternative concepts of performance is explored.

Gross Outcomes. Gross outcomes in employment and training programs refer to measures of status at termination or at some time following termination of participation. Examples of gross outcome measures include job placements, earnings levels and wage rates, elimination of welfare receipt, and attainment of educational credentials (for example, a GED). With the exception of cost measures, the performance measures used for JTPA are gross outcome measures. These outcomes are gross in the sense that they do not necessarily reflect gains from the program. For example, many participants may have obtained jobs in the absence of the program. Thus, the level of placement activity does not necessarily give an indication of a program's success. On the other hand, performance management systems measure outcomes relative to some standard. If the standards are set to take into account what would have occurred in the absence of the program, then gross outcome measures may be useful in assessing the program's impact.

The principal advantage of gross performance measures is that they are relatively easy to obtain and understand. On the other hand, gross measures may not take account of what the program adds to the participant. For example, if a placement rate measure is used, a state might receive the same credit for placing individuals with significantly different characteristics—a person with limited reading skills would be compared to a person with a high school reading level. Such inequities can be partially or fully compensated for by adjusting for client characteristics.

Net Outputs. The direct output of employment and training programs consists of the human capital added to the participants: vocational programs add skills that employers need, basic skills and English as a second language (ESL) programs provide general academic training, and employment programs lead to work experience that provides basic work skills. Although the concept of measuring what is produced has appeal, the obstacles to developing net output performance measures may often be insurmountable.

A basic problem with using net outputs as performance measures is that programs such as JOBS and JTPA offer a variety of programs with different types of skills produced. The development of performance measures related to net program outputs would require some method of comparing programs that provide skills as diverse as job-specific skills (such as welding and clerical skills), pre-employment skills, and basic education skills. In addition, it may be impossible or very difficult to measure the outputs from some types of activities. How, for example, would one measure the output from a work program such as on-the-job training, work supplementation, or work experience?

Value of Net Outputs. An alternative type of performance measure is the market value of skills added, that is, the net earnings gains added from participation in the program. The advantage of this approach over the use of net outcomes is that money is used as a common metric across different outcomes. The performance measurement system need not be concerned with measuring skill gains, only with the value the market places on such gains.

Unfortunately, measuring net earnings gains is not a simple matter. Nonexperimental evaluations of CETA programs produced widely divergent estimates of program impacts; using virtually the same data, some analysts concluded that CETA programs increased earnings by as much as $1,000, while other researchers found that the programs actually reduced earnings.[6] Recent improvements in nonexperimental meth-

6. To illustrate the range, Dickinson, Johnson, and West (1984) obtain statistically significant overall earnings impacts of about $-$600 for men, while Westat (1984) obtains statistically significant estimates for men that are about equal in magnitude but opposite in sign. See Barnow (1987a).

ods have made some researchers confident that good nonexperimental estimators will be developed for determining impacts in training programs, while other observers remain more pessimistic.[7]

Regardless of whether experimental or nonexperimental methods are used, conducting evaluations at every program site in the nation or even a reasonable sample of sites would be a formidable task—well beyond the evaluation levels that have been sustained in the past.[8] Moreover, if a sample of sites is used, the evaluation would have to be conducted after the fact (ruling out the possibilities of conducting an experiment or gathering nonexperimental data contemporaneously), or there would be a risk of program operators putting their best programs in the sites used to measure performance.

Inputs and Process Measures. Programs have sometimes used inputs or process variables to measure performance. For example, programs can be judged on the characteristics of the participants enrolled (for example, a higher rating for serving more disadvantaged participants), the levels of enrollment, attendance rates, and costs. An obvious advantage of using inputs and process variables to measure performance is that they are relatively easy to obtain. In addition, the federal government may have statutory requirements to assure that the programs serve particular types of people or provide certain types of services.[9] Of course the limitation of such measures is that they provide no information on program outcomes or effectiveness.

Cost Measures. To make valid comparisons among programs, it is important to take acccount of the resources used. One approach is to define outcome measures per dollar spent, for example, placements per dollar spent. Alternatively, separate cost measures can be included. Until the program year beginning July 1, 1990, the JTPA Title II-A performance management system has included cost measures (such as cost per

7. Heckman, Hotz, and Dabos (1987) appear most optimistic. They conclude, "We are confident that reliable nonexperimental evaluation methods can and will be developed for all subsidized employment and training programs." At the other extreme, Burtless and Orr (1986) are pessimistic about the utility of nonexperimental methods.

8. The JTPA experiment, which is the Department of Labor's major effort to evaluate JTPA, is being conducted in fewer than 20 sites. Moreover, the sample consists of volunteers rather than a randomly selected sample.

9. Both JTPA and JOBS have requirements of this type. Under JTPA, welfare recipients, youths, and high school dropouts are to be served equitably. The Family Support Act specifies mandatory participation rates for the JOBS program to qualify for the enhanced federal matching rate.

entered employment). The advantage of having a separate cost measure, particularly for a public program such as JTPA or JOBS, is that it calls specific attention to unit costs. The disadvantage, in terms of promoting economic efficiency, is that unless the cost measure is properly combined with outcome measures, it may promote underinvesting in participants and serving participants who require less training.[10] Omitting costs from the performance measurement system avoids the unintended bias toward shorter and less intensive programs, but if expenditures are not included in some manner there will be a possible bias toward overinvesting in participants.[11]

Multiple Performance Measures

If a program has more than one performance measure, a method must be developed for assessing overall performance. Conceptually, it is possible to develop a single overall measure of the economic gains from employment and training programs. For example, a single performance measure could be defined as the present value of all earnings gains resulting from the program or the present value of earnings gains plus welfare savings.[12] Although economists might argue for a single measure to maximize economic efficiency, employment and training programs, and other government programs as well, usually have other goals of interest.[13] Even if the program has a single objective, it may be advantageous to use several measures as proxies if an ideal measure cannot be developed.

10. The January 5, 1990, *Federal Register* notice proposing the elimination of the JTPA Title II-A cost measures (in spite of the fact that they are required by the statute) states that "research and experience have shown that the use of cost standards in the awarding of incentives has had the unintended effect of constraining the provision of longer-term training in many SDAs."

11. The Department of Labor's response to comments received on its January 5, 1990, *Federal Register* proposal to drop the cost measures states that "treating costs as a compliance issue rather than as a performance standards issue—through more rigorous state oversight of SDA fiscal practices, and greater SDA monitoring of local service providers—is a more direct approach to ensuring fiscal accountability and sound program management." See *Federal Register,* April 13, 1990, p. 14013.

12. The problems involved in obtaining the present value of earnings gains are discussed later in this section.

13. For further discussion of the social goals of government training programs, see Barnow (1987b).

As noted previously, if equity of services is a program objective, performance measures can be developed to promote services to participants with particular characteristics. For example, both the JTPA and JOBS statutes contain provisions that call for providing equitable levels of services to particular types of eligible individuals. Performance measures can be developed to encourage enrolling individuals with desired characteristics by including participation standards (such as minimum levels of enrollment) for the groups of interest. To encourage outcomes as well as participation for selected groups, separate outcome measures can be developed for categories of interest. For example, JTPA includes separate performance measures for all adults, adult welfare recipients, and youths.

Government programs may have other social goals that may be promoted through performance measurement systems. For example, employment may be valued by society beyond whatever earnings gains are produced. Likewise, reduction or elimination of receipt of transfer payments may be valued as a goal in itself.[14]

The presence of multiple performance measures requires that a method be developed for linking the measures to develop overall levels of performance and establishing criteria for rewards and sanctions. A relatively simple method of dealing with multiple performance measures is simply to count all performance measures equally. An overall performance score can then be computed by summing the scores on the various measures.

However, simply adding scores on individual measures may be undesirable for several reasons. First, some measures may be considered more important than others. Second, there may be more variation in some measures of performance, and the government may wish to take this factor into consideration. These concerns can be accommodated by weighting the measures differently. Other, more complex methods can be used, and the states have adopted a number of approaches in the JTPA system. For example, the performance measures can be grouped and programs can be required to meet a certain number of standards in each group.

---

14. In a benefit-cost framework, transfer payments are usually netted out. From the perspective of taxpayers, however, a reduction in welfare payments represents a benefit. See Mallar et al. (1982).

Rewards and Sanctions

Another key component of a performance management system is the concept of rewards for exceeding standards and punishment or sanctions for failing to achieve adequate performance. Rewards and punishments can be made in several ways. The simplest method is simply to issue an "honor roll" or give certificates to programs with high levels of achievement. Another approach is to provide additional program funds, perhaps with fewer strings attached than in the general funding for the program, as is done in JTPA programs. In instances where funding is shared by the federal and state levels of government, as in the JOBS program, the matching rate can be varied; for example, for good performers, the federal government would pay a greater share of the program costs. An approach that is commonly used in the private sector but rarely used for government programs is to tie compensation to performance.[15]

Failure to perform adequately can be dealt with using the same types of incentives. In the extreme case, inadequate performers can be stripped of the right to operate programs. In programs where the state and federal governments share funding responsibilities, the federal government can reduce the matching grant. In JTPA, local programs that fail to meet performance standards may receive "technical assistance" from the state or may ultimately be stripped of the right to operate a program; the possibility of sitting through lectures on how to perform better may serve as an incentive to perform well.

Because of the nature of government training programs, care must be taken in establishing reward and punishment systems. One JTPA official stated, only half joking, that getting more funding was more of a punishment than a reward because it was difficult to find potential participants in his low-unemployment area. More seriously, putting more funding in better-managed programs may put participants in poorly run programs at a double disadvantage—not only do they have inferior program managers, but less funding is provided as well.

---

15. Three of the 30 SDAs included in the Dickinson et al. (1988, p. 118) study of the impacts of JTPA performance standards used additional funds received from performance standards rewards to provide raises or bonuses to SDA staff. Also, the U.S. Department of Labor conducted a demonstration in the 1970s in which state employment service employees were eligible for bonuses for high levels of performance, but the results of the evaluation were inconclusive.

In addition to determining the size of potential rewards, a decision must be made about whether the size of the award should vary with the extent to which standards are exceeded. The JTPA statute calls for such a system, and many states have used this approach. The problem with giving larger rewards for more success is that unless the performance management system takes appropriate account of participant characteristics, such a system will encourage enrolling participants who are most likely to do well in the labor market without the program, that is, "creaming."

Objectives of Employment and Training Programs

Employment and training programs in the United States involve a number of different agents who may have differing objectives. In the JTPA Title II-A program, for example, the federal government, state government, local government, the private sector, and service providers all play important roles in shaping the system. If all the agents had the same objectives, then the main purpose of performance management would be to monitor how well those responsible for running the programs are meeting the objectives. If, on the other hand, the objectives differ, the performance standards system can be used to help channel behavior in the direction desired by the federal government.

One of the key objectives at all levels is likely to be the promotion of economic efficiency. Because scarce federal resources are used to finance such programs, they should be judged in part on the return to the investment. Measuring the earnings gains of the programs requires long-term follow-up of participants or the development of reasonable proxies. However, measuring earnings gains attributable to the program requires some means of estimating what earnings would have been in the absence of the program—which would require impact evaluations at each site subject to the performance measures.

Two interesting efficiency issues must be considered in determining how to define the economic value of the programs: dealing with reductions in transfer payments and substitution effects. A common procedure in benefit-cost analysis is to view welfare payments as transfer payments, and the loss of income for participants resulting from reduction in transfer payments is assumed to be offset by a gain in income to taxpayers. From the perspective of taxpayers, however, a reduction in welfare payments represents a benefit.[16] In addition, the statutory language in most employment and training programs indicates that society views reductions in welfare payments as a benefit, regardless of what economic theory may say. Thus, reductions in receipt of welfare should generally be considered a positive benefit of the program.

The substitution problem is more complex. If the gains in earnings accruing to participants are at the expense of other workers, then not all of the private gains are also social gains. Most evaluations of training programs have concentrated on the private returns to the programs and ignored the substitution issues, but to assess the true social gains of a program the losses to nonparticipants should be taken into account.[17]

Several types of equity issues may arise. First, earnings gains to some participants may be considered more valuable by society than the same gains to others. Thus, it may be considered socially desirable to give preference to more disadvantaged groups even if they gain the same or possibly less than other participants. Another equity issue is whether programs should be indifferent, other things being equal, between serving a large number of people and providing a small amount of service versus serving fewer people but providing longer or more intensive training. As I note in the next section, a performance standards system can be structured to promote one approach more than another. Local governments might have an interest in serving a greater number of people to improve political support, but the interests of the federal government and society as a whole may be toward serving fewer people but having a greater impact on those served.[18]

Performance Management in Government Programs

In this section I provide a review of the performance management systems used in other government programs, with particular emphasis on the system used for the JTPA Title II-A program for disadvantaged youth and adults. Emphasis is placed on the JTPA system for three reasons. First, the client base of JTPA overlaps with the JOBS client base

16. See Mallar et al. (1982).

17. Evaluations of countercyclical programs, such as public service employment and revenue sharing, on the other hand, have often focused on the substitution issue.

18. For a discussion of possible objective functions and their implications, see Barnow (1979).

significantly: welfare recipients are a primary target group in JTPA and constitute more than 20 percent of the participants. Second, the JTPA system includes performance measures for welfare participants; thus, the JOBS program could build upon an existing system if it desired. Finally, the JTPA performance management system is well established. Preliminary efforts aimed at developing performance measures and standards began during the days of JTPA's predecessor, the Comprehensive Employment and Training Act (CETA), and the JTPA statute included provisions for a performance management system. In addition, the JTPA system has been developed with a great deal of participation by state and local program officials; the system appears to be generally accepted as reasonable by federal, state, and local program officials.

Performance Management in the Job Training Partnership Act

The JTPA program for economically disadvantaged youth and adults (Title II-A) has distinct roles for federal, state, and local levels of government and for the private sector. The country is divided into more than 600 local areas called service delivery areas (SDAs); some states have elected to have a single SDA serve the entire state. Funding is passed through from the federal government to the states and then to the local level by formula. The states pass through 78 percent of the funds and retain 22 percent for funding older worker programs (3 percent), coordination grants for education (8 percent), administration (5 percent), and performance standards awards and technical assistance (6 percent). In contrast to CETA, states play a major role in JTPA. States monitor the performance of the SDAs and administer the performance standards system subject to guidance from the federal government.

Each SDA is overseen by a private industry council (PIC) whose members are selected by the chief elected official(s) in the SDA. A majority of the PIC membership must be representatives of business, selected by the chief elected official from nominations made by a local general-purpose business organization. The PIC may either run the program itself or act as a board of directors to the program.

Participants are generally enrolled in vocational or basic skills classroom training, on-the-job training, job search assistance, or work experience. SDAs may provide activities themselves, but generally they make use of vocational education institutions, nonprofit institutions, and proprietary schools. Stipends, need-based payments, and supportive services are permitted, but the amounts spent on non-training activities are capped by provisions in the statute.

Performance management in JTPA grew out of pilot efforts that were started when the CETA program was in effect. Some senior Department of Labor officials were concerned that although the program's emphasis was on serving the economically disadvantaged, there were no explicit incentives for local programs to maximize the gains to participants. Department of Labor analysts and contractors analyzed data collected for administrative purposes and evaluations to estimate models of placement rates, wages at placement, and earnings after termination. As this work was being carried out, the Reagan administration came into office and began considering how to replace CETA with a new training program. CETA's poor image created an environment conducive to implementing a performance management system that would help make the new program more accountable. Along with the increased role of the private sector in overseeing the programs through the private industry councils, a formal performance management system was seen as an important tool for focusing local programs' attention more on outcomes. State and local program officials were included in discussions about the performance measurement system that was being developed, and by the time JTPA was passed, the concept of including a performance management system was generally accepted by state and local officials and both political parties.

The JTPA Performance Management System. Section 106 of the Job Training Partnership Act describes the performance standards system that is to be established. The statute notes that "job training is an investment in human capital and not an expense." The statute then states that the basic measures of return to be used are increased employment and earnings of participants and their reduction in welfare dependency. The statute than provides measures that must or may be used to determine if the basic goals are achieved. For adults, the statute mentions placement and retention in unsubsidized employment, increases in wage rates and earnings, and reductions in the number of families receiving welfare and the amounts received. For youth, the measures are to include attainment of "employment competencies" established by the PIC; completion of elementary, secondary, or postsecondary education; and enrollment in other training programs, apprenticeships, or the armed forces. In addition, standards are to be issued relating costs to the performance measures. Finally, the performance standards are to include

Table 8.1 National performance measures and standards for Title II-A of JTPA for program years 1989 and 1990

Measure	PY 89 standard	PY 90 standard
Adult measures		
Entered employment rate	68%	N/A
Cost per entered employment	$4,500	N/A
Average wage at placement	$4.95	N/A
Welfare entered employment rate	56%	N/A
Follow-up employment rate	60%	62%
Welfare follow-up employment rate	50%	51%
Weekly earnings at follow-up	$177	$204
Weeks worked in 13-week follow-up period	8	N/A
Welfare weekly earnings at follow-up	N/A	$182
Youth measures		
Entered employment rate	45%	45%
Positive termination rate	75%	N/A
Cost per positive termination	$4,900	N/A
Employability enhancement rate	30%	33%

provisions governing the base period prior to participation that will be used and a representative post-program period to measure performance.

The performance management system that has been implemented for Title II-A of JTPA is similar but not identical to what is called for in the statute. The Department of Labor establishes performance measures and issues standards that governors may adopt. In addition, the Department of Labor issues optional adjustment models that governors may use to adjust SDAs' expected performance for variations in participant characteristics and local labor market conditions.

The current performance measures and national standards for program year 1989 (July 1, 1989, through June 30, 1990) and the measures and standards for program year 1990 for Title II-A are shown in Table 8.1.[19] The national standards are set, based on experience in prior years, so that approximately 75 percent of the nation's SDAs will exceed the standards; thus the JTPA standards are based on relative rather than

19. There were initially seven performance measures for the program. The youth competencies measure was added after some program experience, and the post-program standards were added more recently.

absolute levels of performance. The changes for 1990 indicate an intention to simplify the system by reducing the number of standards, a shift away from measurement of status at termination to post-program measures, and the elimination of cost standards. The general shift in emphasis is intended to encourage more emphasis on longer-term training and away from "quick fixes" such as job search assistance.

Most states make use of the optional adjustment models rather than the national standards. The goal of the optional adjustment models is to put all SDAs in a state on a level playing field where they are held harmless for local conditions and for the types of participants they serve.[20] For the system to work, the SDAs must understand the trade-offs involved in changing their mix of participants and services and the effects that changes will have on their measured performance. The optional adjustment models are based on regression analyses conducted on data collected in previous years. The regression models are estimated annually using the most recent administrative data available. When estimated coefficients have an unexpected sign, the variables are dropped from the models and the regressions are reestimated. All the adjustment models except the model for the youth employability enhancement rate are based on PY 1988 data submitted in the JTPA Annual Status Reports (JASR) by the SDAs. The adjustment models provide governors with one means of adjusting expected performance for differences in participant characteristics and local conditions.

Table 8.2 shows the worksheet that is used to compute an SDA's performance on the adult welfare follow-up entered employment rate measure when the adjustment model is used. The column labeled F lists the variables in the regression model. In this case, the model includes demographic variables (percentage of participants who are female, percentage black, and percentage other minority), background characteristics of the participants (percentage who are high school dropouts, percentage of long-term unemployed, percentage not in the labor force, and percentage receiving general assistance or refugee assistance), and local labor market characteristics (unemployment rate, annual earnings in retail and wholesale trade, employment in manufacturing, mining, and agriculture, and the three-year growth rate in earnings in wholesale

---

20. The intent of the *current* system is to hold SDAs harmless for their choice of which participants they enroll. I address the question of whether the system can, does, or should achieve this goal later in this section.

and retail trade). The models for the other measures contain many of the same variables and other similar variables.[21]

To compute its performance standard for this measure in a state using the adjustment model, an SDA inserts its values for the variables in column G of the worksheet. The SDA then subtracts the national average for the variable (found in column H) and multiplies the difference by the regression coefficient (called a weight) in column J. By summing these products and adding the adjusted intercept, the SDA obtains its adjusted performance standard.[22] To illustrate, if an SDA increased the proportion of its participants that are female from 40 to 50 percent, the adjustment model would lead to a reduction in the entered employment rate of 0.89 percentage point, holding other things equal.

At this point, states have a number of options. As noted above, they may use the national standards or the adjustment models. Whatever option is used, they must decide how to weight the measures and set appropriate rewards and sanctions for SDAs that meet, exceed, or fall short of expected performance. States can modify the standards set by the model to require higher performance or to provide a tolerance for error in the model or omitted variables (item O on the worksheet). States also have the option of adding additional measures, developing their own adjustment models, and/or modifying the Department of Labor's models in a manner that is considered equitable by the Department.[23]

Initially, many states used the national standards (that is, they did not make use of the adjustment models), but over time states came to realize that the national standards created strong incentives to "cream" (enroll participants who would be easiest to place). Now the vast majority of states use the national adjustment models or similar procedures to adjust SDAs' expected performance for the characteristics of participants and local conditions.

In January 1990, the Department of Labor proposed modifying the data reporting requirements of SDAs to explore the feasibility of adding

21. Other variables in the adult models include employment in mining and manufacturing, percentage who have postsecondary education, percentage Hispanic, percentage who are unemployment insurance exhaustees, population density, the employee/resident ratio in the SDA, and the percentage of families in the SDA with income below the poverty level.

22. The adjusted intercept is set equal to the national standard so that approximately 75 percent of the SDAs will exceed the standard.

23. For example, Illinois has developed its own models based on participant-level data for participants in state JTPA programs.

Table 8.2 JTPA worksheet used to compute performance on the follow-up welfare employment rate

PY 90 JTPA Performance Standards Worksheet			A. Service Delivery Area's Name	B. SDA Number
C. Performance Period PY 90	D. Type of Standard [ ] Plan [ ] Recalculated	Date Calculated ———	E. Performance Measure Follow-Up Welfare Employment Rate (Adult) (Method I)	

F. LOCAL FACTORS	G. SDA FACTOR VALUES	H. NATIONAL AVERAGES	I. DIFFERENCE (G minus H)	J. WEIGHTS	K. EFFECT OF LOCAL FACTOR ON PERFORMANCE EXPECTATIONS (I times J)
1. % Female		79.5		−.089	
2. % Black		32.5		−.089	
3. % Other Minority		10.8		−.051	
4. % Dropout		29.4		−.112	
5. % Long-Term AFDC Recipient		33.0		−.028	
6. % Unemployed 15 or More Weeks		56.8		−.044	

7. % Not in Labor Force	22.8	−.086
8. % GA/RCA Recipient	12.9	−.092
9. Unemployment Rate	5.9	−.547
10. Annual Earnings in Retail and Wholesale Trade (000)	13.5	−.754
11. 3-Year Growth Rate in Real Annual Earnings in Retail and Wholesale Trade	1.1	.347
12. Employment in Manufacturing, Mining, and Agriculture	23.4	−.262

L. Total	
M. NATIONAL DEPARTURE POINT	51.0
N. Model-Adjusted Performance Level (L + M)	
O. Governor's Adjustment	
P. SDA Performance Standard	

additional performance measures and variables for the adjustment models.[24] The proposed additional outcomes for youth are: remained in school, completed a major level of education, entered non–Title II training, and returned to school.[25] For adults, the Department of Labor has proposed collecting information on skill attainment in basic education and occupational training similar to the data already collected for youth. Additional adjustment data items on participants to be collected are: lack of significant work history (has not worked for the same employer for longer than three months in the prior three years), homelessness, and having multiple barriers to employment (at least three out of twelve). Finally, there is a proposal to collect more detailed information on the length of training.

The *Federal Register* notice indicates that "most of the additional reporting items and redefinitions relate to the Department's focus on serving the hardest-to-serve by making quality training investments which underscore long-term employability development." Thus, the Department of Labor will be developing standards and adjustment models for measures relating to skill attainment and adding more explanatory variables to the adjustment models.

In most aspects the JTPA performance standards system is responsive to the statutory language. Initially, the measures dealt with status at termination because of the burden of collecting post-program data. Over time, however, post-program follow-up was introduced because termination measures were believed to promote short-term approaches such as job search assistance rather than longer-term vocational and educational training, and the Department has now eliminated the termination measures and replaced them with post-program measures in spite of the extra expenses associated with collecting post-program data.

The major deviation from the statutory requirements for the performance management system is that the statute calls for measures based on the *increase* in earnings due to participation, but the current system uses the *level* of post-program earnings as the measure of performance. The difficulty in establishing performance measures of earnings gains is that data are available only for participants. Short of conducting evalu-

---

24. See the *Federal Register,* vol. 55, no. 4, January 5, 1990.
25. Only the "remained in school" measure is completely new. The other measures were previously components of the completed program objective measure, which has been dropped.

ations at every site, there does not appear to be a simple way to use impact as a performance measure.[26]

An Assessment of the JTPA Performance Standards System. The success of the JTPA performance measurement system can be assessed along several dimensions. In terms of practicality and acceptance, the system is clearly successful. By including state and local government officials in the process of developing the system, the Department of Labor has achieved the goal of getting states and SDAs to pay attention to program outcomes. The data items collected for the adjustment models are useful for assessing whether the program is reaching the appropriate target group, and JTPA now has far richer data on its participants than any other federal training program.[27]

On the other hand, the performance standards system is likely to have encouraged creaming to some extent. The evidence on this topic is mixed, but the initial studies of JTPA implementation indicated that the emphasis on performance did lead to efforts to enroll participants who were easy to place.[28] It is difficult, however, to separate the importance of performance standards from other factors such as the increased role of the private sector in overseeing programs and the limitations on supportive services and stipends. In addition, as more states began switching from use of the national standards, where no adjustments in standards are made for characteristics of the participants, to the regression adjustment models, one would expect the gains from creaming to decrease.

The JTPA statute required the National Commission for Employment Policy (NCEP) to conduct a study of the effect of the performance management system on who is served by JTPA, how they are served, and the cost of services. NCEP funded Dickinson and colleagues (1988) of SRI International to conduct this mandated study. It was not possible to evaluate the performance management system through an experimental design where SDAs were randomly assigned to different performance measures and standards, so SRI had to rely on the naturally occurring variation across states. The SRI study included both qualitative and

---

26. Friedlander (1988) has conducted research on developing performance standards based on program impact in the context of work-welfare experiments. Friedlander's work is discussed in the final section of this chapter.

27. See Barnow and Aron (1989) for a summary of federally sponsored training programs.

28. See the discussion on creaming in Johnston (1987), pp. 77–81.

quantitative components. The qualitative study was based on site visits to a stratified sample of 10 states, 30 SDAs, and 87 service providers.

The quantitative study was based on analysis of SDA-level data obtained from the JTPA Annual Status Report (JASR), administrative data on state performance standards policies, 1980 census data, and a special mail survey of SDAs. Ordinary least squares regression analysis was used to assess the effects of performance standards on clients, services, and costs. The dependent variables for the client models were the proportion of participants who were members of selected hard-to-serve groups: welfare recipients, dropouts, minorities, females, individuals with other barriers to employment, and individuals age 55 and older. These variables were regressed on a set of variables characterizing the performance standards system for the state in which the SDA was located, the influence and concerns of the local private industry council, the influence and concerns of the local elected official, and characteristics of the local environment including the characteristics of the JTPA-eligible population. Separate regressions were run for adults and youth. Similar models were estimated for activities provided (job search assistance, basic skills training, occupational classroom training, and on-the-job training), average length of participation, and average cost per terminee.

Dickinson and colleagues found that although the performance management system still creates some incentives for creaming, SDAs with other goals can overcome the incentives to cream. Based on field studies and quantitative analysis, Dickinson and colleagues found that SDAs were influenced by three sets of objectives: (1) commitment to serving certain types of clients, (2) commitment to responding to local employer needs and interests, and (3) commitment to achieving specific levels on JTPA performance standards. The study concluded that SDAs vary significantly in terms of which areas they emphasize. SDAs that place a great deal of emphasis on achieving high scores in the performance standards system are likely to engage in creaming. On the other hand, SDAs that emphasize other areas find the performance management system to be of little hindrance in achieving their goals because most SDAs have little trouble meeting the standards.

The SRI evaluation has several shortcomings, but given the complexity and diversity of the performance standards adopted by the states and the inability of the researchers to systematically vary the performance measures, standards, and reward and sanction policies, it is unlikely that an ideal evaluation could have been conducted. One major problem with the evaluation is that SRI was only able to look at the impact of performance standards on groups for which data were reported (such as minorities, women, and dropouts). Because these characteristics are already captured in the adjustment models and SDAs in most states already have their standards adjusted for serving individuals with these characteristics, the impact on services to these groups is likely to be smaller than for individuals with barriers not included in the adjustment models. A second problem with the SRI evaluation is that because the characteristics of the states' performance standards systems are reduced to a manageable number of variables, the full range of incentives is not captured. Finally, as the SRI researchers note, the use of independent ordinary least squares regression models does not capture the simultaneous nature of the decisions made about clients, services, and costs.

In recent years the Department of Labor has made strong efforts to minimize creaming and the provision of "quick-fix" services. Through policy directives and speeches, Department officials have encouraged states and SDAs to serve individuals with greater barriers to employment. The Department has also distributed material on how states can encourage more services to the most disadvantaged.[29] Recent changes in the performance measures used and the adjustment models have reinforced these efforts. The addition to the adjustment models of explanatory variables that better reflect earnings capacity has also been an important factor in encouraging more services to the most disadvantaged. Dropping the cost standards has also sent a strong message to the states and SDAs that providing inexpensive services and enrolling participants who need minimal services are not the Department of Labor's policies.

Although the ability of local programs to "play the system" should not be underestimated, it is extremely unlikely that more than a minority of the SDAs understand the incentives produced by a complex system involving more than half a dozen linear equations and a dozen variables.[30] To play the performance standards game correctly, SDAs must solve this complex system of equations and assess how their overall ranking will be affected by serving, say, more women and fewer men. Be-

29. See Barnow and Constantine (1988).
30. The conclusions in this section are based on interviews by the author with more than 20 federal, state, and local employment and training officials conducted in 1987 and 1988.

cause "percentage of females" is in all the adjustment models, the SDA must look at all the equations simultaneously and take account of the particular manner in which performance across measures aggregated in the state to determine the overall score.

Although it may be obvious to an economist with a year or more of graduate study in econometrics, most state and local officials I have spoken with did not realize that to maximize measured performance they must have an idea of what the true regression coefficients in the model are.[31] Some officials indicated that if a regression coefficient in the entered employment rate model is negative, they will improve their measured performance by serving more of that group; they found it difficult to grasp the concept that the coefficient might not be negative enough to make serving more members of the group worthwhile in improving their measured performance. Some states have assisted their SDAs in dealing with the complex system of equations by providing floppy disks for personal computers with the performance standards equations already programmed. To see what happens to its performance standards when the SDA changes the characteristics of its participants, all the SDA has to do is type in alternative values of the explanatory variables in the model.

Three critical questions regarding the JTPA performance standards system relate to (1) whether it promotes maximizing gains in earnings and employment and reductions in welfare receipt, (2) whether it achieves its goal of holding SDAs harmless for serving individuals with different characteristics, and (3) more fundamentally, whether it *should* be designed to make SDAs indifferent, insofar as performance is concerned, regarding whom they serve.

Because the JTPA performance standards system is not tied to any measures of impact, the system cannot produce performance standards that relate to the program's impact. The system might still be useful, however, if it provides good relative rankings of SDAs. The implicit model underlying the performance standards adjustment models is of the form:

(1) $Y_{ijn} = \beta_0 + \Sigma \beta_i X_{ijn} + \Sigma \tau_{jn} Z_j + u_{ijn},$

31. Fortunately, the JTPA system has been spared dealing with logarithmic models. In contrast, performance standards adjustment models for the employment service used natural logarithms. Although the worksheet instructions explained how to find and use the natural log keys on a calculator, probably no more than a handful of officials truly understood the structure of the models.

where the X variables represent the explanatory variables in the model, the Z variables are a set of dummy variables representing the $j + 1$ SDAs, and u is a random error term.[32] If all the explanatory variables are available without measurement error (a heroic assumption which will be revisited shortly), then relative impacts can be estimated by regressing Y on the X and Z variables; the τ coefficients will provide estimates of the relative impacts.

The actual procedure used in developing the JTPA performance standards adjustment models differs in several ways. The data are collected at the SDA level rather than the individual level (although individual-level data are collected by the SDAs), and regressions of Y on the X variables are run at the SDA level. The expected performance is then calculated by subtracting the fitted Y value from the actual Y value. In addition to the possible bias introduced by grouping the data,[33] bias is potentially introduced by omitting the Z variables. If the omitted SDA dummy variables are correlated with the other explanatory variables, then the coefficients of the included variables will be biased.[34]

A second potential cause of bias is that the set of explanatory variables in the models is almost certainly incomplete.[35] Although the model contains a number of demographic, human capital, and labor market variables that are expected to affect earnings and the other outcomes, there are undoubtedly other variables that affect the outcomes of interest. Traits such as intelligence, work motivation, and experience are all likely to affect earnings but are not in the models. Information on some of the omitted variables is likely to be available to the local JTPA staff, making it relatively easy to engage in creaming to beat the performance standards. For example, intake interviewers can assess motivation and obtain information on the applicant's job history. It has been reported that some SDAs require participants to go through a job search workshop before they are admitted to the program; this provides the SDA the opportunity to screen out bad risks.

32. If we assumed a uniform effect across SDAs, as is often done in program evaluations, there would be no need for a performance management system.

33. Trott and Baj (1987) found that some of the regression coefficients changed significantly for their data in five midwestern states when grouped SDA data rather than individual data were used.

34. Another difference is that the models used for measuring performance are developed on data from earlier years. This would also introduce bias if the coefficients change over time. Because performance standards and adjustments must be established in advance, there is no practical way around this problem.

35. I postpone until later a discussion of Friedlander's research on models where program impact interacts with the explanatory variables.

The Department of Labor has omitted program activity variables from the models because they are believed to be under the discretion of SDA officials. Trott and Baj (1987) have pointed out that this is not always the case because SDAs are limited, at least in the short run, in terms of what service providers they can use and what activities they can provide. More important, as Trott and Baj note, if the activity variables are omitted and they have an effect on the outcomes, then omitting them from the regression models is likely to bias the remaining coefficients.

A third source of potential bias is that the regression analyses are performed on participants in JTPA rather than on the eligible population. Although this may be necessary for practical reasons, if there are systematic differences between the eligible population and the participant population, the resulting models may produce incentives that discourage enrollment of the most disadvantaged eligible individuals.

The National Commission for Employment Policy (1990) has illustrated how this problem might have occurred with respect to enrollment of Hispanics in JTPA. The NCEP study noted that none of the current outcome adjustment models include an adjustment for enrolling Hispanics. The reason is that when the models were estimated, the coefficients for percentage of Hispanics generally had the "wrong" sign; if a variable for Hispanics were included in the models, SDAs would be expected to achieve better outcomes for Hispanics than others. The issue is that the proportion of Hispanics not proficient in English is nearly twice as high in the JTPA-eligible population as it is among program participants. Given the strong emphasis on outcomes during the early days of JTPA, creaming was probably strong then, and the base population for developing the models may not have been representative of the eligible population. Thus, the adjustment models have no way of controlling for variation in characteristics of the eligible population rather than among actual participants. States have the flexibility to make some ad hoc adjustments, but the models, as currently constructed, cannot be used to make such adjustments.

Although it is easy to offer criticisms of the adjustment models, it is important to keep in mind the theoretical and practical limitations in developing good models of earnings and employment. Judging from the recent review of the literature by Willis (1986), the economics profession has not come a long way since Mincer's 1974 model with education, experience, and experience squared as the determinants of earnings.

Moreover, each new variable added to the adjustment models requires SDAs to collect the information for all participants. Finally, as the models grow in complexity, they become unwieldy to implement. The Department of Labor has begun collecting some potentially important additional variables in recent years—lack of reading skills and poor work history, for example—and these variables may lead to a reduction in disincentives to serve people with severe barriers.

Next consider whether the goal of the adjustment models should be to hold SDAs harmless for their choice of participants. It is not obvious that all earnings gains are equally valued by society, and several provisions in the JTPA statute require equitable provision of services to some highly disadvantaged groups (dropouts and welfare recipients) and give states the opportunity to provide additional funding to SDAs that enroll the hard-to-serve.[36]

Some states have directly addressed this issue by adding standards for participation rates for particular groups, and others have added standards for outcomes for such groups.[37] Given the statistical limitations of the models discussed above, it is worth strongly considering whether rewards and sanctions should be based entirely on regression equations. In the recent past, the Department of Labor has been reluctant to approve state performance standards systems in which the regression coefficients are modified on a nonstatistical basis. Consideration should be given to approaches such as giving "extra credit" for hard-to-serve individuals and permitting modifications in the regression coefficients to take account of characteristics not included in the models.

An issue implicit in the development of a performance management system is whether the performance measurement should be made on a per-terminee basis or on the basis of aggregate outcomes: should an SDA be judged on the basis of the proportion of terminees that are placed in jobs or on the total number of people placed for a given budget? The current JTPA performance standards system uses the per capita approach, but the employment service performance standards system uses aggregate numbers. Depending upon how expenditures are

36. Both the performance standards incentive funds and the hard-to-serve incentive funds come from the same pool of money (the 6 percent funds), and states that wish to increase target group incentive funds must do so at the expense of performance standards incentive funds.

37. See Barnow and Constantine (1988) for illustrations of potential and actual approaches that states have used or could use to encourage increased enrollment of the hard-to-serve.

taken into account (recall that the Department of Labor is abolishing the cost standards), the use of per capita standards may encourage serving fewer people more intensively than the use of aggregate measures. This raises another equity consideration: is it better to produce large gains for a small number of participants or to produce smaller gains but spread them over more of the eligible population? The current JTPA system favors the former strategy, and a number of arguments can be made to support this position; the point is that the decision should be made explicitly.

Performance Management Systems in Other Employment and Training Programs

Although the JTPA Title II-A performance standards system is the most highly developed system among federally supported employment and training programs, several other programs also have performance standards systems.[38] The JTPA Title III program for dislocated workers includes one performance standard (entered employment rate) and an optional goal (average wage at placement) for use in judging substate area performance, but the Department of Labor has not implemented a rewards/sanctions system for the Title III program.

Performance standards systems have also been developed for the national programs supported under Title IV of JTPA—the Job Corps, the Native Americans program, and the Migrant and Seasonal Farmworker program. The Job Corps program is notable because the standards are used to assess the performance of private-sector center operators who can lose their franchise if their performance is inadequate. A performance standards system has been developed for the public employment service to measure state and substate performance, but the system has not been actively promoted by the federal government; governors have the option to distribute discretionary employment service funds on the basis of performance standards. The Food Stamp program, administered by the Department of Agriculture, currently has performance standards for participation, and a contractor is assisting the Department of Agriculture in developing an outcome-oriented performance standards system.

---

38. The discussion in this section is based on King (1988).

Performance Measurement for the JOBS Program

The Department of Health and Human Services is required to develop a performance standards system for JOBS by October 1, 1993. Because performance standards have already been developed for JTPA and other human service programs, HHS can learn from the positive and negative experiences of other agencies that have preceded it along this path.

JOBS and JTPA have a number of common features. Both programs provide employment, training, and supportive services to economically disadvantaged youth and adults. Welfare recipients, the target group for JOBS, is one of the major groups served by JTPA. There are, however, some important differences between JOBS and JTPA that may affect how the performance standards system should be developed. First, JOBS is a state program rather than a local program; thus, there are about 50 units of government rather than 600 to be rated. Second, the JOBS program is funded jointly by federal and state governments, which has several potential implications for JOBS performance standards. Because of the joint funding, the federal government can vary the match rate for the program. If the Department of Health and Human Services varies the match rate on the basis of measured performance, states may be more sensitive to measured performance under JOBS than SDAs are under JTPA, where monetary rewards are small. On the other hand, because states put in a great deal of their own funding, they may be more inclined to operate the program as they choose rather than as the federal government tells them to.

On the basis of observations of the JTPA performance standards system and research from HHS-supported work-welfare programs, both federal and state AFDC officials are wary of the JTPA performance standards system. Two major concerns have been expressed. First, many welfare officials believe that largely because of the JTPA performance standards system, SDAs have been reluctant to enroll AFDC recipients, especially those with major labor market barriers. Second, results from the work-welfare experiments have indicated that gross outcomes are not highly correlated with program impacts.

As noted earlier, the JTPA performance standards system probably resulted in substantial creaming during the early years, and although there still may be creaming at some SDAs, the Department of Labor has taken steps to alleviate the problem: the Department has begun collecting more data on barriers such as lack of work experience and basic skills; the cost standards have been abolished effective July 1, 1990; encouragement has been given to states to concentrate more on the hard-to-serve; and data will be collected on the attainment of basic education and occupational skills for adults.

Part of the perceived problem with JTPA may result from a difference in philosophy between JTPA and AFDC programs rather than from the performance standards system per se. In a recent study of coordination between JTPA and other human service programs, many of the 60 SDAs interviewed noted that welfare programs often have more of a social service orientation, while JTPA is more concerned with getting people trained and into a job.[39] This difference in philosophy stems from more than just the role of performance standards; for example, it may involve an effort to overcome the poor image of CETA or the strong influence of employers through the private industry councils.

The concern about the divergence between gross outcomes and program impact stems from important recent work by Friedlander (1988), who analyzed data from experiments conducted in five sites to evaluate the effects of job search and work experience programs. Rather than constraining program impacts to be identical for all participants, Friedlander classified participants and control group members into three tiers: (1) AFDC applicants with no prior AFDC experience, (2) applicants with prior AFDC experience, and (3) ongoing AFDC participants. Because it permits treatment impact to interact with participant characteristics, Friedlander's model is a variant of Equation (1) above:

$$(2) \quad Y_{ijn} = \beta_0 + \Sigma\beta_i X_{ijn} + \Sigma\gamma_{jn} Z_j + \Sigma\delta_{jn} Z_j X_{ijn} + u_{ijn}.$$

Friedlander found that, generally speaking, the relationship between impact and welfare dependency is quadratic in form, with those in the middle range of dependency receiving the greatest benefits. The fact that program impact is not constant across participant characteristics complicates the performance standards process, but it is not surprising. What we are probably observing is something similar to teaching to the middle of the class—the teacher sets the level of a course to maximize gains by the average student, and those at either extreme gain less. The impact for a given participant is then a function of her characteristics

39. See Trutko et al. (1990).

and the type of program she is enrolled in, and when enough programs are observed, the overall relationship between participant characteristics and impact may look quite different from what we observe in a few sites with a narrow range of treatments.

Although the JTPA experience indicates that performance standards can encourage undesired behavior, my belief is that on the basis of the JTPA experience, a reasonable system can be developed for JOBS. My strongest recommendation is that the JOBS program begin collecting more data on participants and outcomes in all states. The initial data collection system does not include much outcome data. It is unlikely that simply collecting data on outcomes would encourage creaming, and when the time comes to develop a performance standards system there will be no national data base available if the current system is continued.

The second recommendation is that whatever performance standards system is established, rewards and sanctions should be kept to a minimum initially, and efforts should be made to avoid encouragement of creaming. The recent experience in JTPA should be helpful in meeting these goals.

The third recommendation is that the performance standards not be based on the evaluations at a small number of sites. Friedlander wisely cautions against extrapolating his results to other sites with different programs, and using only the 10 experimental JOBS sites for developing the performance standards system would also be unwise. In particular, I do not believe it is likely that any treatment-participant characteristic effects found at experimental sites will necessarily be valid for other sites.

It is clear that an ideal performance management system is beyond our reach for the foreseeable future. Nonetheless, a reasonable system has been developed and refined for the JTPA program, and an acceptable system can probably also be developed for JOBS. The basic question that must be addressed is whether the dangers of providing improper incentives through imperfect models outweigh the benefits of providing program direction and accountability. Many observers have blamed the decline in the nation's educational system on a lack of accountability, and a performance management system offers the best chance of dealing with conflicting objectives between the federal government and state and local governments. As Niskanen (1971) pointed out, it is naive to assume that bureaucracies will seek to act in a manner consistent with achieving economic efficiency. Indeed, Niskanen suggested a system similar to the JTPA performance management system as an option to deal with bureaucratic behavior.[40] Although a performance management system must be implemented carefully, I believe that the benefits are likely to exceed the costs.

References

Barnow, Burt S. 1979. "Theoretical Issues in the Estimation of Production Functions in Manpower Programs." In *Evaluating Manpower Training Programs: Research in Labor Economics*, Supplement 1, ed. Farrell Bloch. Greenwich, Conn.: JAI Press.

——— 1987a. "The Impact of CETA Programs on Earnings: A Review of the Literature." *Journal of Human Resources*, 22 (no. 2): 157–193.

——— 1987b. "Government Training as a Means of Reducing Unemployment." In *Rethinking Employment Policy*, ed. D. Lee Bawden and Felicity Skidmore. Washington, D.C.: Urban Institute Press.

Barnow, Burt S., and Laudan Y. Aron. 1989. "Survey of Government-Provided Training Programs." In Commission on Workforce Quality and Labor Market Efficiency, *Investing in People: A Strategy to Address America's Workforce Crisis*. Background Papers, vol. 1. Washington, D.C.: U.S. Department of Labor.

Barnow, Burt S., and Jill Constantine. 1988. *Using Performance Management to Encourage Services to Hard-to-Serve Individuals in JTPA*. Washington, D.C.: National Commission for Employment Policy.

Burtless, Gary, and Larry L. Orr. 1986. "Are Classical Experiments Needed for Manpower Policy?" *Journal of Human Resources*, 21 (no. 2): 606–639.

Dickinson, Katherine P., Terry R. Johnson, and Richard W. West. 1984. "An Analysis of the Impact of CETA Programs on Participants' Earnings." Menlo Park, Calif.: SRI International.

Dickinson, Katherine P., Richard W. West, Deborah J. Kogan, David A. Drury, Marlene S. Franks, Laura Schlichtmann, and Mary Vencil. 1988. *Evaluation of the Effects of JTPA Performance Standards on Clients, Services, and Costs*. Washington, D.C.: National Commission for Employment Policy.

40. Niskanen's preferred strategy is to introduce competition between agencies, but if that is not possible he suggests providing financial incentives to managers or agencies as alternatives.

Friedlander, Daniel. 1988. *Subgroup Impacts and Performance Indicators for Selected Welfare Employment Programs.* New York: Manpower Demonstration Research Corporation.

Heckman, James J., V. Joseph Hotz, and Marcelo Dabos. 1987. "Do We Need Experimental Data to Evaluate the Impact of Manpower Programs on Earnings?" *Evaluation Review,* 11 (August): 395–427.

Johnston, Janet W. 1987. *The Job Training Partnership Act: A Report by the National Commission for Employment Policy.* Washington, D.C.: National Commission for Employment Policy.

King, Christopher T. 1988. *Cross-Cutting Performance Management Issues in Human Resource Programs.* Washington, D.C.: National Commission for Employment Policy.

Mallar, Charles, Stuart Kerachsky, Craig Thornton, and David Long. 1982. "Evaluation of the Economic Impact of the Job Corps Program: Third Follow-Up Report." Princeton, N.J.: Mathematica Policy Research.

Mincer, Jacob. 1974. *Schooling, Experience, and Earnings.* New York: Columbia University Press, for the National Bureau of Economic Research.

National Commission for Employment Policy. 1990. *Training Hispanics: Implications for the JTPA System.* Washington, D.C.: National Commission for Employment Policy.

Niskanen, William A., Jr. 1971. *Bureaucracy and Representative Government.* Chicago: Aldine Publishing Company.

Trott, Charles E., and John Baj. 1987. *Development of JTPA Title II-A Performance Standards Models for the States of Region V.* DeKalb, Ill.: Center for Governmental Studies, Northern Illinois University.

Trutko, John, Larry Bailis, Burt Barnow, and Stephen French. 1990. *An Assessment of the JTPA Role in State and Local Coordination Activities.* Arlington, Va.: James Bell Associates.

Westat. 1984. "Summary of Net Impact Results." Rockville, Md.: Westat.

Willis, Robert J. 1986. "Wage Determinants: A Survey and Reinterpretation of Human Capital Earnings Functions." In *Handbook of Labor Economics,* vol. 1, ed. Orley Ashenfelter and Robert Layard. Amsterdam: North-Holland.

9 Case Management in Welfare Employment Programs

Fred Doolittle and James Riccio

Case management has been increasingly cited as a crucial part of a reformed welfare system, but because the term has been used to refer to a wide variety of staff responsibilities and behaviors, the concept remains somewhat nebulous. Moreover, the operation and effects of alternative approaches to case management in welfare employment programs are little understood, since researchers have only recently begun to study these issues. This chapter provides some background information on the common meanings of the concept and highlights issues that researchers should take into account in evaluating the role of this activity in the programs of the 1990s.

Why Care about Case Management?

Case management has come to the fore in several related contexts. In 1987 the American Public Welfare Association (APWA) identified case management as a "key component" of its proposed welfare reform plan (American Public Welfare Association, 1987). Moreover, case management has been a major feature of several state welfare employment initiatives that began operating during the late 1980s and that sometimes had very different operating premises.[1] The Job Opportunities

1. For example, in Massachusetts' Employment and Training (ET) Choices progam, clients' participation is voluntary and their service plans are completely individualized (for a summary of ET Choices, see Behn, 1989), while in California's Greater Avenues for Independence (GAIN) program, their participation is mandatory and must follow legislatively prescribed sequences of activities, which vary according to individuals' educational, employment, and welfare histories. (The GAIN program is described in more detail later in this chapter.) Yet in both of these programs, case managers play a central role.

and Basic Skills Training (JOBS) program of the Family Support Act of 1988 (FSA) also recognized the potential value of case management. It gave states the option of instituting a case management system and receiving matching federal funds for its support. But—reflecting the diversity of opinion about the nature of an appropriate case management approach and a desire to allow state flexibility—the U.S. Department of Health and Human Services (HHS) explicitly declined to define case management or to mandate any specific approach in implementing regulations.[2] Most states, however, have identified case management as a central part of their program, although the diversity of systems continues to be great.[3]

Why should *evaluators* of welfare employment programs care about case management? Basically, there are three reasons:

1. *To understand the nature of a program's "treatment" in practice.* In many states, case managers become the agents of the policymakers and give a program model its concrete meaning. They operationalize the relationship between the client and the program by applying, in specific situations, legislative and regulatory directives about who must participate, what activities they should participate in, and what support services they should receive. How case managers do this will have a great effect on what the program looks like in practice.

2. *To inform policy questions concerning the most efficient and effective ways of providing a program's treatment.* Despite the central role it can play, very little is known conclusively about the consequences for programs and clients of different ways of providing case management. In particular, rigorous scientific evaluations of the relative cost-effectiveness of alternative approaches are virtually nonexistent. Thus, even basic questions such as the relationship between the level of resources devoted to case management and program participation and impacts[4] remain unan-

2. See U.S. Department of Health and Human Services (1989), pp. 42153–4, for the discussion of case management in the comments on the JOBS regulations. These regulations also allow states to provide case management to only some recipients. The Department reached this conclusion despite comments urging it to specify a case management model and to mandate universal coverage.

3. This statement is based on information collected as part of the MDRC's technical assistance on the implementation of the JOBS program and on conversations with state and other officials involved in implementing the program. The APWA has proposed a National Institute on Family Self-Sufficiency, which would focus on case management in JOBS and would try to develop standards for it.

4. By impacts we mean the difference the program makes in terms of such outcomes as employment rates, earnings, and levels of welfare receipt. Since some program partici-

swered at this point. Learning more about these relationships would help to identify some "best practices" for achieving the common goal of welfare employment programs: moving clients into jobs and off welfare.

3. *To conduct successful evaluations.* Because the actions of case managers will so fundamentally influence clients' experiences in many state programs, evaluators of those programs must obtain case managers' cooperation with research objectives. In some situations, this can be difficult because of the incentives deriving from performance criteria under which case managers work. If these incentives conflict with those inherent in a particular research design, the integrity of the research could be undermined.

In this chapter, we discuss each of these issues and propose a future research agenda for the study of case management in welfare employment programs. We summarize what has been learned from past research, identify a number of "open questions" for future inquiry, and highlight some practical considerations to guide evaluators as they design such studies. In the process, we address four major themes:

1. *Case management has several core functions, but the prominence of each one, and the way it is executed, depend in part on a program's overall design.* Such program features as the number and types of service components, the degree to which activity sequences are standardized for all clients or individualized, and whether participation by eligible individuals is mandatory or voluntary influence the kind of case management system that is appropriate for operating any particular program model. Consequently, a great variety of approaches is found across programs.

2. *Case management approaches also vary widely when they are used to operate the same program model, reflecting alternative beliefs among administrators about how best to achieve the program's ultimate goals.* The actual character of a welfare employment program is influenced heavily by administrative decisions about case management that are often made at the local level.

---

pants would have found a job on their own or left welfare without the program, rates of post-program employment and welfare receipt are not measures of the difference the program made. Evaluators must compare the experiences of those given access to the program with the experiences of a similar group not given access. As discussed elsewhere in this book, many techniques—both experimental and nonexperimental—have been used to do this.

For example, local administrators often must decide on the division of labor among case managers, the types of people to hire for those positions, and the number of clients to assign to them. These and other choices will directly affect the substance and tone of clients' experiences in the program, and often entail important resource trade-offs.

3. *Because so little is known about the influence of different case management approaches on program participation and impacts, administrators' methods of assessing their case managers' performance may not always encourage staff behavior that best serves the program's goals.* How staff are evaluated will influence how they spend their time on the job, including how they interact with clients and what efforts they make on their behalf. To date, research findings offer little empirical guidance on what kinds of staff behavior are best suited to the objectives of the program, making it difficult to design appropriate staff incentives and performance criteria.

4. *Case managers play a central role in evaluations of programs, so evaluators cannot ignore their perceptions of the research design.* Case managers are likely to be particularly concerned about research designs that impinge upon their professional discretion to make what they believe are decisions in the best interests of their clients. Thus, researchers need to be sensitive to these concerns, to provide a compelling rationale for the goals and techniques of the research, and to monitor the implementation of those techniques very closely.

We begin by describing how the main functions common to case management systems in a variety of social service settings have been adapted to welfare employment programs. In doing so, we highlight alternative approaches for organizing and staffing these functions, and the trade-offs associated with each approach. In particular, we consider the implications of having the welfare agency provide case management itself versus subcontracting it to an outside agency; the trade-offs of dividing case management duties into a set of specialized tasks performed by multiple staff versus combining them into a single role; and some ramifications of setting different client-to-staff ratios and staff qualifications for the case manager position. We then turn to a discussion of the challenges of designing a performance evaluation system for case managers and the incentives faced by case managers under common types of systems. Finally, we summarize the implications of case management practices for conducting research on welfare employment programs and highlight some important open questions for future inquiry.

What Is Case Management?

Case management is not new; it has been an important part of social work practice for at least two decades. However, most experience with it has been in contexts other than welfare employment programs, especially in mental health services for the chronically mentally ill, in the care of the aged or disabled, and in child welfare. In fact, the most recent edition of the *Encyclopedia of Social Work*, published in 1987, discusses case management solely in these contexts (Rubin, 1987). The federal Work Incentive (WIN) program, begun in 1967, did use social workers and employment specialists to assist welfare recipients in entering the work force, but in most states this program consisted primarily of short-term job search assistance requiring little ongoing case oversight. The emergence of more complex, multi-component welfare employment programs, such as California's GAIN program and Massachusetts' ET Choices program, and the ambitious scope of services urged by the JOBS legislation have inspired a new application of the approach.

What Do Case Managers Do?

Most definitions of case management identify four core functions:[5] (1) assessing a client's service needs and setting goals, (2) developing an action plan to reach those goals, (3) arranging and coordinating the services to carry out the plan, and (4) monitoring the use of those services and assessing the continuing appropriateness of the plan. How these functions are put into practice tends to vary widely across social service programs, reflecting their different goals, philosophies, resources, target populations, service options, and other conditions.

Function 1: Identifying factors that will affect the client's progress toward self-support. The assessment function is the starting point of case management. It involves an examination of such factors as the circumstances that led the client to apply for welfare, current skills relevant to employment such as education and past work experience, needed support services such as child care or transportation assistance, and the client's interests and goals.[6] In some cases, as urged by the APWA, assessment

5. Rubin (1987) and American Public Welfare Association (1987), for example, use this framework.
6. Regulations implementing the Family Support Act's JOBS program contain a similar list.

might also be used to increase a client's motivation by helping her identify her special strengths and by portraying the options available to her in a positive manner (American Public Welfare Association, 1987). Even when case managers themselves do not conduct all the tasks in this assessment—for example, when assessment experts are hired for some of the work—they attempt to use the information in subsequent planning for the client.

Not all welfare programs conduct either a complete assessment of clients or an assessment of all clients, reflecting differences in their overall designs. For example, some programs with specified sequences of services may not conduct a full up-front assessment, focusing instead on support service needs and grounds for temporarily excusing—that is, "deferring"—clients from program participation. In contrast, programs that offer clients a wide choice of activities, without strict rules regarding the sequences in which they may be entered, tend to conduct a full assessment upon entry to the program.

GAIN and ET Choices illustrate how a program's overall design can influence its approach to assessment. In GAIN, the complex legislative compromise balancing services and obligations outlines how a welfare recipient's educational, employment, and welfare history is to be translated into service decisions.[7] An individual registers for the program at the welfare department's income maintenance office and is then referred to the GAIN office. There she attends an orientation session and is evaluated for assignment to an initial activity and for support service needs such as child care. This process also includes her taking a basic reading and mathematics test. In most cases, she will be (1) assigned to one of two primary service tracks, (2) allowed to continue in an education or training program in which she had previously enrolled, or (3) temporarily deferred from participation. On the basic education track, one of the two primary service tracks, registrants who do not have a high school diploma or General Educational Development (GED) certificate, do not speak English, or fail the skills test usually go into an adult education, GED, or English language program.[8] On the second

7. The unusual specificity on the GAIN statute as to the program model reflects an agreement between liberal and conservative legislators in California on a balance of program services and recipient obligations. The legislation was intended to describe in detail the terms of this compact. See Wallace and Long (1987) for background on the legislation and implementation regulations.

8. They have the option of participating in job search assistance first. However, they must later enroll in an education class if they do not find a job.

track, registrants who are determined not to need basic education are usually referred first to a job search activity. In most cases, only individuals who do not find a job after basic education or job search are given a full career assessment of their skills and service needs in order to develop an action plan—over which they are to have considerable choice—for further education and training.[9]

In ET Choices, where participation is voluntary and service plans are individually determined, a full-scale assessment is conducted up front. The ET caseworker even has the option of referring the participant to an outside vocational counseling agency, under contract with the welfare department, for an "in-depth evaluation of her skills, aptitudes, interests, and needs" (Behn, 1989, p. 3-1).

Because a full-scale assessment can be costly, these two approaches highlight an important set of issues: Should such an assessment be done for all clients? If not, for whom? How intensive should it be? To answer these questions, it is important to distinguish between a person's "job-readiness" and her potential for being helped by a program. Assessment tools and procedures that are effective in identifying individuals who are most job-ready will not necessarily indicate whether they are likely to benefit from a given type of program or from any of the service options it makes available. For example, some research suggests that job search and work experience programs may have no effect on the employment and earnings of eligible clients judged at the time of enrollment to be the most job-ready (based on their previous work and welfare experience) but can be effective for those in the middle range of job-readiness. The study found that those considered most job-ready were indeed more likely to enter employment than was the less job-ready group—but not at a higher rate than the most job-ready individuals in a randomly selected control group that did not have access to the program.[10] How clients with different levels of preparation for the job market would be affected by other types of programs, such as those emphasizing basic education and skills training, is not known.

9. Participation in an initial component and any subsequent activities is expected to continue until the individual finds employment, leaves welfare, or, for other reasons, is no longer required to participate.

10. This study found that, although sample members at the high end of job-readiness were more likely than those in the middle range to be employed after leaving the program, the experimental-control *differences* in employment were lower and not statistically significant for that more job-ready subgroup. See Friedlander (1988).

The difficulty of using up-front assessments to predict whether particular types of clients will benefit from participating in specific employment-related activities raises the question of whether the best approach is simply to require part or all of the caseload to participate in job search assistance for a period of time and then conduct a full assessment and arrange more intensive services only for those who do not find employment in this first step.[11] Advances have probably been made in assessment techniques in recent years,[12] but the issue remains important and controversial. Future studies of the relationship of alternative techniques—and their placement in a program's activity sequence—to post-program impacts would be especially valuable.

Other research suggests that formal testing, which is often a major part of assessment, may not always provide information that is useful to case managers in helping clients to select training activities. (A likely exception is testing for reading and math skills.) Recently, the Manpower Demonstration Research Corporation (MDRC) studied the early experiences of eight California counties in implementing the GAIN program (see Riccio et al., 1989). Many GAIN staff indicated that the career assessments provided by outside specialists did not add much to their knowledge of clients' training interests and capabilities; they already had information from talking with the clients themselves about their educational background, experiences, and aspirations. In some counties, moreover, the range of training and job options available in the community was fairly narrow. In these cases, some case managers questioned the value of detailed test data on clients' vocational interests and personality characteristics.

However, a number of the staff at the assessment agencies maintained that they received little feedback on the types of training activities that registrants ultimately entered or on registrants' success in those programs. Thus, they felt uncertain as to how to improve their performance. Further research on testing and other assessment tools for welfare employment programs should more closely examine how the

11. One example of this approach is the San Diego Saturation Work Initiative Model (SWIM). See Hamilton (1988).

12. See Center for Remediation Design (1989) for a discussion of recent lessons on assessment. One important point made in recent literature is that assessment and testing are not synonymous. Testing is only one of several assessment tools available. The JOBS program regulations, for example, also identify other methods such as interviews, counseling, and self-assessment instruments.

information they yield is being used by case managers, or why it is not being used.

Function 2: Developing an action or service plan specifying concrete activities to be undertaken by both the agency and the client. This is usually referred to as an employability plan. Under JOBS, it must specify a client's employment goal; the job search, education, or training activities to be undertaken in pursuit of that goal; and the support services (such as child care) to be provided to facilitate the client's participation in those activities. In some state programs such as GAIN, the case manager (on behalf of the welfare agency) and the client sign an agreement outlining each party's responsibilities under the plan. JOBS regulations leave the use of such a formal agreement up to the states.[13]

Programs vary greatly in the extent to which client preferences guide the development of the employability plan. JOBS regulations require the agency to "consider the needs and preferences of the participant in the context of agency goals and constraints (including program resources, available services and local employment opportunities)." But they specify that "the final determination of the contents of the employability plan rests with the state IV-A agency"—that is, the agency overseeing the administration of the Aid to Families with Dependent Children (AFDC) program.

Creating a plan appropriate to a client's needs and preferences requires not only a careful assessment, but also an effort to help the client make an informed choice. This does not mean "rubber-stamping" clients' requests but, rather, teaching them about options they might not have thought about. It also involves helping them make realistic judgments about their abilities and experiences and about the types of jobs available in the local labor market.

Under JOBS, the expected proliferation of employability plans will offer fertile ground for learning much more about how this function is put into practice and what factors influence the decision-making process. Of particular interest is understanding how other characteristics of a program influence case managers' efforts to tailor service assignments to clients' interests, capabilities, and preferences. These characteristics include the program's service options, linkages with outside service providers, approaches to assessment, case management systems,

13. The comments accompanying the regulations discuss the practice in some programs of viewing the resulting client/agency agreement as a contract enforceable under applicable state contract law.

and standards for evaluating case managers' performance, in conjunction with the characteristics of the local job market.

Function 3: Arranging and coordinating the services necessary to carry out the plan. This case management function refers to putting the plan into action—that is, helping the client enter the selected activities and obtain the necessary support services. Opinions differ on the extent to which case managers should assume the burden of arranging services or require clients to take on some or all of these responsibilities.[14]

In some cases, arranging services means simply referring clients to service providers—giving them the names and locations of schools or training centers and telling them what to do when they get there. In at least three kinds of situations, however, case managers may play a more active role. First, some providers may be reluctant to serve welfare recipients. In these circumstances, case managers may have to be advocates for their clients.[15] Second, some clients may be reluctant to participate, and case managers may have to encourage—or even more forcefully "push" for—involvement.[16] Finally, some types of services—such as counseling for personal or family problems—may not be available, and case managers may themselves seek to provide what is needed.

As is true for the planning process itself, much remains to be learned about what conditions influence how case managers put an employability plan into action, and what the implications of their efforts are for clients' experiences in the program.

Function 4: Monitoring the client's receipt of services and participation in

14. American Public Welfare Association (1987) states that "preference is given to having the client take the lead in arranging for the appropriate services or resources." JTPA service providers sometimes perceive welfare employment programs as doing too much "hand-holding" and urge more of a "self-help" approach so that those clients who do participate are "motivated." This orientation may be linked to their operating under performance standards based on post-program placement and wages. See Riccio et al. (1989).

15. For example, under Title IIA of JTPA, service providers face performance standards based on rates of post-program employment and wages. This can make them hesitant to serve clients with serious barriers to employment. The prevalence of this problem is uncertain, but where it exists case managers may have an advocacy role in getting welfare recipients into JTPA-funded programs. See National Commission for Employment Policy (1988) and Job Training Partnership Act (JTPA) Advisory Committee to the Secretary of Labor (1989) for discussions of the seriousness of this problem.

16. While the distinction is often drawn between mandatory and voluntary programs, case managers in both types of settings often play a role in "pushing" clients to participate. Of course, in mandatory programs, they may have the threat of sanctions (involving grant reductions) to reinforce their efforts at persuasion.

activities, enforcing any participation obligation, and assessing the continued appropriateness of the original service plan. Monitoring participation in a welfare employment program can be quite complex, particularly if the program has multiple components and special eligibility criteria for each of them. The program design for GAIN is one of the most complicated and illustrates the monitoring challenge facing case managers. A simplified version is presented in Figure 9.1.

As this figure shows, GAIN registrants can be assigned to a variety of activities or can be temporarily deferred from participation. Moreover, they can exit from the program at many different points. An analysis of participation during an early period in the program's history in eight counties found that, within six months of registering for the program, about 71 percent of the individuals referred to GAIN orientation and appraisal actually showed up, while 34 percent (or almost half of the orientation attenders) went on to enter an initial program activity such as basic education, job search, or self-initiated education or training (Riccio et al., 1989). Many of those who did not participate in orientation and appraisal or in an initial activity were temporarily excused from participation because of part-time employment, illness, or a family emergency, or were no longer required to participate because they had left welfare, given birth, or met other exemption criteria.

As this example illustrates, many individuals initially targeted by a program may not participate in it for a variety of reasons. Thus, case managers must not only monitor participation, for example, by obtaining information on attendance from service providers, but also investigate reasons for nonparticipation. Often they will need to initiate contacts with the registrants themselves by mail, phone, or in person. In mandatory programs, they must distinguish reasons for nonparticipation that are acceptable (that is, for "good cause") from those that are not, and they must apply the penalty process as required by the program regulations, which might include efforts at conciliation and financial sanctions.[17] Case managers must also continue to monitor the appropriateness of deferrals to determine when registrants who have been temporarily excused from participation should be assigned to an activity.

In programs such as GAIN, it is not easy to obtain the information needed to track participation in required activities. It is usually necessary

17. These issues also arose under the WIN program and were addressed in regulations and litigation. The JOBS program follows many of the definitions developed under WIN.

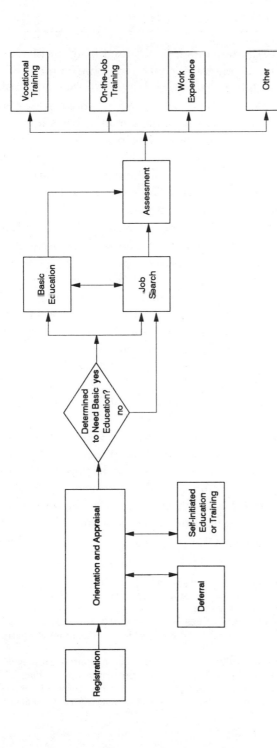

Figure 9.1. Simplified depiction of the GAIN program model. Registrants can leave the GAIN program at any point because of employment or deregistration from GAIN for other reasons. *Source:* Adapted from James Riccio et al., *GAIN: Early Implementation Experiences and Lessons* (Manpower Demonstration Research Corporation, 1989), Figure 1. Copyright © 1989 by the Manpower Demonstration Research Corporation and used with its permission.

for welfare departments to develop new information linkages with many different service providers. To meet this challenge, some counties have required the service providers to collect attendance information and communicate it to the case managers (thus raising those providers' costs). Some have also sought to develop complex management information systems (MIS) in an attempt to track participation accurately and efficiently.[18] These experiences are relevant for other states because the JOBS program participation standards require extensive reporting on recipient activities. In most states, this will require considerable new investments for data collection and reporting.

In general, the procedures for monitoring participation in welfare employment programs can impose a substantial burden on case managers, particularly in large-scale, multi-component programs emphasizing a continuous participation requirement. Available research suggests considerable variety in the way programs adapt the case manager role to handle this burden and to enforce a participation obligation. This reflects different philosophies as well as structural features such as the size of staff caseloads (as discussed in the next section).[19]

Organization and Staffing for Case Management

In this section we discuss several major dimensions along which the organization and staffing of case management tend to vary across welfare employment programs. These variations are important because they affect how the program "treatment" is delivered, the experiences of clients in the program, and the use of resources. The dimensions are the following: the degree of specialization of functions; the use of in-house staff versus a subcontracted agency to perform these functions;

18. Riccio et al. (1989) provide some examples from GAIN on how counties addressed this problem. Hamilton (1988) discusses the SWIM demonstration in San Diego, in which an elaborate MIS was created especially for the project in order to monitor and document participation in required program activities. Such an extensive MIS was necessary to support the explicit program goal of obtaining the highest possible level of continuous participation in program activities.

19. Findings from a number of MDRC's studies of mandatory welfare employment programs illustrate this. For example, in the San Diego SWIM program, financial sanctions were imposed on about 11 percent of AFDC single-parent registrants, whereas none were imposed on those enrolled in a Baltimore program. See Hamilton (1988) and Friedlander et al. (1985).

client-to-staff ratios; and staff qualifications. Past research and experience suggest that the alternative approaches along each of these dimensions generate important trade-offs that policymakers and program administrators must understand if they are to make informed choices in designing and operating programs. However, evaluators have only begun to study these trade-offs, and this is an important area for continued research.

Generalist versus Specialist Case Managers

Three models for distributing case management responsibilities among staff appear to be commonly used. Which one is chosen depends on many factors, such as a program's overall design, the larger network of services within which it must operate, and the desired relationship between staff and clients.

1. *Generalist model.* A case manager begins working with a client at intake and continues to work with her throughout her tenure in the program. This single case manager performs all of the core case management functions. Sometimes the case manager is assigned to work with only particular kinds of clients, such as young mothers or heads of two-parent families. This model allows the case manager to know the client better, provides continuity of treament, and establishes clear responsibility for reassessments and adjustments of service plans over time. In complex, multi-component programs, however, generalist staff may have difficulty developing expertise on all aspects of the program. Furthermore, this approach may be inefficient when the monitoring function requires ongoing communication with outside service providers, since case managers could have clients enrolled at numerous agencies.

2. *Sequential, specialist model.* As a person passes through the program, different case managers assume responsibility. For example, specialists may conduct orientation and assessment, monitor clients in different activities (such as basic education or skills training), or implement the penalty process in response to noncompliance. Staff qualifications (and expense) can vary according to the functions they are assigned, reflecting the level of difficulty and training required to perform those duties. Under this model, case managers may find it easier to master specific aspects of the program and to treat participants at each stage consistently. However, they may have less understanding of clients'

overall needs. Furthermore, there may be gaps in coverage if the transition of clients from one stage to the next is not made carefully. Also, specialists may emphasize their part of the program rather than overall program success.[20]

3. Team-of-specialists model. One person serves as the coordinator and continuously works with the client, but specialists in specific aspects of the program are involved as needed. While this approach combines the advantages of each of the previous two approaches, it can lead to higher administrative costs. The ET Choices program gradually evolved from a generalist model to this team approach in order to combine the close personal relationship between staff and client with expertise on the many services available in this multi-component program (see Behn, 1989).

The available research does not indicate that any one of these models is more effective than the others in securing higher participation from clients or more positive longer-term welfare and employment outcomes. As already suggested, however, each approach offers certain operational advantages and disadvantages.[21] Further research could help to identify these trade-offs.

In-House versus Subcontracted Case Management

In welfare, as in other domains of public administration, state and local officials have the option of subcontracting services. The JOBS regulations explicitly authorize subcontracting for case management, although they do impose some limits on the particular tasks that can be delegated by the welfare department. Both in-house and subcontracted case management have strengths and weaknesses.

In-house case management allows welfare agency officials to control directly a task that is central to defining the practical meaning of the program. Because of the involvement of agency staff in case management, agency managers will find it easier to learn how the program is

20. For example, in some programs, client assessment has been assigned to specialists in education, resulting in a very high proportion of participants being referred to basic education and the goal of employment being downplayed.

21. Several of the larger counties in the recent GAIN study, which operated more complex programs, gradually moved to the specialist model in order to provide the expertise needed at each step in the program. See Riccio et al. (1989). The SWIM program in San Diego also used this approach to case management. See Hamilton (1988).

being implemented. More important, this type of management allows the welfare agency greater flexibility to revise the program model as agency staff acquire experience in operating it and as funding and other conditions change. Similarly, in-house case management may provide greater flexibility in defining performance assessment measures and changing them as the need arises. With in-house case management, such program procedures and assessment systems do not need to be formalized in contracts with other agencies, and changes do not require contract amendments. (However, as discussed below, collective bargaining agreements may limit administrators' discretion.) This flexibility may be particularly important to newly implemented programs. Typically, they evolve over several years, adjusting their design and procedures through trial and error, before reaching a period of "steady-state" operations.

In-house case management does present potential problems, though. It may call for skills the current agency staff does not have, and civil service rules may limit the flexibility of hiring staff who have the most relevant prior experience. Alternatively, extensive staff retraining may be needed. Because of the separation of eligibility determination and services in the early 1970s and the decline in WIN funding in the 1980s, many welfare departments may have little recent experience with case management tasks required by multi-component employment programs. Furthermore, collective bargaining agreements or civil service rules may constrain agency managers from implementing or changing performance assessment systems within the welfare department. In new programs, in-house case management can involve a significant expansion of agency staff, raising concerns if policymakers oppose growth in the public sector or if future funding is uncertain and later cutbacks may occur.[22]

Subcontracting case management—which to date is extremely rare in welfare employment programs—may provide an opportunity to circumvent these problems. In addition, if more than one potential bidder for the case management contract exists, competition could lead to cost savings. And if funding drops, cutbacks are easier—politically and managerially—when services are provided by contract. .

22. States and localities have traditionally been cautious about assuming that federal aid will not decline in the future. Often, federal funds have been used in ways designed to lessen state and local commitment to maintain services if federal support does drop. See Nathan and Doolittle (1985) for a summary of this argument.

Purchase of case management by contract does pose some challenges, however. First, subcontracting requires agencies to develop detailed guidelines for contractor activity and to remain involved in certain aspects of case management. At a minimum, federal regulations prohibit the welfare agency from delegating to officials other than its own functions "involving discretion in the overall administration or supervision of the program." Agencies may subcontract functions that "involve decisionmaking with regard to individual participants" so long as "there are specific rules and regulations issued by the state agency governing their implementation" and contractors do not "review, change, or otherwise substitute their judgment for that of the IV-A agency" (U.S. Department of Health and Human Services, 1989, p. 42154).

These requirements mean that subcontracting case management is more feasible in a program such as GAIN, with clearly prescribed activity sequences, than in a program with minimal rules governing activity assignments. And within this framework, certain tasks related to case management *must* still be performed by the welfare agency, including determining exemptions from participation requirements, determining "good cause" for failure to participate, and imposing sanctions for failure to comply with program requirements.

Second, outside contracts complicate a welfare agency's efforts to develop and revise performance assessment systems.[23] Since contracts for new services may be in place for a considerable time, welfare officials need to understand the key measures of program performance to include in the contract *before gaining experience operating the service*. In practice, initial contracts may include relatively crude performance measures, and it may prove impossible to change the definition of desired performance in the short run, while the contract is in place.

Finally, subcontracting individual parts of program administration to the most experienced agency may lead to excessive fragmentation of overall program administration and of case management in particular.

Two examples from the GAIN program help to illustrate the use of alternative arrangements. Most California counties chose to keep within the welfare department almost all the crucial case management functions for most registrants. These included conducting orientations and appraisals, selecting appropriate service providers, monitoring participa-

---

23. "Performance-based contracts" are common in the employment services area. Such contracts tie payments to the achievement of particular types of performance; measures of performance can be quite simple or complex, as discussed later in this chapter.

tion, and enforcing rules. For many GAIN positions, they chose to hire existing income maintenance workers and former WIN workers and train them in their new jobs (Riccio et al., 1989).[24] This reflected the welfare agencies' positive expectations of GAIN and the pivotal role they believed case management would play. Many county welfare directors, for example, saw GAIN as a means of reorienting their agency's core role in the community from simple income maintenance (with its necessary emphasis on fraud prevention) to the more constructive goal of helping welfare recipients become self-supporting. GAIN, it was further believed, could reduce the stigma of being a recipient of welfare or an employee of the welfare department (Wallace and Long, 1987).

The Los Angeles County GAIN program offers a contrasting example. Here the county Board of Supervisors, although supportive of GAIN, opposed expansion of the welfare department and required it to subcontract case management under a 36-month contract. Under this contract, a private firm is paid a monthly fee that varies according to the number of people actually served. It also receives incentive payments if GAIN participants are placed in unsubsidized jobs that meet specified criteria.[25] In addition, the contract specifies standards for the performance of case management tasks (for example, required services for each client and permitted time lags before required services are performed).[26]

Subsequent events have affected the administration of the contract. County officials discovered that a lower than expected proportion of persons referred to GAIN were *active* in program components such as education and job search.[27] They wished to increase that number but

24. Many counties, however, chose to subcontract the formal assessment, which required special training. An example is administration of vocational interest tests. Typically, though, the case managers maintained responsibility for developing the employability plan, using the results of the assessment to guide them.

25. The contractor is paid $150 for each placement in full-time unsubsidized employment that lasts six months and results in AFDC grant termination or reduction by at least 50 percent; the subcontractor has chosen to give $100 of this incentive payment to the GAIN case manager whose client found work.

26. If the contractor fails to meet these standards, the county can require a corrective action plan, assess financial penalties, or (in certain circumstances) suspend the contract.

27. This occurred because of the type of "drop-off" in participation reviewed earlier in this chapter. The lower-than-expected number of persons active in education, job search, and training components posed serious problems for the contractors of these services who had made staffing decisions based on the original projections of clients. It also meant that the county was unable to spend its GAIN service funds and risked losing funding in subsequent years.

could not force the contractor to revise the intake procedures or staff caseloads.[28] In contrast (see Riccio et al., 1989), county welfare departments with in-house case management have been able to institute a wide variety of program changes with much less difficulty.

Under JOBS, more welfare agencies than in the past may choose to subcontract some or all case management functions to outside agencies. If they do, evaluators should be able to learn much more about the advantages and disadvantages of this arrangement.

Client-to-Staff Ratios

Another important decision facing JOBS planners concerns client-to-staff ratios. MDRC's study of GAIN's early implementation found that caseload sizes can have important implications for staff interactions with clients and thus for clients' experiences in the program (Riccio et al., 1989).

In the California counties that were studied, the average number of registrants assigned to staff for ongoing case oversight ranged from roughly 50:1 to over 200:1. In the county with the highest ratio, GAIN administrators had sought to stretch program resources in this way. In other counties, administrators believed that lower caseloads and closer individual attention would be essential to GAIN's effectiveness, and some decided to serve only a portion of the county's total pool of registrants in order to keep staff caseloads low.

High ratios did not prevent case managers from knowing about their clients' attendance at GAIN activities because in most counties service providers were responsible for supplying that information. However, they did delay case managers' responses to nonattendance. High ratios also impeded the use of persuasion instead of (or in addition to) penalties to increase program participation. On the other hand, high ratios permitted some counties to enroll a greater proportion of their GAIN-eligible caseloads with a given level of resources.

The evidence from GAIN does not reveal a simple relationship between a county's client-to-staff ratio and its participation outcomes. Counties whose staff had smaller caseloads did not have consistently

28. This situation was further complicated when other county officials (including members of the state legislature) who opposed contracting out GAIN administration to a private firm succeeded in enacting a state ceiling on payments to the contractor. The ceiling was later removed.

higher rates of registrant attendance at orientation or entry into service components during the early period of implementation. A variety of county conditions and practices affected these outcomes, with staff caseload size not necessarily being the most important. However, lower ratios may have had other benefits that were not studied. For example, many GAIN staff reported that closer monitoring and more intensive involvement with registrants—practices facilitated by smaller caseloads—improved registrants' attendance while enrolled in activities.

In general, the relationship between client-to-staff ratios and clients' participation in program activities and longer-term post-program outcomes is not well understood and is an important area for future research. MDRC is studying this issue in one California county (Riverside), using an experimental design according to which registrants are randomly assigned to two groups of staff having different caseload sizes.

Staff Qualifications

What sorts of people make the best case managers in welfare employment programs? Opinions differ, with some groups, such as the APWA, urging specific educational credentials as a minimum requirement.[29] Of particular interest is how easily income maintenance workers—one likely source of job candidates—can make the transition to this role. The interactions they are used to having with clients—which emphasize eligibility determination, fraud detection, and low "error rates"—are quite different from what is required of case managers who must help clients prepare for jobs.[30]

However, the limited available research evidence suggests that eligibility workers have indeed been able to make this switch. This has been the case, for example, in GAIN, Massachusetts' ET Choices program, and New Jersey's REACH program. Experience suggests that the most important characteristics are a problem-solving attitude, clear orienta-

29. For example, as a general rule, the APWA urges states initially to require an associate's (AA) degree and eventually a bachelor's degree. It also recognizes the need for flexibility, since some people with no formal education beyond high school (including former welfare recipients) may be effective case managers. See American Public Welfare Association (1987).

30. Riccio et al. (1989) found that income maintenance workers and GAIN case managers had different attitudes toward clients. The former were more likely to hold negative views of the capabilities of welfare recipients and more likely to blame them for their poverty.

tion to the goal of self-sufficiency, communication skills, and a willingness to see "working the system" in the interests of the client as part of the job.[31] Some evidence does suggest that, on average, these attitudes may be less common among income maintenance workers, so administrators of welfare employment programs may have to select their workers very carefully and provide training with a clear statement of the special mission of the program and recommended ways to relate to clients (see Riccio et al., 1989; Behn, 1989).

Some research suggests that combining the case management and traditional income maintenance duties in the same staff role can lead to role conflict. This can result in the former being subordinated to the latter, particularly if client-to-staff caseloads are high and—as is typical—the standards for assessing performance for income maintenance duties are more concrete, carefully reviewed, and firmly enforced (as are "error rate" standards) than are the performance criteria used to judge case management.[32]

Some of the difficulties inherent in assessing the performance of case managers are discussed in the next section.

Performance Evaluation for Case Managers

Often managers of welfare employment programs have introduced numerical performance standards as a means to assess the overall accomplishment of program goals. Examples of such standards include goals for the number of persons served by the program or the number placed in jobs.

Performance assessment systems are likely to become even more common in the future. The JOBS regulations include client participation standards at the state level starting in fiscal year 1990, and these are linked to federal matching fund rates. Furthermore, the statute calls for the introduction of broader performance standards in the mid-1990s. States may, in turn, translate these standards into measures of ongoing performance of case managers in order to create operational incentives for the achievement of these goals.

31. See Frazier (1989), who prepared training materials for New Jersey's REACH program (under contract to MDRC), for an example of this emphasis.

32. This combination was tried in one county included in MDRC's study of GAIN. After a while, program administrators decided to reassign some GAIN functions to specialized GAIN staff in an effort to ensure that those tasks would be performed more effectively.

Measurement systems have been developed in the absence of firm evidence on what kinds of case management actions lead to positive program impacts—such as an employment rate that is higher than what would have been achieved in the absence of the program. Indeed, one of the most important—though elusive—contributions of evaluation researchers would be to help lay an empirical foundation for constructing performance measures that (1) provide signals to case managers on how best to spend their time and (2) are linked to the impact of programs.

Most measures of case managers' performance in welfare employment programs fall into five categories: number of persons served, program inputs (for example, types of services provided), recipient participation, program outcomes (such as the number who are placed in jobs or who leave welfare), and—the most sophisticated measure—attainment of the program's goals. In practice, programs often use a combination of these measures.

Client-Count Assessment Systems. These are relatively crude systems that include such measures as the total number of cases assigned to each case manager. (This measure is embedded in the Los Angeles GAIN program's outside contract for case management.) By themselves, aggregate client-count systems implicitly assume that the benefits of providing case management services are the same for every family receiving assistance. They make no attempt to reward staff more for assisting families in which the payoff may be greater. They also assume that the cost of this service is the same in every case. In effect, caseload is assumed to be a measure of workload. Consequently, unless counteracted by other agency policies or contract clauses, client-count systems may create incentives to treat all cases in the program similarly, or even to attempt to enroll in the program those cases that seem easier to serve (such as volunteers for the program).[33]

Input-Based Assessment Systems. These rest on judgments about what constitutes a good set of procedures and services. They range in formality and encompass such measures as the number of contacts with clients, the completeness of the documentation supporting various case management decisions on behalf of clients, and the "quality" of the individual service plans that are developed for clients.

One illustration is the approach adopted by one county for GAIN. Here, program administrators audit a sample of each case manager's

---

33. This problem could be addressed by establishing separate service goals for different types of cases.

case files, determining the proportion of cases for which individual forms are properly completed. Individual performance is assessed partly on the error rate in documenting services.

Unless counteracted by other incentives for staff, systems that emphasize "inputs" could devolve into a test of the documentation of service actions rather than of the quality of service. Such systems, in addition to creating the classic social worker's dilemma of time spent on service versus documentation, might also lead case managers to apply the same procedures to all cases rather than concentrating their attention on cases with problems and giving lower priority to cases in which things are going well.

Client Participation–Based Systems. These systems place special value on the "welfare bargain" struck between the client and the agency, which links payment of the welfare grant to the client's participation in employment-related activities. They measure participation as a way to determine if the terms of the bargain have been implemented. They also implicitly assume that participation in activities is the major mechanism leading to increases in impacts on employment and welfare receipt, which may not always be the case.[34] Case managers are assessed on the extent to which they are involving recipients in program activities. The JOBS regulations also set participation standards and link them to federal matching fund rates. Quite likely, these standards will be translated into operational measures of case manager performance in some states.[35]

Although participation standards may appear simple in theory, in practice they can be quite complicated.[36] First, questions arise concerning what activities are to be counted in measures of participation. For example, is participation in assessment counted? Are all forms of job

34. For example, in mandatory programs, the participation requirement itself may lead people to find employment or leave welfare (or both) in order to avoid the "hassle" of participation. At this time, no careful research has shown a consistent link between overall levels of program participation and program impacts on employment, earnings, and welfare receipt, although a recent study of the SWIM program did show both high participation rates and strong program impacts. See Hamilton and Friedlander (1989).

35. A similar situation involved federal eligibility error rate standards, which were linked to federal payments for assistance costs. Many states translated these into error rate standards for office operations. See Behn (1989) for an example.

36. The recent SWIM evaluation and the debate over the JOBS regulations illustrate this. See Hamilton (1988) and U.S. Department of Health and Human Services (1989), p. 42198, for a brief summary of the comments on the proposed regulations defining participation rates in JOBS.

search, education, and training activities acceptable? Will the amount of time scheduled for a client to participate in a given activity during each week matter? (It does under the JOBS regulations.) Second, the measures can be "snapshots" of the participation rate among the program-eligible population at a point in time (such as during a given month), or longitudinal measures of the proportion of the eligible group participating in an activity within a specified period after becoming eligible for the program. Third, standards can include ongoing attendance measures, rather than simply focusing on rates of entry into an activity. Fourth, standards can take account of activities *other than participation* that indicate the program is operating as intended. Examples of this would include employment while still on welfare, departure from welfare entirely, and sanctions for noncompliance with program rules.[37]

While simple measures of participation ignore the complexity of program operations, more complicated ones pose a danger of their own: excessive data requirements. Indeed, sophisticated point-in-time participation measures have so far been available only for the Saturation Work Initiative Model (SWIM) in San Diego, a specially funded demonstration intended to measure participation carefully and test its upper limits.[38] Yet even this program found it extremely difficult to create a data system through which the participation rates of clients on individual staff members' caseloads could be monitored on a regular basis. Many states will have to upgrade their data systems substantially in order to comply with the participation reporting requirements of the JOBS regulations.

Client Competency–Based Systems. Some performance assessment systems focus on the attainment of employment-related competencies while clients are in the program. Such systems are rare in welfare employment programs, but they are a central feature of Job Training Partnership Act (JTPA) programs. Under federal regulations for JTPA, recognized youth competencies include completion of a major level of education (as represented, for example, by receipt of a high school diploma or

37. In its past studies of welfare employment programs, MDRC has developed the concept of program coverage of the caseload, which measures the proportion of program-eligibles who participate, are sanctioned for nonparticipation, find employment, or leave welfare. See Hamilton (1988) for a comparison of this with other measures of participation.

38. During typical months of the demonstration, approximately one-half of the mandatory caseload subject to the participation requirement were active in a program component or employed while still registered for the program.

GED) and attainment of pre-employment skills such as knowledge of job search techniques.[39]

Such competency-based systems could prove very useful. If research is able to determine a relationship between program impacts and the attainment of specific employment-related competencies, this approach could send clear signals about the types of changes in clients' levels of education and training that case managers should encourage.[40]

Outcome-Based Systems. These typically focus on the number of people placed in jobs or the proportion of people with post-program "success stories," often defined as placement in an unsubsidized job. ET Choices offers an example of an increasingly refined system that evolved as program designers identified new problems. Originally, program performance was judged solely on the number of participants placed into jobs. As officials gained experience in operating the program and identified new goals, they gradually adopted more complex measures of performance, which included wage standards and separate placement goals for different types of participants (Behn, 1989). Program managers rewarded local offices that achieved these goals with formal recognition awards and improvements in working conditions. Title IIA of JTPA uses an even more sophisticated system. Not only does it focus on post-program placement rate and wage levels, but it also adjusts the standards that apply in each locality according to local labor market conditions and client characteristics.

While this type of system has the advantage of shifting attention from services provided to clients to what actually happens to them after leaving the program, it raises two concerns. First, short-run placement goals create incentives for case managers to arrange short-term services (such as job search activities) likely to generate jobs quickly. To the extent that more intensive education or training would promote longer-term job stability and greater earnings, this could lessen the overall effectiveness of the program. Second, the focus on post-program success rates (especially when there is a short follow-up period) creates incentives for pro-

39. Initially the U.S. Department of Labor, which administers the JTPA program, allowed local officials to define these competencies, but gradually the federal agency has sought greater national consistency in definitions. In addition, the department has recently allowed credit for attainment of youth competencies only when the youth served originally lacked more than one competency; the department feared that programs were deliberately enrolling youth with a single, easily remedied deficiency in order to do well on the performance standards.

40. See Center for Remediation Design (1989) for one call for such a system.

gram operators to avoid enrolling or working with persons less likely to achieve success, even though some research evidence from several different settings suggests that program impacts may be very small or even nonexistent for more job-ready participants (Friedlander, 1988).[41]

Ideally, one might argue for a case manager performance assessment system that is linked closely to research findings on program impacts, yet even this presents difficulties. Although there is gradually growing research evidence on the types of services and target groups for whom impacts are larger and benefit-cost ratios are best, very little is known about how more "micro" program implementation decisions (such as those made by a case manager) are related to impacts. In the foreseeable future, it is unlikely that impact findings can provide anything more than very gross signals, such as a guideline that discourages programs from limiting their enrollment to only those potential clients who appear to be the more employable ones in the welfare population, or guidance on the types of services to which clients with particular background characteristics should be assigned.

The Role of Case Managers in Program Evaluation

In this section we discuss some of the problems that can arise with case managers when an evaluation of a welfare employment program—and not just an evaluation of case management within that program—is superimposed on the ongoing operation of the program. In particular, we will illustrate how some of the day-to-day incentives under which case managers perform their duties can conflict with research demands and, if not carefully handled, can undermine the integrity of the research.

One such problem concerns the way in which clients are selected for a program. Many experts believe that evaluation of a program's overall effectiveness is best accomplished through random assignment of clients to the program or to a control group that does not receive program services. Yet, in situations where case managers previously had some discretion over program entrance, they may resist random assignment because it eliminates that discretion and forces them to implement deci-

41. The JTPA system has faced this charge of "creaming," though recent changes in performance standards and statements by the Department of Labor have reduced these incentives to avoid the hard-to-serve.

sions that they may find unpalatable, at least in part because of the performance systems in place. In particular, random assignment will invariably require them to assign to the control group—and thus deny program services to—some clients who appear highly motivated, eager to be in the program, and very likely to help the program in meeting performance standards such as job placement goals.[42]

Case managers might also resist the random assignment of clients to alternative treatments within the same program. Such a design would be used to evaluate the *relative* effectiveness of alternative treatments—for example, a sequence of program activities that includes basic education compared to a sequence that does not. However, in a program that otherwise permits the case managers some discretion over the initial selection of an activity and the authority to change an assignment as a client's circumstances or interests change, random assignment may be viewed as an unwelcome intrusion on their professional judgment.

Because case managers often play a central role in implementing random assignment, evaluators using this technique will need to be sensitive to their perspectives in setting up such a study. For example, evaluators should make special efforts to assure that case managers understand the purposes of the study and why random assignment is a valuable tool for measuring their program's effectiveness. In addition, they should institute procedures to monitor the intake process closely and build in safeguards against any attempts to circumvent it.

The problem of staff resistance to random assignment arose recently in the implementation of a random assignment impact evaluation of Title IIA of JTPA. In JTPA, local program performance is assessed using measures such as the proportion of people enrolled in the program who find a job and the wages they receive. Since random assignment would interfere with staff members' discretion over which individuals to admit into the program, they feared it might lead to the enrollment of less skilled persons and might lower their program's measured performance. The evaluators therefore spent a considerable amount of time explaining why random assignment was so essential, developed procedures to address staff concerns, and, as a result, were able to obtain the staff's cooperation in participating sites.[43]

42. Some case managers may also object on ethical grounds to a process that allocates program slots to individuals randomly.

43. However, in many potential sites, random assignment continued to be an issue. See Doolittle and Traeger (1990) for a discussion of the implementation of this study and the ways the research team sought to address these concerns.

Problems can also arise when attempts are made to study the differential effects of alternative case management systems (holding a program's service sequences and other features constant). Generally, the preferred design for such a study would include the random assignment of clients to groups that were intended to receive the different types of case management. Any differences observed in clients' participation and post-program outcomes would thus clearly reflect the type of case management, since the groups would be similar in all other ways. Randomly assigning *staff* to each of the groups would also be desirable; this would guard against the possibility that "more effective" staff members would choose or be disproportionately assigned to—inadvertently or by their supervisor's choice—any of the groups, which would confound the results. Of course, the practical constraints against implementing such a research design are many, which is one reason it has so rarely been attempted.

As part of its evaluation of California's GAIN program, MDRC has been conducting such a study in Riverside County. Although not yet completed, the study has already revealed some important practical lessons for evaluators who might wish to use an experimental research design in other analyses of case management. In this project, welfare recipients who were registered for GAIN were randomly assigned to a control group (not subject to GAIN's participation mandates or eligible for its services) or to one of two different case manager treatments, which were defined primarily in terms of staff caseload sizes. Under the "enhanced" treatment, each staff member is responsible for a smaller caseload than in the "regular" treatment; the goal has been to keep the client-to-staff ratio for the enhanced group at about half that for the regular treatment. Staff providing the enhanced treatment are expected to spend the extra available time per case making more frequent contacts with clients, doing home visits, and making special efforts to improve client self-esteem.

The research will compare each treatment group's rate and patterns of participation in GAIN activities and post-program labor market and welfare outcomes. Moreover, it will compare each group's post-program outcomes to those of the control group that did not enter GAIN. Thus, the findings will shed light on whether differences in caseload sizes—which imply different levels of intensity of case oversight and, hence, alternative ways of allocating program resources—influence clients' experiences while in GAIN and after they leave the program. Furthermore, the study will compare the attitudes and case management practices of staff members, who were also randomly assigned to the two treatment groups.[44]

Implementing this research has been complicated. First, the evaluators and county administrators had to be concerned that staff might view the case management workload associated with the two treatment groups as unequal. If this occurred, the staff's cooperation with the study could be jeopardized. Therefore, to avoid the emergence of a belief that the group with the lower caseloads had an "easier" job, guidelines were issued to ensure that their extra time available per case was actually spent on more intensive case management tasks (and not, for example, on longer coffee breaks).[45]

A second problem has been maintaining constant caseload sizes throughout the study period. Because of registrants' departures from the program, an uneven flow of new cases into the program, and staff changes (due both to an expansion of the staff and turnover of personnel), the absolute number of registrants assigned to each case manager has fluctuated considerably over time. More success has been achieved in ensuring that the average client-to-staff ratio in the enhanced group is about half the ratio in the regular group, as intended by the research design. However, this has required ongoing intensive monitoring by both the evaluators and the program staff responsible for implementing the assignment procedures.

The Riverside experience illustrates clearly that operating two different case management systems side by side within the same agency is a difficult task for program administrators as well as for evaluators. It requires an unusually strong commitment to the research by those administrators and staff because it more directly intrudes on their flexibility to reassign staff and change program procedures as circumstances change than does an evaluation of the effectiveness of a program in its entirety.[46] Consequently, setting up a "micro" evaluation of this kind will

44. Findings from this study will be presented in a report to be completed in 1993.

45. The situation is further complicated because the county involved evaluates case manager performance partly on the quality of case documentation, and there is a danger that enhanced case managers will spend the extra time per case on documentation rather than additional services.

46. The constraints against instituting certain changes in program operating procedures are likely to be more frustrating to administrators and staff in newly established programs, which may change quite extensively through a trial-and-error learning process, than in mature ones, in which the process of evolution has peaked.

often require a great deal of direct and ongoing collaboration between researchers, program administrators, and case managers, as well as vigorous monitoring to ensure that the treatment differences are maintained throughout the period of the study.

Implications for Future Research

In this chapter we have attempted to help evaluators navigate the current debate about the role of case management in welfare employment programs. We have shown that little is known about the implications of numerous case management design choices, particularly for client participation in program activities or ultimate program impacts on employment, earnings, welfare receipt, and other outcomes. We now offer some suggestions for future research and review some ongoing work that will inform that agenda.

Assessment Practices

Much remains to be learned about how to identify at an early stage in welfare employment programs which individuals are likely to benefit from which kinds of employment-related activities. As previously noted, this means understanding how a program's impacts vary for different types of clients. For example, are "intensive" program services necessary for all clients? Would some clients do just as well in the labor market with less intensive training or none at all? Answers to these questions would help to take some of the guesswork out of case management. Policymakers could establish guidelines for assigning clients to particular activities and for choosing which individuals to serve (where they have such discretion) if resources preclude serving everyone.

The new JOBS program already moves in the direction of targeting resources according to the characteristics of the eligible population. In particular, it attempts to discourage "creaming" by providing financial incentives to states to focus their JOBS resources on (1) longer-term welfare recipients and (2) young parents without a high school diploma and with little recent work experience. Both of these groups are believed to be less likely to succeed in the labor market without the program's assistance compared to other groups, such as better educated recipients who have worked recently. Yet in some states, funding will not be sufficient to provide intensive services to all who fit this "hard-to-serve" definition. Case managers would therefore benefit from reliable assessment tools to target resources further.

Level of Case Management Resources in Relation to Program Participation and Impacts

Here the issues include the following: Does devoting more resources to case management—which might permit staff to spend more time with registrants, monitor their participation more closely, and encourage or enforce participation more diligently—actually lead to higher rates of participation and more consistent attendance? Does it lead to better post-program impacts, such as effects on labor market and welfare behavior? Are the benefits of this approach greater than the extra cost per client? In particular, would a program be better off serving more clients with less intensive case management or fewer clients with more intensive case management? Findings on these issues would be particularly important for policymakers across the country, since few states are likely to have the financial resources to offer a comprehensive JOBS program to all potentially eligible welfare clients.

As previously noted, MDRC's recent research on the implementation of GAIN in eight counties did not find a clear relationship between client-to-staff ratios and rates at which registrants entered program activities, but suggested that more intensive case management may be related to better attendance. Although the special case management study in Riverside County will help to address these issues more rigorously, it is only one study of one program in one county. Further experimental research on this topic across a variety of program settings would clearly be valuable.

Performance Standards in Relation to Program Impacts

Research that helps clarify the relationship between the criteria that administrators might use to judge case managers' job performance and the program's eventual impact on clients' labor market and welfare behavior would be another very fruitful endeavor. For example, would criteria that encourage case managers to achieve high participation rates, or high job placement rates, or both, also generate large program impacts? Would other performance standards yield larger impacts?

Two ongoing research projects will help to inform, but not fully answer, these questions. The National JTPA Study, examining Title IIA services in a sample of local service delivery areas, provides the first careful look at program impacts in JTPA. Its findings will be used in future refinements of JTPA performance standards, such as job placement rates and educational competencies.[47] Although these standards will apply to the program as a whole, they will influence which individuals staff choose to work with within the general population, and how they assist them. A second relevant project is the recently initiated national JOBS Evaluation funded by the U.S. Department of Health and Human Services, which is expected to yield recommendations for JOBS program performance standards. Together, these projects may move program performance assessment systems more in line with program impact findings; however, much remains to be learned.

Participation and Impacts in Relation to Other Case Management Variations

With the previous two types of research as a foundation, it may be possible to develop performance evaluation systems that provide research-based signals on how case managers should interact with their clients. If case management actions such as frequent contacts with clients, specific counseling techniques, close monitoring of participation, or strong sanctioning policies prove to be related to impacts, case managers could emphasize the appropriate practices. If these case management behaviors are also found to be related to participation, and if participation does influence impacts, this would reinforce the appropriateness of grounding performance assessment systems for case managers in participation standards. Research that examines whether other aspects of case management systems affect participation and impacts, such as the degree to which staff functions are specialized and the kinds of qualifications that are required of staff, might also be profitably examined in future studies.

It is important to recognize, however, that researching the independent effects on impacts of any of these dimensions is difficult because many of them are interdependent, and some combinations of features

---

47. The impact analysis, funded by the U.S. Department of Labor, is being done by Abt Associates, Inc., New York University, and MDRC. See Abt Associates, Inc., Manpower Demonstration Research Corporation, and New York University (1989).

are rare in existing programs. Clearly, this final type of research is far in the future, and much remains to be learned before even approaching this task.

The goal of future work should not be to find the single best case management system. As discussed throughout this chapter, the variety we see in case management practices reflects a complex array of funding decisions, policy choices about the overall goals and emphasis of the welfare employment program, and responses to existing agencies' administrative capacity and relations with other organizations. Research can highlight the implications of choices and the trade-offs among them, but it is unlikely to identify a single best approach.

References

Abt Associates Inc., Manpower Demonstration Research Corporation, and New York University. 1989. *Design Report for the National JTPA Study.* Washington, D.C.: Abt Associates, Inc.

American Public Welfare Association. 1987. "W-Memo: Case Management and Welfare Reform." Washington, D.C.: American Public Welfare Association.

Behn, Robert D. 1989. *The Management of ET Choices in Massachusetts.* Durham, N.C.: Institute of Policy Sciences and Public Affairs, Duke University.

Center for Remediation Design. 1989. "Improving Workplace Skills: Lessons from JTPA." Washington, D.C.: Center for Remediation Design.

Doolittle, Fred C., and Linda Traeger. 1990. *Implementation of the National JTPA Study.* New York: Manpower Demonstration Research Corporation.

Frazier, Donald. 1989. "REACH Program Case Manager Training Design and Notes: Achieving Self-Sufficiency." New York: Manpower Demonstration Research Corporation.

Friedlander, Daniel. 1988. *Subgroup Impacts and Performance Indicators for Selected Welfare Employment Programs.* New York: Manpower Demonstration Research Corporation.

Friedlander, Daniel, Gregory Hoerz, David Long, and Janet Quint. 1985. *Maryland: Final Report on the Employment Initiatives Evaluation.* New York: Manpower Demonstration Research Corporation.

Hamilton, Gayle. 1988. *Interim Report on the Saturation Work Initiative Model in San Diego.* New York: Manpower Demonstration Research Corporation.

Hamilton, Gayle, and Daniel Friedlander. 1989. *Final Report on the Saturation Work Initiative Model in San Diego.* New York: Manpower Demonstration Research Corporation.

Job Training Partnership Act (JTPA) Advisory Committee to the Secretary of Labor. 1989. *Working Capital: Coordinated Human Investment Directions for the 90's.* Washington, D.C.: U.S. Department of Labor.

Nathan, Richard P., and Fred C. Doolittle. 1985. "Federal Grants: Giving and Taking Away." *Political Science Quarterly,* 100 (no. 1, Spring): 53–74.

National Commission for Employment Policy. 1988. *Evaluation of the Effects of JTPA Performance Standards on Clients, Services, and Costs: Final Report.* Washington, D.C.: National Commission for Employment Policy.

Riccio, James, Barbara Goldman, Gayle Hamilton, Karin Martinson, and Alan Orenstein. 1989. *GAIN: Early Implementation Experiences and Lessons.* New York: Manpower Demonstration Research Corporation.

Rubin, Allen. 1987. "Case Management." In National Association of Social Workers, *Encyclopedia of Social Work,* 18th ed. Silver Spring, Md.: National Association of Social Workers.

U.S. Department of Health and Human Services, Family Support Administration. 1989. "Aid to Families with Dependent Children: Job Opportunities and Basic Skills Training Program and Child Care and Supportive Services—Final Rule." *Federal Register,* October 13, pp. 42146–42267.

Wallace, John, and David Long. 1987. *GAIN: Planning and Early Implementation.* New York: Manpower Demonstration Research Corporation.

Acknowledgments

1. What Did the OBRA Demonstrations Do?

We would like to express our appreciation to Dr. Judith Gueron, President of the Manpower Demonstration Research Corporation, and members of the Corporation's staff. We are grateful for the research assistance provided by Matthew Birnbaum and for additional support received by Wiseman from the Centre for Social Policy Research, University of Bremen.

2. Designing an Evaluation of the Job Training Partnership Act

I wish to thank Daniel Black, Norman Bradburn, Robert Chirinko, Fred Doolittle, Irwin Garfinkel, Charles Manski, Robert Michael, Robert Moffitt, Larry Orr, Jeffrey Smith, and Ernst Stromsdorfer as well as seminar participants at the Institute for Research on Poverty at the University of Wisconsin–Madison and the Harris Graduate School of Public Policy Studies at the University of Chicago for their comments. I especially wish to thank Burt Barnow and Jim Heckman not only for their comments on this chapter but also for the extremely useful interactions I have had with them on evaluation analysis.

3. The Role of Evaluation in State Welfare Reform Waiver Demonstrations

We would like to thank Linda Mellgren, Canta Pian, and Reuben Snipper for their assistance with the case studies in this chapter and Steve Carlson, Irwin Garfinkel, Charles Manski, and Isabel Sawhill for their comments and suggestions. We also thank Stephanie Comai-Page for her help with the Evaluation Scorecard and Dorothy Baldwin for her assistance in typing and pulling this chapter together. We would like to pay a special tribute to Carl Dahlman, Deputy Assistant Secretary for Income Security Policy, HHS, from January 1987 to March 1989. Carl is a true believer in the value of good research and always puts principle before politics.

4. Are High-Cost Services More Effective than Low-Cost Services?

We are grateful to the Ford Foundation for supporting the preparation of this chapter and to the Institute for Research on Poverty of the University of Wisconsin—Madison and the Office of the Assistant Secretary for Planning and Evaluation of the U.S. Department of Health and Human Services for additional assistance. However, the views expressed are those of the authors and not the funders. We also benefited from careful reviews of various drafts by Irwin Garfinkel, Mark Greenberg, and a number of our MDRC colleagues, including Gordon Berlin, Fred Doolittle, Barbara Goldman, Gayle Hamilton, Robert Ivry, David Long, Cameran Lougy, Janet Quint, Kay Sherwood, and John Wallace.

5. Randomization and Social Policy Evaluation

This research was supported by NSF Grant SES 87-39151. I have benefited from the comments of Ricardo Barros, Fred Doolittle, Sherry Glied, Joseph Hotz, Thomas MaCurdy, Charles Manski, and James Walker. For a more complete statement of the argument in this chapter, see Heckman (1990b).

6. Evaluation Methods for Program Entry Effects

I would like to thank Stephen Bell, Thomas MaCurdy, and Charles Manski for comments.

8. The Effects of Performance Standards on State and Local Programs

I am grateful for financial support from the Institute for Research on Poverty. Comments and discussions with Charles Manski, Irwin Garfinkel, Kay Albright, Carol Romero, Karen Greene, Joseph Hotz, James

Heckman, Steven Aaronson, and Howard Rolston were very helpful. I am especially grateful to Edward Gramlich, the discussant at the conference, "Evaluation Design for Welfare and Training Programs," for pointing out aspects of the paper that needed strengthening. All opinions expressed here are my own and do not necessarily reflect the views of the Institute for Research on Poverty or the U.S. Department of Health and Human Services.

9. Case Management in Welfare Employment Programs

We would like to thank our colleagues at MDRC for assistance and comments on earlier drafts of this chapter, especially Judith Gueron, Kay Sherwood, and Sharon Rowser.

Contributors

Burt S. Barnow, Lewin/ICF, Washington, D.C.

Fred Doolittle, Manpower Demonstration Research Corporation, New York, New York

Michael E. Fishman, Office of the Assistant Secretary for Planning and Evaluation, U.S. Department of Health and Human Services, Washington, D.C.

Daniel Friedlander, Manpower Demonstration Research Corporation, New York, New York

Irwin Garfinkel, School of Social Work, University of Wisconsin–Madison

David Greenberg, Department of Economics, University of Maryland, Baltimore County

Judith M. Gueron, Manpower Demonstration Research Corporation, New York, New York

James J. Heckman, Department of Economics, University of Chicago, Chicago, Illinois

V. Joseph Hotz, Irving B. Harris Graduate School of Public Policy Studies, University of Chicago, Chicago, Illinois

Charles F. Manski, Department of Economics, University of Wisconsin–Madison

Charles Michalopoulos, Department of Economics, University of Wisconsin–Madison

Robert Moffitt, Department of Economics, Brown University, Providence, Rhode Island

James Riccio, Manpower Demonstration Research Corporation, New York, New York

Daniel H. Weinberg, Housing and Household Economic Statistics Division, U.S. Bureau of the Census, Washington, D.C.

Michael Wiseman, Robert M. La Follette Institute of Public Affairs, University of Wisconsin–Madison

Name Index

Aaron, Henry, 1n, 19n
Akerlof, George, 261n
Appel, Gary Louis, 235
Arnott, Richard, 215n
Aron, Laudan Y., 297n
Asch, Solomon E., 257
Ashenfelter, Orley, 13n, 77, 207, 221, 253
Auspos, Patricia, 70, 162, 163, 186
Axelrod, Robert, 261n

Bailis, Larry, 306n
Baj, John, 301n, 302
Bane, Mary Jo, 159
Barbridge, Lynn C., 42
Barnow, Burt, 8, 13n, 76, 132, 280n, 282n, 284n, 288n, 297n, 299n, 303n, 306n
Bartlome, Jeffrey A., 71
Bassi, Laurie, 13n
Baum, Erica, 26, 62, 63
Behn, Robert D., 31, 310n, 316, 324, 330, 332n, 334
Bell, Winifred, 235
Betsey, Charles L., 13n, 145n
Bloom, Howard, 122, 127
Blum, Barbara, 43n, 62
Boruch, Robert F., 13n, 17n, 122, 127
Bowden, D. Lee, 42
Brandeis, Louis, 9n
Bryant, Jan, 70
Burghardt, John, 162
Burtless, Gary, 123, 145, 253, 268n, 283n
Bushe, Dennis M., 235

Cain, Glen, 202, 207, 223
Campbell, Donald, 201n, 215n

Card, David, 77, 221
Carter, Jimmy, 25
Cave, George, 40, 44, 70, 71, 163, 186
Cella, Margot, 163
Conlisk, John, 202, 223
Constantine, Jill, 299n, 303n
Cook, Thomas, 113n, 201n, 215n
Corbett, Tom, 8n
Cosslett, Stephen, 244n
Cox, David R., 213, 216
Coyle, Susan L., 13n, 17n
Crane, Jonathan, 258
Crutchfield, Richard S., 257
Cunningham, Patrick M., 71

Dabos, Marcelo, 145n, 253, 283n
Deloya, Jeannette, 8n
Demsetz, H., 261n
Dickinson, Katherine P., 145n, 282n, 286n, 297, 298
Doolittle, Fred, 7, 8, 89n, 93n, 95, 96, 99, 102, 219, 221, 325n, 336n
Drury, David A., 286n

Ellwood, David T., 159, 185
Erickson, Marjorie, 72
Evans, Daniel J., 115, 116

Fisher, Ronald A., 213, 227
Fishman, Michael, 13, 246
Fraker, Thomas, 13n, 83, 86, 107, 108, 123, 145n, 202, 212, 213, 219
Franks, Marlene S., 286n
Frazier, Donald, 330n
Freedman, Stephen, 40, 44, 69, 70, 71
Freeman, Howard E., 120
French, Stephen, 306n

Subject Index

Abt Associates, 86, 341n
Administrative data, 244–247
AFDC state programs: in Massachusetts, 33, 58; in Virginia, 40; in Arkansas, 57–58, 159; in Washington, 58; in Illinois, 59; in California, 59, 160; in New Jersey, 131–132; in New York, 133; in Ohio, 134; in North Carolina, 137; in Maryland, 159
AFDC-U (Unemployed Parents), 33, 35, 59, 61, 116, 131–132, 237. *See also* Aid to Families with Dependent Children
AIDS, 221
Aid to Families with Dependent Children (AFDC): and Family Support Act, 1, 143, 277; described, 6, 36, 119, 127, 183, 184, 191, 193; case management, 7–8; evaluations, 12, 127, 140, 233–239, 253; and welfare reform, 25, 26, 39, 116, 126, 127, 145; and OBRA, 33, 38, 39, 42, 44, 50, 52–55, 58, 59, 60, 235–236, 237; and JTPA, 91, 306; benefits, 116, 120n, 134; and Food Stamps, 139; and JOBS, 143, 147, 164, 277, 318; and Supported Work, 163; entry into program, 238, 240; exit effects, 239; administrative records, 244; participation rates, 247–249; and CSAS, 262–263. *See also* Family Support Act; Homemaker–Home Health Aide training; Welfare-to-work programs
Alabama, 130
American Public Welfare Association (APWA), 310, 311n, 314–315, 329

Arizona, 130
Arizona Work Incentive Demonstration, 37, 68. *See also* Omnibus Budget Reconciliation Act demonstrations
Arkansas WORK program: described, 45, 52–58, 68, 151–152, 171–175 passim, 180, 181; and employment, 159; enrollment, 164. *See also* Omnibus Budget Reconciliation Act demonstrations; Welfare-to-work programs
Attrition, 16, 17, 122, 233–234; bias, 48, 49

Baltimore Office of Manpower Resources, 174
Baltimore Options program: described, 34, 36, 45, 52–56, 70, 155, 159, 172–186 passim. *See also* Omnibus Budget Reconciliation Act demonstrations; Welfare-to-work programs
Basic skills education, 146
Benefit-cost analysis, 64–65, 287; of OBRA, 31
Benefit-reduction rates, 233, 235–236
Broad-coverage programs: defined, 146, 149, 161; described, 162–176 passim; and selective-voluntary programs, 163, 179–188; research agenda, 194–195. *See also* Omnibus Budget Reconciliation Act demonstrations; Welfare-to-work programs
Butte, Mont., 96

California, 130
California Greater Avenues for Independence (GAIN): described, 33–34, 69, 310n, 315–338 passim; in Los